To Brenda Webster —
who knows whence I write.
In appreciation, and with
best wishes,

Advance praise for **PSYCHOANALYSIS AT THE MARGINS**

"Paul Stepansky, a broad and gifted historian who also reports as an eye-witness, has written a fresh and compelling intellectual history of psychoanalysis in the United States in the second half of the twentieth century. By using the idea of social marginality, Stepansky offers a clear and persuasive explanation of what has happened to one of the major movements of the recent past—and why it has happened."

—JOHN BURNHAM, PH.D., Research Professor of History, Ohio State University, and author of *Psychoanalysis and American Medicine*

"The uniqueness of *Psychoanalysis at the Margins* derives from a combination of original material not available elsewhere—the history of psychoanalytic publishing and book sales in the United States—and the brilliant scholarship and lucid writing one has come to expect of Dr. Stepansky. He explores concepts of marginalization, fractionation, and so-called theoretical pluralism within a broad cultural and intellectual framework, and ends the book with a surprising suggestion regarding the future role of psychoanalysis. All of this is carried out with the authority that is derived from his nonparochial stance, ranging scholarship, and clear and subtle thinking. Anyone interested in substantive issues in psychoanalysis, including its future status, will have to wrestle with this book."

—MORRIS N. EAGLE, PH.D., Professor Emeritus, Derner Institute of Advanced Psychological Studies, Adelphi University

"Paul Stepansky has written an absolutely stunning book that is as compelling as a good mystery that carries the reader along to a very unsettling conclusion. Alas, the hero of the book as well as the victim is psychoanalysis. Stepansky writes about a subject in the effortless manner of a good author, in the erudite manner of a scholar who has mastered the field, and in the caring manner of someone who loves the subject."

—ARNOLD GOLDBERG, M.D., the Cynthia Oudejan Harris, M.D., Professor of Psychiatry, Rush Medical College, and Training and Supervising Analyst, Chicago Institute for Psychoanalysis

Psychoanalysis at the Margins

Psychoanalysis at the Margins

Paul E. Stepansky

OTHER PRESS • NEW YORK

Passages from Richard M. Gottlieb, "A Psychoanalytic Hypothesis Concerning the Therapeutic Action of SSRI Medication," *Journal of the American Psychoanalytic Association*, 50:969–971, are reprinted by permission of the American Psychoanalytic Association.

Production Editor: Yvonne E. Cárdenas

Book design: Simon M. Sullivan

This book was set in 10.5 pt. Sabon LT Roman by Alpha Design & Composition of Pittsfield, NH.

10 9 8 7 6 5 4 3 2 1

LIBRARY OF CONGRESS CATALOGING-IN-PUBLICATION DATA

Stepansky, Paul E.
  Psychoanalysis at the margins / Paul E. Stepansky.
    p. cm.
  ISBN 978-1-59051-340-8 (hardcover)
  1. Psychoanalysis—United States—History. 2. Psychotherapy—United States—History. I. Title.
  BF173.S816 2009
  150.19'50973—dc22
                                        2009023470

In Memory of My Father
WILLIAM STEPANSKY, M.D.
my hero

Contents

Preface

Does a field make progress because it is a science, or is it a science because it makes progress?[1]

Here is my problem: In a three-decade career as a psychoanalytic editor and publisher, I have worked productively with psychoanalysts and psychoanalytic psychotherapists of many persuasions, and I have admired many of them greatly. I have no doubt at all of their professional bona fides: Their rigorous and lengthy training, their knowledge of human development, their understanding of psychopathology in its developmental, psychological, and interpersonal aspects, and their capacity empathically to engage their patients and help them. In a word, psychoanalysts are men and women of great insight; of this I am certain.

But I have great difficulty making conceptual sense of this insight and the clinical skills to which it is wed. And, in truth, so do they. Psychoanalysts are unique in their century-long discourse about who they are and what they do. What exactly is psychoanalysis? A science like other sciences? A science like some sciences but not others? A sui generis science of the mind? A nonscientific interpretive exercise akin to hermeneutics or linguistics or history? Perhaps the insightful "something" that analysts share is akin to craft knowledge, a pragmatic nuts-and-bolts knowledge of things that are useful to know in a clinical-therapeutic context. And perhaps such knowledge is not only tacit but also incompatible with specific knowledge claims, especially the formal, predictive claims of science.[2]

1. Thomas Kuhn, *The Structure of Scientific Revolutions*, 2nd ed. (Chicago: University of Chicago Press, 1970 [1962]), p. 162.

2. Of course, such knowledge can be scrutinized scientifically as to its applicability and effectiveness in different clinical situations, but it cannot be foundational to a psychoanalytic "theory" of mind, with its accompanying theories of development,

But psychoanalysts, with very few exceptions, have shied away from a clinical pragmatism that reduces their knowledge-claims to the hands-on know-how of craftspeople.[3] And they have not been content to let their field evolve in the modest manner of a craft, i.e., through the handing down and incremental refinement of craft knowledge. Most analysts have conceived of their endeavor differently, as well they might. After all, they come to their analytic training as licensed health care providers intent on entering a profession given over to a particular therapeutic modality. Through psychoanalytic training, they seek to acquire the kind of expert, esoteric knowledge that our culture reserves for licensed professionals. In point of fact, analytic training is typically the capstone of professional training in one or another health care field, whether psychology, psychiatry, or clinical social work. And analysts, no less than psychologists, psychiatrists, and clinical social workers, are culturally authorized to provide expert assistance on the basis of knowledge claims that grow out of this professional training. Licensure, certification, subspecialization, fee for services rendered, consultation, third-party reimbursement—these accouterments of professionalism give us the psychoanalysis we have come to know: A formalized system of psychotherapy that codifies essential truths about the human condition and provides demonstrable and durable relief of human suffering.

This is psychoanalysis as most American psychoanalysts understand it and live it in their literature and their institutions. And this is the

---

psychopathology, technique, and therapeutic action. Incidentally, this is precisely the claim made by Louis Berger in *Psychoanalytic Theory and Clinical Relevance: What Makes a Theory Consequential for Practice?* (1985), one of the first books I published at The Analytic Press. Berger argued that the knowledge of analysts could only be theorized about at the "cognitive level of clinical pragmatism," and that this level was antithetical to what he termed the "state process formalisms" of natural science.

3. John Kerr's riveting history of the early psychoanalytic movement ultimately comes to the conclusion that what was actually a broad and deep growth of craft knowledge was mistakenly identified as scientific progress, a mistake that was perpetuated through socially constructed psychoanalytic institutions. See John Kerr, *A Most Dangerous Method: The Story of Jung, Freud, and Sabina Spielrein* (NY: Knopf, 1993), pp. 508–511 and, with respect to the institution of the training analysis, his subsequent "'The Goody-Goods are No Good': Notes on Power and Authority in the Early History of Psychoanalysis, with Special Reference to Training," *Psychoanal. Inq.*, 24:7–30, 2004.

psychoanalysis whose near-demise I will be documenting and exploring in the chapters to follow.

What do I mean when I speak of near-demise? To the extent that psychoanalysis is a mental health profession, it may be reasonably expected to possess the kind of knowledge shared by the members of any profession. And like the knowledge of other culturally authorized caregivers, psychoanalytic knowledge may be reasonably expected to increase as the shared possession of the entire community of psychoanalysts. But in America this has simply not happened. The profession to which American psychoanalysts belong—the profession that nurtured and trained them and bestowed on them special therapeutic identities—has long fractured into various subcommunities of analysts allied with one or another psychoanalytic school of thought. What we are left with is less a cohesive profession than a loose federation of psychoanalytic subcommunities—what I will term psychoanalytic part-fields—whose proponents see the world in different and often incommensurable ways. The fractionation of the past four decades has occurred in tandem with the dramatic contraction of the field in the wake of the biological turn of American psychiatry, managed care, the cost-effectiveness of nonanalytic therapies, the maturing of psychopharmacology, and the failure of psychoanalysis to provide compelling evidence of its efficacy in relation to other interventional modalities.

As Managing Director of The Analytic Press, I experienced the decomposition of American psychoanalysis firsthand. My authors, all psychoanalysts, all men and women of deep insight, all (presumably) doing effective clinical work with their patients—often seemed to live in different professional worlds. Their divergences were basic and profound. As representatives of one or another psychoanalytic school of thought, they gathered into small enclaves with like-minded colleagues; offered up their own exemplars of great analysts and great analytic work; defined their own standard literature; published their own journals; hosted their own conferences; trained their own successors; and experienced that "relative fullness of communication" that falls to members of a scientific community. Correspondingly, they expressed, to varying degrees and in various combinations, condescension, irritation, anger, disapproval, and incomprehension of colleagues who inhabited different psychoanalytic worlds. To this extent, each of the major American psychoanalytic schools—the ego psychologists, the self psychologists, the interpersonalists, the relationalists, the

Kleinians, the neuropsychoanalysts, the infant researchers, and so forth—acquired the community structure of what Thomas Kuhn famously termed a "paradigm" or a "disciplinary matrix."[4]

As an editor and publisher, I came to know and admire American analysts identified with each of the aforementioned schools of thought. But I was frustrated by them as well. Gifted analysts from different walks of professional life never seemed to add up to a collectivity, much less to a community of like-minded professionals with a common body of knowledge. Their disputes, played out at conferences and in the pages of their journals, could and did become personal.

Infighting among representatives of different psychoanalytic schools spilled over to me. I recall late-night phone calls from an analyst distressed and angry to learn I was working with a colleague of whom he or she disapproved. I was told countless times that certain of my authors did not really "do" psychoanalysis, and that their claims to be contributing to the psychoanalytic canon were fraudulent. On one occasion, a senior analyst expressed concern about his ability to work with me at all if I continued to work with a particular colleague. On another occasion I was asked to remove my name from the editorial board of a journal because it conveyed an alliance with one psychoanalytic group at the expense of another. Over and over I was on the receiving end of angry remonstrance that one author did not read or cite another; that one or another school of thought was not adequately represented in this or that journal article or book chapter or bibliography; that an author's claim to originality was specious because he or she had not considered contributions outside his own psychoanalytic school of thought.

What kind of profession gives rise to a history of institutionalized infighting that takes it to the brink of implosion? How can these different psychoanalysts all be so insightful in such radically different and seemingly irreconcilable ways? This book is my attempt to make sense of a conundrum that I have experienced personally and moved on to explore historically, sociologically, and philosophically. My experiential point of entry to what many term the "crisis" of Ameri-

---

4. See Kuhn, *Structure* (n. 1), especially the "Postscript—1969," pp. 176–210 and "Second Thoughts on Paradigms" (1974), in Thomas S. Kuhn, *The Essential Tension: Selected Studies in Scientific Tradition and Change* (Chicago: University of Chicago Press, 1977), pp. 293–319, at pp. 294–297, quoted at p. 296.

can psychoanalysis underscores a key limitation of this work: I am not attempting a critique of psychoanalysis worldwide but only of psychoanalysis in America. I allow for the fact that psychoanalysis may be thriving in other parts of the world, such as South America, and leave it to others to situate my analysis of the near-demise of American psychoanalysis on a broader international canvas.

Three interrelated ideas guide me through this project. I have been greatly influenced by Thomas Kuhn's work in the history and philosophy of science and also by the many criticisms it has elicited over the decades. I use the Kuhnian term *paradigm* throughout this book to convey the sense of a cohesive community of practitioners whose training into, and acceptance of, a particular theoretical tradition shapes their everyday work. In the case of the basic sciences, a paradigm suggests a certain kind of research program; it identifies the kind of problems to be explored, the range of solutions that can be envisioned, and the methodologies, procedures, and instruments through which problems are explored and solutions sought.

In a field such as psychoanalysis, the notion of paradigm transposes such particulars to a healing discipline. It stipulates the kind of background assumptions and theories that may be properly termed psychoanalytic, and it uses these assumptions and theories to ground a distinctively psychoanalytic modus operandi—a therapeutic modality (whether a method, a procedure, a family of techniques, an interpretive orientation, or simply an investigative sensibility) that can be applied to individuals who come to the psychoanalyst as "patients" in search of professional help for their various problems as these problems are *psychoanalytically* understood.

Normal science typifies the everyday activities of scientists (or scientifically minded clinicians) working within one or another paradigm. In this sense, normal science is nonrevolutionary science that does not question basic paradigmatic assumptions. In Kuhn's original formulation, "normal-scientific research is directed to the articulation of those phenomena and theories that the paradigm already supplies." This is simply to say that scientists normally identify and explore problems with the conceptual and instrumental tools that their paradigm provides. Novelties and anomalies will invariably be encountered in the course of such work, but they are not sought after. For this reason, Kuhn equated the work of normal science with everyday puzzle-solving, and saw the scientist as spurred on by the challenge of "solving a puzzle that no one before has solved or solved so well." "Many of the great scientific minds," he continued, "have devoted all of their professional attention to demanding puzzles of this sort."[5]

The idea of *progress* in science, medicine, psychiatry, and psychoanalysis weaves in and out of my narrative in the manner of a leitmotiv. I am mindful of the tension between Kuhnian philosophy of science and the idea of progress in its usual Whiggish sense. Kuhn began by stressing the incommensurabilities among different paradigms, rendering problematic the notion of cumulative progress across paradigms. His understanding of scientific revolutions and the gestalt-like switches they effected constituted a frontal assault on the logical-empiricist wisdom of his day, the belief "that whole theories can be judged by the same sort of criteria employed when judging the individual research applications of a theory."[6] How, Kuhn mused, can whole theories even be compared if they do not share an axiological and linguistic baseline from which progress can be adjudged, if they are indeed incommensurable?

Kuhn himself was acutely aware of the counterintuitive implications of his vision of revolutionary scientific change. He directly confronted the problem of progress in the final chapters of *The Structure of Scientific Revolutions*, addressed it in subsequent writings, and recurred to it in a lengthy interview conducted the year before his death.[7] It bears noting that over the course of his career he progressively soft-

---

5. Kuhn sketched out the notion of "normal science" in 1959 in "The Essential Tension: Tradition and Innovation in Scientific Research" (reprinted in Thomas S. Kuhn, *The Essential Tension: Selected Studies in Scientific Tradition and Change* [Chicago: University of Chicago Press, 1977], pp. 225–239). He then elaborated the notion at length in *Structure* (n. 1), pp. 10–42, and recurred to it in his critique of Karl Popper in "Logic of Discovery or Psychology of Research" (in Imré Lakatos & Alan Musgrave, *Criticism and the Growth of Knowledge* [Cambridge: Cambridge University Press, 1970], pp. 1–22). Quoted passages are from *Structure*, pp. 24, 38.

6. Kuhn, "Logic of Discovery" (n. 5), p. 12; reprinted in *Essential Tension* (n. 5), p. 280.

7. Kuhn, *Structure* (n. 1), pp. 160-173; Kuhn, "Logic of Discovery" (n. 5), pp. 278–280; Aristides Baltas, Kostas Gavroglu, & Vassiliki Kindi, "A Discussion with Thomas S. Kuhn," in Thomas S. Kuhn, *The Road Since Structure: Philosophical Essays, 1970–1993, with an Autobiographical Interview*, edited by James Conant & John Haugeland (Chicago: University of Chicago Press, 2000), pp. 255–323, at pp. 307–308.

ened the impact of his original formulation, stressing that incommensurabilities were partial and could be overcome when proponents of one paradigm (or theory) took the time and trouble to learn the language of another paradigm (or theory). In the years preceding his death in 1997, he turned to an evolutionary epistemology in order to give a new, positive spin to incommensurability as necessary to the continuous growth of knowledge within the relatively isolated communities of scientific subspecialists.[8] More recent work in the philosophy of science has elaborated the evolution of Kuhn's viewpoint and underscored the manner in which incommensurability is compatible with rational theory change that moves science toward progressively more realistic accounts of one or another aspect of the natural world.[9]

Within normal science, of course, the idea of progress is unproblematic, since it occurs within a dominant paradigm that identifies problems that are resolvable with existing tools and methodologies. I

---

8. Just as one product of Darwinian evolution was speciation, so, for the "late" Kuhn, scientific revolutions were "associated with an increase in the number of scientific specialties required for the continued acquisition of scientific knowledge." The evolution of knowledge thereby resided in the proliferation of such specialties, and the incommensurabilities or conceptual disparities that kept the specialties apart furthered the growth of knowledge within each specialty. "Knowledge production," wrote Kuhn, "is the particular business of the subspecialties, whose practitioners struggle to improve incrementally the accuracy, consistency, breadth of applicability, and simplicity of the set of beliefs they acquired during their education, their initiation into the practice." See Thomas S. Kuhn, "The Trouble with the Historical Philosophy of Science" (1991), in Conant & Haugeland, eds., *Road Since Structure* (n. 7), pp. 105–120, quoted at p. 117 and "Afterwords," in Paul Horwich, ed., *World Changes: Thomas Kuhn and the Nature of Science* (Cambridge: MIT Press, 1993), pp. 311–341, quoted at p. 336. For an illuminating discussion of Kuhn's evolutionary epistemology and its failure to eliminate the relativism that figured so prominently in his original account of incommensurability, see Xiang Chen, "Thomas Kuhn's Latest Notion of Incommensurability," *J. Gen. Phil. Sci.*, 28:257–273, 1997.

9. On the integration of Kuhnian incommensurability, especially as it pertains to the cognitive task of learning new concepts, with a version of scientific realism, see especially Harold I. Brown, "Incommensurability and Reality," in Paul Hoyningen-Huene & Howard Sankey, eds., *Incommensurability and Related Matters* (Dordrecht: Kluwer, 2001), pp. 123–142 and Harold I. Brown, "Incommensurability Reconsidered," *Stud. Hist. Phil. Sci.*, 36:149–169, 2005. Chen emphasizes the critical role of scientific instruments in a revised understanding of incommensurability that avoids the relativism of Kuhn's approach in "Kuhn's Latest Notion of Incommensurability" (n. 8), pp. 268–272.

am all too aware of the controversies that typify the history of Western medicine. Yet, in this work, for heuristic and comparative purposes, I am content to take Western biomedicine as an example of a mature healing discipline that has progressed in the manner of normal science since roughly the final third of the nineteenth century. Over the course of this period, that is, medical progress has been progressive and cumulative within a single paradigm. To contribute to medical progress was, and is, to become part of this tradition and to work within this paradigm.

It goes without saying that experimental and clinical researchers no less than practicing clinicians have encountered a plethora of novelties and anomalies that caused this or that aspect of the modern medical paradigm to be modified or reconceptualized or abandoned. But, in the period of scientific medicine that took hold after the American Civil War, such novelties and anomalies never led to a revolutionary crisis of Kuhnian proportions. Rather, the history of medical discovery over the past century and a half is the history of continuous rearticulation of the dominant biomedical paradigm as it seeks to resolve anomalies and to encompass discoveries and innovations of an experimental, conceptual, and clinical-observational nature. In point of fact, medical history during the modern period is normal science in action. Furthermore, over the course of the twentieth century, each of the medical specialties became an exemplar of normal-science progress. Even psychiatry, a traditionally marginal specialty with a problematic relationship to the medical mainstream, has been cumulatively progressive since the end of World War II.

This last is hardly a ringing endorsement of contemporary "scientific" psychiatry. My claim is simply that psychiatry, no less than cardiology or ophthalmology or surgery, has for more than half a century undergone evolutionary growth in a manner convergent with normal science. One may put whatever normative spin one wishes on this historical reality.

Psychiatry, no less than other medical specialties, has become more cohesive, more like normal science, largely in instrumental and technical ways. And so, many will argue, psychiatry has arguably achieved its paradigmatic integrity at the expense of ontological breadth and clinical resourcefulness. A clinical paradigm, after all, is no less noteworthy for the problems it excludes than for those it deems solvable and targets for research, funding, and clinical intervention.

And this brings us to psychoanalysis, whose disciplinary status has been a topic of ongoing discussion throughout its troublous history. In the quarter century that followed World War II, American psychoanalysis was not only medicalized; it was embraced as the guiding light of psychiatry, its parent specialty. For William and Karl Menninger, Robert Knight, Kenneth Appel, and others who led psychiatry into the postwar era, modern psychiatry, which is to say a psychiatry that incorporated the lessons learned by military psychiatrists during the war, could *only* be psychoanalytic psychiatry. Thus, American psychoanalysis, in its postwar ego-psychological reincarnation, had the appearance of a scientific paradigm; it would, according to the best and brightest of the day, not only lead psychiatry to a new and enviable position among the medical specialties but also guide the nation in a program of social, political, and educational reform. It represented the nation's paradigmatic pathway to mental health and civic renewal.

All this began to fall apart a quarter century later, and, as we shall see in chapter 1, there were incipient signs of paradigmatic breakup even earlier. What I elaborate in chapter 1 bears mentioning here: When I refer to the "marginalization" of psychoanalysis I am using the term in a neutral, sociological sense. The fractionation of American psychoanalysis, the manner in which a once cohesive paradigm has splintered into a number of contentious psychoanalytic schools of thought, is not tantamount to marginalization but, as I hope to demonstrate, it has fed into and thereby accelerated it. Certainly one might argue that psychoanalysis has become marginal in the manner I suggest but not for the reasons I suggest. My argument is that in America the internal fractionation of psychoanalysis into rivalrous and even sect-like groupings and the marginalization of the field have proceeded in tandem over the past three decades; historically, the two trends are intertwined.

My point of entry to the intertwining of fractionation and marginalization is the history of psychoanalytic book publishing in America since World War II. This part of the book is a case study of the role of books, journals, and publishing in the rise and fall of a small, historically insular profession. The chapters that follow bring a more historical, sociological, and philosophical purview to bear on the eclipse of American psychoanalysis by other approaches to mental healing. The American psychoanalytic community has been aware of its retreat to the margins for a good quarter century, and a number of

American psychoanalytic subcommunities have developed their own strategies of survival and renewal in the face of this ineluctable trend. The central chapters of this book explore and critique the most important of these strategies, each of which provides a different perspective on why American psychoanalysis is threatened with extinction. These strategies, briefly noted, are: The effort to reestablish "common ground" among psychoanalysts on the basis of heuristic clinical assumptions; the recourse to what analysts term "theoretical pluralism" as a viable resting place for their profession; the use of contemporary research from nonclinical disciplines (such as attachment theory, neurobiology, and dynamic systems theory) to provide an integrative framework through which psychoanalysis can be rendered scientific and the disparate psychoanalytic schools of thought brought together in common purpose; and the belief that psychoanalysis can survive and even thrive if it is simply taught and used in a comparative manner, i.e., as "comparative psychoanalysis."

What would otherwise end as a cautionary story of the inevitable marginalization of any profession that resists integration into the scientific mainstream takes a somewhat unexpected turn in the final chapters, and this ending attests to my belief that there is more to marginalization than meets the eye. The history of alternative medicine in America, and the assimilationist dynamic through which it has simultaneously approached the mainstream and drawn the mainstream toward it, is exemplary of what sociologists term "optimal marginalization." Perhaps, however improbably, psychoanalysis can learn something useful from the history of alternative approaches to health care as they emerged and matured in the late-nineteenth and twentieth centuries. I do not compare psychoanalysis to homeopathy, osteopathy, naturopathy, and chiropractic to disparage it by association, but rather to point out that life at the margins has more to offer than one might suppose.

Psychoanalysis at the Margins

Chapter 1

Psychoanalysis and Its Crises, Publishing and Otherwise

Now, of course, what was put together has come apart: the professional authority of psychoanalysis is in tatters. Psychoanalysis has
lost its preeminent standing in psychiatry, barely holding its own as
one treatment modality among many. Many question whether it is
scientific at all, belonging among the other medical procedures and
practices supported by empirical research. Analysts themselves
question what has come to be called "the medical model." More-
over, the reputation of Freud has suffered a shattering reversal. Not
only has the public come to view him with suspicion, but analysts
themselves have come to be dispersed among so many varied analytic
schools that Freud no longer represents the authoritative center of
psychoanalysis that he once did.[1]

If a history of scholarly publishing in the final decades of twentieth-
century America is ever written, psychoanalytic publishing—the
publishing of specialized books and journals for psychoanalysts, psychoanalytic psychotherapists, and psychoanalytically engaged academics—
will be consigned, deservedly, to a footnote. And the story of The
Analytic Press (TAP), a minuscule publishing enterprise in Hillsdale,
New Jersey, that struggled to stay afloat from 1982 to 2006, will be a
footnote to that footnote. And yet TAP is at the heart of my story. I
ran the firm from 1984 until its offices closed on December 22, 2005,
and my 22 years at the helm of this tiny ship are the experiential well-
spring of this book.

1. Kenneth Eisold, "The Splitting of the New York Psychoanalytic Society and the
Construction of Psychoanalytic Authority," *Int. J. Psycho-Anal.*, 79:871–885, 1998,
quoted at p. 882.

1

For TAP, the epitome of a small specialty publisher that catered to a small professional readership, opens to a large and intriguing story. It not only provides a window into the recent history of American psychoanalysis but also tells us something about a set of issues that ranges well beyond psychoanalysis. TAP's rise and fall gathers into itself valuable lessons about America's culture of mental health and mental healing, about America's enduring but hesitant embrace of mainstream science, about contemporary medicine, and even about the idea of progress. TAP's story fuels my story: It guides me to historical, sociological, and philosophical reflections on the role of psychoanalysis and "talking" treatment in general in the ever-evolving landscape of American health care. Finally, the history of TAP is an intriguing microcosm of fundamental changes in book publishing that occurred during the brief period of its existence. These changes, to borrow the title and subtitle of a book by André Schiffrin, revolve around "the business of books," with "how the international conglomerates took over publishing and changed the way we read."[2]

The setting forth of this history in such exemplary respects must be reserved for a later date. Here it suffices to note that the history of TAP coincides with the implosion of American psychoanalysis over the past three decades into a congeries of small, rivalrous, and—until very recently—isolated professional communities. TAP was a casualty of the fractionation of American psychoanalysis into these entrenched "part-fields," and its rise and fall speaks to the special quandary of disciplines and professions that successfully resist absorption into the scientific mainstream of a particular society in a particular time and place. And TAP was also a casualty of the sea change in American mental health that, beginning in the 1970s, increasingly marginalized psychoanalysis and psychoanalytically oriented therapies, a reality to which Kenneth Eisold, writing a decade ago, eloquently attests.

Marginalization, as we shall see in our final chapters, is not a death warrant for a profession or discipline. Far from it. In the case of American psychoanalysis, however, marginalization has intensified what historians and journalists have long characterized as the "cri-

2. André Schiffrin, *The Business of Books: How the International Conglomerates Took Over Publishing and Changed the Way We Read* (NY: Verso, 2000).

sis" of the field. Its long-standing isolation from academia, universities, and the world of normal science has been well and repeatedly documented.[3] I believe my background as a publisher and historian of ideas provides a different vantage point from which to understand an evolving crisis that has at long last reached, well, crisis proportions. As we shall see in the final two chapters, the kind of crisis that now imperils the very existence of American psychoanalysis is the shared quandary of all alternative (i.e., unorthodox) approaches to health care.

This crisis has been long in the making; its tributaries are plentiful. In 1964, the Chicago analyst Maxwell Gitelson was writing about the "identity crisis" in American psychoanalysis, which he understood as the reflection of an irresolvable tension between analysis as a therapeutic modality pragmatically aligned with psychiatry and analysis as a basic science committed to investigating mental life with due scientific rigor. As the sixties progressed, it was precisely the absence of a credible connection between the field's scientific assumptions, however rigorously pursued, and its clinical operation in the everyday world that fueled a perception of crisis. According to the historian Nathan Hale, the crisis of psychoanalysis originated in the mid-60s, when the dominant school of American psychoanalytic thought, the "ego psychology" of the postwar generation, was strenuously challenged on methodological and scientific grounds by George Klein and Robert Holt, two Menninger-trained psychologist-psychoanalysts. Hale's reading turns on its head the perspective of Erich Fromm who, writing in 1970, equated the crisis of psychoanalysis with the ascendancy of this selfsame ego psychology, which he berated as a conformist dilution of European psychoanalysis. The crisis, for Fromm, signified

---

3. Nathan G. Hale's *The Rise and Crisis of Psychoanalysis in the United States: Freud and the Americans, 1917–1985* (NY: Oxford University Press, 1995) exemplifies the "crisis" literature, but it stops short of the broadening and deepening of the crisis over the past quarter century. For a more recent exposition from the standpoint of contemporary psychiatry, see Joel Paris, *The Fall of an Icon: Psychoanalysis and Academic Psychiatry* (Toronto: University of Toronto Press, 2005). Writings that link the crisis of psychoanalysis to its failure to become a normal science form a virtual industry. Adolf Grünbaum, *The Foundations of Psychoanalysis: A Philosophical Critique* (Berkeley: University of California Press, 1985) and Marshall Edelson, *Psychoanalysis: A Theory in Crisis* (Chicago: University of Chicago Press, 1988) are preeminent examples of this crisis-related subgenre that I briefly consider in chapter 7.

the exchange of the radically transformative goals of Freudian treatment for an ameliorative approach to everyday problems of living.[4]

Depending on how one defines the term, the "crisis" of American psychoanalysis may be moved forward to virtually any point in time from 1960 to the present. A case can be made that the critique of metapsychology of the mid-60s cleared away a conceptual space for the internal crisis that erupted in the late 70s, when Heinz Kohut's "psychoanalytic self psychology" emerged as a rival theoretical and clinical paradigm that would be neither absorbed into, nor marginalized by, the then psychoanalytic mainstream. Here, perhaps, we discern a crisis in professional cohesion over the continuing centrality of Freud's own theories to psychoanalysis.

And what of psychoanalysis in relation to its American "parent" specialty, psychiatry? Joseph Schildkraut's "The Catecholamine Hypothesis of Affective Disorders," published in the *American Journal of Psychiatry* in 1965, stands out as a seedbed of psychoanalytic crisis. Skillfully weaving together a decade of laboratory and clinical research, Schildkraut suggested that the metabolism of catecholamines—the family of biogenic amines that function as neurotransmitters—provided an understanding of affective disorders that accounted for the effectiveness of the first-generation antidepressants iproniazid and imipramine, both of which, via different mechanisms, prevented cellular reuptake of norepinephrine at receptor sites in the brain.[5]

For American psychiatry, Schildkraut's paper, in David Healy's words, was "the right article at the right time." For American psychoanalysis, however, it heralded the sea change that led to margin-

4. Hale, *Rise and Crisis* (n. 3), pp. 360–363; Erich Fromm, "The Crisis of Psychoanalysis," in *The Crisis of Psychoanalysis: Essays on Freud, Marx, and Social Psychology* (NY: Holt, Rinehart & Winston, 1970), pp. 11–41.

5. J. J. Schildkraut, "The Catecholamine Hypothesis of Affective Disorders: A Review of Supporting Evidence," *Am. J. Psychiatry*, 122:509–522, 1965. The biogenic amines comprise epinephrine, norepinephrine, dopamine, and serotonin. Schildkraut's paper of 1965 dealt primarily with levels of brain norepinephrine, and his findings, which dominated American psychiatry during the 1970s and early 1980s, led to what is now termed the norepinephrine version of the catecholamine theory of depression. From the mid-1980s on, following the marketing of Prozac and other selective serotonin reuptake inhibitors (SSRIs), the serotonin version of the theory supplanted the norepinephrine version in popular consciousness. See David Healy, *The Creation of Psychopharmacology* (Cambridge: Harvard University Press, 2002), p. 209.

ality. The catecholamine hypothesis of affective disorder, especially depression, would dominate American psychiatry and set psychiatric research agendas for the two decades to follow; for all its shortcomings, the hypothesis helped propel American psychiatry to a non-analytic explanatory paradigm, one that "made some effort to account for the fact that antidepressants worked and afforded some predictions that could be tested about the mechanism of action of those drugs." Throughout the 60s and 70s, American psychiatrists, whatever their orientation, joined together in prescribing tricyclic antidepressants whose action appeared to be explained by the hypothesis. Not so the analysts, whose marginalization was foretold by "the advent of the psychiatric researcher who was conversant with the details of neuro-transmitter metabolism, receptor binding, and endocrine changes—a researcher who spoke a different language from the analyst."[6]

Nineteen seventy-seven, the year of publication of Kohut's *The Restoration of the Self,* was also the year Gerald Klerman and his colleagues at the National Institute of Mental Health began planning the series of studies on depressive disorder that would be implemented from 1982 through 1986 and would eventually yield (arguably) the first methodologically rigorous data on the comparative effectiveness of different treatment approaches to clinically significant depression. The NIMH protocol, which began with a two-year period of training workshops for participating clinicians, compared imipramine (Tofranil) and placebo, both administered in an "optimal therapeutic encounter," with cognitive therapy and interpersonal therapy, the two modalities that had sparked renewed interest in "talking therapies" throughout the 1970s. Psychodynamically informed treatment, much less full-blown psychoanalysis, was never on the planners' drawing board. For the historian, these two signs of external marginalization dovetail, respectively, with the scientific critique of ego psychology in

---

6. David Healy, *The Antidepressant Era* (Cambridge: Harvard University Press, 1997), pp. 157, 159. Cf. pp. 70–71, where Healy claims that the catecholamine hypothesis of depression "sounded the death knell for analysis . . . it did so because though it was in many ways far more simplistic and unidimensional than analytic notions about depression, it provided an alternative framework that was seen by many both within the profession and among the lay public as having a better chance than analytic theories of accounting for one of the new central facts about depression—its response to drug treatments."

the mid-60s and the internal crisis of cohesion marked by Kohut's *Restoration of the Self* (1977) and continuing with his final writings.

Nineteen eighty is a nodal point of crisis: It marked the unveiling of the third edition of the American Psychiatric Association's *Diagnostic and Statistical Manual* (DSM-III). The triumph of Robert Spitzer and his contingent of neo-Kraepelinian diagnostic methodologists at Washington University (St. Louis) and Columbia University, DSM-III jettisoned the psychobiological and psychoanalytic framework of its earlier editions and replaced it with a diagnostic system organized around observable symptoms and behaviors. In a nutshell, DSM-III successfully remedicalized psychiatric diagnosis. The effort at psychoanalytically inspired conceptualization that had gained expression in DSM-I and fairly dominated DSM-II gave way to a classification aimed at standardizing psychiatric assessment, rendering psychiatric diagnoses more reliable from clinician to clinician, and enabling psychotropic drug researchers to formulate inclusion and exclusion criteria for study subjects in psychotropic drug trials targeted at specific syndromes.[7] DSM-III, as Healy pithily observes, "was the Trojan horse by which they [the neo-Kraepelians] effected entry into the citadel of psychoanalysis."[8] And this reincarnation of the Trojan horse, like its ancient Greek forebear, was celebrated far and wide—in this case by the pharmaceutical industry and FDA, by government regulators and HMO administrators, by psychotherapists allied with behaviorism and cognitive therapy—by everyone, that is, but the analysts. Surely the publication of DSM-III, which encased in concrete the wedge that had been driven between American psychiatry and psychoanalysis as far back as 1965, was, for the analysts, a blossoming of the crisis foretold by the NIMH's decision to exclude psychodynamic approaches from its massive, comparative studies of depression. A crisis of relevance was at hand.

In the following year, the crisis of relevance sealed by DSM-III sprouted crisis nodes in several directions. Nineteen eighty-one was

---

7. The history of DSM-III—the confluence of problems internal and external to psychiatry that gave rise to it; the work of Washington University methodologists throughout the 1970s that laid the foundation for it; and the struggles and compromises within American psychiatry attendant to its adoption—is ably recounted by Mitchell Wilson, "DSM-III and the Transformation of American Psychiatry: A History," *Am. J. Psychiatry*, 150:399–410.

8. Healy, *Antidepressant Era* (n. 6), pp. 231–237, quoted at p. 233.

marked by Heinz Kohut's death; Jeffrey Masson's dismissal as projects director of the Sigmund Freud Archives; and Peter Swales's original presentation to the psychology faculty of New York University on Freud's alleged affair with, and impregnation of, his sister-in-law, Minna Bernays.[9] For the analysts, the crisis of diagnostic relevance was now aggravated by a collateral crisis in professional authority that apparently extended to Freud's own person.[10] Less well known but equally portentous, 1981 marked the editorial decline of International Universities Press (IUP), long the psychoanalyst's professional publishing firm of choice. Founded by the Russian expatriate Abram Saulovich Kagan in 1943, IUP was the premier independent publisher of psychoanalytic books from the 1950s through the 1970s and was closely allied with the American Psychoanalytic Association.[11] The

9. Swales's presentation, which I attended and recall as quite dazzling, was at an NYU clinical psychology colloquium on the evening of November 18, 1981, and was entitled "Freud, Minna Bernays, and the Conquest of Rome: New Light on the Origins of Psychoanalysis." It was published under the same title a year later in *The New American Review*, Spring/Summer 1982, pp. 1–23.

10. The *New York Times* brought the early work of Masson and Swales to the attention of a wide readership in back-to-back lead stories on page 1 of the "Science Times" sections of August 18 and August 25, 1981. Then, in its issue of November 30, 1981, *Newsweek* brought the crisis in professional authority to national attention with a cover story on "The Hidden Freud: His Secret Life; His Theories Under Attack." The story, like the earlier *Times* pieces by Ralph Blumenthal, reviewed the recent wave of Freud scholarship that revolved around the grounds of Freud's repudiation of the seduction hypothesis (Jeffrey Masson; Marianne Krüll); Freud's early relationship to, and dependency on, Wilhelm Fliess (Jeffrey Masson; Frank Sulloway; Peter Swales); Freud's therapeutic integrity (Milton Klein & David Tribich); and Freud's personal life and character (Peter Swales). Masson's dismissal from the Freud Archives, which followed his unauthorized use of then unpublished Freud-Fliess correspondence in a lecture at Yale at which he argued that Freud's repudiation of his seduction theory in 1897 was opportunistic and clinically disastrous, also rated a page in *Time* magazine, "Muffling the Master's Voice," *Time*, November 23, 1981, p. 59.

11. A graduate of the Law Faculty of St. Petersburg University, Kagan had a career in academic and literary publishing that began in pre-revolutionary Russia, where he worked for *Nauka I Shkola* (*Science and School*), a cooperative publishing enterprise of prominent St. Petersburg-based Russian scholars, and then, with two literary scholars, cofounded the Petropolis publishing house. Following his deportation by the Bolsheviks in 1922, Kagan resettled in Berlin, where he was active in several publishing ventures, the transplanted Petropolis among them. Kagan and his wife fled Germany in 1938, spent two years in Belgium, and arrived in New York (via Paris and Toulouse) in June, 1942. Kagan's interest in psychiatry and psychoanalysis

firm's quickening descent in the early 80s, which encouraged other small publishers to enter the publishing fray, compounded the afore-mentioned crises of relevance and authority with an impending crisis in the field's venues of professional communication, in its ability to disseminate the written word.

In the mid-80s, we discern four additional signposts of crisis, the first two in the form of two very different but equally unsettling publications: Janet Malcolm's *In the Freud Archives* of 1984, a compromising portrait of the field's political underbelly initially serialized in *The New Yorker*, and Adolf Grünbaum's *The Foundations of Psychoanalysis: A Philosophical Critique* of 1985, an uncompromising critique of the field's scientific pretensions. Nineteen eighty-five was also the year that four psychologist-psychoanalysts filed a class-action lawsuit against the American Psychoanalytic Association, two of its member societies, and the International Psychoanalytical Association. The suit alleged a monopolization of psychoanalytic training, to the detriment of psychologists and of the analyst-seeking public, in viola-

---

long antedated his founding of IUP in 1943: He was the first to publish Freud in Russian in the 1910s. More than a decade after his death in 1983, Kagan received a brief tribute in *JAPA* written by Charles Brenner ("Tribute to Abram S. Kagan," *JAPA*, 44:1015–1016, 1996), but it contains many errors. I am grateful to Professor Olga Demidova of Herzen State Pedagogical University (St. Petersburg, Russia), the editor of Kagan's diaries, who generously answered my various questions about him and whose archival research is the basis of the brief remarks given here. IUP, which at the time of my employment had only 15 employees, managed to compete more or less successfully with several university presses (Harvard, Yale, Chicago) and a major trade imprint (Basic Books) for top-tier psychoanalytic titles. IUP's decline followed Dr. Kagan's retirement in the mid-70s, at which time management of the firm passed to Kagan's daughter, Irene, and her husband, Martin Azarian. Shortly thereafter, Azarian divorced Kagan's daughter (who remarried the analyst Samuel Guttman in 1978), bought out her interest in the company, and became president and owner of IUP. I began my career in psychoanalytic publishing as editor at IUP in 1979–1980 and witnessed firsthand the disintegration of this once distinguished imprint. The "crisis" of 1981 followed the efforts of the IUP staff to unionize, which led to Azarian's firing of employees. A year after I left the firm, IUP had undergone a complete turnover of staff. Around this same time, new independent firms, principally Guilford Press and then TAP, entered the scene, compounding the desertion of authors from IUP. I left IUP shortly before the crisis of unionization but was fully apprised of events by my IUP colleague and friend, Nick Cariello.

tion of the Sherman Antitrust Act of 1890.[12] Finally, in 1985 a Baltimore arbitration panel awarded $250,000 to Dr. Raphael Osheroff, a nephrologist who in 1982 brought suit against Chestnut Lodge, the esteemed, psychoanalytically oriented treatment facility where Osheroff had been hospitalized for seven months in 1979. The suit alleged malpractice owing to the Chestnut Lodge staff's misdiagnosis of Osheroff's severe biological depression as the affective coloring of an underlying "narcissistic personality disorder," which the staff elected to treat with psychoanalytic psychotherapy alone. Osheroff was not prescribed any antidepressant medication over the course of a prolonged institutionalization during which his condition continuously worsened.[13] The Chestnut Lodge staff held to its psychoanalytic course despite Osheroff's manifest deterioration and despite evidence that a previous course of medication, privately prescribed, had been helpful to him. After seven months, Osheroff's family removed him from Chestnut Lodge and had him admitted to the Silver Hill Foundation in New Canaan, Connecticut, where he was rediagnosed as psychotically depressed and treated with a combination of phenothiazine and tricyclic antidepressants. He evinced marked improvement in three weeks, was discharged in three months, and experienced no relapse in the decade to follow.[14] Taken together, these four events

---

12. The plaintiffs' action represented the large class of clinical psychologists desirous of psychoanalytic training and was supported by the Psychoanalysis Division of the American Psychological Association. The outstanding study of this signal event in the political history of American psychoanalysis, including its anlagen and sequelae, is Robert Wallerstein, *Lay Analysis: Life Inside the Controversy* (Hillsdale, NJ: Analytic Press, 1998). For a clear synopsis of these particulars, see Robert S. Wallerstein & Edward M. Weinshel, "The Future of Psychoanalysis," *Psychoanal. Quart.*, 58:341–373, 1989 at pp. 341–349.

13. Over the course of his seven months of inpatient care at Chestnut Lodge, Osheroff experienced major weight loss (up to 40 pounds), severe insomnia, and marked psychomotor agitation.

14. Both parties appealed the arbitration panel award to court, but settlement for an undisclosed amount was reached prior to trial. The verdict in *Osheroff v. Chestnut Lodge* (Civil Action No. 66024, Circuit Court for Montgomery County, Maryland, 1984) triggered an animated debate within American psychiatry that centered on the defensibility of exclusive psychodynamic management of severe psychopathology (typically diagnosed as personality disorders) in an era of psychotropic agents

seemed to instantiate the aforementioned crises of relevance and authority and to fuel them with contiguous crises of scientific legitimacy
and civil accountability.

We may, if we choose, jump forward another five years to 1990,
the year fluoxetine hydrochloride (Prozac), released in December,
1987, achieved its "most prescribed" status in American psychiatry
and heralded a revolution in psychopharmacology that would eventually seal the marginalization of psychoanalysis through a coalescence
of patient expectations, insurer requirements, and pharmaceutically
driven research agendas. Over the course of the 90s, many medical
psychoanalysts, no less than their patients, would embrace Prozac and
its successors—the family of selective serotonin reuptake inhibitors
(SSRIs)—as useful, and for certain "analyzable" patients, even essential, treatment adjuncts. Within the world of psychoanalysis, these
events suggest a crisis of belief in therapeutic efficacy, certainly of
therapeutic self-sufficiency, that aggravated the preexisting crises of
scientific legitimacy and civil accountability. Summing up a decade

---

whose effectiveness had been demonstrated by randomized controlled trials (RCT).
The debate played itself out in the pages of the *American Journal of Psychiatry* with
major articles by Gerald L. Klerman ("The Psychiatric Patient's Right to Effective
Treatment: Implications of Osheroff v. Chestnut Lodge," *Am. J. Psychiatry*, 147:409–
418, 1990) and Alan A. Stone ("Law, Science, and Psychiatric Malpractice: A Response to Klerman's Indictment of Psychoanalytic Psychiatry," *Am. J. Psychiatry*,
147:419–427, 1990), which generated a raft of letters to the editor. The facts of the
case and its import on psychotherapeutic practice have been thoughtfully reviewed
by J. D. Malcolm, "Treatment Choices and Informed Consent in Psychiatry: Implications of the Osheroff Case for the Profession," *J. Psychiatry Law*, 14:9–107, 1987
and Wendy L. Packman, Mithran G. Cabot, & Bruce Bongar, "Malpractice Arising
from Negligent Psychotherapy: Ethical, Legal, and Clinical Implications of *Osheroff
v. Chestnut Lodge*," *Ethics Behav.*, 4:175–197, 1994. The implications of the case
rate continuing mention in more recent literature, e.g., David Healy, *The Antidepressant Era* (n. 6), pp. 245–251; Daniel Widlöcher, "Quality Control, Condensed Analysis
and Ethics," *Int. J. Psycho-Anal.*, 79:1–11, 1998; Michael Robertson, "Power and
Knowledge in Psychiatry and the Troubling Case of Dr. Osheroff," *Austral. Psychiatry*, 13:343–350, 2005; Paris, *Fall of an Icon* (n. 3), pp. 95–98; and John M. Oldham,
"Editorial: Psychodynamic Psychotherapy for Personality Disorders," *Am. J. Psychiatry*, 164:1465–1467, 2007. The anthropologist Theresa Luhrmann makes good use
of the Osheroff case in her consideration of the split between psychoanalysis and
"psychiatric science" in American psychiatry in the 70s and 80s; she deems it "the
most famous instance of the ideological struggle" between the two orientations. See
T. M. Luhrmann, *Of Two Minds: The Growing Disorder in American Psychiatry*
(NY: Knopf, 2000), pp. 232–235, quoted at p. 232.

of frustration attendant to the ascendancy of the SSRIs, which fed into a cultural ambience that demanded what he termed "'fast-fast-fast' relief," the analyst Richard Chessick imputed the crisis of psychoanalysis to a failure of nerve "in the teeth of the abusive behavior of insurance companies regarding the payment for psychoanalysis."[15]

By the final years of the last century, signs of crisis abounded in all directions. We beheld the dearth of analytic trainees and analytic patients; the financial crisis of the august Menninger Clinic; and the controversy attendant to the Library of Congress exhibition on Freud's life and work.[16] In psychoanalytic publishing, my own small neck of these crisis-ridden woods, we beheld the drastically diminished readership of psychoanalytic books, which resulted in the withdrawal of university presses such as Harvard and Yale from this long-established genre of scholarly publishing. And spanning all the crisis-related particulars given above, indeed rising above them in the manner of a grand *arc de crise*, is the decade-by-decade documentation of the (singly, and in various combinations) organizationally flawed, conformity inducing, creativity stifling, and psychologically crippling structure of traditional psychoanalytic training. One need not look to contemporary literature for elaboration of the "organizational and educational crisis in psychoanalysis," which encompasses, inter alia, "the problems of excessive orthodoxy, idealization and intimidation, at least in the lives of candidates."[17] These themes were sounded in the 1940s by Michael Balint; in the 1950s by Greta Bibring and Clara Thompson;

15. Richard D. Chessick, "The Contemporary Failure of Nerve and the Crisis in Psychoanalysis," *J. Am. Acad. Psychoanal.*, 29:658–678, 2001, quoted at p. 676.

16. The crisis, search for a financial partner, and near-demise of the Menninger Clinic in the late 90s were charted in the pages of the *Topeka Capital-Journal*. See, for example, Harold Voth, "Menninger Is Dead; I Saw the Menningers Kill It," *Capital-Journal*, December 29, 2001; Ira Stamm, "Menninger Has a Distinguished Past but What Is Its Future?" *Capital-Journal*, January 6, 2002; and Michael Hooper, "Menninger Board to Discuss Partnership," *Capital-Journal*, November 15, 2002. On the crisis attendant to the Freud exhibit at the Library of Congress, see Margaret Talbot, "The Museum Show Has an Ego Disorder," *New York Times*, October 11, 1999.

17. César Garza-Guerrero, "'The Crisis in Psychoanalysis': What Crisis Are We Talking About?" *Int. J. Psycho-Anal.*, 83:57–83, 2002, quoted at p. 76; Kenneth Eisold, "The Intolerance of Diversity in Psychoanalytic Institutes," *Int. J. Psycho-Anal.*, 75:785–800, 1994, quoted at p. 786.

in the 1960s by Anna Freud and Phyllis Greenacre; in the 1970s by Jacob Arlow and Daniel Widlöcher; and in the 1980s and 1990s by Arlow, Kenneth Eisold, John Gedo, Arnold Goldberg, Otto Kernberg, Robert Wallerstein, Edward Weinshel, and Helmut Thomä.[18] This tradition of crisis-exposition is alive and well in the crisis-bloated new century, with especially trenchant critiques of psychoanalytic education and its relationship to the deepening crisis in the field by Kernberg, Eisold, and César Garza-Guerrero, among others.[19]

One could argue endlessly about when exactly any or all of the aforementioned events and developments culminated in a *real* crisis in psychoanalysis. Equally, one could debate ad nauseam whether or not "crisis" is the best way to characterize whatever it is that has been happening to psychoanalysis within the healing professions, the mental health research establishment, academia, and the general culture over the past four decades. As a historian, I choose not to add to desultory musings that convey, variously, exasperation, anger, hand-

---

18. Michael Balint, "On the Psycho-Analytic Training System," *Int. J. Psycho-Anal.*, 29:163–173, 1948; Greta Bibring, "The Training Analysis and Its Place in Psycho-Analytic Training," *Int. J. Psycho-Anal.*, 35:169–173, 1954; Clara Thompson, "A Study of the Emotional Climate of Psychoanalytic Institutes," *Psychiatry*, 21:45–51, 1958; Anna Freud, "The Ideal Psychoanalytic Institute: A Utopia," in *Writings of Anna Freud*, vol. 7 (NY: International Universities Press, 1966–1970), pp. 73–93; Phyllis Greenacre, "Problems of Training Analysis," *Psychoanal. Quart.*, 35:540–567, 1966; Jacob Arlow, "Some Dilemmas in Psychoanalytic Education, *JAPA*, 20:556–566, 1972; Daniel Widlöcher, "The Ego Ideal of the Psychoanalyst," *Int. J. Psycho-Anal.*, 59:387–390, 1978; Jacob Arlow, "Psychoanalytic Education: A Psychoanalytic Perspective," in *Ann. Psychoanal.*, vol. 10 (NY: International Universities Press, 1982), pp. 5–20; John Gedo, "Essay on Psychoanalytic Education," in *Psychoanalysis and Its Discontents* (NY: Guilford, 1984), pp. 167–178; Otto Kernberg, "Institutional Problems of Psychoanalytic Education," *JAPA*, 34:799–834, 1986; Robert S. Wallerstein & Edward S. Weinshel, "The Future of Psychoanalysis," *Psychoanal. Quart.*, 58:341–373, 1989; Arnold Goldberg, "Authentic Analysis," in *The Prisonhouse of Psychoanalysis* (Hillsdale, NJ: Analytic Press, 1990), pp. 133–149; Helmut Thomä, "Training Analysis and Psychoanalytic Education: Proposals for Reform," in *Ann. Psychoanal.*, vol. 21 (Hillsdale, NJ: Analytic Press, 1993), pp. 3–75; Kenneth Eisold, "The Intolerance of Diversity in Psychoanalytic Institutes" (n. 17); Otto Kernberg, "Thirty Methods to Destroy the Creativity of Psychoanalytic Candidates," *Int. J. Psycho-Anal.*, 77:1031–1040, 1996.

19. Otto Kernberg, "A Concerned Critique of Psychoanalytic Education," *Int. J. Psycho-Anal.*, 81:97–120, 2000; Garza-Guerrero, "'Crisis in Psychoanalysis'" (n. 17); Kenneth Eisold, "The Profession of Psychoanalysis: Past Failures and Future Possibilities," *Contemp. Psychoanal.*, 39:557–582, 2003.

wringing, and denial. Excepting occasional works of historical reflection and infrequent media coverage, writings about the "crisis in psychoanalysis" have been internal to the field and therefore less than edifying. My own concerns lead me to the sociological concept I invoked at the outset, viz., marginalization, as a perfectly adequate descriptor of what has happened to psychoanalysis in America since the 1970s.

Marginalization, as I will use it throughout this work, has clear quantitative and qualitative referents in relation to the socioeconomic and political "center" of mental health care. Equally important, it has a dynamic, relational component that captures positive as well as negative meanings.[20] In my final chapters, I will suggest that life at the margins need not be disastrous. Indeed, it offers contemporary psychoanalysts unique opportunities to optimize their marginality in ways that may pull the mainstream toward it. But the strategic use of marginality is predicated on acceptance of marginal status as a sociological fact of life. Many analysts will be unhappy with the verdict that they have indeed become marginal men and women, but the facts of the matter, sociologically speaking, leave little room for disputation.

It is difficult to demur from the finding of an unbiased anthropologist that a confluence of ideological tensions and economic forces is "pushing the psychodynamic approach out of psychiatry with a nearly

---

20. Sociologists, for example, theorize that marginalization can be a "valuable strategic tool" that encourages self-definition, group cohesion, and innovative thought absent institutional constraints. In this conceptual sense, one may speak of an "optimal marginality" in which alternate sources of cultural and political authority put marginal forces in "dialectical interaction" with the mainstream. Jaap Bos and Neil McLaughlin argue that just this sense of positive marginality typifies particular psychoanalytic theorists such as Erich Fromm and particular periods in psychoanalytic history. See Neil McLaughlin, "Revision from the Margins: Fromm's Contributions to Psychoanalysis," *Int. Forum Psychoanal.*, 9:241–247, 2000 and "Optimal Marginality: Innovation and Orthodoxy in Fromm's Revision of Psychoanalysis," *Soc. Quart.*, 42:271–288, 2001 and Jaap Bos, David W. Park, & Petteri Pietikainen, "Strategic Self-Marginalization: The Case of Psychoanalysis," *J. Hist. Behav. Sci.*, 41:207–224, 2005. Note that this dynamic conception of marginality differs from the older sense of the term as signifying depreciated outsider status. In this latter sense, Harvey Smith wrote a half century ago of psychiatry as a marginal medical specialty and of psychiatrists as embattled "marginal men of medicine" who labored under stresses in scientific orientation, collegial relationships, and self-definition that might take them to a professional "break[ing] point." Harvey L. Smith, "Psychiatry in Medicine: Intra- or Inter-Professional Relationships?" *Am. J. Sociol.*, 63:285–289, 1957.

irresistible force."[21] More specifically, it is difficult to contest the increasingly marginal role of psychoanalysis (indeed, of psychotherapy in general) in the training of American psychiatric residents. It is difficult to argue away the vanishingly small number of psychiatric residents who choose to pursue psychoanalytic training and become psychoanalysts. It is difficult to dispute the nonanalytic backgrounds and orientations of psychiatry chairpersons at major universities, which contrasts greatly with the situation a half century ago. It is difficult to dispute the primacy of biological psychiatry and psychopharmacology, for better or worse, in contemporary psychiatric training and practice. At the level of national policy, it is difficult to deny the progressively less analytic, and—by the end of the 1980s—thoroughly biological orientation of the National Institute of Mental Health both in its leadership and research agenda.[22]

Such historical trends attest to the marginalization of psychoanalysis within American psychiatry. They attest further to a recent, heightened *sense* of crisis about the political and economic viability of the profession among health care policy makers, legislators, government funding agencies, private foundations, and "patients" or "clients" who exercise freedom of choice by selecting one kind of mental health "provider" and one kind of treatment over another.

All this is in stunning contrast to the status of psychoanalysis in American mental health in the two decades following World War II. Prior to the war, American psychiatry was organizationally and politically beleaguered. Lacking the scientific grounding of other medical specialties, it was eclectic by default and hovered noncommittally among its somaticist, holistic (Meyerian), Kraepelinian (classifying), Freudian, and community-oriented constituencies. The war radically changed the power relationships among these groups. As Healy notes, it "led to an influx of clinicians into psychiatry, whose experience in the management of combat reactions led to a decisive switch in orientation from a disease model to Meyerian and analytic approaches." These military psychiatrists—perhaps less than a third of whom had received specialty training before the war—were amazingly success-

---

21. T. M. Luhrmann, *Of Two Minds* (n. 14), p. 203.

22. Analysts writing about the future of their field have acknowledged these interrelated developments for at least a quarter century. See, for example, Wallerstein & Weinshel, "Future of Psychoanalysis" (n. 12), pp. 353–354, 363.

ful in treating combat soldiers with neuropsychiatric disorders with supportive techniques informed by psychodynamic and psychoanalytic concepts. Roughly 60% of the neuropsychiatric "casualties" thus treated returned to duty within two to five days.[23]

With this astonishing record of treatment success in hand, American psychiatry rid itself of its prewar malaise and grew heady with postwar expectations. As both William and Karl Menninger, Roy Grinker, and others averred, wartime experience provided the foundation for renewed therapeutic optimism and social activism under the aegis of psychoanalysis.[24] At war's end, American psychiatry embarked on a period of external expansion (as to residency programs, departments, and professorships) that coincided with the internal dominion of its psychoanalytic contingent. From the 1940s through the 1960s, psychoanalysis, in the Americanized guise of psychodynamic psychiatry, was, in Gerald Grob's words, "virtually synonymous with the psychotherapies." Indeed, the burgeoning role of psychiatry in American life—as trumpeted in a Special Supplement to *The Atlantic* of July, 1961—was equated with the medical, educational, and cultural impact of psychoanalysis.[25]

23. Healy, *Antidepressant Era* (n. 6), pp. 222–223. The percentages given in this paragraph come from Gerald N. Grob, "Origins of DSM-I: A Study in Appearance and Reality," *Am. J. Psychiatry*, 149:421–431, 1991, at p. 427.

24. See William C. Menninger, "Psychiatric Experience in the War, 1941–1946," *Am. J. Psychiatry*, 103:577–586, 1947; William C. Menninger, "The Role of Psychiatry in the World Today," *Am. J. Psychiatry*, 104:155–163, 1947; Leo H. Bartemeier, Lawrence S. Kubie, Karl A. Menninger, et al., "Combat Exhaustion," *J. Nerv. Ment. Dis.*, 104:358–389, 489–525, 1946; and Roy R. Grinker & John P. Spiegel, *War Neuroses* (Philadelphia: Blakiston, 1945), pp. 113–114. Gerald N. Grob provides the best brief account of the transformation of American psychiatry that grew out of its wartime experience in "Psychiatry and Social Activism: The Politics of a Specialty in Postwar America," *Bull. Hist. Med.*, 60:477–501, 1986 and "Origins of DSM-I" (n. 23).

25. Healy, *Antidepressant Era* (n. 6), pp. 222–223; Gerald Grob, "Psychiatry's Holy Grail: The Search for the Mechanisms of Mental Disease," *Bull. Hist. Med.*, 72:189–219, 1998, quoted at p. 213. In his preamble to *The Atlantic*'s rich collection of essays that spanned clinical, institutional, developmental, historical, and applied-analytic topics, editor Charles J. Rolo placed all the contributions under the psychoanalytic umbrella. In America, he remarked, the Freudian Revolution was a matter of "psychoanalysis and psychiatry in general," which conjointly "influenced medicine, the arts and criticism, popular entertainment, advertising, the rearing of children, sociology,

The draw of psychoanalytic training was great, even among psychiatrists who aspired only to general psychiatric practice. Throughout the 50s, the American Psychoanalytic Association had more people in training than it had members. Its annual meetings received national attention. In April, 1956, President Eisenhower sent greetings to the analytic assemblage, remarking that "Its deliberations and conferences will, I'm sure, advance and improve our knowledge and methods and our skills for the betterment of the nation's mental health."[26] This was the period of analysis triumphant,

> when medical analysts achieved dominance within the psychiatric mainstream, shaping residency training programs and the content of psychiatric textbooks, spearheading efforts at psychiatric reform, and occupying positions of regional and national leadership within the profession. Further, it was the period that witnessed the flowering of psychosomatic medicine, when, owing to psychoanalytically guided recognition of the causal role of emotional factors in various functioning disorders, "psychotherapy gained a legitimate entrance into medicine proper and could no longer be restricted exclusively to the field of psychiatry."[27]

---

anthropology, legal thought and practice, humor, manners and mores, even organized religion." See Rolo, "The Freudian Revolution," *The Atlantic*, July, 1961, p. 62.

26. For example, in 1951 the APsaA had 428 active members, 150 associate members of affiliate societies, and over 700 candidates at its various training institutes. Seven years later, in 1958, its 800 analysts in practice were matched by 1,000 in training. See "Increase Is Shown in Psychoanalysts," *New York Times*, May 4, 1951, p. 22; "Rapid Gains Seen in Psychoanalysis," *New York Times*, May 10, 1958, p. 14. Eisenhower's greeting to attendees of the April, 1956 APsaA Conference is quoted in "Physician Urges No-Fee Analysis," *New York Times*, April 29, 1956, p. 42.

27. Paul E. Stepansky, *Freud, Surgery, and the Surgeons* (Hillsdale, NJ: Analytic Press, 1999), p. 207. The passage ends with a quotation from Franz Alexander, *Psychosomatic Medicine: Its Principles and Applications* (NY: Norton, 1950), p. 43. I stop short of Kenneth Eisold's stronger claim that "psychoanalysis did indeed virtually take over psychiatry, as the core discipline, the discipline within the discipline," but I commend Eisold's well-wrought analysis of the historical reasons analysis came to dominate psychiatry in the postwar years, viz., the ability of second-generation orthodox analysts in New York and elsewhere to fuse the professional authority of medicine with Freud's charismatic authority (as represented by senior refugee analysts who reached American shores in the late 30s). See Kenneth Eisold, "Splitting of New York Psychoanalytic Society" (n. 1).

Analytic training was especially important to, almost a sine qua non for, advancement in the world of academic psychiatry. "From 1945 to 1955," reminisced Bertram Brown, Director of NIMH from 1970 to 1978, "it was nearly impossible for a nonpsychoanalyst to become chairman of a department or professor of psychiatry."[28] By 1948, three-quarters of all committee posts in the American Psychiatric Association were held by analysts, and by 1962, 13 of the 17 most recommended psychiatric texts were psychoanalytic in orientation.[29] In the 1980s and 1990s, a single generation later, those few analysts who occupied leadership roles in academic and research establishments—Herbert Pardes, Shervert Frazier, Gerald Klerman, and John Gunderson among them—had sequestered their analytic identities and achieved eminence as nonanalytic, biologically oriented researchers. "Thirty or forty years ago," mused the analyst Marshall Edelson in 1985, "it would have been inconceivable for a group on the frontier of investigations of anxiety and the anxiety disorders to report their ideas and findings, as has been done in Tuma and Maser [editors of the book *Anxiety and the Anxiety Disorders*], largely without any reference—without feeling any need even to refute—the ideas and findings of psychoanalysis." The exclusion of analysis from this research frontier, Edelson continued, could be imputed largely to "certain attitudes toward scientific work that are representative of the psychoanalytic community." Exactly two decades later, Joel Paris, a Canadian research psychiatrist and one-time analytic fellow-traveler, deemed analysis so far outside the research Zeitgeist that "even mentioning analytic theory in a grant application can be as good as poison."[30]

The marginalization of psychoanalysis within American psychology is no less telling. The refugee psychoanalysts who emigrated to America in the late 1930s and early 1940s included analyst-researchers whose

28. Bertram S. Brown, "The Life of Psychiatry," *Am. J. Psychiatry*, 133:489–495, 1976, quoted at p. 492.

29. These and other indices of the hegemony of psychoanalysis within American psychiatry are provided by Edward Shorter, *A History of Psychiatry: From the Era of the Asylum to the Age of Prozac* (NY: Wiley, 1996), chap. 5.

30. Joel Paris, *Fall of an Icon* (n. 3), p. 143; Marshall Edelson, "Psychoanalysis, Anxiety, and the Anxiety Disorders," in A. H. Tuma & Jack D. Maser, eds., *Anxiety and the Anxiety Disorders* (Hillsdale, NJ: Erlbaum, 1985), pp. 633–644, quoted at p. 633.

familiarity with the European tradition of empirical psychological research made for a convivial reception on American shores. Among the refugees, the psychologist-analyst Else Frenkel-Brunswik, the analytically oriented educator Bruno Bettelheim, and the medical analyst René Spitz had been Viennese students of no less an academic psychologist than Karl Bühler.[31] In the U.S., they were joined by Käthe Wolf, Erik Erikson, Heinz Hartmann, and Ernst Kris, all of whom collaborated with university-based colleagues on research projects informed by psychoanalysis but incorporating the methods and measures of academic psychology. Kris in particular urged an empirical research program on his American colleagues in the hope of bridging psychoanalysis and cognitive psychology. He was drawn to Yale's Child Study Center, where he joined the faculty and participated in various observational studies on normal childhood development in the 1950s and 1960s.

The refugees' general commitment to ego psychology, with its ambitious, long-term project of a "general psychology" that would bridge the assumptions of analysis and nonanalytic psychology, aided and abetted these collaborative forays.[32] Equally important to psychoanalytic outreach to American psychology was the work of the neo-Marxist refugees aligned with the Institute for Social Research of the University of Frankfurt am Main, the analyst Else Frenkel-Brunswik among them.[33] Newly massed at New York's New School for Social Research, these transplanted members of the Frankfurt School jointly authored *The Authoritarian Personality* (1950), a massive contribution to the understanding of anti-Semitism that integrated psychoanalytic theory of personality with quantitative assessment based on questionnaires, surveys, and a battery of psychological tests; it was the pinnacle of the postwar literature predicated on the

31. Jean Matter Mandler & George Mandler, "The Diaspora of Experimental Psychology: The Gestaltists and Others," in Donald Fleming & Bernard Bailyn, eds., *The Intellectual Migration: Europe and America, 1930–1960* (Cambridge: Harvard University Press, 1969), pp. 371–419 at p. 411.

32. Lewis A. Coser, *Refugee Scholars in America: Their Impact and Their Experiences* (New Haven: Yale University Press, 1984), pp. 49–50.

33. The analyst Erich Fromm was a member of the Frankfurt School from 1928–1938 but severed his ties with it prior to emigration to the U.S. See Coser, *Refugee Scholars* (n. 32), pp. 70–71.

complementarity of psychoanalytic theory and academic psychology.[34] In the decade to follow, psychoanalysis not only inspired the development of the new generation of projective tests, it also fueled the dramatic growth of clinical psychology, an emerging profession "profoundly influenced by psychoanalytic ideas."[35] How matters have changed. The psychologist-psychoanalyst Frank Summers recently observed that

> Psychoanalysis is virtually ignored in psychology textbooks. Whereas at one time most clinical psychology internships were psychodynamically focused or at least contained psychoanalytic representation, now few programs have even a modicum of psychoanalytic influence. Whereas in 1960, more than one-third of clinical psychologists regarded themselves as psychodynamic, by 2000 the number had dropped to only 18% (Masling, 2000). Furthermore, the number of candidates admitted to psychoanalytic institutes has declined so precipitously that it is not uncommon for many programs to be unable to fill their classes every year.[36]

It requires little imaginative leap to link these marginalizing trends to the progressively diminished sales of psychoanalytic books. In chapter 2, in documenting the rise and fall of psychoanalytic book publishing in America, we will give special consideration to trends that have shaped the nature of the books analysts have written, published, and bought over the past three decades. Here the briefest summary will suffice: In a challenging time of transition, struggling with the omnipresence of third-party reimbursement and managed care, analysts of the 1980s and 1990s refashioned their professional identities in a manner that weakened their reliance on the kind of books

34. T. W. Adorno, Else Frenkel-Brunswik, Daniel J. Levinson, & R. Nevitt Sanford, *The Authoritarian Personality* (NY: Harper, 1950).

35. See Marie Jahoda, "The Migration of Psychoanalysis: Its Impact on American Psychology," in Fleming & Bailyn, eds., *The Intellectual Migration* (n. 31), pp. 420–445, quoted at p. 441.

36. Frank Summers, "Theoretical Insularity and the Crisis of Psychoanalysis," *Psychoanal. Psychol.*, 25:413–424, 2008, quoted at p. 413. Summers's reference is to Joseph Masling, "Empirical Evidence and the Health of Psychoanalysis," *J. Am. Acad. Psychoanal.*, 28:665–685, 2000.

that had traditionally sustained them. In an era of economic retrenchment in which cultural forces progressively eroded professional self-determination and hemmed in practice-related prerogatives, books that gave pride of place to staples of the older psychoanalytic book literature—expositions of the analytic "method" and the "theories" of technique and therapeutic action that grew out of it—became less and less central to the kind of psychotherapeutic doctoring that analysts found themselves doing. Psychoanalysis, which formerly signified a patient free-associating on an analytic couch at a frequency of four or five sessions weekly, came to envelop a more conversational face-to-face psychotherapy at a frequency of one or two sessions weekly. The difference between psychoanalysis proper and psychoanalytically informed psychotherapy—a topic over which analysts spilled abundant ink in the 50s and 60s—became all but irrelevant. For the vast majority of institute-trained analysts from the 1980s on, analysis increasingly denoted a particular genre of psychotherapy informed but not constrained by Freud's psychoanalytic method.

From the early 80s on, marginalization from without was matched by sectarian splintering from within. And both processes occurred in tandem with the overall contraction of the field, as fewer and fewer psychiatrists and clinical psychologists entered analytic training programs with the goal of becoming psychoanalysts. This was a recipe for disaster for those publishing firms that served the traditionally robust psychoanalytic marketplace. Beginning in the 80s, as we shall see, psychoanalytic books of general interest to the entire profession became few and far between. Publishers such as TAP had to content themselves with specialized monographs aimed at one or another of the proliferating psychoanalytic schools of thought. The typical psychoanalytic book not only failed to draw a meaningful readership from mental health professionals unallied with psychoanalysis; it also failed to interest psychoanalytic readers unallied with the particular school of thought of the author. Throughout the 80s and into the 90s, sales of the vast majority of psychoanalytic books were unexceptional, and then modest. By the late 90s—allowing for the occasional exception—sales were vanishingly small.

Psychoanalysis is hardly the only field whose marginalization has gained expression in, among other things, a publishing crisis. In point of fact, academic publishing in general has been in crisis mode for at least the past two decades. Academic publishers too look back nostalgically on a glory era, in their case a glory era in which cold-war anxiety fueled enormous governmental expenditures on behalf of higher education. University press publishing was galvanized by the Soviet Union's launching of Sputnik in 1957 and the National Defense Education Act (NDEA) that arose in its wake. The NDEA's charge was to plant educational seeds that would enable the nation to stock-pile scientific knowledge and technological know-how in the manner of nuclear weapons. Federal money poured into universities, which channeled a portion of it to their libraries, which proceeded to amass collections of scholarly monographs with unparalleled vigor. Through-out the 1960s, as Peter Givler, Executive Director of the American Association of University Presses, has observed, "Money poured into higher education as never before: money for teaching, for research and publication, and for building library collections. NDEA and programs like it created a golden age for publishers of scholarly research in the 1960s. The institutional market boomed, and university presses boomed along with it."[37] But the boom would not outlive the decade. The tri-umphant moon landing of 1969, which signaled America's victory in the space race, and the deepening quagmire in Vietnam, which by 1970 was beginning to strain federal budgets, signaled the beginning of the end of the postwar expansion of academic publishing.

Throughout the 60s, as noted, university presses prospered because federal funding sustained the purchasing power of university librar-ies, the primary institutional market for their books. When the fed-eral government cut back its educational outlays in the early 70s, libraries were no longer able to sustain across-the-board purchases of scholarly books. And careful allocation of dwindling federal monies favored serials in the natural sciences over scholarly monographs in the humanities and social sciences. In their acquisitions priorities, li-brarians had little choice but to support the research infrastructure and faculty research appointments that were the legacy of the federal largesse of the 60s.

University presses were clearly the loser in the reduction and rede-ployment of library acquisition funds that began in 1970 and has

---

37. Peter Givler, "University Press Publishing in the United States," in Richard E. Abel & Lyman W. Newman, eds., *Scholarly Publishing: Books, Journals, Publishers and Libraries in the Twentieth Century* (NY: Wiley, 2002), pp. 107–120, quoted at p. 110. I draw on Givler's overview in the two paragraphs to follow.

continued ever since. By the end of the 70s, the presses' loss of revenue from library purchases was compounded by reduced operating subsidies from their newly budget-conscious universities. By 1980 the era of academic plenty was gone and all but forgotten. University presses, under mounting pressure from their universities to acquire titles with an eye to profitability, devised flexible survival strategies to cope with the loss of revenue from their long-standing institutional customer, the university library, and greatly diminished subsidies from their long-standing institutional partner, the sponsoring university. Outside funding from the National Endowment for the Humanities, the National Endowments for the Arts, the Andrew W. Mellon Foundation, and the NEH Challenge Grant Program enabled university presses to continue with their historic mission of publishing scholarly works that advanced knowledge, regardless of salability. Complementary with the search for outside funding was a willingness to deviate from this selfsame mission in quest of profits that would sustain growth and ensure survival. Beginning in the 80s and continuing into the present, university presses systematically cultivated their nonscholarly book lists, publishing a plethora of titles of local and regional interest. They also began publishing popular trade books on sports and entertainment topics, the very kind of "midlist" titles that the large commercial houses had forsaken.[38]

Small, for-profit professional publishers differ from university presses in critical ways that explain their respective trajectories of decline. As for-profit corporations, professional publishers are not constrained by a historical mission that privileges scholarly content over commercial promise. In order to implement their historical mission, university presses, as noted, have traditionally received substantial subsidies from their sponsoring universities. When university funding dried up, they sought and received financial relief from foundations. Now, as times grow harder and their survival is imperiled once more, they receive the outspoken support of university administra-

---

38. Within trade publishing midlist titles are relatively recent books of secondary importance, i.e., books that lack the commercial promise of, and therefore command less editorial and promotional attention than, a firm's latest titles, i.e., its frontlist. Midlist books are in the middle, between the frontlist and the list of older, in-print titles that make up the backlist. André Schiffrin discusses university presses' commercially driven turn to midlist trade titles in *The Business of Books* (n. 2), pp. 139–140.

tors and scholars who propose ingenious strategies by which scholars and scholarly organizations can give back to these presses in financially consequential ways.[39] Further, as nonprofit corporations, university presses have enjoyed the kinds of indirect subsidization available to all nonprofits: Noncommercial mailing rates and exemption from corporate tax on inventories.

Small, for-profit publishers receive no such benefits, nor are they beneficiaries of the kind of foundation grants that have provided university presses with an additional measure of financial relief. But then, most small, for-profit publishers, psychoanalytic publishers among them, have never relied on institutional sales to university libraries to render books profitable. Their books, their variant of "scholarly monographs," are aimed at individual members of the professions they serve. Institutional purchases, which are limited to a small network of libraries that serves mental health professionals,[40] have always been secondary to sales to individuals. The contraction of the institutional market is therefore of lesser importance to the commercial fate of psychoanalytic books than of academic books published for scholars. It is for this very reason that major university presses such as Harvard, Yale, and Chicago pursued their psychoanalytic book lists through the 70s and 80s. These books were primarily sold to a small but stable market of high-income professionals whose book-buying was integral to their professional identity and unrelated to the global downturn in sales of scholarly books.

In the small world of psychoanalytic publishing, the 80s emerge as the key transitional decade. Senior authors identified with traditional, aka "classical," psychoanalysis continued the theoretical project they had begun in the 50s and 60s of refining and amending Freud's theories and explanatory concepts in the tradition of American ego psychology and object relations theory. And their trainees did likewise,

39. See, for example, Cathy N. Davidson, "Understanding the Economic Burden of Scholarly Publishing," *Chron. Rev.*, 50(6):B7–B10, October 3, 2003. Professor Davidson, Vice Provost for Interdisciplinary Studies and Professor of English at Duke University, initially presented this paper at the 2003 meeting of the American Council of Learned Societies.

40. The libraries of psychoanalytic and psychotherapy training institutes are the core of this small institutional market. For select titles, and especially through the 1970s, this market was enlarged by the libraries of medical school psychiatry departments and university psychology departments.

publishing their own theoretical articles in the pages of the *International Journal of Psycho-Analysis*, the *Journal of the American Psychoanalytic Association*, and the *Psychoanalytic Quarterly*. But the kind of abstractive psychoanalytic writing greatly in vogue in this country from the 40s through the 70s was, by the 80s, increasingly irrelevant to analytic practitioners.[41] As American psychoanalysis embraced newer "postclassical" perspectives and a more pragmatic publishing venue, authors of the previous generation, especially classical analysts devoted to the ego psychology that blossomed in the 50s, continued to publish within the circumscribed realm available to them. Specifically, the 80s witnessed a recrudescence of two genres of book publication that are coterminous with the history of psychoanalytic book publishing in America, but, with exceedingly rare exceptions, have been marginal to the growth of psychoanalytic knowledge and the publishing enterprise that sustains it. I refer to books of "selected" or "collected" papers, all of which have previously appeared in the journal literature, and to Festschriften that pay homage to senior figures of the previous generation. The 80s saw the publication of many such collections of "selected papers" of the psychoanalytic old guard. Likewise, it was the decade of encomiastic Festschriften celebrating the contributions of these selfsame figures. Selected papers volumes[42] and Festschriften[43] tend to celebrate the work of a generation of theo-

41. At the first meeting of the American Psychoanalytic Association that I attended as Editor at International Universities Press in December, 1979, I reverentially approached Merton Gill and told him how much I had learned from his *Topography and Systems in Psychoanalysis* (NY: International Universities Press, 1963), to which he crustily replied, "Really? You liked that book? I've had it with all that metapsychological horseshit."

42. Representative examples from the 80s include: Margaret Mahler, *Selected Papers*, vols. 1 & 2 (NY: Aronson, 1979); Rudolph Loewenstein, *Practice and Precept in Psychoanalytic Technique: Selected Papers* (New Haven: Yale Univesity Press, 1982); Leo Stone, *Transference and Its Context: Selected Papers on Psychoanalysis* (NY: Aronson, 1984); Mardi Horowitz, *Nuances of Technique in Dynamic Psychotherapy: Selected Clinical Papers* (Northvale, NJ: Aronson, 1989); and Jacob Arlow, *Psychoanalysis: Clinical Theory and Practice* (Madison, CT: IUP, 1991).

43. At TAP, I published one such Festschrift in 1986—Arnold Richards & Martin Willick, eds., *Psychoanalysis: The Science of Mental Conflict: Essays in Honor of Charles Brenner* and another in 2000, Doris Silverman & David Wolitzky, eds., *Changing Conceptions of Psychoanalysis: The Legacy of Merton M. Gill*. Both books,

rists that, by the time of publication, has already been sequestered within the field; the books themselves are of interest primarily to colleagues, students, and friends of the honorees and rarely sell more than a few hundred copies (if that).

In point of fact, by the late 80s, the entire corpus of American ego psychology, "classics" and all, was becoming an artifact of the mindset associated with a kind of psychoanalytic training and socialization that bore less and less relationship to the realities of psychoanalytic practice in a time of transition. As clinicians, analysts became pragmatists about their work and about their "calling." It is arguable whether or not they came to read less in general; it is more certain that they became increasingly selective about what they read and increasingly selective about the kind of books they bought. During this same decade, library sales, which in the 60s and 70s had extended into medical school and general university libraries, significantly contracted, often to the point of numerical insignificance.

TAP, which published its first two books in 1983,[44] was a casualty of these interrelated developments. Taken together, they led to a sea change in book publishing that corresponded to a weakening need among analysts and analytically oriented psychotherapists for high-priced specialty books published in small, sometimes tiny, print runs and offered to them at high list prices. This weakening had both structural and psychological components. The former included the burgeoning of an increasingly fragmented journal literature that gave expression to the sectarian propensities of analytic therapists and, over time, rendered books, especially edited compilations, marginal to

---

unsurprisingly, were commercial failures. Other representatives of this genre from the 80s and 90s are: James Masterson, ed., *Object and Self: A Developmental Approach: Essays in Honor of Edith Jacobson* (NY: IUP, 1981); Harold Blum, ed., *Fantasy, Myth, and Reality: Essays in Honor of Jacob Arlow, M.D.* (NY: IUP, 1988); Edward Weinshel, Harold Blum, & F. Robert Rodman, eds., *The Psychoanalytic Core: Essays in Honor of Leo Rangell, M.D.* (NY: IUP, 1989); Arlene Richards, Martin Bergmann, & Arnold Richards, *The Spectrum of Psychoanalysis: Essays in Honor of Martin S. Bergmann* (Madison, CT: IUP, 1994); and Jorge Ahumada et al., eds., *The Perverse Transference and Other Matters: Essays in Honor of R. Horacio Etchegoyen* (Northvale, NJ: Aronson, 1997).

44. Emanuel Peterfreund, *The Process of Psychoanalytic Therapy: Models and Strategies* (Hillsdale, NJ: Analytic Press, 1983) and Joseph Masling, ed., *Empirical Studies of Psychoanalytical Theories*, vol. 1 (Hillsdale, NJ: Analytic Press, 1983).

analysts' reading habits. The proliferation of what I term part-journals, which we consider in chapters 3 and 4, helped render the very idea of general-interest specialty books all but oxymoronic.

Commensurate with the marginalization of "general-interest" specialty books throughout the 80s was the growth of the Internet, which generated a plethora of nonprint possibilities for consolidating a professional identity and augmenting a professional knowledge base. By the mid-90s, it was relatively easy to learn about books, to sample books, and to discuss books via online workshops, panels, and discussion groups. Electronic dissemination, which, via various online forums, made it possible to sample recently published journal issues and books with maximal ease (and without the material inducement to purchase that follows from perusing an actual journal issue or book at a conference exhibit or a bookstore), augmented this trend.

As the purchasing and reading of books was supplanted with a menu of online opportunities for professional growth, analytic readers felt less need to purchase books; they were certainly less inclined to purchase books on impulse. With this last, we segue into the psychological dimension of the weakening market for psychoanalytic books. Beginning in the mid-80s and continuing into the 90s, the purchasing of books came to matter less to issues of professional socialization and professional well-being. Analysts no longer needed to amass a library of psychoanalytic books to feel at home in their professional calling. More specifically, analysts no longer felt driven to buy books written and published especially for them as members of a cohesive professional community. Book buying, by which I mean global, continuing book buying, was progressively drained of its professional raison d'etre. A library of general-interest psychoanalytic books was no longer the material concomitant of an analytic identity, which is to say it no longer provided necessary confirmation that one thought like, acted like, and practiced like a psychoanalyst in some generically inclusive sense of the term. Increasingly, from the mid-80s on, American analysts bought books identified with a particular school of analytic thought. This transformation of analytic book-buying habits and the sales data that sustain it are at the heart of chapter 2.

The difficulties presented to publishers by a simultaneously contracting and fractionating market for their books and journals was aggravated by author indifference to those very marginalizing trends that progressively rendered virtually all psychoanalytic-type books "specialty" publications. TAP, no less than other small professional firms, was a casualty of an indifference that occasionally became outright denial. Indeed, among the lessons learned during my career as a psychoanalytic publisher, the persisting strength of authorial denial in the face of tectonic cultural and economic shifts holds pride of place. Warding off the increasing marginalization of their role within the mental health profession and the wider culture, analytic authors have until very recently proven remarkably oblivious to the commercial marginalization of their books. Many analytic authors through the 1990s clung to a mind-set developed during the glory era of psychoanalytic publishing, when psychoanalytic books had a mainstream currency within mental health publishing and a cultural salience among highly educated lay readers, for whom analysis was not only the treatment of choice but de rigueur as an instrument of cultural and literary analysis.

During the very period when the Internet was transforming the possibilities, indeed the very meaning, of small-market publication, many American analysts clung to a vision of traditional, high-overhead publishing in which intensive editorial and production labor was freely available to all authors, independent of the salability of their respective books. This mind-set, which was becoming an archaism by the end of the 1980s, militated against understanding that by the 1990s analytic books were produced in tiny print runs (and with commensurately high retail list prices) for very narrowly conceived, and hence very small, audiences. As such, they required the economies, editorial and otherwise, attendant to specialty publication.[45] Under these circumstances, analytic authors were forced to choose, whether or not consciously,

45. Lynne Withey, Director of the University of California Press, addressed this reality in 2003: "I would hardly downplay the editorial value offered by publishers. But I would like to argue that we need to think carefully about how, and in what circumstances, the editorial value of publishers is most effectively deployed. . . . my point is that while we might believe that scholarship deserves to reach its audience no matter how small, it doesn't necessarily need to reach that audience being published by high-overhead book publishers. . . . We should allow professional editors to focus on books with that kind of broad appeal. Very specialized work, intended for an audience largely confined to the author's peers, can just as well be edited according to the journals model." Lynne Withey, "Remarks," in *Crises and Opportunities: The Futures of Scholarly Publishing*, American Council of Learned Societies Occasional Paper, No. 57, 2003, pp. 45–52, quoted at p. 49.

among three alternatives: (1) They could resign themselves to the marginalization of their books and gracefully accept the concomitants of specialty publishing in relation to production, design, pricing, and sales. (2) They could accept the marginalization of their books as a commercial fact of life for their publishers but work energetically to counteract it through self-promotion, usually in the form of conventional professional activities. (3) They could deny the reality of professional-cum-commercial marginalization, retain expectations of mainstream publicity and sales, and ascribe disappointingly modest sales to their publishers' complaisance, nonresponsiveness, and/or ineptitude.

Over the course of my three decades in the field, I have encountered my fair share of authors in all three categories. But the predominance of authors in category 3 has accelerated the very marginalizing forces that these authors are at pains to deny. Instead of working in concert with their publishers to maximize the visibility and salability of their books within the specialty market, these authors have been content to sulk on the sidelines, aghast and demoralized that a labor of many years, sometimes of a lifetime, has resulted in a book that has created nary a ripple in their own profession and sold a scant 300 to 400 copies.

The ascendancy of the online booksellers, especially Amazon.com and BarnesandNoble.com, has increased the disjunction between author and publisher expectations by feeding into a cultural myth about authorship that bedevils all small publishers and boils down to the claim that an author is an author is an author. Many authors confront their publishers with a global estimation—analysts might term it an undifferentiated estimation—of what it means to be an author. They tend to ascribe the publicity, excitement, and sales attendant to popular trade books to newly published books per se. Indeed, many first-time authors "present" to their publishers with a veritably Platonic vision of authorship. For these people, authorship, i.e., the fact of having written a book that a publisher—any publisher—has gone to the trouble and expense of publishing, is a pure condition of being that any and all earthly authors equally partake of. And so specialty book authors, hearkening back to their mainstream forebears of the postwar era, come to expect recognition—even if only intraprofessional recognition—analogous to, if not actually commensurate with, the celebrity of successful trade authors.

Without doubt the Internet has been a transformative experience for book-buyers of all sorts. At the time of this writing, I work as an independent scholar without university affiliation. Without the limitless catalog of (usually affordable) specialty used books available to me through the Amazon Marketplace and BookFinder.com, I could not have amassed the library of books in the history of medicine, psychiatry, and psychoanalysis that I will draw on in the chapters to follow. Without access to the extensive journal literature provided electronically to my local university library by various journal-literature aggregators (Project Muse, Ebsco, JSTOR, PEP, and the like), I could not locate, print out, and read the many journal articles, old and new, to which my research directs me. Without Google's powerful search engine, I could not quickly locate relevant online sources on the crisis in scholarly and professional publishing that buttress my remarks about the near-demise of psychoanalytic book publishing. For me the Internet has been empowering. And yet the same Internet that enables me to write about the rise and fall of psychoanalytic book publishing plays a key role in the story I am telling. For the Internet has empowered the scholar at the expense of the small scholarly/professional publisher. That is, it has destroyed the marketplace as small specialty publishers, indeed as specialty distributors of all sorts, have traditionally understood it and approached it.

My use of the Internet as a research tool for locating and acquiring tiny-print-run, obscure, and usually out-of-print books and articles from back volumes of low-circulation, highly specialized journals is a small example of what Chris Anderson famously terms the "long tail" of Internet commerce.[46] By democratizing the production and distribution of goods, and by devising algorithms that make it simple for people to travel down the long tail of the marketplace to locate most any product, including tiny niche products, the Internet serves the consumer in wondrous ways. Consumers—academics and other specialty book buyers among them—need no longer be their own aggregators, perusing countless book catalogs of in-print and out-of-print books and canvassing used book stores near and far for the books they need. Now the major online aggregators—Amazon.com, Alibris .com, BarnesandNoble.com, BookFinder.com—do the work for us in

---

46. Chris Anderson, *The Long Tail: Why the Future of Business Is Selling Less of More* (NY: Hyperion, 2006).

the digital domain, and the resulting catalog of books instantly available to the consumer on his screen becomes the mega-catalog of a continuously expanding universe of publisher catalogs and brick-and-mortar store inventories. There are no effective limits to catalog length when individual books are simply digital entries; for all practical intents and purposes, the new mega-catalog instantaneously accessible from one's computer is limitless.

The new mega-catalog is characterized not only by its inclusiveness but also by its leveling of distinctions among long-established categories of authors and publishers. For the online marketplace is a digitally leveled playing field able to give equal space (in bandwidth) to books of all kinds, published by firms of all kinds (and, increasingly, self-published), and published in all times and places. Internet visionaries such as Anderson hail these interrelated developments as a "democratization" of the marketplace and, from the perspective of the consumer, they are absolutely right. Relying on the online aggregators, I have no more difficulty locating and purchasing an obscure half-century-old university press title than the latest best-selling novel by Danielle Steel. I have no more difficulty locating and purchasing a self-published manual than a nationally advertised title by Random House. This is good.

But the democratization of the online marketplace has come at a price, and that price has been borne disproportionately by small scholarly and professional firms whose authors come to them with the same expectations of online advertising and online availability as successful trade authors. Of course small scholarly firms, no less than huge trade houses, must have their websites. How could it be otherwise? So we have this vast universe of publisher websites that gives the appearance of electronic parity among all publishers, large and small, general and specialist. But the parity is specious: Small scholarly firms, unlike corporate trade houses, lack the resources to create websites that actually attract visitors and generate meaningful revenue. Websites are a key element in the democratizing of the marketplace for consumers, but websites hardly attest to an equal playing field among producers; they simply transpose to the electronic domain profound disparities of scale and resources that predated online advertising and sales. I am of a mind here with Pantheon's former publisher André Schiffrin, for whom "[t]here is every reason to assume that larger firms, with greater marketing clout, will dominate the Internet in the same way they have asserted themselves in more conventional publishing." And Schiffrin is more ominous still about the future, for the larger firms, he believes, "may also ultimately control our access to that medium."[47]

For small scholarly and professional publishers, there is a different burden wrought by a democratized online marketplace, and it has less to do with the economics of publishing than with the psychology of authorship. It is inarguable that the Internet has established a democratized venue in which consumers may browse products and place orders with astonishing electronic ease. The burden is intrinsic to this venue: The same Internet that presents book buyers with a continuously expanding universe of book titles has progressively eroded long-established differences of kind among authors and their respective publishers. The major online sellers, especially Amazon.com and BarnesandNoble.com, enter the picture here, for they have hastened the homogenization of authorship through their own democratization of the electronic marketplace. Within the universe of online selling, after all, each and every author has instantaneous access to his or her online "page," typically with cover graphic, promotional copy, and endorsements. Each and every author is equally able to—and equally prone to—monitor online sales via a continuously updated sales ranking. Each and every author feels the same sense of urgency to keep the online presentation as pristine and up-to-date as possible. After all, the online page is the public face of the book, available to anyone in the world with a screen and an Internet provider.

What is obscured by the appearance of parity in online listings is the paltry size of the "public" served by the overwhelming majority of academic and professional books. Nor are authors of these books easily persuaded that online sales contribute very little to overall sales and hence are of minor interest to their publishers.[48] The visual and emotional appeal of one's Amazon.com page, the instantaneity with which the page can be accessed and savored, the addictive urge to monitor the continuously fluctuating sales ranking—these dimensions

47. Schiffrin, *Business of Books* (n. 2), pp. 148–149.

48. In 2002, members of the American Association of University Presses received an underwhelming 4.7% of their revenue from online retailers. For publishers of specialized professional books, the percentage is no doubt less. See http://aaupnet.org/aboutup/upfacts.html.

of Internet selling have clouded the numerical insignificance of Internet sales for specialty books per se. And, in the case of a field such as psychoanalysis, they have made it harder still for authors to accept and work productively with the reality of marginalization.

Small academic and professional publishers have, with few exceptions, toed the line and exerted themselves to meet their authors' expectations of trade-like online advertising via the Internet sellers. But the electronic transmitting, amending, and updating of book information to Internet sellers have diverted limited promotional resources to a sales venue that, at least to date, has been largely irrelevant to the marketing, distribution, and sales of many specialty books, psychoanalytic titles among them. Simply coping with the steady stream of author phone calls and emails regarding errors or omissions in Amazon.com listings has become a chronic burden for the already overburdened staffs of small professional publishers.

At TAP, I had several authors whose daily Amazon.com sales ranking became a veritable obsession in the year or so following publication. These authors not only tracked their ranking on a daily basis but also felt it necessary to share their numbers with me on a regular basis and to complain to me when their respective sales rankings slipped. Often, they believed, it was some failure on the publisher's part, whether of omission or commission, that accounted for ebbing online sales as reflected in declining sales rankings. The inevitability of declining sales rankings over time and the minuscule sales reflected in the numeric ranges captured by their books were realities not easily grasped. The autonomy of the online sellers, the fact that publishers do not control their use (or misuse) of book files transmitted to them electronically in accord with the sellers' own procedures—this reality proved more elusive still. Why hadn't TAP supplied Amazon with revised jacket copy or with this or that collegial endorsement? Why didn't their listings include all the promotional copy we had submitted to them? Where was the picture of the dust jacket that we had electronically transmitted to Amazon two days ago? Why didn't Amazon offer their book at higher discount? Why had Amazon paired their book (as in "buy this book and that book for this price") with another book not to this or that author's liking? All such matters, these authors held, were the publisher's responsibility, and failure to amend or enhance this or that online presentation would lead to further decline in sales ranking for which the publisher alone would bear the onerous responsibility.

Like other small presses beholding the Internet juggernaut, TAP was responsive to author vigilance in the matter of online presentation, patiently explaining the Amazon system to authors, continuously sending the online sellers corrections and additions, and urging them, both online and via phone calls, to implement submitted changes as quickly as possible. Sadly, this very responsiveness has had an ironic effect: It has militated against an understanding of the unique place of specialty publications within the universe of books and the kind of local promotional initiatives (including local online initiatives) that continue to be appropriate to their distribution and sale. In an era of cultural shift, economic retrenchment, and professional redefinition, the homogenization of authorship encouraged by the online sellers has forestalled a meeting of minds between professional book authors and their publishers. In the case of psychoanalytic publishing, it has buttressed author indifference to forces of marginalization and fragmentation that, as noted, have progressively eroded the market for psychoanalytic-type books and forced previously unheard of economies on their publishers. It has provided narcissistic gratification at the expense of the commercial reality principle. It has been in the service of authorial denial.

And it has been in the service of denial about the status of psychoanalysis as a profession. The lure of traditional authorship, now electronically enhanced, has pulled would-be leaders of the field away from alternative initiatives (or from the writing of alternative kinds of books) capable of strengthening a profession ensconced on the margins. Over the course of my career and continuing into the present, leading analysts of all persuasions continue to write books that proffer new theories, new permutations of psychoanalytic technique, new theories of therapeutic action and cure, as if a half-century-old soapbox were still in place.

In the case of psychoanalysis, author expectations have proven especially resistant to deflation for good historical reasons. For the books psychoanalysts have authored have not always been marginal. Far from it. In the three decades following World War II, psychoanalytic books were very much part of the publishing mainstream. They had widespread appeal among psychiatrists, psychologists, and social workers who lacked analytic training but championed analysis and adapted it to their own professional lives. During this period many analytic books even achieved commercial success among lay readers—enormous success in the case of analysts such as Karl Menninger, Erich Fromm, Erik Erikson, and Karen Horney, who became cultural icons.

In chapter 2, we launch our examination of the glory era of psychoanalytic book publishing with the end of World War II, but it bears noting that America's cultural enshrinement of psychoanalytic books has its own prehistory. Karl Menninger's *The Human Mind*, the first major popularization of Freudian theory presented to the American public, was published in January, 1930, by the firm of Alfred A. Knopf. The book was a hasty assemblage of lectures Menninger offered to freshmen at nearby Washburn College in an introductory course on mental hygiene. Nor was the Karl Menninger of 1930 a paragon of authority within the psychoanalytic establishment. At the time of the book's publication, his actual experience of psychoanalysis consisted of one or two sessions of trial analysis with Smith Ely Jelliffe, his psychiatric mentor, a decade earlier. But *The Human Mind* had as cultural backdrop the mental hygiene movement of the 1920s, which whipped up public enthusiasm for Menninger's brand of avuncular psychoanalytic pedagogy. The book was superficial, homiletic, moralizing, and unrelentingly optimistic; Menninger himself expressed regret at having written it two weeks prior to publication.[49] Yet the literary critic Carl Van Doren was sufficiently impressed to persuade his colleagues on the advisory board of the Literary Guild of America to adopt it at once as a Guild main selection. The Literary Guild edition was a great success, with sales of 200,000 copies.[50]

In early May, 1930, Menninger, along with a host of American psychiatric and psychoanalytic luminaries, convened in Washington

---

49. Lawrence J. Friedman, *Menninger: The Family and the Clinic* (NY: Knopf, 1990), p. 59. Menninger's relatively brief training analysis in Chicago with Franz Alexander began in the winter of 1931, after publication of *The Human Mind*.

50. I located this sales figure at www.menningerclinic.com/about/early-history.htm. In the brochure announcing publication of the second edition of the book, the publisher, Alfred A. Knopf, headlined "over 165,000 copies of first edition sold." My thanks to Sara J. Keckeisen, Librarian, Kansas State Historical Society, for sending me a copy of the brochure along with copies of correspondence and royalties reports from the Karl Menninger papers pursuant to publication of *The Human Mind* (KAM-PRO 6.20; 102-03-03-03, back row). Incidentally, Menninger was fully aware of Van Doren's sponsorship and wrote to him directly to express his gratitude to the Literary Guild. See Menninger to Van Doren, February 7, 1930, in Howard J. Faulkner

for the first International Congress on Mental Hygiene. They were joined by representatives from 40 other countries; the crush at registration was so great that many more than the 3,042 official registrants got through the doors and graced the proceedings.[51] Americans were surely ready for Menninger and his gently meliorative vision of psychoanalysis as the medically scientific pathway to mental health. According to Lawrence J. Friedman, *The Human Mind* was on its way to becoming "the best-selling mental health volume in American history."[52] *Man Against Himself* (1938) and *Love Against Hate* (1942), Menninger's painfully sanitized revisionings of Freud's theory of life and death instincts, followed in its wake.

Menninger quickly became American psychiatry's premier spokesperson. Indeed, with his popular advice column in the *Ladies Home Journal*, which also commenced in 1930,[53] he became the nation's psychiatric pater familias, its foremost guide to—as his column was titled—"Mental Hygiene in the Home." Psychoanalysis, as he under-

---

& Virginia D. Pruitt, eds., *Selected Correspondence of Karl A. Menninger, 1919–1945* (New Haven: Yale University Press, 1988), pp. 107–109.

51. On the first International Congress on Mental Hygiene, See Norman Dain, *Clifford W. Beers: Advocate for the Insane* (Pittsburgh: University of Pittsburgh Press, 1980), pp. 244–253 and for a contemporary popular account of the proceedings, "Mental Hygiene," *Time*, May 19, 1930.

52. Friedman's claim that *The Human Mind* is the best-selling mental health volume in America, which is not supported by any sales data (and which I find highly dubious in view of the staggering sales of Erich Fromm's books in the 50s and 60s, as related in chapter 2) is in *Menninger* (n. 49), p. 56. I provide sales estimates of Fromm's books below, p. 45.

53. Virginia D. Pruitt and Howard Faulkner have edited an illuminating selection of Menninger's advice to readers of *Ladies Home Journal* that includes the questions that prompted his columns. See Virginia D. Pruitt & Howard J. Faulkner, eds., *Dear Dr. Menninger: Women's Voices from the Thirties* (Columbia, MO: University of Missouri Press, 1997). We now know that Jean Lyle, the personal assistant Menninger hired to help him with the advice column, actually composed Menninger's replies to the letters sent to him in care of the magazine. Menninger himself "often made only a few scant suggestive notations" before handing the letters over to her. After Menninger ended his column in 1932, Lyle stayed with him, becoming his second mistress and in 1941 his second wife. See Howard J. Faulkner & Virginia D. Pruitt, "The Unpublished Menninger: Divorce, Marriage, and Analyses," *Am. Imago*, 64:145–212, 2007, at pp. 152, 154, 157–158, quoted at p. 157.

stood it and misunderstood it, was his calling card. Menninger's books attested to the public's receptiveness to Freudian theory as a method of self-examination that would lead to self-understanding under the auspices of modern, scientific psychiatry. Ironically, Menninger used psychoanalysis to popularize psychiatry at the very time psychiatry was, among American medical specialties, a weak second-cousin that lacked a unifying purpose and coherent therapeutic agenda. The transformation of the field that began taking shape in combat aid stations in the final years of World War II and blossomed in the late 40s and 50s was a decade away. Throughout the 30s and into the 40s, psychiatry comprised several special interest groups, each with its own understanding of, and approach to, mental illness and psychiatric treatment. As such, it labored under the onus of what American psychoanalysts would later term "theoretical pluralism."

And yet, Menninger's early books laid the groundwork for the glory era of psychoanalytic publishing by establishing that writerly exponents of America's "new psychiatry"—a psychiatry that leaned on psychoanalysis and thereby became psychodynamic psychiatry—had arresting and even luminous insights to share with educated lay readers. Menninger was an icon but also a cheerleader. If *The Human Mind* were to achieve popularity, he mused to William Alanson White shortly after the book's release, "it's going to be because psychiatry is great stuff and not because of any creation of mine."[54] By psychiatry, of course, Menninger always meant psychoanalytic psychiatry, psychiatry informed by psychoanalytic principles, outpatient psychotherapy conducted along psychoanalytic lines. It was psychoanalysis that infused the "new psychiatry" with its newness; psychoanalytic discoveries, his brother Will observed many years later, "are probably the most important contributions to our [i.e., psychiatrists'] technical knowledge in the history of psychiatry."[55]

Menninger's three early books were harbingers of good things to come for publishers of psychiatric and, more especially, of psychoanalytic books. American psychiatry, an anemic medical specialty going into World War II, emerged from the war with greatly enhanced

54. Karl Menninger to White, March 6, 1930, in *Correspondence of Karl A. Menninger* (n. 50), p. 109.

55. William Menninger, *Psychiatry in a Troubled World* (NY: Macmillan, 1948), p. 6.

clinical credibility. Along the way, as we have observed, it also become socially activist and confidently psychoanalytic.[56] The glory era of psychoanalytic book publishing began in earnest after the war years and picked up momentum with Norton's publication of Erik Erikson's *Childhood and Society* in 1950. The era crested in the 1960s and began to taper off in the early and mid-70s.

In 1979, when I began my career in psychoanalytic publishing as an editor at International Universities Press, the glory era was over, but psychoanalytic book publishing remained robust and highly competitive. Membership in the American Psychoanalytic Association had grown over 50% during the 70s, from 1,287 in the fall of 1970 to 1,979 in the summer of 1979. In September, 1979, the American Psychological Association's (APA) Division of Psychoanalysis came into being; it reported 926 members in 1980 and 1,175 the following year.[57] The postwar ego-psychological framework of American psychoanalysis was broadened by influential and strong-selling titles, such as John Gedo and Arnold Goldberg's *Models of the Mind: A Psychoanalytic Theory* (University of Chicago Press, 1973) and Roy Schafer's *A New Language for Psychoanalysis* (Yale University Press, 1975). This framework was challenged more focally by Otto Kernberg and virtually jettisoned by Heinz Kohut. Each published two books in the 70s, all four of which were great commercial successes for their respective publishers, Jason Aronson, Inc. and International Universities Press.[58] Margaret Mahler, Fred Pine, and Anni Bergman's *The Psychological Birth of the Human Infant: Symbiosis and Individuation* was published by Basic Books in 1975. This readable exposition of Mahler's theory of early development, which incorporated several decades of

56. In chapter 3, I recur to the social activism of American psychiatry after World War II and contrast it with the relative indifference of American psychoanalysis to the social and political issues of the day.

57. The circumstances attendant to the founding of APA's Division 39 are recounted in Robert C. Lane & Murray Meisels, eds., *A History of the Division of Psychoanalysis of the American Psychological Association* (Hillsdale, NJ: Erlbaum, 1994).

58. Otto Kernberg, *Borderline Conditions and Pathological Narcissism* (NY: Aronson, 1975); Otto Kernberg, *Object Relations Theory and Clinical Psychoanalysis* (NY: Aronson, 1976); Heinz Kohut, *The Analysis of the Self: A Systematic Approach to the Psychoanalytic Treatment of Narcissistic Personality Disorders* (NY: IUP, 1971); Heinz Kohut, *The Restoration of the Self* (NY: IUP, 1977).

observational research and revolved around her concept of the separation-individuation process, was a successful professional/trade crossover book for its publisher, Basic Books. Over the course of the decade, small independent firms such as IUP, Jason Aronson, and Brunner-Mazel competed with university presses such as Harvard, Yale, Chicago, Johns Hopkins, and Columbia, and also with the professional book divisions of large trade houses such as Basic Books (sold to Harper & Row in 1972), Free Press (sold to Macmillan in 1961), and W. W. Norton.

In 1982 The Analytic Press entered the fray. It was founded by the psychology publisher Lawrence Erlbaum, who was convinced that the decline of IUP following its labor-related difficulties of 1981 had cleared the way for a new, profitable psychoanalytic imprint. He approached me in the fall of 1982 and invited me to become affiliated with TAP, initially as a consultant but later, when it suited me, as editorial director. This book began as a meditation on my ill-fated career as a publisher of psychoanalytic books and journals. It has taken shape as something quite different, but the experiential anlagen of my history and critique should always be borne in mind. My experience at The Analytic Press initially led me to the history of psychoanalytic book publishing in America, a heretofore unexplored topic that proves immensely revealing of the rise and fall of American psychoanalysis since World War II. And this is where my story begins.

Chapter 2

The Rise and Fall of Psychoanalytic Book Publishing in America

Let's make this as explicit as possible: If books with small print runs disappear, the future will die. Kafka's first book was published with a printing of 800 copies. Brecht's first work merited 600. What would have happened if someone had decided that was not worth it?[1]

War-weary Americans hardly had to await the surrender of Japan on September 2, 1945, before losing themselves in their books. Many on the home front, partly for want of other things to do, had read their way through the war—Book-of-the-Month-Club membership increased from 508,000 in 1941 to 848,000 in 1946—and the cessation of hostilities only increased book buying among the populace.[2] For the most part, Americans reached for the same escapist fare that had distracted them over the preceding five years. Historical novelists of the time fashioned, as they say, swashbuckling adventures in remote times and distant places. In 1945, Americans lost themselves in Thomas Costain's *The Black Rose*, a story of the bastard son of an English peer who took part in riots at Oxford University in 1273 and fled to China, and Samuel Shellabarger's *Captain from Castile*, which chronicled the adventures of a young Spanish nobleman who accompanied Cortés to Mexico in the early sixteenth century. A year later, they reveled in Daphne du Maurier's *The King's General*, a novel about militaristic love and tragedy during the English civil war (1642–1646).

1. Klaus Wagenbach, noted German publisher and Kafka scholar, writing in the Wagenbach book catalog of 1999, quoted in André Schiffrin, *The Business of Books: How International Conglomerates Took Over Publishing and Changed the Way We Read* (London: Verso, 2000), p. 147.

2. Joseph C. Goulden, *The Best Years: 1945–1950* (New York: Atheneum, 1976), p. 181.

Such historical exotica was infinitely more entertaining than the realities of North Africa, Normandy, and Hiroshima. Closer to home but no less distant from wartime preoccupations were Adria Langley's *A Lion Is in the Streets*, an earthy, novelistic rendering of Louisiana's Huey P. Long (it preceded by a year Robert Penn Warren's *All the King's Men*), and the Canadian Gwethalyn Graham's *Earth and High Heaven*, the story of an ill-fated romance between a Jewish lawyer of modest circumstances and the daughter of one of Montreal's upper-crust Gentile families.

The first nonfiction book of 1945 to reach the number one spot on the *New York Times* Bestseller List engaged racial realities that clouded the rush to postwar escapism. In March of that year, Harper & Brothers released Richard Wright's autobiographical *Black Boy: A Record of Childhood and Youth*, a lancing chronicle of Wright's coming-of-age in the Jim Crow south of rural Tennessee, Arkansas, and Mississippi. *Black Boy*, so viscerally premonitory of postwar racial tensions, was the first Book-of-the-Month-Club selection by an African American author and received a photo spread in *Life* magazine. It was an instant best seller.

The second best-selling nonfiction work of the year used humor to detoxify the wartime mentality. Famed wartime combat artist Bill Mauldin's *Up Front!*, which hit the number one spot on August 5, 1945, was a selection of Mauldin's comically barbed output for the military's *Stars and Stripes* magazine. Four months later, on December 23, Betty MacDonald's *The Egg and I*, published by Lippincott earlier in the year, rocketed to number one, where it would remain securely ensconced for four months. This ingratiating tale, which gave American readers something to laugh about, chronicled the author's hilarious adventures as a backwoods farmer's wife in Washington State's remote Chimacum Valley. MacDonald and her book became all the rage: *The Egg and I*, which summoned Americans to an infinitely simpler time and place, became a runaway international bestseller, with sales of 1,038,500 copies. It would be translated into more than 30 languages and spawn a series of movies. MacDonald and her family became instant celebrities and were accorded the ultimate postwar accolade: A multipage spread in the March 18, 1946, issue of *Life* magazine.

December, 1945, was also the month W. W. Norton released Otto Fenichel's *Psychoanalytic Theory of Neurosis*, a work far removed from the bucolic misadventures of *The Egg and I*. Fenichel's book was an outgrowth of his lectures on psychopathology at the Berlin Psychoanalytic Institute in the 30s; Sandor Rado, his mentor, claims to have given him the assignment.[3] Austerely written and copiously documented, *The Psychoanalytic Theory of Neurosis* is "an encyclopedia of stupendous completeness,"[4] a dauntingly comprehensive distillation of mainstream Freudian theory as it gained expression in Freud's corpus and in the writings of his first- and second-generation followers.

Following Fenichel's arrival in the United States in 1938, his radical politics were progressively displaced onto a politically inspired defense of Freudian orthodoxy against the incursions of "reactionary" neo-Freudian culturalism.[5] He brought to the task remarkable intellectual ardor suffused with obsessionality. For Fenichel was a compulsive tabulator and organizer of information; Russell Jacoby refers to him as the supreme "man of lists." No event of quotidian existence escaped his systematizing zeal. Every movie seen, every concert attended, every restaurant frequented, every piece of correspondence received—all were recorded, dated, numbered, and cross-referenced. Fenichel's obsessional zeal was harnessed to the preparation of his chef d'oeuvre, *The Psychoanalytic Theory of Neurosis*, which presented the reader with a daunting bibliography of 1,600 references. But, alas, the published

3. Paul Roazen & Bluma Swerdloff, *Heresy: Sandor Rado and the Psychoanalytic Movement* (Northvale, NJ: Aronson, 1995), p. 101.

4. The phrase comes from Hans Sachs, who reviewed the book for the *Psychoanalytic Quarterly*. "Everything that has been written on any subject related to the psychoanalytic theory of neurosis," Sachs continued, "is contained in it, in an abbreviated and condensed, but perfectly lucid presentation. It might be said that almost the whole psychoanalytic literature is made easily accessible by this book and that many contributions toward it in future will be at the disposition of every student who wishes to acquire general information before starting on a laborious and time-consuming special study." Hans Sachs, "Review of *The Psychoanalytic Theory of Neurosis* by Otto Fenichel," *Psychoanal. Quart.*, 15:369–371, 1946, quoted at p. 369. Sandor Rado's more cynical estimation, which he claims was shared by Heinz Hartmann, was that Fenichel's book "was a remarkable record of all the errors in psychoanalysis." See Roazen & Swerdloff, *Heresy* (n. 3), p. 101.

5. Fenichel believed the culturalists and ego psychologists were threatening to destroy psychoanalysis from within. Neo-Freudianism, he remarked in May, 1942, "was similar to fascism and other reactionary movements starting with 'left' ideologies." See Benjamin Harris & Adrian Brock, "Otto Fenichel and the Left Opposition in Psychoanalysis," *J. Hist. Behav. Sci.*, 27:157–164, 1991, quoted at p. 160.

bibliography gave Fenichel no pleasure; it was a pale facsimile of the comprehensive bibliography he had prepared for the book but which Norton could not print owing to the wartime paper shortage.[6]

Fenichel's text does not invite casual perusal. Even for classical psychoanalysts it is a far from pleasurable read. For what Fenichel gives us is, from our contemporary vantage point, a virtual parody of "classical" psychoanalytic writing—dry, turgid, and scientistic in the extreme. And yet *The Psychoanalytic Theory of Neurosis,* in its original cloth edition, sold 80,000 copies. Even Norton's fiftieth anniversary reissue of the book in 1995, newly introduced by Leo Rangell, sold over 1,500 copies, far more than the typical modern psychoanalytic book of our own decidedly post-Fenichel, postclassical era.

I am not aware of any contemporary English-language psychoanalytic book that has sold 80,000 copies. But in the decade following World War II, sales of this magnitude were not unheard of. Indeed, they were far exceeded by prominent analysts and psychiatrists who offered accessible expositions of Freudian or neo-Freudian theory to larger audiences, both inside and outside the mental health field. Harry Stack Sullivan's *Interpersonal Theory of Psychiatry,* released by Norton in 1953, sold over 95,000 copies in the paperback edition alone. Without doubt, Charles Brenner's immensely readable *An Elementary Textbook of Psychoanalysis,* published by International Universities Press in 1955 and reissued by Doubleday Anchor as a mass-market paperback in 1957, vastly outsold Fenichel and Sullivan. Sales data on Brenner are alas unavailable, but the New York psychoanalytic grapevine of the 60s had it that the Doubleday Anchor paperback edition sold over 1,000,000 copies.[7] Throughout the 50s and 60s, large trade houses were quick to appreciate the popularity of psychoanalysis among educated lay readers and to license paperback reprint rights from small professional firms. *An Elementary Textbook of Psychoanalysis* is a case in point. Robert Waelder's popu-

6. Fenichel is an interesting émigré analyst who still awaits his biographer. Until then, one must rely on Russell Jacoby's illuminating *The Repression of Psychoanalysis: Otto Fenichel and the Political Freudians* (NY: Basic Books, 1983). The information in this paragraph is gleaned from pp. 30–36.

7. The New York analyst David Wolitzky related this fact to me after my presentation of a version of this chapter to the Rapaport-Klein Study Group in Stockbridge, Massachusetts, on June 10, 2007.

lar *Basic Theory of Psychoanalysis* is another example. It was published in cloth by IUP in 1960, but republished and widely distributed as a trade paperback four years later by Schocken Books, a German imprint that began publishing in the United States in 1945.

And then there is Erik Erikson, whose literary gifts and appealingly optimistic vision of the human life cycle struck a responsive chord in the war-weary American public. Before popular psychology was debased into pop psychology, there was Erikson. In 1950, Norton released his *Childhood and Society*. Anna Freud dismissed the book as mere "sociology," and her anger at what she took to be Erikson's revisionist intentions was shared by Kurt Eissler, Robert Waelder, Ernst Kris, and Géza Roheim, among others.[8] The cloth edition got off to a discouragingly slow start, with sales of only 1,500 copies the first year, mainly from a small market of social scientists. Analysts and psychiatrists paid little heed to the book although, as the decade progressed, it increasingly turned up on the reading lists of American psychiatric residency programs. By January, 1955, bolstered by course adoptions at major research universities, sales of *Childhood and Society* topped 16,000 copies, and by the fall of 1961 the number had risen to between 40,000 and 50,000.

In 1963, Norton published a revised edition of the book in both cloth and paperback. The revised cloth edition sold 85,000 copies, success enough for any trade book. But the revised paperback edition, a response to burgeoning course adoptions throughout the country, put Erikson on the road to cultural celebrity.[9] Norton wisely made the paperback available at a "college textbook" discounted price of $3.45; in this format and with this pricing, *Childhood and Society* was

8. Daniel Burston, *Erik Erikson and the American Psyche: Ego, Ethics, and Evolution* (Lanham, MD: Jason Aronson, 2007), pp. 36–37; Lawrence J. Friedman, *Identity's Architect: A Biography of Erik H. Erikson* (Cambridge: Harvard University Press, 1999), p. 239. To be sure, Erikson also had his psychoanalytic defenders, David Rapaport and Robert Knight, the closest of his colleagues at the Austen Riggs Center, foremost among them. See Friedman, pp. 238, 286–291.

9. Erikson himself proposed the college paperback edition of *Childhood and Society* to Norton after his friend at Harvard, David Riesman, explained to him "that the paperback revolution under way was based on a college market. The undergraduates were a captive audience, and the professor's order for required course reading guaranteed the sales of a book." As it happened, the Norton staff had already been considering this very possibility, and Erikson's editor, George Brockway, was quick to accede to Erikson's suggestion. See Friedman, *Identity's Architect* (n. 8), pp. 334–335.

an immediate success. It sold almost 28,000 copies during the 1964–65 academic year, and Norton reports total cumulative sales since 1963 of around 750,000 copies.[10]

Erikson would go on to become the psychoanalytic standard-bearer for college students of the 60s and 70s (I was among them). None of his later books approached the dizzying sales of *Childhood and Society*, but all qualify as trade successes. *Young Man Luther*, published by Norton in 1958, sold over 260,000 copies in the paperback edition of 1962. *Insight and Responsibility*, a commercial disappointment, sold over 11,000 copies in cloth and over 80,000 copies in paperback. Erikson and his publisher rebounded with *Identity: Youth and Crisis* (1968), a collection of essays less coherent but trendier in tone and tenor than *Insight and Responsibility*. Aided by Norton's effective promotion, which "resonated to the catch themes and visions of contemporary American college students,"[11] sales were strong: 18,000 copies in cloth followed by 290,000 copies in paperback; a paperback reissue of 1994 sold another 25,000 copies.

Another Norton author, Karen Horney, whose neo-Freudian bent brought her into conflict with the orthodox New York psychoanalytic establishment of the postwar years, had little difficulty finding her way to a wide and appreciative audience of lay readers. As early as 1939, her *New Ways in Psychoanalysis,* one of the early culturalist reinterpretations of Freudian theory, sold 37,000 in cloth and another 78,000 in paperback. In 1945, the year Fenichel's orthodox tome was published, Horney's *Our Inner Conflicts* was released; it would sell 67,000 copies in cloth and over 150,000 in paperback. Horney's trials and tribulations among her New York colleagues notwithstanding, she had staying power among her American readers. Her best book, *Neurosis and Human Growth*, published in 1950, sold over 125,000 copies in paperback (cloth figures are not available). When Norton released the fortieth anniversary edition of the book in 1990, it sold another 35,000 copies.

10. I am relying here on information provided by Friedman in *Identity's Architect* (n. 8), pp. 237, 240–241, 334–335. Friedman puts hardcover sales of the first edition of *Childhood and Society* at 50,000 on p. 237 and 40,000 on p. 335. The figure for total paperback sales of the revised 1963 paperback edition is the result of my own queries to the book's publisher, W. W. Norton.

11. Friedman, *Identity's Architect* (n. 8), p. 351.

Sales of Erikson and Horney, impressive as they were, pale alongside the postwar sales of Erich Fromm, whose psychoanalytically informed social criticism was immensely popular with professional and lay readers wrestling with postwar political tensions, especially the specter of totalitarianism. There is no possibility of retrieving cumulative sales data from first publication of Fromm's series of trade books of the 40s, 50s, and 60s, but Rainer Funk, Fromm's literary executor, has provided me with his personal sales estimates of all of Fromm's titles. His listing gives no less than 14 titles from this period with worldwide sales in all languages of at least 1,000,000 copies. Funk allows that his estimates of Fromm's early books may be on the high side, but there is, in my judgment, little question that each of his three most popular books, *Escape from Freedom* (1941), *The Sane Society* (1955), and *The Art of Loving* (1956), sold millions of copies in English.[12] In the case of *The Art of Loving*, according to Funk, U.S. sales from 1970 on total a staggering 5,000,000 copies.[13]

One need not be a Fromm, Erikson, or Horney to garner trade success during the glory era of psychoanalytic publishing. In the quarter century that followed the end of World War II, hundreds and hundreds of commercially successful psychoanalytic books were published. Theodor Reik immigrated to the United States in 1938 and immediately formed a publishing relation with the firm of Farrar, Straus and Company (today Farrar, Straus and Giroux). The collaboration yielded some 13 books over the next two decades. Most notable in the years following World War II were *Listening with the Third Ear* (1948/1952) and *The Search Within* (1956). Farrar sold around 9,000 copies of a paperback edition of *Listening*; other sales data on Reik's books cannot be retrieved. But his books were obviously very successful for his publisher. *The Search Within* began with a publisher's preface in which John Farrar pronounced the book the first of a series of volumes from Reik's works. Tellingly, he mentioned that Reik "did

12. Funk's estimates of worldwide sales of these three volumes, which he acknowledges may be higher than actual sales, are: *Escape from Freedom* (1941, 5,000,000 copies); *The Sane Society* (1955, 3,000,000 copies); *The Art of Loving* (1956, 25,000,000 copies). According to Funk, Fromm also had two multimillion-copy best sellers in the 70s: *The Anatomy of Human Destructiveness* (1973, 3,000,000 copies) and *To Have or to Be?* (1976, 10,000,000 copies).

13. Rainer Funk to Paul Stepansky, August 15, 2007.

not wish to edit these books himself," so that Farrar, Straus itself had undertaken the task.[14] Needless to say, publishers do not undertake such tasks for commercially marginal authors.

Wilhelm Reich was another European analyst who filled the Farrar, Straus coffers, albeit in the 60s and 70s. Reich arrived on American shores in August, 1939, and immediately set about providing the American public with English-language editions of his books. He began by writing a new book with an old title[15]—*The Function of the Orgasm*—and then, with his former patient and translator, Theodore Wolfe, set up his own publishing house, the Orgone Institute Press, to publish it. The book appeared early in 1942, received little promotion, and enjoyed steady but unexceptional sales. But Reich was unfazed. His publishing house went ahead with Wolfe's translations of *The Sexual Revolution* and *Character Analysis* in 1945 and *The Mass Psychology of Fascism* in 1946.[16]

From these humble publication beginnings, Reich found an appreciative, if resolutely nonanalytic, American readership, and English editions of his early works, translated by Wolfe and later by Vincent Carfagno, found their way into the Farrar, Straus catalog in the 60s and 70s. Beginning in 1961, Farrar, Straus reissued *The Function of the Orgasm* and *Character Analysis*.[17] Additional titles would follow. A decade later Farrar licensed paperback rights to *The Function of the Orgasm* to Simon & Schuster, which released a mass-market "pocket book" edition of the book in 1975. Reich, a leftist sexual revolutionary who ended his days in the Lewisburg (Pennsylvania) Penitentiary[18] in a full-blown paranoid psychosis, became a popular

14. John Farrar, "Publisher's Preface," in Theodor Reik, *The Search Within: The Inner Experiences of a Psychoanalyst* (NY: Farrar, Straus, 1956), pp. vii–viii.

15. In 1927, Reich had published in German a different book with this same title.

16. Myron Sharaf, *Fury on Earth: A Biography of Wilhelm Reich* (NY: St. Martin's Press, 1983), pp. 266–268.

17. Colin Wilson, *The Quest for Wilhelm Reich: A Critical Biography* (NY: Anchor Press, 1981), pp. 230–231.

18. On May 25, 1956, Reich was sentenced to two years in federal prison for refusing to obey a federal court injunction to cease shipping his "orgone energy accumulators" across state lines and to recall and destroy those accumulators already shipped. See Sharaf, *Fury on Earth* (n. 16), pp. 410ff.; Wilson, *Quest for Reich* (n. 17), pp. 217ff.

counterculture author during the decade of the permissive society and student activism directed at the Establishment and its war in Vietnam.

With best-selling authors like Erikson, Horney, Fromm, and credible trade authors like Reik and Reich, it was a matter of psychoanalysts who achieved commercial success in one of two ways. Erikson, Horney, Fromm, and Reik simply wrote about psychoanalysis in accessible and engaging ways. On the other hand, in the case of Erikson's psychobiographies, Fromm's social criticism, and Reich's sexual politics, these authors chose to address nonanalytic subjects analytically. What is equally impressive is the manner in which psychoanalysis in the postwar years entered into mainstream medical discourse. This was the era in which psychoanalysis helped transform the nature of medical history-taking. Early in the century, medical students learned to take patient histories via an outline that solicited yes-no replies to standardized questions; the point of the exercise was to minimize time-consuming digressions about irrelevant experiences. After the war, influenced by the popularity and prestige of analysis, medical history-taking became newly sensitized to the diagnostic importance of dialogic inquiry that invited patients to relate their stories in their own words. The history evolved into an "interview" aimed at uncovering aspects of illness opaque to more traditional forms of medical information-gathering.[19] In this general context, primary care physicians and specialists alike became interested in what psychoanalysis had to offer.

Unsurprisingly, analysis had its greatest impact on psychiatry. In chapter 1, we briefly outlined the circumstances in which psychiatry came to lean on psychoanalysis in the two decades following World War II. A complementary dynamic was also at work: Psychoanalysis, albeit more haltingly, reached out to psychiatry. Two Berlin-trained, Hungarian émigrés, Franz Alexander and Sandor Rado, were principal architects of this initiative. Invited in 1930 by Robert Hutchins, President of the University of Chicago, to become a Visiting Professor of Psychoanalysis, Alexander accepted the offer and permanently settled in Chicago two years later. He lost no time in founding the Chicago Institute of Psychoanalysis. Securely ensconced in Chicago, Alexander, prodded by the Rockefeller Foundation's Alan Gregg,

19. Stanley Joel Reiser, *Medicine and the Reign of Technology* (Cambridge: Cambridge University Press, 1978), pp. 180–181.

devoted himself to a topic that bridged his early training in experimental pathology and his subsequent conversion to psychoanalysis: Psychosomatic medicine. Throughout the 30s and 40s he focused especially on the putatively psychodynamic causes of a broad range of psychosomatic symptomatology.[20] Beginning in 1935, the Chicago Institute was the beneficiary of Rockefeller Foundation largesse—three annual $100,000 grants—aimed at promoting Alexander's psychosomatic research and thereby fostering the relationship of psychoanalysis to medicine and psychiatry. Alexander's first American book, *The Medical Value of Psychoanalysis*, was released by Norton in 1936.[21]

Rado too visited the States in 1930, in his case as a guest of A. A. Brill and the New York Psychoanalytic Society. His permanent relocation to New York was in 1933, a year after Alexander's move to Chicago. By 1935, Rado had formed a friendship with Adolf Meyer, then dean of American Psychiatry, and his deepening appreciation of Meyer's integrative biopsychosocial perspective is the anlage of his rancorous dealings with his New York colleagues during the late 30s.[22]

20. Alexander's other major focus, which dates back to his *Psychoanalysis of the Total Personality* (1927), was the elaboration of a Freudian variant of Alfred Adler's social theory of neurosis. See Paul E. Stepansky, *In Freud's Shadow: Adler in Context* (Hillsdale, NJ: Analytic Press, 1983), pp. 225–230.

21. Alexander's training in experimental pathology was in the laboratory of the Budapest physiologist Franz Tangl. See Franz Alexander, *The Western Mind in Transition* (New York: Random House, 1960), pp. 15–16, 287–288. On Alan Gregg's measured support of, and subsequent disillusionment with, Alexander's psychosomatic research, see especially Theodore M. Brown, "Alan Gregg and the Rockefeller Foundation's Support of Franz Alexander's Psychosomatic Research," *Bull. Hist. Med.*, 61:155–182, 1987 and, additionally, Wilder Penfield, *The Difficult Art of Giving: The Epic of Alan Gregg* (Boston: Little, Brown, 1967), p. 274; Dorothy Levenson, *Mind, Body, and Medicine: A History of the American Psychosomatic Society* (Baltimore: Williams & Wilkins, 1994), pp. 29–30; and Katherine Angel, "Defining Psychiatry: Aubrey Lewis's 1938 Report and the Rockefeller Foundation," in Katherine Angel, Edgar Jones, & Michael Neve, eds., *European Psychiatry on the Eve of War: Aubrey Lewis, the Maudsley Hospital, and the Rockefeller Foundation in the 1930s* (London: Wellcome Trust, 2003), pp. 39–56, at pp. 50–54.

22. Craig Tomlinson has written perceptively on Meyer's influence on Rado and the latter's vision of psychoanalytic education in "Sandor Rado and Adolf Meyer: A Nodal Point in American Psychiatry and Psychoanalysis," *Int. J. Psycho-Anal.*, 77:963–982, 1996. On Rado's "rancorous dealings" with his colleagues at the New York Psychoanalytic Institute see George Daniels, "History of the Association for Psychoanalytic Medicine and the Columbia Psychoanalytic Clinic," *Bull. Assn. Psychoanal. Med.*,

Influenced by the multidisciplinary orientation of Meyer's Johns Hopkins–based Phipps Clinic, to which he traveled on a weekly basis to attend clinical conferences throughout 1938, Rado formed the idea of a new psychoanalytic institute attached to a university clinic and hospital by 1939. Three years later, he led the group of New York Psychoanalytic Society members who, frustrated with the atmosphere of "bickering, slander, and gossip"[23] prevalent in the society, founded the Association for Psychoanalytic and Psychosomatic Medicine. Throughout 1943, Rado and George Daniels discreetly negotiated with the American Psychoanalytic Association for a revision of by-laws that would permit his new association to establish an APsaA-approved psychoanalytic training center.[24] Anticipating a positive outcome, Rado and his associates simultaneously met, albeit informally, with Nolan D. C. Lewis, Chairman of the Department of Psychiatry at Columbia University and Director of the university's Psychiatric Institute; together they laid the groundwork for integrating the new training institute with Columbia's College of Physicians and Surgeons.

By June, 1944, with the promise of a Columbia affiliation in place, the Association for Psychoanalytic and Psychosomatic Medicine was drafting its constitution and articles of incorporation. Later in the summer, Rado, accompanied by Abram Kardiner, David Levy, and George Daniels, left the New York Psychoanalytic Society to found Columbia University's psychoanalytic training program, initially dubbed the Psychoanalytic and Psychosomatic Clinic for Training and Research of the Columbia Department of Psychiatry. There, Rado later

---

11:12–15, 26–31, 47–53, 1971–1972; Marianne Horney Eckardt, "Organizational Schisms in American Psychoanalysis," in Jacques M. Quen & Eric T. Carlson, eds., *American Psychoanalysis: Origins and Development* (NY: Brunner/Mazel, 1978), pp. 152–156; and John Frosch, "The New York Psychoanalytic Civil War," *JAPA*, 39: 1037–1064, 1991. Rado's own reminiscences of these developments are in Roazen & Swerdloff, *Heresy* (n. 3), pp. 116–127.

23. Letter of Carl Binger, representing the group of seceding New York analysts, to Leonard Blumgart, president of the New York Psychoanalytic Society, June 12, 1942, quoted in Eckardt, "Organizational Schisms in American Psychoanalysis" (n. 22), p. 153.

24. Prior to the bylaw revision, which was implemented in 1946, the APsaA allowed only one authorized training institute in a given city.

recollected, he "forced psychoanalytic students to learn psychiatry" within the broader shared goal of "bring[ing] psychoanalysis out of its isolation and into contact with medicine, as well as to teach doctors the connection with psychoanalysis."[25]

The vision of a psychoanalytically informed "psychodynamic psychiatry" as a "Cinderella" specialty that absorbed and even transcended the explanatory perspectives of medicine and surgery had been articulated in the 30s, especially by Karl Menninger.[26] But it was during the war and its aftermath that medicine seemed responsive to Menninger's special pleading and reached out to analytically trained—or at least analytically oriented—psychiatrists for elucidation of "psychodynamic science" in relation to any number of medical conditions. Books of the era paid special attention to psychodynamic anlagen of peptic ulcer, asthma, allergies, hypertension, and neurodermatitis, but typically invoked case examples involving these conditions to sustain a globally psychoanalytic approach to psychosomatic medicine. For Helen Flanders Dunbar, the approach culminated in distinct "psychosomatic profiles" of patients suffering from any number of ostensibly medical conditions, including fractures, rheumatic disease, diabetes, and various subtypes of cardiovascular disease.[27]

Dunbar, a polymath whose medical training at Yale was preceded by a Columbia doctorate in medieval philosophy and a Bachelor of

25. Roazen & Swerdloff, *Heresy* (n. 3), p. 126. The residency training program attached to the new Psychoanalytic and Psychosomatic Clinic opened January 15, 1945, and was described in *Psychosomatic Medicine* the following May. See "Note: Graduate Residency Training in Psychoanalysis and Psychosomatic Medicine," *Psychosom. Med.*, 7:44, 1945. For a thoughtful assessment of the institutional and political tensions that gained expression in the several splits within the New York Psychoanalytic Society in the early 40s, Rado's among them, see Kenneth Eisold, "The Splitting of the New York Psychoanalytic Society and the Construction of Psychoanalytic Authority," *Int. J. Psycho-Anal.*, 79:871–885, 1998.

26. Stepansky, *Freud, Surgery, and the Surgeons* (Hillsdale, NJ: Analytic Press, 1999), pp. 179–186. I return to postwar psychiatry's Cinderella status below, pp. 127–128.

27. Helen Flanders Dunbar, *Psychosomatic Diagnosis* (NY: Hoeber, 1943), chaps. 4–10. Dunbar's "psychosomatic profiles" were directly influenced by the internist George Draper, who devised his four panels of personality at Columbia College of Physicians and Surgeons, where, with a three-year Rockefeller grant, he established the College's Division of Medical Anthropology in 1936. See Sarah W. Tracy, "George Draper and American Constitutional Medicine, 1916–1946: Reinventing the Sick Man," *Bull. Hist. Med.*, 66:53–89, 1992, at pp. 78–83.

Divinity degree from Union Theological Seminary, was the most prolific psychosomaticist of the era and the recipient of successive grants from the Josiah Macy Foundation. In 1935, Columbia University Press released her *Emotions and Bodily Changes: A Survey of the Literature on Psychosomatic Interrelationships*; with its bibliography of 2,251 entries summarized in a text of 432 pages, the book "quite literally launched the 'American psychosomatic movement'" and rated a second edition, expanded and updated, in 1938.[28] A year later, the Commonwealth Fund funded and published George Canby Robinson's *The Patient as a Person: A Study of the Social Aspects of Illness*. It was the culmination of a major psychosomatic project of the mid-30s: Robinson's Rockefeller-funded "Study of the Accessory Factors on Health" that analyzed a series of 174 new patients admitted to Johns Hopkins Hospital during 1936 and 1937; the goal of the study was to link "faulty habits" and maladjustment—especially those associated with "adverse social conditions"—to a host of medical conditions.[29]

Two substantial textbooks were released under major medical imprints in 1943 while the fighting raged: Dunbar's own comprehensive *Psychosomatic Diagnosis* (741 pages), published by Paul B. Hoeber, and Edward Weiss and O. Spurgeon English's *Psychosomatic Medicine: The Clinical Application of Psychopathology to General Medical Problems*, published by W. B. Saunders. Two years later, with the end of hostilities in sight, The Blakiston Company, a Doubleday imprint, released Roy R. Grinker and John P. Spiegel's *Men Under Stress*, · with its abundant examples of psychophysical dysfunction pursuant to the "ego depletion" of battlefield stress among American aviators. Dunbar's *Mind and Body: Psychosomatic Medicine*, published by

28. Theodore M. Brown, "The Rise and Fall of American Psychosomatic Medicine," presented to the New York Academy of Medicine, November 29, 2000, www.human-nature.com/free-associations/riseandfall.html, p. 21; Levenson, *Mind, Body, and Medicine* (n. 21), p. 31.

29. On the methodology of the study, the criteria of patient selection, and the definition of "adverse social conditions" employed in the study, see G. Canby Robinson, *The Patient as a Person: A Study of the Social Aspects of Illness* (NY: Commonwealth Fund, 1939), chap. 2. On Robinson and the Hopkins study, see Theodore M. Brown, "George Canby Robinson and 'The Patient as a Person,'" in Christopher Lawrence & George Weisz, eds., *Greater Than the Parts: Holism in Biomedicine, 1920–1950* (NY: Oxford University Press, 1998), pp. 135–160, especially at pp. 144–145, 149–151.

Random House in 1947, is an excellent example of the psychosomatic genre in its popularized postwar incarnation; it is entertaining, informative, and vastly overreaches itself in ways that, 60 years later, are comical.[30] A more sober work, Harold Abramson's *Psychodynamics and the Allergic Patient*, was published by The Bruce Publishing Company a year later. It was, so its front cover proclaimed, "An Official Publication of the American College of Allergists, Inc."

Two years later, in 1950, Norton released Franz Alexander's *Psychosomatic Medicine: Its Principles and Applications*, the capstone of the postwar psychosomatic literature. It would sell 18,000 copies in the original paperback edition; a cloth reissue in 1987 sold another 1,000 copies. Lest the trade success of authors such as Fromm, Erikson, and Horney leave us unmoved by professional-book sales of 18,000, we should bear in mind that *Psychosomatic Medicine* was published at a time when the American Psychiatric Association had fewer than 5,900 members and the American Psychoanalytic Association just over 400. It would be a full three decades before the Psychoanalysis Division of the American Psychological Association came into being.

In relation to the professional-book market of its time and place, Alexander's *Psychosomatic Medicine* was most certainly what publishers refer to as a "big book." It reached out to the entire American community of analysts and psychiatrists and was bought by many nonpsychiatric physicians as well. But then American psychoanalysis as a field has historically been given to big books. In the postwar era, it is difficult to imagine any analyst (or aspiring analyst or psychodynamic psychiatrist) who would not have bought, very early in the going, a copy of Fenichel's *Psychoanalytic Theory of Neurosis*. It is equally difficult to imagine an American analyst (or aspiring analyst or psychodynamic psychiatrist) of the 1960s who would not have

---

30. Dunbar claimed, inter alia, that at least 80% of major accidents are due to "accidentitis," a bona fide ailment, the sufferers of which have much in common: "They are generally decisive to the point of giving an impression of impulsiveness. They concentrate upon daily pleasures with little interest in long-term goals. They display a relatively cavalier attitude toward sex and family, but take very good care of their own health. Their illness rate is well below that of the general population. Even in their extramarital sex relationships they maintain enough concern for their own welfare to have a very low rate of venereal-disease infection or unwanted pregnancy, yet are not bothered by exaggerated fears on either score" (Helen Flanders Dunbar, *Mind and Body: Psychosomatic Medicine* [NY: Random House, 1947], pp. 96, 101).

prized his or her copies of Anna Freud's *Ego and the Mechanisms of Defense* and of Heinz Hartmann's *Ego Psychology and the Problem of Adaptation.*

The last major trade success of the glory era of psychoanalytic publishing attests to the manner in which psychoanalysis, especially in its descriptive characterology, dominated American psychiatry and engaged educated lay readers. David Shapiro began writing *Neurotic Styles* in 1960, the final year of his eight-year stint as chief psychologist at the Austen Riggs Treatment Center. At least one presentation of his material was made to Riggs staff members—Erik Erikson, Robert Knight, and David Rapaport among them—and the resulting book was published by Basic Books in 1965 as the fifth volume in the Austen Riggs Monograph Series.[31] The psychoanalytic grounding of Shapiro's rich character descriptions obviously passed muster with his mentors at Riggs; Robert Knight, in his Foreword to the first edition, opined that the book would "come to be widely regarded as an outstanding contribution to psychoanalytic ego psychology and characterology."[32] And yet Shapiro aimed at a broad readership of "analytically interested people" and intentionally wrote the book in "English rather than Psychoanalese."[33] In the four decades following publication, Basic Books sold over 250,000 copies of the paperback edition. Sales of the original cloth edition would enlarge this number. Clearly, the psychoanalytic character of *Neurotic Styles* did not limit its appeal among nonanalytic clinicians and lay readers.

From the dizzying heights of Shapiro's *Neurotic Styles*, we descend to sales of more conventionally strong-selling professional titles of the 1970s. Even in the limited span of my own career, I recall books such as Margaret Mahler's *The Psychological Birth of the Human Infant*

31. I am indebted to Craig Piers, a current member of the Rapaport-Klein Study Group, for apprising me of the circumstances in which Shapiro conceived and wrote *Neurotic Styles* and for putting me in touch with Dr. Shapiro.

32. Robert P. Knight, "Foreword," in David Shapiro, *Neurotic Styles* (NY: Basic Books, 1965), p. vii.

33. David Shapiro to Paul Stepansky, August 2, 2007. Shapiro is at pains to differentiate the style of *Neurotic Styles* from psychoanalytic writing per se: "It [*Neurotic Styles*] is also clear in its psychological understanding (for example, of projection) where psychoanalysis frequently offers only revered formulas preserved from its days of adventure." Quoted with permission.

(1975), which sold over 21,000 copies, and, on a smaller scale, Roy Schafer's *A New Language for Psychoanalysis* (1976), which sold over 9,100 copies. A year later, Basic Books released Paul Wachtel's *Psychoanalysis and Behavior Therapy: Toward an Integration* (1977), which initiated a new subgenre of psychoanalytic literature aimed at integrating disjunctive psychotherapeutic modalities in the service of pragmatic clinical goals. *Psychoanalysis and Behavior Therapy*, which helped launch the "psychotherapy integration" movement, sold 17,000 copies; a revision of the work, *Psychoanalysis, Behavior Therapy, and the Relational World*, published by American Psychological Association Press in 1997, has sold an additional 4,500 copies.

Neither Mahler nor Schafer nor Wachtel were "trade" successes in the manner of Fromm, Erikson, Horney, or Shapiro. Yet, within the United States, Mahler and Schafer spoke to the entire psychoanalytic profession. Wachtel, for his part, spoke as an analytically oriented academic psychologist to a broad psychotherapy readership willing to explore integrative approaches to clinical practice. Mahler and Schafer count as general-interest psychoanalytic books. Wachtel, on the other hand, is a special-interest psychoanalytic book that is simultaneously a general-interest psychotherapy book. And it is just such books—general-interest in one of these two senses—with sales in the 10,000 to 20,000 range, that have grown scarcer decade by decade. Now, three decades later, books of general significance to the profession as a cohesive discipline have effectively vanished. Nor does the occasional integrative book authored by a psychoanalyst enjoy commercial success.[34] Very occasionally, as we shall see, a professional book falls within, or even sells beyond, this range. But such books have the status of novelties; they ride the crest of a particular trend or innovative disciplinary approach to psychoanalysis. They are no longer psychoanalytic books per se. They do not speak to the field at large in

---

34. This, at any event, was my experience at The Analytic Press. In the 1990s, I published two fine books in the spirit of Wachtel, Mary-Joan Gerson's *The Embedded Self: A Psychoanalytic Guide to Family Therapy* (1996) and Kenneth Frank's *Psychoanalytic Participation: Action, Interaction, and Integration* (1999). Each book has sold around 750 copies. In my final year at TAP, I returned to this genre with Mary Connors's excellent *Symptom-Focused Dynamic Psychotherapy* (2006), a work that revisited the role of cognitive-behavioral techniques in psychoanalytically oriented treatment and received Wachtel's strong written endorsement. Sales of Connors as of the end of 2008 were also at 750, half of which were book club sales.

the manner of Anna Freud, Fenichel, Hartmann, Mahler, and Alexander because the field no longer exists in the way it existed for these exemplars of an earlier generation.

Even within the history of dissent within psychoanalysis, one has little difficulty summoning a handful of important books that had to be engaged—which is to say they had to be purchased and read—by the profession at large. In the United States, where the hegemony of the ego-psychological paradigm went largely unchallenged until the 1970s, substantive articulations of alternative psychoanalytic Weltanschauungen tended to become big books through the simple fact of their rarity. John Gedo and Arnold Goldberg's *Models of the Mind* (9,500 copies sold) and Heinz Kohut's *Analysis of the Self* (around 42,000 copies sold) and *Restoration of the Self* (around 36,000 copies sold)[35] are outstanding examples from the 1970s;[36] Jay Greenberg and Stephen Mitchell's *Object Relations in Psychoanalytic Theory*, with sales of over 49,500 copies, and Daniel Stern's *The Interpersonal World of the Infant*, with sales of 23,000 copies, had considerable profession-wide impact in the 1980s, and sales to match.

In the mid-80s, the field's fragmentation was less advanced than it would be a decade hence, so that big books could still be pegged to the part-agendas of what were understood to be major dissident viewpoints. Two books of the mid-80s and one of the late-80s exemplify this publishing reality with respect to self psychology: Kohut's posthumously published *How Does Analysis Cure?* (University of Chicago Press, 1984), a reprise on psychoanalytic self psychology, sold over 16,000 copies and is still in print. Stolorow, Brandchaft, and Atwood's *Psychoanalytic Treatment: An Intersubjective Approach* (Analytic Press, 1986), an influential articulation of the treatment implications

35. I was unable to obtain sales totals of Kohut's *Analysis of the Self* and *Restoration of the Self* from the publisher, International Universities Press, and thank Professor Thomas Kohut for reviewing his father's royalty statements in order to provide me with these estimates.

36. Otto Kernberg's *Borderline Conditions and Pathological Narcissism* (NY: Jason Aronson, 1975) and *Object Relations Theory and Clinical Psychoanalysis* (NY: Jason Aronson, 1976) were also major titles of the 70s, but I was unable to obtain sales data on these books.

of self-psychologically inspired "intersubjectivity theory," sold over 12,000 copies and is still available. Two years later, in 1988, Guilford Press released Ernest Wolf's elementary exposition of self psychology, *Treating the Self: Elements of Clinical Self Psychology*. It has sold over 14,000 copies in its cloth and paperback editions.

Other influential books of the period were sober-minded critiques of traditional analytic claims about the possibility of objective knowledge. Donald Spence's *Narrative Truth and Historical Truth* (Norton, 1982), which rode the crest of an emerging postclassical, relativistic epistemology, sold over 7,000 copies in cloth and paperback editions. Adolf Grünbaum's *The Foundations of Psychoanalysis: A Philosophical Critique* (University of California Press, 1984), a trenchant critique of the field's scientific claims that provided an epistemic wake-up call to many psychoanalysts, sold around 9,000 copies.

Other rigorous examinations of the scientific challenges before the field of the mid-80s also sold respectably well. Indeed, in the 80s the scientific status of psychoanalysis seemed to matter much more to members of the profession than it would in the years to follow. Morris Eagle's *Recent Developments in Psychoanalysis: A Critical Evaluation*, published by the trade firm of McGraw-Hill in 1984 and reprinted in paperback by Harvard University Press in 1987, sold around 6,000 copies. Marshall Edelson's *Psychoanalysis: A Theory in Crisis* (1988), in part an extended dialogue with, and reply to, Grünbaum, sold around 2,900 in cloth and paperback editions.

Among psychoanalytic books of comparable epistemological import, such numbers could not be approached in the 90s or 00s. In fact, by the 90s, small mental-health publishing firms generally avoided books about psychoanalysis, science, and philosophy like the plague. Only major university presses, whose offerings were ipso facto credible to a larger academic audience, occasionally ventured into these perilous waters. Harvard University Press enjoyed moderate success with Marcia Cavell's *The Psychoanalytic Mind: From Freud to Philosophy* (1993; 1,800 copies sold). At TAP, I remained committed to this type of publication but felt obligated to limit myself to works that were (so I thought) clinically consequential. Donnel Stern's excellent *Unformulated Experience: From Dissociation to Imagination in Psychoanalysis* (1997) embodies this subgenre and was a rare success with sales of 2,500 copies. More typical, sadly, were such fine books as Philip F. D. Rubovits-Seitz's encyclopedic *Depth-Psychological Understanding: The Methodologic*

Ground of Clinical Interpretations (1998) and Marilyn Charles's evocative, beautifully written *Patterns: Building Blocks of Experience* (2002), both of which sold fewer than 300 copies.

A major commercial success of the late 80s was a professional/academic crossover book, Jessica Benjamin's *The Bonds of Love: Psychoanalysis, Feminism, and the Problem of Domination*, which drew sales from a multidisciplinary readership of analysts, feminists, social scientists, and gender theorists. Pantheon Books, the distinguished Random House imprint, released the book in 1988. Benjamin estimates sales at between 30,000 and 35,000 copies, with continuing annual sales of between 1,000 and 1,500 copies. *The Bonds of Love*, with its broad academic appeal to feminist scholars and other academics,[37] conveys a sense of the sea change in psychoanalytic publishing that would gain momentum in the 90s. Whereas the outstanding commercial success of the early 80s, Greenberg and Mitchell's *Object Relations in Psychoanalytic Theory*, was a traditional psychoanalytic book in tone, tenor, and content, Benjamin's *Bonds of Love*, a major commercial success of the late 80s, was avowedly multidisciplinary in all these respects. It used psychoanalytic theory to frame and bolster an analysis of gender, power, and desire relevant to a broad nonclinical readership.

What were the commensurately big analytic books of the 1990s? Burness Moore and Bernard Fine's *Psychoanalytic Terms and Concepts*, an enlargement of the American Psychoanalytic Association's self-published *Glossary of Psychoanalytic Terms and Concepts* (1968), was released by Yale University Press in 1990 and sold 14,000 copies in cloth and paperback editions. It is significant as perhaps the last dictionary-like compendium to enjoy commercial success across the various psychoanalytic communities.[38] Another bona fide big book that launched the decade is Carol Basch and Michael Basch's *Understanding Psychotherapy*. This analytically, and more especially self

---

37. The exceptional sales of the German edition of *Bonds of Love* (about 25,000 copies) attest to this fact. Jessica Benjamin to Paul Stepansky, March 10, 2007.

38. Moore's subsequent effort at an edited, dictionary-like work, *Psychoanalysis: The Major Concepts*, was published by Yale in 1996 and reprinted in paperback in 1999. The two editions together sold a scant 3,200 copies. The drop-off is symptomatic of the fractionation of the field that proceeded apace during the 90s.

psychologically, oriented examination of psychotherapy would sell, under the guiding hand of Basic Books' trade division, some 17,500 copies—over 10,000 copies fewer than Michael Basch's *Doing Psychotherapy* of 1980, but still a resounding commercial success by professional book standards. Theoretically, *Understanding Psychotherapy* benefited from the impact of psychoanalytic self psychology on American psychoanalysis and its diffusion within American psychotherapy throughout the 1980s. Commercially, it benefited from the attentiveness of a major house convinced of the book's trade potential and able to present it to a broad mental-health readership through bookstore distribution. In both senses, *Understanding Psychotherapy* was a swan song to an earlier era in psychoanalytic publishing, when psychiatry and clinical psychology espoused a psychodynamic viewpoint that gained expression in many psychotherapy texts written by psychoanalysts.

The sales of both Basch titles, impressive as they are, pale alongside sales of two other books of the mid-90s. Both, in their respective ways, are introductory textbooks, and both appeal to readers far outside the typical audience for psychoanalytic publications. Nancy McWilliams's *Psychoanalytic Diagnosis* was released by Guilford Press in 1994. Spurred on by her graduate students in clinical psychology, McWilliams wrote the book for an audience of "students and trainees, mostly people who were unfamiliar with analytic ways of thinking about personality."[39] Flying beneath the radar of the various psychoanalytic schools of thought, *Psychoanalytic Diagnosis* brought a psychoanalytic mode of conceptualization to a large market of nonanalytic mental health professionals. It was an enormous commercial success, with total sales, as of February, 2008, of 54,000 copies[40] and it established McWilliams as a premier expositor of psychoanalytically oriented therapy for nonanalysts hungry for a comprehensible, depth-psychological modus operandi in an era of brief therapy, psychopharmacology, and managed care. McWilliams, who clearly addressed herself to nonanalytic readers, expresses surprise at the book's collateral (and continuing) success among trained analysts and other experienced clinicians.

39. Nancy McWilliams to Paul Stepansky, February 22, 2007 and February 16, 2008. Quoted with permission.

40. Of these sales of *Psychoanalytic Diagnosis*, 3,450 were book club sales.

Almost as successful as *Psychoanalytic Diagnosis* was Stephen Mitchell and Margaret Black's *Freud and Beyond: A History of Modern Psychoanalytic Thought*, published by Basic Books in 1995. Unlike McWilliams's book, which side-stepped the fractious and fractionated state of the field in conveying to nonanalysts a pragmatic way of thinking and working analytically, the latter book absorbed fractionation into a Whig history that pointed to, and culminated in, the "postclassical" (viz., two-person, interactive, participatory) sensibility of which the authors were major proponents. It follows that the anlagen of Mitchell and Black's commercial success were very different from those of McWilliams. Mitchell's stature within postclassical psychoanalysis; his strikingly successful publication record of the 80s and early 90s (of which more, below); and his writerly ability to describe and compare psychoanalytic theories with lucidity and even grace—these attributes made him the ideal expositor of contemporary psychoanalysis in its sundry theories and clinical approaches for academics and lay readers interested in a single, authoritative overview of the field. Basic Books has sold around 7,000 copies of the original cloth edition; the paperback reprint has sold over 40,000 copies.

I am not aware of any university or mental-health press psychoanalytic-type books that enjoyed commensurate success in the early or mid-90s. Nor, for that matter, am I aware of any psychoanalytic-type books published by larger houses that approached the sales figures of the books by Basch, McWilliams, and Mitchell and Black. And all three books, as noted, adopted a mode of conceptualization and level of presentation appropriate to nonanalytic psychotherapists. There are other successful books by analysts during this period, but they tend to be crossover projects with greater appeal to the literati than to clinical readers. The several collections of Adam Phillips's evocative essays are a case in point. By academic book standards, Phillips is a very successful author. Harvard University Press sold 21,000 copies of *On Kissing, Tickling, and Being Bored* (1993), 10,000 copies of *On Flirtation* (1994), and 6,200 copies of *Terrors and Experts* (1996).

Yale, for its part, was successful with the books of Robert Stoller, whose subject area was ready-made for trade promotion and crossover sales. In 1985, Yale published Stoller's *Observing the Erotic Imagination* and *Presentations of Gender*, each of which was aimed at analytic readers and each of which sold about 2,100 copies. But Stoller's more commercially pegged *Porn*, published by Yale in 1991, sold over 6,400 copies. Leonard Shengold's *Soul Murder* (1989) is another successful crossover book by an analyst. Yale sold around 5,900 copies of the book before licensing paperback rights to the Random House imprint Ballantine Books. Ballantine did not provide me with sales data, but it is safe to say they sold many thousands of copies of the paperback edition. Textbooks and academic or trade crossover books—such were the royal roads to commercial success for analytic publishers from the late 80s on. To be sure, the vast majority of textbooks and crossover books sold like typical analytic books, i.e., very modestly. But the textbook and crossover genres at least provided the possibility of strong sales.

If we turn to the more focal realm of psychoanalytic book publishing, which excludes textbooks and academic/trade crossover books, we find a very different situation by the late 80s. Here the very notion of success was being recalibrated to the smaller markets of particular psychoanalytic schools of thought. Analytic books of this time could still be successful, indeed *very* successful, but they were no longer analytic books in the generically inclusive sense of the term; the most successful books of the late 80s grew out of, and gave articulate expression to, one or another school of thought.

Christopher Bollas is a case in point. In 1987, Columbia University Press published Bollas's *The Shadow of the Object: Psychoanalysis of the Unthought Known*. A representative of the British Independent Group influenced by Winnicott, Khan, and Balint, among others, Bollas provided a creative extension of object-relational thinking that was especially congenial to two American schools of thought. In setting forth the mother as a "transformational object" whose particular "idiom" of mothering was reactivated, analyzed, and ultimately relinquished in treatment, he subsumed an important theme of American self psychology. For Bollas, as for the American self psychologists, psychopathology was developmentally grounded in the mother's failure—whether through impingements or an absence of empathy or nurturance—to provide the kind of attuned maternal "process" that sustained psychological growth. Simultaneously, in presenting an interactively cogwheeling vision of countertransference, in which the analyst's ability to feel him- or herself into the patient's childhood role in a particular family environment interlocked with the patient's progressive ability to think about heretofore "unthought knowns," Bollas anticipated a central emphasis of the American relational orientation of the 90s. The result was a long-term commercial success. Columbia reports sales of over 16,000 copies of the book in cloth and paperback editions; in 2006, a full two decades after publication, it sold another 450 copies.

Stephen Mitchell, the outstanding proponent of the relational orientation, was the other commercially successful author of the late 80s and early 90s. Mitchell, whose sophisticated grasp of British object relations theory was supplemented by mastery of the American interpersonal tradition, elaborated a therapeutic perspective that had broad appeal inside and outside of analytic circles, and he did so in lucid, accessible language. His *Relational Concepts in Psychoanalysis: An Integration* (1988), which sold over 12,000 copies for Harvard University Press, and *Hope and Dread in Psychoanalysis* (1993), which sold 13,000 copies for Basic Books, laid the foundation for the commercial success of his textbook (with Margaret Black), *Freud and Beyond* (1995). Bollas and Mitchell presided over the last revitalizing wave of psychoanalytic theory that swept across a sea of analytically oriented psychotherapists. The other commercially successful author of the 90s, Nancy McWilliams, wrote *loosely* analytic books that conveyed a broad and user-friendly analytic sensibility to therapists without analytic training.

Within American psychoanalysis itself, important books were increasingly books that took sides, however cogently and persuasively. Commercial success could be achieved by books that acknowledged the "sides" and tried to amalgamate them in clinically productive ways. Fred Pine's *Developmental Theory and Clinical Process*, published by Yale University Press in 1987, was among the first such efforts; it was widely and appreciatively read, with sales of 9,200. But Pine's effort to distill a pragmatic common ground out of theoretical disparities was the exception to the rule. By the late 80s, most analytic books were content simply to take sides at a time when the field in toto continued to shrink and faced progressive marginalization from without.

Even books that tried to capture, in more theoretically meditative ways, the broadly analytic sensibility that informed McWilliams's programmatic strategies could not reach out to the profession at large. Ironically, general-interest analytic books, excepting only occasional releases of historically noteworthy material,[41] were of diminishing interest to analysts. Consider the books of Roy Schafer, a mainstream American analyst widely admired for his broad-mindedness and literary craftsmanship. His *A New Language for Psychoanalysis* (1976), as noted above, sold 9,100 copies for Yale University Press. But *The Analytic Attitude*, published by Basic Books in 1983, sold under 3,400 copies. Commercially speaking, Schafer had become a conventionally strong author by the early 90s; *Retelling a Life*, published by Basic Books in 1992, sold over 4,000 copies. And his most recent book, *Bad Feelings* (2003), has sold just over 1,200 copies for Other Press.

The intersecting trends of internal fractionation and external marginalization continued into the mid-90s. Mitchell and Black's *Freud and Beyond* (1995), with sales of 47,000, did extraordinarily well for its time and place. But these sales pale alongside the sales and profession-wide impact of Fenichel's *Psychoanalytic Theory of Neurosis* (1945) and Charles Brenner's *Elementary Textbook of Psychoanalysis* (1955) a half-century earlier. Fenichel and Brenner gave authoritative (and in the case of Fenichel, encyclopedic) expression to an understanding of psychoanalysis that was consensual and spoke to most of the English-speaking psychoanalytic world. Mitchell and Black, on the other hand, revisited the history of psychoanalytic theory and practice from the standpoint of a postclassical sensibility that accommodated disparate traditions, theories, and technical preferences. Their admirably contemporary purchase on psychoanalysis, which revolved around a postclassical epistemology alien to Fenichel and Brenner and developmental research unavailable to them, may be fairly adjudged "progressive" in the conventional sense of the term. The point is that, by the mid-90s, the very idea of psychoanalytic "progress" had been drained of the disciplinary cohesiveness of the postwar era; it existed only at the level of part-perspectives—classical, relational, self-psychological, Kleinian, Lacanian, or otherwise.

Sales trends attest to the fact that by the early 90s, psychoanalytic thinking itself had evolved along a series of parallel tracks, no one of

41. In 1989, Harvard University Press published Winnicott's *Psycho-Analytic Explorations* (edited by Clare Winnicott, Ray Shepherd, and Madeleine Davis), which has sold over 11,000 copies. Of course, Winnicott, an analyst whose work is appreciatively recruited by proponents of various psychoanalytic schools of thought, is a uniquely appealing historical figure.

which spoke for, or even commanded the attention of, the profession at large. Evolutionary advance became understandable only within intradisciplinary paradigms, the proponents of which increasingly spoke different languages and made partly incommensurable claims about what psychoanalysis was and how and why it purportedly worked. As always, there are exceptions to the rule, but by the late 80s they were becoming few and far between. It required an analyst of the international stature of Otto Kernberg, whose object-relational perspective was imbricated with elements of classical and Kleinian analysis and addressed the psychotherapeutic (as opposed to analytic) management of severely disturbed patients, to achieve relative success by pulling sales from several analytic schools of thought and a broader psychiatric market as well. His *Severe Personality Disorders*, published by Yale University Press in 1993, sold 9,700 copies, whereas his *Love Relations*, published by Yale in 1995 and reprinted in paperback in 1998, has sold 5,800 copies. Christopher Bollas's international reputation was securely in place by the early 90s, and his successive books have all been successful. *Being a Character*, published by Hill & Wang (an imprint of Farrar, Straus and Giroux) in 1992 and reissued by Routledge in 2003, has, between the two imprints, logged sales of over 13,000 copies. *Cracking Up* (1995), another Hill & Wang publication reissued by Routledge in 2003, has sold around 8,800 copies. Like Kernberg, Bollas, an evocative writer whose work is difficult to classify, has had staying power throughout the decade and into the new century although, as with Kernberg, Schafer, and others, sales of his books have eased off considerably in recent years. *Hysteria* and *The Mystery of Things*, both published by Routledge in 1999, have sold 5,500 copies and 4,000 copies, respectively.

My own firm, The Analytic Press, achieved more modest success with books that exemplified the postclassical sensibility, particularly in its interpersonal, relational, and infancy research–grounded dimensions. It fell to Harvard University Press and Basic Books, respectively, to publish the two major books by Stephen Mitchell that put relational psychoanalysis on the map, *Relational Concepts in Psychoanalysis: An Integration* (1988; 12,000 copies); and *Hope and Dread in Psychoanalysis* (1993; 13,000 copies). The interpersonal tributary of the relational sensibility, with its emphasis on the analyst's emotional availability to the analysand and emotional participation in the here-and-now therapeutic interaction, gained expression in Darlene

Ehrenberg's popular *The Intimate Edge: Extending the Reach of Psychoanalytic Interaction*, published by Norton in 1992. *Intimate Edge* sold around 5,500 copies in paperback and probably several thousand more in cloth.

TAP's relational offerings were more analytic in tone and tenor and, with two exceptions, could not equal these sales. But these books, many of which were published within the Press's Relational Perspectives Book Series, still did quite well within the declining market for theoretically rigorous analytic books. Our offerings from the late 90s included Karen Maroda's *Seduction, Surrender, and Transformation* (TAP, 1999), with sales of over 3,900 copies; Stephen Mitchell's *Influence and Autonomy in Psychoanalysis* (TAP, 1997), with sales of over 3,500 copies; Philip Bromberg's *Standing in the Spaces* (TAP, 1998), with sales of over 4,500 copies; Irwin Z. Hoffman's *Ritual and Spontaneity in the Psychoanalytic Process* (TAP, 1998), with sales of over 3,100 copies; Lewis Aron's *A Meeting of Minds* (1996), with sales of over 3,000 copies; and Donnel Stern's *Unformulated Experience* (1997), with sales of around 2,500. Bromberg's *Awakening the Dreamer* (2006), one of the final books published during my tenure at TAP, sold over 2,400 through the end of 2008. The first volume in our series of relational psychoanalysis readers, *Relational Psychoanalysis: The Emergence of a Tradition* (1999), edited by Stephen Mitchell and Lewis Aron, has sold over 6,800 copies. Mitchell's *Relationality: From Attachment to Intersubjectivity*, published shortly before the author's untimely passing in December, 2000, has sold over 5,700 copies.

Lacanian psychoanalysis has its own hierarchy of better- and worse-selling titles in America. Lacanian theory had considerable intellectual currency through the 80s, with correspondingly strong-selling books by academics who came to Lacan's work from comparative literature and French studies. Stuart Schneiderman's *Jacques Lacan: The Death of an Intellectual Hero* (1983) and Shoshana Felman's *Jacques Lacan and the Adventure of Insight: Psychoanalysis in Contemporary Culture* (1987), both published by Harvard University Press, sold over 12,700 copies and over 9,500 copies, respectively. Into the early 90s, successful Lacanian titles, whether or not written by analysts with a clinical orientation, continued to pull a significant readership from academics in literary and critical studies. Malcolm Bowie's *Lacan*, released by Harvard University Press in 1991, sold 4,600 copies.

The books of Bruce Fink, an American who received Lacanian training with Jacques-Alain Miller at the Ecole de la Cause freudienne, have been even more successful. His *The Lacanian Subject: Between Language and Jouissance* was published by Princeton University Press in 1995 and has sold over 7,000 copies in cloth and paperback editions. Princeton, in the words of its sales director, has "little reach into the psychoanalytic community," and he surmises that these strong sales come from "the literary theory crowd."[42] Fink's second book, *A Clinical Introduction to Lacanian Psychoanalysis: Theory and Technique* (1997) was decidedly pragmatic in tone and tenor but equally successful. Harvard University Press has sold over 7,500 copies of the book in cloth and paperback. Lacanian book sales fall off thereafter, though a small number of titles continue to be reasonably successful. Joel Dor's *Introduction to the Reading of Lacan*, published by Aronson in 1997 and reprinted by Other Press in 1998, has sold over 3,600 copies for the latter.

Within psychoanalysis proper, more impressive sales could only be achieved with textlike presentations that either finessed the splintering of the field by conveying a globally "analytic" modus operandi to nonanalytic mental health readers, or synthesized and interpreted the voluminous literature associated with one or another psychoanalytic perspective. Nancy McWilliams continues to be by far the most successful of the first type of textbook writer. Her *Psychoanalytic Case Formulation* (Guilford, 1999) has sold approximately 28,000 copies and her more recent *Psychoanalytic Psychotherapy* (Guilford, 2004) is approaching sales of 17,000 copies.[43]

Recent textlike presentations have garnered small fractions of the readership of McWilliams's text of 2004. Herbert Schlesinger's two "intermediate" textlike offerings, *The Texture of Treatment: On the Matter of Psychoanalytic Technique* (TAP, 2003) and *Endings and Beginnings: On Terminating, Psychotherapy, and Psychoanalysis* (TAP, 2005) are broadly psychoanalytic, highly accessible, and wonderfully illuminating; sales through the end of 2008 have been around 950 and 750, respectively. Owen Renik's recent effort at a reader-friendly overview for professional and lay readers, *Practical Psycho-*

---

42. Eric Rohmann to Paul Stepansky, February 27, 2007. Quoted with permission.

43. Sales of *Psychoanalytic Case Formulation* (1999) and *Psychoanalytic Psychotherapy* (2004) include book club sales of 3,000 and 3,400, respectively.

analysis for Therapists and Patients (Other Press, 2006) has sold over 4,000 copies, whereas Person, Cooper, and Gabbard's *American Psychiatric Publishing Textbook of Psychoanalysis* (2005), an edited compilation conceived of and sponsored by American Psychiatric Press, has sold over 2,400 copies.[44] Edward Erwin's *The Freud Encyclopedia: Theory, Therapy, and Culture*, published by Routledge in 2002, has sold just over 1,400 copies. Commercially, there is no longer the possibility of a book such as Moore and Fine's *Psychoanalytic Terms and Concepts* (Yale, 1990), with sales of 14,000 copies. To achieve commercial success of this order, the "psychoanalytic" appellation must be diluted to "psychodynamic," and the psychodynamic "terms" and "concepts" offered in a user-friendly format intended to broaden rather than supplant other diagnostic frameworks. This is the very formula that has made the recently self-published *Psychodynamic Diagnostic Manual*, collectively authored by an "Alliance of Psychoanalytic Organizations," a stunning success, with sales, as of March, 2008, of over 20,000 copies.

Within the second, more narrowly gauged type of text, sales cannot aspire to the lofty heights of McWilliams and Mitchell and Black, although, over the past 15 years, they have exceeded the modest numbers of the most recent introductory (e.g., Renik) and comprehensive (e.g., Person et al.) overviews. Such texts provide more rigorous and/or comprehensive surveys of particular psychoanalytic traditions and their respective clinical approaches. They are written for analysts and analytic therapists, not for therapists, counselors, and students interested in analysis and desirous of learning how analysts think and work in some generic sense of thinking and working. TAP made two noteworthy offerings to this latter genre: Ronald Lee and J. Martin Colby's *Psychotherapy After Kohut: A Textbook of Self Psychology* (1991), with sales of over 4,400 copies, and Frank Summers's *Object Relations Theories and Psychopathology: A Comprehensive Text* (TAP, 1994), with sales of over 4,300 copies. Another representative example

---

44. I was intent on comparing the sales of these several psychoanalytic texts with sales of recent psychoanalytically oriented psychodynamic texts aimed at a broader psychiatric readership. Two books by Glen Gabbard, viz., *Long-Term Psychodynamic Psychotherapy: A Basic Text* (2004) and *Psychodynamic Psychiatry in Clinical Practice* (1989, 2005 [4th ed.]), exemplify this genre. Sadly, neither the publisher of these books, American Psychiatric Press, Inc., nor the author, Glen Gabbard, would share sales data of these titles with me.

is Neil Altman et al., *Relational Child Psychotherapy* (Other Press, 2002), with sales of over 2,000 copies.

In general, with the noteworthy exception of McWilliams's successive books, the textbook subgenre has been coordinate with fractionation into part-fields, with diminishing sales of increasingly specialized introductions to smaller and smaller parts of the analytic pie. In the future, it will be exceedingly difficult for any analytic text, whether school-specific, practical, or comprehensive, to approach the sales of a typically good-selling nonanalytic therapy text, such as Henry Pinsker's *A Primer of Supportive Psychotherapy* (TAP, 1997, over 6,000 copies sold), much less an accessible, integrative psychotherapy text that traverses various therapeutic modalities in prescribing strategies of communication, such as Paul Wachtel's *Therapeutic Communication: Knowing What to Say When* (Guilford, 1993, over 16,000 copies sold).[45]

Where do matters now stand? I submit that the very idea of a big *psychoanalytic* book no longer exists, for the simple reason that the field is neither big enough nor cohesive enough nor influential enough to yield indigenously big books. Psychoanalysis, whether in its parts or in its dispiritedly pseudoentirety, does not have the shaping impact on contiguous mental-health professions that it had through the 1970s. So publishers can no longer rely on nonanalytic therapists (and nonanalytic libraries) to seek out and buy and elevate to bigness conventional psychoanalytic books. In a field fractionated to a virtually atomic level, publishers have no place even to look for big books. They can still aspire to give the field bigger "little" books that capitalize on the smaller but still viable readerships associated with individual theoretical and clinical perspectives: Interpersonal psychoanalysis, relational psychoanalysis, object relations theory, neuropsychoanalysis, intersubjectivity theory, "modern" Freudian psychoanalysis, Kleinian psychoanalysis, psychoanalytic self psychology, Lacanian psychoanalysis. They can also give books to the field that are au courant because they seek to revivify psychoanalysis from the nonanalytic

45. Wachtel tells me that his royalty reports for *Therapeutic Communication* give U.S. sales of approximately 6,000 copies in cloth and 10,500 copies in paperback through June, 2008, but that his personal sales tally, which includes book club sales and sales of overseas editions, gives total sales of over 23,000 copies. Paul Wachtel to Paul Stepansky, June 11, 2007, and December 9, 2008.

disciplinary vantage point of the moment, be it feminism, dynamic systems theory, infancy research, neuroscience, linguistics, semiotics, attachment theory, or metaphor theory. Such books can be important, but they are less and less psychoanalytic in the traditional, strong sense of the term.

Books of this latter sort can still on occasion be successful. Mark Solms and Oliver Turnbull's *The Brain and the Inner World*, probably the best interpretive overview of the convergences between neurobiology and psychoanalysis (the terrain of neuropsychoanalysis), has sold over 6,000 copies for Other Press. Peter Fonagy's *Attachment Theory and Psychoanalysis* (Other Press, 2001) has sold over 12,000 copies, but, as we shall see in a later chapter, it adopts an essentially juxtapositional strategy that compares and contrasts attachment theory with each prominent psychoanalytic school of thought. Fonagy's coauthored work (with György Gergely, Elliot L. Jurist, and Mary Target) *Affect Regulation, Mentalization, and the Development of the Self* (Other Press, 2000), a comprehensive overview of cognitive and emotional development consonant with attachment research and data from other tributaries of developmental psychology, has sold 9,000 copies in cloth and paperback editions. This book is a provocative contribution to several contiguous literatures—its coauthors include a prominent developmental researcher and a philosopher—but it is not really a psychoanalytic book. I hazard the guess that the psychoanalytic contribution to overall sales of a book such as *Affect Regulation* is limited to research-savvy and philosophically oriented subgroups within the field. This is another way of saying that the occasional "big" psychoanalytic book has, over the past three decades, become less and less a big "psychoanalytic" book in the categorical sense of the term.

What would be involved in the creation of a big psychoanalytic book circa 2010? Many psychoanalytic groups would have to come together and attest to the fundamental importance of a particular book to the field at large. In so doing, they would perforce be setting aside theoretical, clinical, and institutional commitments that sustain their identities as proponents of particular psychoanalytic schools of thought and members of particular psychoanalytic communities. Put differently, each group, each faction, would have to overcome the narcissistic loading of its particular purchase on Freud, the psychoanalytic method, and psychoanalytic therapy. What Robert Wallerstein terms the "common ground" linking all psychoanalysts would have to mute particularized commitments—and their economically consequential sequelae—and the reading habits they have engendered over the past three decades. The tacit knowledge that (arguably) links psychoanalysts of all times and places would have to become public, codifiable, and hence publishable knowledge that sustained a coherent idea of psychoanalytic progress.[46]

Can it happen? Perhaps, but I have become a skeptic. Publishers may aspire to publish interesting books, even significant books. But with only a handful of recent exceptions, all such books have become intrinsically small books, where smallness has relatively little to do with the content of the book. It has much more to do with the contraction of the field over the past three decades and the way this numerically diminished field has become a conglomerate of still smaller part-fields. Potentially important books that reframe the field's theoretical infrastructure in empirically credible and clinically consequential ways—books such as Lichtenberg's *Psychoanalysis and Motivation* (TAP, 1989) and Beebe and Lachmann's *Infant Research and Adult Treatment* (TAP, 2002)—are increasingly lucky to sell several thousand copies. And, sadly, this is as good as it gets. Not these books, not any books, can effect a coalescence of disciplinary fragments that are narcissistically encased. Nor, with the rare exception of textbooks such McWilliams's *Psychoanalytic Diagnosis* and Mitchell and Black's

---

46. And this, in a nutshell, is the problem. Different analysts, working within different traditions, have their respective visions of the field's progressive evolution. But the field itself lacks a unified idea of progress able to gather together these traditions and order the disjunctive literatures that have grown out of them. In the language of the philosophy of science, psychoanalysis lacks a consensually agreed upon axiology against which judgments of progress can be measured. On the history of the idea of progress, see the classic study of J. B. Bury, *The Idea of Progress: An Inquiry into Its Origin and Growth* (London: Macmillan, 1920). For a contemporary exposition of progress in terms of problem-solving—with an appraisal measure of effectiveness keyed to empirical problems, anomalous problems, and conceptual problems—see Larry Laudan, *Progress and Its Problems: Towards a Theory of Scientific Growth* (Berkeley: University of California Press, 1977). On the axiological presuppositions of scientific progress, see the dialogue in Laudan's *Science and Values: The Aims of Science and Their Role in Scientific Debate* (Berkeley: University of California Press, 1984), especially chapter 3. For a rich analysis of the ways scientific ideas advance that attends to the dialectic interplay of experimental, conceptual, and aesthetic dimensions of progressive theory building, see Gerald Holton, *Thematic Origins of Scientific Thought: Kepler to Einstein*, rev. ed. (Cambridge: Harvard University Press, 1988).

Freud and Beyond, can such books speak to a broad contingent of mental health workers unallied with psychoanalysis.

Let me be clear on this matter of big books. Commercially speaking, psychoanalyst authors can still, albeit rarely, produce big books. But, as I have argued above, the very occasional big book has over the past three decades been *psychoanalytic* in a progressively diluted and even eccentric sense of the term. Psychoanalysis itself is neither unitary enough nor large enough to yield big books, but the residual community of analytic-friendly psychotherapists, counselors, and knowledgeable lay readers that surround the field can still sustain a commercially successful book. And so they have in the case of McWilliams's texts and Mitchell and Black's *Freud and Beyond*. In the depressed world of academic-professional publishing, these titles are bona fide best sellers. But they are neither *as* big nor as focally *psychoanalytic* as noteworthy psychoanalytic titles from the glory era of psychoanalytic publishing, roughly speaking, the 30 years following the end of World War II.

Furthermore, given the sheer volume of psychoanalytic books published over the past 35 years, the number of commercially successful titles has been microscopically small. My sales tally to date gives a scant 12 books with total English-language sales over 20,000, which I give here chronologically: Kohut, *Analysis of the Self* (1971; 42,000); Mahler, *Psychological Birth of the Human Infant* (1975; 21,000); Kohut, *Restoration of the Self* (1977; 36,000); Basch, *Doing Psychotherapy* (1980; 27,500); Greenberg and Mitchell, *Object Relations Theories in Psychoanalytic Theory* (1983; 49,500) Stern, *Interpersonal World of the Infant* (1985; 23,000); Benjamin, *Bonds of Love* (1988; 30–35,000); Phillips, *On Kissing, Tickling, and Being Bored* (1993; 21,000); McWilliams, *Psychoanalytic Diagnosis* (1994; 54,000); Mitchell and Black, *Freud and Beyond* (1995; 47,000); McWilliams, *Psychoanalytic Case Formulation* (1999; 20,000); and Mitchell, *Can Love Last?* (2002; 20,000).

If the net is broadened to include psychoanalytic books with sales of over 10,000 copies, we add another 13 titles over this same period: Wachtel, *Psychoanalysis and Behavior Therapy* (1977; 17,000); Kohut, *How Does Analysis Cure?* (1981; 16,000); Bollas, *Shadow of the Object* (1987; 16,000); Stolorow et al., *Psychoanalytic Treatment* (1987; 12,000); Wolf, *Treating the Self* (1988; 14,000); Mitchell, *Relational Concepts in Psychoanalysis* (1988; 12,000); Winnicott,

Psycho-Analytic Explorations (1989; 11,000); Basch and Basch, *Understanding Psychotherapy* (1990; 17,500); Moore and Fine, eds., *Psychoanalytic Terms and Concepts* (1990; 14,000); Bollas, *Being a Character* (1992; 13,000) Mitchell, *Hope and Dread in Psychoanalysis* (1993; 13,000); Phillips, *On Flirtation* (1994; 10,000); and Fonagy, *Attachment Theory and Psychoanalysis* (2001; 12,500). There are no doubt other psychoanalytic books published since 1970 that have sold 10,000 or more copies, but probably not a great many.[47] The afore-mentioned books are those for which I have been able to retrieve hard sales data that meet this baseline.

But even if these numbers were doubled or tripled, it would still not alter the basic fact that the era of big *psychoanalytic* books has come and gone, professionally, culturally, and commercially. Of the 25 books given above, seven (both Basch books; both McWilliams books; Wachtel; Wolf; Mitchell and Black) are accessible textbooks that reach out to nonanalysts; three (Mitchell's *Can Love Last?* and both Phillips books) are trade books intended for educated lay read-ers; and one (Benjamin) is a crossover book with primary sales to academic readers. So we are left with 14 big analytic books in the strong traditional sense of the term: Focally analytic studies that present and discuss clinical "data," analytic research, and/or analyti-cally relevant findings from contiguous fields to elaborate new theo-ries and new clinical strategies that seek to advance the field.

Chronologically, of the 25 books whose sales I can document, four were published in the 70s; ten in the 80s; eight in the 90s; and two in the 00s. There are almost certainly additional big books from the 70s,

---

47. Shengold, *Soul Murder* (New Haven: Yale University Press, 1989), has probably sold well over 10,000 copies if Yale's cloth edition (around 5,900 copies) and the Ballantine trade paperback edition (sales unknown) are totaled. Partial sales data and author reports suggest that Gedo and Goldberg, *Models of the Mind* (Chicago: Uni-versity of Chicago Press, 1973) and Ehrenberg, *The Intimate Edge* (NY: Norton, 1992) have sales of around 10,000 copies. One or more of Robert Langs's books from the 1970s—e.g., *The Technique of Psychoanalytic Psychotherapy*, 2 vols. (NY: Aronson, 1973/1974); *The Bipersonal Field* (NY: Aronson, 1976); and *The Listening Process* (NY: Aronson, 1978)—may have sold 10,000 or more copies. Sales data on these books are unavailable. Finally, as noted in the text, Schafer, *A New Language for Psychoanalysis* and Pine, *Developmental Theory and Clinical Process* (New Haven: Yale University Press, 1985) have reported sales of over 9,000 copies. Fonagy et al., *Affect Regulation, Mentalization, and the Development of the Self* (NY: Other Press, 2000) has also sold over 9,000 copies, though I do not consider this multidisciplinary book "psychoanalytic" in the strong sense of the term.

but sales data from this decade are quite difficult to obtain. My own candidates for psychoanalytic books from this decade that were commercially successful (but for which sales data are not available) include Edgar Levenson's *The Fallacy of Understanding* (1972), Otto Kernberg's *Borderline Conditions and Pathological Narcissism* (1975), Otto Kernberg's *Object Relations Theory and Clinical Psychoanalysis* (1976), and Thomas Ogden's *Matrix of the Mind* (1977). Crossing into the 80s, David Shapiro's *Autonomy and Rigid Character* (1981), which built on the success of his earlier *Neurotic Styles* (1965), was without doubt a trade-level commercial success for Basic Books. Others will no doubt have their own candidates for big book status. But it matters little. The fact is that the era of major psychoanalytic books has come and gone. It is now for historians to chronicle the three decades that followed the end of World War II and produced the textbooks of Fenichel, Brenner, and Waelder; the writings of Anna Freud, Heinz Hartmann, D. W. Winnicott, and Harry Stack Sullivan; the psychosomaticist literature of Franz Alexander, Roy R. Grinker, Sr., and others; and the immensely salable professional/trade books of Erikson, Fromm, Menninger, Horney, Reik, and Reich. The 25 or so big books published over the past four decades pale alongside these impressive forerunners, and now, a decade into the twenty-first century, even the more recent genre of big books has virtually disappeared.

The progressive disappearance of big psychoanalytic books—of books that speak to the American psychoanalytic profession and to the community of psychiatrists and psychotherapists influenced by it—is one sign of the fractionation of the profession into rival part-fields. It is a commercial consequence of "theoretical pluralism." But it is not the heart of the matter. It is not the reason psychoanalytic book publishing has severely contracted and seems to be at the brink of collapse. Big books, after all, are rare, breakaway successes; such books belie sales projections and the understanding of markets that underlies them. The absence of big books in recent decades is a telling symptom of the problem, but it is not the problem per se.

Far more portentous than the near-extinction of big books is the fate of what publishers consider credible books, and which I will henceforth term, in proper Winnicottian parlance, "good enough" books. After all, academic/professional books that sell 2,000 copies or 4,000 copies or 40,000 copies are all profitable books. It is the lesser sales range of the vast number of adequately informative and competently written books—books that are good enough to publish but destined to sell only averagely well—that tells the tale. From the end of World War II through the mid-70s, psychoanalysis was not only an influential subfield of psychiatry but also academically and culturally de rigueur. I believe that the vast majority of psychoanalytic books published during this time were profitable in the baseline sense of generating revenue that exceeded editorial and manufacturing costs, marketing expenses, and staff overheads; institutional sales alone (to university, medical school, and psychiatry department libraries) made them so.

In the realm of high-level mental-health publishing, this situation began to change in the late 70s and the pace of change accelerated in the early and mid 80s. I began my career in psychoanalytic publishing at International Universities Press in 1979 just as the sea change was gathering force. Throughout the 80s, in lockstep with the progressive marginalization of analysis within medicine, psychiatry, and academic psychology, the institutional market for the vast majority of psychoanalytic books shrank to the point of numerical insignificance. By the early 90s, library sales of most analytic books were tantamount to sales to small (and financially strapped) specialty libraries affiliated with psychoanalytic training institutes and psychotherapy training programs; these sales were tallied in tens rather than hundreds.

During the same period in which the transanalytic institutional market for analytic books became marginal to overall sales, the market of individual analytic book buyers, as we have discussed, simultaneously contracted and fractionated into the various analytic part-fields. Analytic publishers found they were publishing books targeted at specific analytic schools of thought, not at analysts in general. As sales weakened across the board, print runs shrank, unit manufacturing costs escalated, retail list prices began their skyward ascent, and price resistance arose. Edited books, which, by their nature, are costly and labor intensive to produce and invite only modest sales, were the first casualties of these interlocking developments. By the early 90s, the market for edited compilations had virtually dried up, so that, excepting only the occasional timely and thematic collection, edited books could be relied on to sell only several hundred copies. They could be undertaken by commercial publishers only with financial assistance in the form of royalty waivers, subventions, guaranteed buyback sales, and the like.

At TAP, I prided myself on publishing only tightly edited thematic collections of the first rank. Like all publishers, we enjoyed the occasional success. Stephen Mitchell and Lewis Aron's *Relational Psychoanalysis: The Emergence of a Tradition* (1999), as mentioned above, has sold over 6,600 copies. Susan Goldberg, Roy Muir, and John Kerr's *Attachment Theory: Social, Developmental, and Clinical Perspectives* (1995) was another successful edited book, with sales of over 3,500 copies. Lewis Aron and Frances Sommer Anderson's *Relational Perspectives on the Body* did well with sales of over 1,800 copies.

But the occasional edited collection that caught on was sadly overshadowed by the many excellent, topically focused edited books that generated meager sales. A lengthy listing is beside the point (and would be depressing for all concerned!) but consider, in descending order: Susan Coates, Jane Rosenthal, and Daniel Schechter's superb *September 11: Trauma and Human Bonds* (2003), with sales of 1,000 copies; Arnold Goldberg's worthy *Errant Selves: A Casebook of Misbehavior*, with sales of 700; Mark Blechner's exemplary *Hope and Mortality: Psychodynamic Approaches to AIDS and HIV* (1997), with sales of 600 copies; Allison Rosen and Jay Rosen's timely and provocative *Frozen Dreams: Psychodynamic Dimensions of Infertility and Assisted Reproduction* (2005), with sales of around 500 copies; and Bruce Sklarew et al.'s socially responsive and responsible *Analysts in the Trenches: Streets, Schools, War Zones* (2004), another 500 copy seller. The massive, authoritative *Handbook of Interpersonal Psychoanalysis* (1995), edited by Marylou Lionells et al., and many years in the making, has sold around 700 copies. Anand Pandya and Craig Katz's *Disaster Psychiatry: Intervening When Nightmares Come True* (2004), the debut publication of Disaster Psychiatry Outreach and winner of a prestigious "Ken" Book Award in 2005 from the National Alliance for the Mentally Ill of New York City, has sold all of 1,100 copies.

When I arrived at The Analytic Press in 1983, my default print run for authored and edited books alike was 1,500 copies. That is, I could reasonably expect to sell at least 1,500 copies of everything we published. Between 1983 and 2006, this default print run fell successively to 1,200 copies, then 1,000 copies, and ended up at 700 to 800 copies for many authored books. And, bear in mind, I continued to publish what I considered top-tier authored books to the bitter end. For edited books, the print runs shrank faster and ended up in the 600 range for the very few edited books I chose to undertake. Over the span of my career in psychoanalytic publishing, from 1979 through 2006, the market for good-enough authored books shrank more or less continuously. My impression, reflecting back, is that the kind of good-enough book that sold 1,500 to 2,000 copies in 1980, sold 1,000 to 1,200 copies in 1990, 800 to 1000 copies in 1995, 600 to 800 copies in 2000, and 200 to 500 copies in 2005. A publishing firm whose *typical* book sells 200 to 500 copies is no longer commercially viable. Even with cut-rate, cookie-cutter production, bare-bones marketing, and inflated list prices, it cannot recover the costs of doing business, much less achieve modest profitability. Unless the publisher receives outside funding or is the beneficiary of university sponsorship or not-for-profit incorporation, it simply cannot stay in business.

Psychoanalytic publishing is not failing because it cannot produce big books that pull together the various theoretical islands into which the field has drifted. It is failing because, owing to this selfsame fractionation and the simultaneous contraction of the field, its good-enough books are no longer good enough to keep small professional firms in business.

Chapter 3

Psychoanalytic Journals and the Road
to Fractionation: I. The Case of *JAPA*

> One could, in fact, write a large part of the history of the APA
> [American Psychoanalytic Association] in terms of the dispute over
> lay analysis.[1]

The role of journals in the fractionation of American psychoanalysis
and the particularized reading preferences that have grown out
of it takes us on a long and twisty journey. We shall see that psychoanalytic journals have been part-journals from the beginning of the
field, and that this judgment applies even to, and perhaps *especially*
to, journals that have attempted to represent the psychoanalytic mainstream. This latter claim will lead us to the historical circumstances
attendant to the birth of the *Journal of the American Psychoanalytic
Association* (*JAPA*), the best-known and most influential of the American psychoanalytic journals. Aspiring to a stature analogous to the
New England Journal of Medicine for internists or the *American Journal of Psychiatry* for psychiatrists, *JAPA* embodied the heightened
desire of the postwar American analytic community to fashion itself
into a psychiatric subspecialty. And this very desire, which was so antithetical to Freud and *his* vision of psychoanalysis, foretold its failure.

To grasp the nature and perduring effects of this failure, we must
turn to the role of psychiatry in World War II and the relationship of
psychoanalysis to psychiatry that was born of the war and came to
fruition in the decade to follow. Founded in 1953, *JAPA* brings into
focus central tensions that gain expression in extremis in the fractionated landscape of contemporary American psychoanalysis. In particular, it concretizes one central fault line in the field—that separating

1. G. W. Pigman, III, "Review of Nathan G. Hale, Jr., *The Rise and Crisis of Psychoanalysis in the United States: Freud and the Americans, 1917–1985,*" *J. Hist.
Behav. Sci.*, 34:101–105, 1998, quoted at p. 103.

medical analysts from their nonmedical or "lay" colleagues. Owing to this divide and the collateral fractures that radiated out from it, *JAPA* emerged as, and in important respects remains still, a part-journal in a sea of part-journals.

Even the British *International Journal of Psycho-Analysis*, founded by Ernest Jones in 1919, could not escape the insider-outsider dynamics of early psychoanalytic institutional life. Jones's first order of business was to maneuver out of participation one Samuel Tannenbaum, an American analyst of "no good standing in N.Y." who had proposed the journal to him a year earlier but was judged unfit for collaboration by Freud's American standard-bearer, A. A. Brill. Freud, who saw the journal partly as an outlet for translated articles from the Vienna-based *Internationale Zeitschrift für Psychoanalyse*, personally passed on all colleagues proposed for journal affiliation. Needless to say, the selection of associate and assistant editors was fraught with politics; Jones was especially concerned about offending participating Americans by placing too many nonmedical or lay analysts on the official staff.[2]

Be this as it may, Jones, who founded the journal in the aftermath of a divisive and disruptive world war, sought a publication that rose above continental cabals and provided an umbrella for an English-speaking psychoanalytic community of various stripes and persuasions. It has been far more successful in this regard than its American counterparts. American psychoanalytic journals, despite grand-sounding names that convey profession-wide inclusiveness, have from the outset been part-journals that serve specific groups within the field and, as such, provide an imprimatur to the proliferation of part-fields that has had such dire consequences for book publishers. This contemporary reality has historical antecedents: From the very inception of the field a century ago, psychoanalytic journals embodied in-group out-group tensions in a manner that presaged the explosion of the field into its many rival subgroups.

2. Jones to Freud, May 2, 1919; Freud to Jones, July 16, 1920; Jones to Freud, November 12, 1920; Jones to Freud, November 25, 1920; Freud to Jones, April 10, 1922; Jones to Freud, April 1, 1923, in R. Andrew Paskauskas, ed., *The Complete Correspondence of Sigmund Freud and Ernest Jones, 1908–1939* (Cambridge: Harvard University Press, 1993), pp. 343–344, 386–387, 398–400, 402–403, 465–467, 470–473.

Psychoanalytic journal publishing dates back to Freud's announcement of the *Jahrbuch für psychoanalytische und psychopathologische Forschungen*, an annual yearbook, at the first psychoanalytic congress in Salzburg, Austria, in 1908. It was a political maneuver of the first order. By making Carl Jung editor of the journal and Eugen Bleuler the "codirector" (with Freud himself) of the publication, Freud made the *Jahrbuch*'s political raison d'etre transparently clear: It was intended to cement the alliance with Swiss gentiles better positioned to propagate analysis throughout Europe than the Viennese Jews of his own Wednesday Evening Circle. The disgruntlement of Freud's Viennese colleagues came to a head at the Nuremberg Congress of 1910, when Freud proposed that Jung be elected lifetime president of the newly established International Psychoanalytical Association. As a sop to his bitterly disaffected Viennese contingent, Freud went along with Alfred Adler's and Wilhelm Stekel's announcement of a second journal outside of Jung's control, the *Zentralblatt für Psychoanalyse*, which Adler and Stekel would edit out of Vienna. Less than two years later, Stekel resigned his membership in the Vienna Psychoanalytic Society but, with the support of the publisher, J. F. Bergmann, refused to relinquish control of the *Zentralblatt*.[3] Freud responded to this challenge to his authority by writing current and prospective contributors to the *Zentralblatt*; he urged them to cease any involvement with the journal and to throw their support to a new journal shortly to be announced. The journal in question was the *Zeitschrift für Psychoanalyse*, which, under the more reliable stewardship of Sándor Ferenczi, Otto Rank, and Ernest Jones, supplanted the *Zentralblatt* as the authorized forum for Freudian ideas and the official publication of the International Psychoanalytical Association (IPA).[4]

3. "After our separation, Freud was confident that he would get the editorship of the Zentralblatt for himself and Tausk, but Bergmann did not cooperate. I remained the sole editor of the Zentralblatt. We lost some subscribers but I enlarged the circle of interest and the journal became a platform for all kinds of psychotherapy" (Wilhelm Stekel, *Autobiography*, ed. Emil A. Gutheil [NY: Liveright, 1950], p. 145).

4. On the political-cum-editorial regrouping that followed Adler's and Stekel's tenure as editors of the *Zentralblatt*, see Freud to Ferenczi, October 27, 1912, November 26, 1912, and December 9, 1912, in Eva Brabant et al., *The Correspondence of Sigmund Freud and Sándor Ferenczi, Volume 1, 1908–1914*, trans. P. T. Hoffer (Cambridge: Harvard University Press, 1993), pp. 417–418, 433, 440.

These particulars of early psychoanalytic history are sadly revelatory of the politicization of journal publishing that has marked the field's century-long existence in America. Journals have typically served to delineate specific groupings within the field. The *Psychoanalytic Review*, founded by Smith Ely Jelliffe and William Alanson White in 1913, carved out a niche as a publishing outlet for social workers and psychoanalytic eclectics of various theoretical persuasions. The *Review* enshrined the pragmatic, problem-solving eclecticism of early American analysis; it willfully shunned what Jelliffe termed the "currents and cross-currents" of European analysis and the controversies to which they gave rise.[5] Rather, as Jelliffe reminisced in 1932, the *Review* "has gone its way with a certain eclecticism which has taken into consideration a broader group of home environmental factors than many of our confreres or colleagues have even as yet understood."[6]

The *Psychoanalytic Quarterly*, on the other hand, was founded in 1932 to give expression to doctrinal orthodoxy as construed by the most conservative wing of the New York Psychoanalytic Society. "Home environmental factors" played no part in its mission. The four founding editors of the *Quarterly*—Frankwood Williams, Dorian Feigenbaum, Bertram Lewin, and Gregory Zilboorg—had an average age of 42 and a narrow vision of analysis that put them in conflict with A. A. Brill and was even more anathema to eclectic American forebears such as Jelliffe and White and contemporaries such as Harry Stack Sullivan. In fact, as the historian Nathan Hale pointedly observes, the founding of the *Quarterly* "crystallized the split between generations."[7] Equally orthodox, though under the control of the

5. See Nathan Hale, *Freud and the Americans: The Beginnings of Psychoanalysis in the United States, 1876–1917* (NY: Oxford University Press, 1971), pp. 329–330, and *The Rise and Crisis of Psychoanalysis in the United States* (NY: Oxford University Press, 1995), pp. 120–121.

6. Smith Ely Jelliffe, "Glimpses of a Freudian Odyssey," *Psychoanal. Quart.,* 2:318–329,1932, quoted at p. 325. For elaboration, see John C. Burnham, *Jelliffe: American Psychoanalyst and Physician and His Correspondence with Sigmund Freud and C. G. Jung*, edited by William McGuire (Chicago: University of Chicago Press, 1983), pp. 61–63.

7. Hale, *Rise and Crisis of Psychoanalysis* (n. 5), p. 120. The key role of the *Quarterly*'s editors in the machinations that led to Paul Schilder's disqualification as training analyst by the New York Psychoanalytic Institute and subsequent resignation from

European old guard, was the *American Imago*, the English-language journal of applied psychoanalysis that supplanted the defunct German-language *Imago*,[8] edited by Otto Rank and Hanns Sachs, two of Freud's "bright and honest boys," and published in Vienna from 1912 until the *Anschluss* of 1938. With Freud's grudging blessing, Sachs, who had left Vienna for Boston in 1932, transposed the *Imago* to American soil in 1939.[9]

Harry Stack Sullivan, who disparaged the *Psychoanalytic Quarterly* as a "private organ" of the conservative New York analysts and was unsuccessful in his effort to purchase White and Jelliffe's eclectic *Psychoanalytic Review*, founded in 1938, in collaboration with Ernest Hadley, *Psychiatry: Journal for the Study of Interpersonal Process*. It began as an interdisciplinary journal, psychoanalytic in character, but Sullivan's commitment to publishing papers that were not purely psychoanalytic, teamed with his unwillingness to be dictated to by the American Psychoanalytic Association, soon caused the conservative analysts to shun it. *Psychiatry* moved decisively in the direction of Sullivan's own interpersonal psychiatry, which evolved into interpersonal psychoanalysis. In the decade following Sullivan's death in 1949, the journal gradually abandoned its focus on Sullivan's work and evolved into the eclectic publication it remains to this day.[10]

---

the New York Psychoanalytic Society in 1935 is a matter of record. See Hale, pp. 121–124.

8. The full title of the original German-language journal was *Imago: Zeitschrift für Anwendung der Psychoanalyse auf die Geisteswissenschaften* (*Imago: Journal for the Application of Psychoanalysis to the Human Sciences*).

9. Freud's blessing was grudging because he was loath to accept the impossibility of German-language journal publication in Nazified Austria. See Ernest Jones, *Life and Work of Sigmund Freud*, vol. 3 (NY: Basic Books, 1957), p. 233 and Peter Gay, *Freud: A Life for Our Time* (NY: Norton, 1988), p. 634. Freud's reference to Rank and Sachs as "bright and honest boys" is in a letter to Ernest Jones of February 12, 1912, in Paskauskas, ed., *Correspondence of Sigmund Freud and Ernest Jones* (n. 2), p. 133.

10. On June 13, 1934, Sullivan wrote William Alanson White that the *Quarterly* was "a private organ of the group here [in New York] with which I am most completely lacking in sympathy." Quoted in Helen Swick Perry, *Psychiatrist of America: The Life of Harry Stack Sullivan* (Cambridge: Harvard University Press, 1982),

Psychoanalysis: The Journal of Psychoanalytic Psychology, launched by the National Psychological Association for Psychoanalysis (NPAP) in 1952, was a later reaction to East Coast psychoanalytic orthodoxy. It was the brainchild of the lay analyst Theodor Reik, whose indifferent reception by the medicalized New York psychoanalytic establishment more than a decade earlier led to his lifelong feud with the New York Psychoanalytic Society and to his creation in 1948 of NPAP as the first American training institute for nonphysicians.

In the decades following World War II, Reik's *Psychoanalysis* (which absorbed Jelliffe and White's *Psychoanalytic Review* in 1956)[11] would be followed by the *American Journal of Psychoanalysis*, the *Journal of the American Academy of Psychoanalysis*, *Modern Psychoanalysis*, *Contemporary Psychoanalysis*, *Psychoanalytic Psychology*, and *Psychoanalytic Dialogues*.[12] All these journals have served as vehicles of institutionalization through which one-time outsider groups have reframed exclusion from the medical psychoanalytic mainstream and evolved into robust mini-establishments of their own. This trend continues right down to the present, with The Analytic Press's launching of the *International Journal of Psychoanalytic Self Psychology* in 2006.

To be sure, such developments, as we shall see below, are not entirely specific to psychoanalysis. What is more unique to American

---

p. 382. The incident through which Sullivan established his independence from the APsaA was Karl Menninger's expression of keen displeasure at Sullivan's publication of Erich Fromm's "The Social Philosophy of 'Will Therapy'" in *Psychiatry*, 2:229–237, 1939 (pp. 380–382). Menninger's letter of complaint to Sullivan and Hadley of June 20, 1939 is in Howard J. Faulkner & Virginia D. Pruitt, *The Selected Correspondence of Karl A. Menninger, 1919–1945* (New Haven: Yale University Press, 1988), pp. 289–290.

11. From 1958 to 1962, the journal that grew out of the merger was published as *Psychoanalysis and the Psychoanalytic Review*. Beginning with the first issue of 1963, it became *The Psychoanalytic Review*.

12. I intentionally exclude from this listing the journal *Psychoanalytic Inquiry*, which has occupied a unique place in the journal literature for more than a quarter century. Each issue of *PI* is a collection of invited papers on a particular topic prepared by a designated "issue editor." Thus, the journal is equivalent to a paperback monograph series. Consistent with the journal's goal of providing a range of opinion on specific topics, *PI* issues (i.e., monographs) often contain contributions by representatives of different psychoanalytic schools of thought.

psychoanalysis is the manner in which the theoretical preferences and exclusionist proclivities of "mainstream" psychoanalytic journals rendered them part-journals no less than the part-journals that formed in reaction to them. *The Psychoanalytic Quarterly*, whose editorial policies were liberalized in the 1980s, was for more than a half century a print medium for the kind of narrowly Freudian psychoanalysis associated with the New York Psychoanalytic Society. Its identification with American psychiatry and hoped-for alliance with American medicine were clearly enunciated in its first issue.[13] Throughout this period, the *Quarterly* did little if anything to provide a forum for emergent psychoanalytic theories that were "progressive" or "dissident," depending on one's psychoanalytic point of view and institutional allegiances. Through the 1970s and even into the early 1980s, proponents of interpersonal psychoanalysis, psychoanalytic self psychology, intersubjectivity theory, and a critically feminist psychoanalytic theory had to look elsewhere for publication outlets. Nor did the *Quarterly* provide a congenial home for a new generation of empirical studies that, for many influential analysts, proved foundational to a thoroughgoing critique of traditional Freudian theory and practice.

Allowing only for a more truncated time frame, the same may be said of the *Journal of the American Psychoanalytic Association*, the official organ of the American Psychoanalytic Association. The his-

---

13. In his review of Franz Alexander's *The Medical Value of Psychoanalysis* (1932), *Quarterly* editor Dorian Feigenbaum observed that "Dr. Alexander's book could accomplish nothing more useful than the introduction of psychoanalytic study in medical schools, and it is hoped that his propagation of the idea will meet with success in time, although one may be justified in taking a less optimistic view than the author of the possibilities of such a reformation in the present medical curriculum (*Psychoanal. Quart.*, 1:177, 1932). Elsewhere in issue 1, the *Quarterly* reprinted the New York Psychoanalytic Society's "Regulations for the Training of Analysts," with its proviso that the nonmedical applicant for training "shall pledge himself in writing to conduct no analysis without having the diagnosis and indications established by a medical analyst" (*Psychoanal. Quart.*, 1:187, 1932). In the final issue of the first volume of the *Quarterly*, Carl Binger, in his appreciative review of Henry Sigerist's *Man and Medicine* (1932), offered the following penultimate observation: "Professor Sigerist's evaluation of the importance of Freud's work in relation to man and medicine may be estimated not only from the context of his book, but from the fact that only the writings of Aristotle, Galen and Harvey are allotted more space than Freud, whose name vies with Vesalius, Sydenham, Laënnec, v. Behring, Koch and Pasteur. When we consider that the book deals with the whole history of medicine, this must impress us as a striking commentary" (*Psychoanal. Quart.*, 1:739, 1932).

torical developments that gave rise to *JAPA* encapsulate medical exclusionism, the institutional conflicts and part-commitments that grew out of it, and more recent, belated efforts to distill a "common ground" among practitioners whose fractionation into rival groups was a product of the APsaA's own policies and practices. As such, the history of *JAPA* is a microcosm of recent trends that have had such dire consequences for psychoanalytic book publishers and for the field in general. It deserves special consideration.

JAPA was launched in 1953, when the postwar crusade of the American Psychoanalytic Association (APsaA) against the incursions of non-medical or lay analysis was approaching fever pitch. Four years earlier, the International Psychoanalytical Association convened its first postwar Congress in Zurich. There, in striking testimony to the altered balance of power that followed the ravages of World War II and the emigration of prominent European analysts to American shores, the APsaA was granted the special relationship to the parent organization it had demanded 11 years earlier, when the last prewar IPA Congress had met in Paris. To wit, the APsaA was elevated from a "component society" to a sui generis "regional association" of the IPA. As such, it was granted an "exclusive franchise" on American psychoanalysis, according to which the IPA ceded to the APsaA total autonomy in the establishment and enforcement of training standards in the United States, absent the oversight it exercised over its component societies. And it further meant that the IPA would recognize no training bodies in the United States other than those affiliated with the APsaA.[14]

The success of the medicalized APsaA at the Zurich Congress of 1949 is one small manifestation of the unparalleled power of organized

14. The terms of this modus vivendi, which were never submitted to an IPA membership vote, were hammered out informally in 1948 at a meeting in Anna Freud's London home attended by senior officials of the American Psychoanalytic Association and the International Psychoanalytical Association. Robert Wallerstein, a senior member of the APsaA who held the presidency of the IPA between 1985 and 1989, provides an admirably balanced, detailed review of these historical developments in *Lay Analysis: Life Inside the Controversy* (Hillsdale, NJ: Analytic Press, 1998), pp. 23–74. Judging from TAP's meager sales (400 copies) of this masterful overview of the lay analysis controversy in psychoanalysis, analysts of all persuasions remain sadly uninterested in the very history that helps explain the current state of their field.

American medicine in the years immediately following World War II. On the home front, this power gained expression in the adroit political maneuverings of the American Medical Association, which not only thwarted congressional efforts to implement structural changes in the provision of medical care in the United States, but also dominated newly formed international bodies (i.e., the World Medical Association and the World Health Organization) attempting to revitalize health care in the war-torn nations of Europe. The AMA's role in the defeat of successive versions of the Wagner-Murray-Dingell Bill, which, from 1943 to 1949, sought to extend Social Security coverage through disability and invalidity insurance and benefits for medical care, is the best-known aspect of its crusade against any and all measures even remotely suggestive of federally sponsored compulsory health insurance. Less well known is the AMA's role in defeating legislation—including legislation in which it had formative input—that extended federal assistance to professional groups beyond the pale of medical orthodoxy. In the years immediately following World War II, the AMA successfully attacked all "the bastions of sectarian medical practice," so that irregular schools of practice, excepting only a handful of schools of osteopathy and chiropractic, had by decade's end "all but disappeared." One example among many will suffice: The AMA's opposition to Senator Claude Pepper's proposed legislation of 1949 (S. 1453), which provided an extension of federal aid to medical schools, was fueled by resentment "that the bill made osteopathic schools eligible for federal assistance."[15]

When the APsaA flexed its muscles at the Zurich Congress, it did so as an arm of American psychiatry, a long-established but weak medical specialty that had limped ineffectually into the war years, ceding leadership in the war effort, in child psychiatry, and in mental hospital improvement to the National Committee for Mental Hygiene. In the years immediately preceding the Zurich Conference, the American Psychiatric Association's (APA) efforts at organizational reform, an aspect of its effort to upgrade the status of psychiatry within American medicine, were aided and abetted by its identification with psychoanalysis, which, as of 1949, was one of six sections within the

15. See James G. Burrow, *AMA: Voice of American Medicine* (Baltimore: Johns Hopkins Press, 1963), pp. 317–318, 322.

Association.[16] The APA's Committee of Reorganization took shape in 1945 under the chairmanship of Karl Menninger. The Young Turks who formed the Group for the Advancement of Psychiatry (GAP) in 1946 to further the APA's reform agenda were by and large friends of analysis. William Menninger was their first president. Daniel Blain, the chief of neuropsychiatry of the Veterans Administration and a founding member of GAP, became the APA's first medical director in 1948; William Menninger credited him with giving "a new life and direction to the activities of the Association." With the incorporation of the short-lived, social-activist Psychiatric Foundation in 1946 and Menninger's election to the APA presidency in 1949, the reform agenda, which sought to extend psychiatry's social role at the same time as it promoted its integration into general medicine, was locked into place.[17]

16. The other five sections were convulsive disorders, forensic psychiatry, military psychiatry, private practice, and child psychiatry. In his APA Presidential Address of 1948, Winfred Overholser intoned that "The understanding of mental mechanisms, thanks largely to the work of Freud, has been in great measure responsible for the success of psychiatry; the gains in treatment could hardly have been envisaged by a worker in the field even 25 years ago." Three years later, APA President John White-horn noted the perception of many European psychiatrists that "the psychoanalytic movement had captured American psychiatry" and attested to its basic accuracy: "It is true, I believe, that a considerable majority of American psychiatrists have come to appreciate and to acknowledge the general value of certain Freudian concepts and methods, which have broadened and deepened the study of many psychiatric problems. In this sense, there has been an assimilation of much of psychoanalysis into general psychiatry." See the Presidential Addresses of Winfred Overholser (1948) and John C. Whitehorn (1951) in *New Directions in American Psychiatry, 1944–1968: The Presidential Addresses of the American Psychiatric Association over the Past Twenty-five Years* (Washington, DC: American Psychiatric Association, 1969), pp. 53, 97.

17. On the American Psychiatric Association's organizational reforms in the five years following World War II, which aimed, inter alia, at integrating psychiatry into general medicine, see Walter E. Barton, *The History and Influence of the American Psychiatric Association* (Washington, DC: American Psychiatric Press, 1987), pp. 170–181. The Psychiatric Foundation was sponsored by the American Psychiatric Association and, shortly thereafter, the American Neurological Association, whose members conjointly donated 13% of the total contributions it received. In the words of Leo Bartemeier, its first president, it sought to raise funds "with which to assist psychiatry to become more effective for the general good." Its first project, commenced in 1948, was a preliminary study of the problems of rating and inspecting mental hospitals. In 1950 The Psychiatric Foundation merged with The National Committee for Mental Hygiene and The National Mental Health Foundation into The National Association for Mental

Small wonder, then, that the American psychoanalysts attending the Zurich Conference were medically minded psychiatrists for whom membership in the APsaA, as Robert Knight observed several years later, was "equivalent to certification in a specialty within a specialty." For Ives Hendrick, who followed Knight into the APsaA Presidency in 1953, analysis was not merely another medical specialty, but primus inter pares, a specialty "widely recognized to be a necessity for the scientific advancement of some fields of modern medicine."[18] Psychoanalysis, in its own small way, basked in the glow of triumphant American medicine, and the latter's postwar energies were devoted, inter alia, to the suppression of both medical "irregulars" and non-medical usurpers—excepting only dentists—of all kinds. In this historical context, it is unsurprising that the fons et origo of the APsaA's demand for "regional association" status, eventually codified in 1963, was the exclusionary impulse—the APsaA's nonnegotiable insistence on excluding from psychoanalytic training and practice anyone in the United States who was not a licensed physician.

The protracted efforts of medically trained American psychoanalysts from the early 1920s through the 1970s to medicalize the psychoanalytic method—arguably a question of economic competition—was a relatively recent flare-up of a century-long debate about the scope of

---

Health. See Leo H. Bartemeier, "The Psychiatric Foundation: Introductory Remarks," *Am. J. Psychiatry*, 104:145–147, 1947; Arthur H. Ruggles, "The Foundation and the American Psychiatric Association," *Am. J. Psychiatry*, 104:148–150, 1947; and Austin M. Davies, "The Psychiatric Foundation," *Am. J. Psychiatry*, 106:866–867, 1950. Bartemeier is quoted by Davies, p. 866.

18. Knight made the remark in his Presidential Address to the APsaA of December 7, 1952, published in the first issue of *JAPA* (1:197–221, 1953) as "The Present Status of Organized Psychoanalysis in the United States." The remark is at p. 211 and precedes Knight's attesting to the fact that in the United States "classical psychoanalysis has come to be more and more identified with medicine and psychiatry" (pp. 212ff). Hendrick's remarks came in his own Presidential Address of May 8, 1955, published as "Presidential Address: Professional Standards of the American Psychoanalytic Association," *JAPA*, 3:561–599, 1955, quoted at pp. 561, 562. The notion of psychoanalysis as a subspecialty of psychiatry was common in the 1940s and 1950s. See, e.g., Leo H. Bartemeier, "The Contribution of Psychiatry to Psychoanalysis," *Am. J. Psychiatry*, 101:205–209, 1944; Robert P. Knight, "The Relationship of Psychoanalysis to Psychiatry," *Am. J. Psychiatry*, 101:777–782, 1945; and Karl Menninger, "The Contribution of Psychoanalysis to American Psychiatry" (1953), in *A Psychiatrist's World: Selected Papers* (NY: Viking, 1959), pp. 834–853 at p. 839.

the "practice of medicine" and the prerogative of physicians to claim a functional and financial monopoly over any and all aspects of the healing art. Long before A. A. Brill and his cohorts wrestled Freud's psychoanalytic procedure away from American nonmedical or lay analysts, their physician forebears, struggling to map the territory of emergent medical specialties, waged similar battles against well-established and culturally sanctioned nonmedical competitors. In the last two decades of the nineteenth century, battle lines were drawn between obstetricians and nonmedical midwives, between medical anesthesiologists and nurse anesthetists, and most especially between "refracting opticians" (subsequently called optometrists) and "medical oculists" (subsequently called ophthalmologists). This final battle, which has attracted the attention of medical historians, raged from the mid-1890s until about 1912, by which time optometry had emerged as a separate profession, "internally organized and supported by the public."[19]

The mutual distrust of optometrists and ophthalmologists, which began to abate only in the mid-1960s, mimics the mutual anathema of American lay and medical analysts in the years following World War II. In 1934, four years before American medical analysts initially and unsuccessfully demanded an exclusive franchise on analytic training at the IPA Paris Conference of 1938, the AMA attempted to prevent optometrists from prescribing glasses in hospitals. A year later, ever sensitive to the optometric encroachment, the AMA deemed it unethical for any AMA member to teach or consult with nonphysicians.[20] In 1949, as noted, the APsaA finally received the "exclusive franchise" on psychoanalytic training and research it had

19. Rosemary Stevens, *American Medicine and the Public Interest: A History of Specialization* (Berkeley: University of California Press, 1998 [1971]), pp. 106, 107. Notable among full-scale treatments of the emergence of ophthalmology as a medical specialty are Alvin A. Hubbell, *The Development of Ophthalmology in America 1800–1870* (Chicago: Keener, 1908) and George Rosen, *The Specialization of Medicine With Particular Reference to Ophthalmology* (NY: Arno, 1972 [1944]).

20. The constraints placed on AMA members with respect to nonmedical practitioners such as optometrists, be it noted, were no different than the long-standing constraints on members apropos alternate medical providers. It was only in 1961 that the AMA permitted its members to associate voluntarily with osteopathic physicians and to teach at osteopathic schools. See Irwin A. Blackstone, "The A.M.A. and the Osteopaths: A Study of the Power of Organized Medicine," *Antitrust Bulletin*, 22:405–440, 1977.

demanded 11 years earlier; in that same year, mimicking the AMA's prohibition of member training of optometrists a decade earlier, it dealt with the surreptitious training of laymen by medical analysts by passing a resolution forbidding APsaA members from training students of analysis "except under the direct auspices of a recognized Institute of this Association." The policing of its own membership was relegated to a Committee on Ethical Standards founded a year later.[21] *JAPA*, which was launched in 1953, gave expression to these institutional developments. At this same moment in medical history, the AMA undertook further efforts to cut off any contact between optometrists and ophthalmologists, excepting only that the latter might accept and retain optometric referrals.

But there is a key difference between the opposition of emergent medical specialties to nonmedical providers and the opposition of medical psychoanalysts to their lay counterparts, and the difference is this: The turf-related battles of medical specialists typically involved the development and use of scientifically advanced instrumentation. It is difficult to envision the medicalization of childbirth in mid-eighteenth-century Britain and the progressively diminished role of midwives among Europe's urban population absent the refinement and sale of Chamberlen forceps.[22] In the mid-nineteenth century, just as the stethoscope and other mechanical aids in physical examination were gaining general acceptance in Britain and the United States, the professionalization of ophthalmology was stimulated by Helmholtz's invention in 1851 of the ophthalmoscope. As Rosemary Stevens notes, it "gave the physician visual access to the retina, proved useful in measuring refractions of the eye, and gave the 'oculists' (as the medical eye specialists were termed) an instrumental focus for their specialty." More than 60 years later, George Crampton's development of the battery-handled ophthalmoscope brought retinal inspection within the purview of internists and neurosurgeons but still reserved for ophthalmologists the task of interpreting clinical findings.[23] The

21. Hendrick, "Presidential Address" (n. 18), p. 569.

22. See Adrian Wilson, *The Making of Man-midwifery: Childbirth in England, 1660–1770* (Cambridge: Harvard University Press, 1995).

23. Stevens, *American Medicine and the Public Interest* (n. 19), pp. 100, 109.

instrumental focus provided to oculists by the ophthalmoscope extended to other emerging specialties in the second half of the nineteenth century. The role of the Dudgeon sphygmograph and James Mackenzie's clinical polygraph in the professionalization of cardiologists is one such example; the role of the reflex hammer and dynamometer in the identity formation of neurologists is another.[24]

But "medical" psychoanalysis involved no such instrumentation, because psychoanalysis, when all is said and done, is the application in a clinical setting of a specialized mode of listening and talking (and not talking). The analyst, whose professional bona fides fall back on his own personal analysis and the kind of listening and talking that emerged therein, is his own "analyzing instrument." Medical training bears no discernible relationship to the skills and sensibilities born of this process. In certain respects, such as the medically conditioned avoidance of uncertainty, it is quite anathema to them.[25] Finally, and most tellingly, the championing of medical training as the sine qua non of analytic training flew in the face not only of Freud's own unequivocal endorsement of lay analysis but also of the postwar emergence of clinical psychology and psychiatric social work

24. On pulse measuring instruments in the development of cardiology, see Christopher Lawrence, "Physiological Apparatus in the Wellcome Museum: 2. The Dudgeon Sphygmograph and Its Descendants," *Med. Hist.*, 23:96–101, 1979 and Audrey B. Davis, *Medicine and Its Technology: An Introduction to the History of Medical Instrumentation* (Westport, CT: Greenwood, 1981), pp. 117–137. On the role of instrumentation in the emergence of neurology as a specialty in the late nineteenth century, see the following articles by Douglas J. Lanska: "The History of Reflex Hammers" (*Neurol.*, 39:1542–1549, 1989); "The Role of Technology in Neurologic Specialization in America" (*Neurol.*, 48:1722–1727, 1997); "William Hammond, the Dynamometer, the Dynamograph," (*Arch. Neurol.*, 57:1649–1653, 2000); "The Romberg Sign and Early Instruments for Measuring Postural Sway" (*J. Hist. Neurosci.*, 10:202–216, 2001); "J. L. Corning and Vagal Nerve Stimulation for Seizures in the 1880s" (*Neurol.*, 58:452–459, 2002). See also Christopher Goetz, Teresa Chmura, & Douglas Lanska, "Part I: The History of 19th-Century Neurology and the American Neurological Association" (*Ann. Neurol.*, 53[suppl 4]:2–26, 2003, esp. pp. 24–25).

25. See Jay Katz, *The Silent World of Doctor and Patient* (Baltimore: Johns Hopkins University Press, 2002[1984]), chap. 7 on physicians' "flight from uncertainty" as an aspect of medical training, socialization, and specialization. The sociologist Donald Light's *Becoming Psychiatrists: The Professional Transformation of Self* (NY: Norton, 1982) explores the manner in which psychiatric residents, in the course of becoming psychiatrists, must unlearn the very kind of medical reasoning that anchors their recently consolidated identity as physicians.

in American mental health—two "vibrant, rapidly growing mental health professions, which soon burst institutional bonds and began to enter the private-practice market."[26]

American psychiatry grappled with the challenge of the newly vitalized nonmedical providers by establishing committees to explore the relationship of psychiatry with "ancillary disciplines" such as psychology and psychiatric social work. A Committee on the Relations of Psychiatry and Clinical Psychology, established in 1946, supplemented earlier committees that attended to psychiatric social work and psychiatric nursing. The clinical psychology committee was to "confer with leading psychologists on the relations between their discipline and ours." APA leadership did not question the legitimacy, even the importance, of such disciplines, which included their right to work with psychiatric patients. In 1946, it even entertained the possibility of a type of associate membership in the APA for clinical psychologists, psychiatric social workers, psychiatric nurses, and other groups who worked with psychiatric patients.[27]

To be sure, there was considerable ambivalence in the APA's attitude toward lay providers. Psychiatrists, so its leadership enjoined, were to deal with the members of auxiliary and associated professions "on the same high ethical and professional plane as those exhibited in relations with other physicians." With respect to psychologists in particular, "much overlapping of function" was acknowledged. Yet, with psychologists no less than psychiatric social workers and psychiatric nurses, it was psychiatrists who would determine the "proper place" of nonmedical professionals within the medicalized universe of mental health and illness. William Menninger, who had encouraged psychologists to undertake diagnosis and treatment during the war years, captured the acceptance of, and autocratic condescension toward, the ancillary disciplines when, in August, 1945, he extolled the team relationship of psychiatrist, clinical psychologist, and psychiatric social worker established during the war as a model for postwar planning. "If we want the job done well," he lectured colleagues at a Convalescent Hospital Conference in Battle Creek, Michigan, "it

26. Wallerstein, *Lay Analysis* (n. 14), p. 64.

27. APA Presidential Addresses of Samuel W. Hamilton (1947) and Karl M. Bowman (1946) in *New Directions in American Psychiatry* (n. 16), pp. 39, 21.

is just as essential to have these ancillary personnel as it is for the surgeon to have the X-ray technician and the laboratory technician." Among the three team members, there was never any question about whose professional model captured the job at hand and who would be captaining the team.[28]

When in 1949 the APA's Committee on Clinical Psychology finally issued its report, it was unequivocal about sequestering the valued lay colleagues outside the realm of private psychotherapeutic practice. "The American Psychiatric Association," it held, "is strongly opposed to independent private practice of psychotherapy by the clinical psychologists; and The Association believes that psychotherapy, whenever practiced, should be done in a setting where adequate psychiatric safeguards are provided."[29]

But this verdict flew in the face of what by 1949 was a fait accompli. Clinical psychologists' competence as independent providers had been amply demonstrated during the war years, when personnel shortages curbed professional rivalries and drew psychologists away from administrative work and testing programs and into the clinical

28. APA Presidential Addresses of Winfred Overholser (1948) , Karl M. Bowman (1946), and William C. Menninger (1949), in *New Directions in American Psychiatry* (n. 16), pp. 57, 27, 71. Menninger's remarks to the Convalescent Hospital Conference of August 21, 1945, were published as "Problems Confronting Psychiatry in the Army Convalescent Hospital," *Am. J. Psychiatry*, 102:732–734, 1946, and are quoted here at p. 734. On Menninger's notion of a team approach and the role of the psychiatrist as team quarterback, see further his *Psychiatry in a Troubled World: Yesterday's War and Today's Challenge* (NY: Macmillan, 1948), pp. 461–463 and Gerald N. Grob, *From Asylum to Community: Mental Health Policy in Modern America* (Princeton: Princeton University Press, 1991), pp. 107–108. Most psychologists, for their part, were only too happy to accept their subordinate role on the team and to criticize the "very few" colleagues who demurred from this assignment. See, e.g., Clarence O. Cheny & Edward I. Strongin, "The Psychologist's Contribution to the Psychiatric Hospital," *Am. J. Psychiatry*, 103:65–68, 1946, quoted at p. 65. The situation changed greatly over the next decade, as clinical psychologists were brought onto chronic wards and given responsibility—always under psychiatric supervision—for the development and implementation of treatment programs. For a report on one such pilot program undertaken in 1951, see Earl P. Brannon & J. Arthur Waites, "The Role of the Clinical Psychologist in Ward Administration: An Extension of the Therapeutic Team Concept," *Am. J. Psychiatry*, 111:497–501, 1955.

29. Report of the Committee on Clinical Psychology, quoted by John C. Whitehorn in his APA Presidential Address of 1951, in *New Directions in American Psychiatry* (n. 16), p. 95.

trenches. There, aided by personality inventories and projective tests, they undertook diagnosis and treatment alongside their psychiatric colleagues. By July, 1945, 1,710 psychologists were employed by the military, a majority of whom assumed clinical responsibilities.[30] Questionnaire research attested to the continuing therapeutic role of psychologists in general hospitals and convalescent hospitals at war's end and into 1946.[31]

The war not only offered many psychologists their first opportunities for clinical training and practice; it also persuaded them "that the field of individual treatment was the place to be in the future."[32] Their clinical responsibilities with the exploding population of VA hospitals were subject to lengthy discussion following the cessation of hostilities. How would the overwhelming demand for clinical psychological services be met? In 1946 and 1947, clinical psychologists wrote at length of the need to standardize clinical training programs and to enlarge training opportunities in personality dynamics and psychotherapy. Clinical externships attached to medical school clinics, such as that of the University of Chicago, were offered as models of training. The Veterans Administration, for its part, initiated an ambitious externship program in collaboration with universities: Clinical psychology graduate students supplemented academic training with 22 hours a week of "practicing clinical psychology" at one or another VA station.[33]

30. See Steuart Henderson Britt & Jane D. Morgan, "Military Psychologists in World War II," *Am. Psychol.*, 1:423–437, 1946, especially Table 8 at p. 429. Of the 968 military psychologists who returned the authors' questionnaires, 687 or 71% reported the development and/or use of clinical and counseling procedures among their military duties.

31. See Max L. Hutt & Emmette O. Milton, "An Analysis of Duties Performed by Clinical Psychologists in the Army," *Am. Psychol.*, 2:52–56, 1947.

32. Ellen Herman, *The Romance of American Psychology: Political Culture in the Age of Experts* (Berkeley: University of California Press, 1995), pp. 84, 92–95, quoted at p. 84.

33. Anna S. Elonen et al., "Training the Clinical Psychologist: Externships in Medical School Clinics," *Am. Psychol.*, 1:50–54, 1946; Robert R. Sears, "Graduate Training Facilities: I. General Psychology II. Clinical Psychology," *Am. Psychol.*, 1:135–150, 1946; James G. Miller, "Clinical Psychology in the Veterans Administration," *Am. Psychol.*, 1:181–189, quoted at p. 187; John G. Darley & Dael Wolfle, "Editorial

In October, 1946, the School of Clinical Psychology collaboratively undertaken by the Menninger Foundation and Kansas University welcomed its first class of psychology graduate students to Topeka; in the words of Karl Menninger, the school embodied the "irrevocable affiliation" of psychology and psychiatry. So "heavily stimulated" was the procurement of clinical psychologists that the Editors of the *American Psychologist* expressed concern lest "a trend toward defining applied psychology as primarily a clinical and therapeutic endeavor" work to the detriment of other research and applied activities "in which psychologists have made real contributions." Their concern was not unfounded. By the fall of 1947, psychotherapy was deemed the preeminent interest of clinical psychologists. In the same year, the American Psychological Association established its Board of Examiners in Professional Psychology as a vehicle of professional certification, and the Association's Committee on Training in Clinical Psychology, chaired by David Shakow, voiced its support for state certification, while maintaining that no clinical psychologist "can be considered adequately trained unless he has had sound training in psychotherapy."[34]

Reading between the lines of the American Psychiatric Association Committee injunction of 1949, then, one discerns grudging acceptance of psychologist practitioners who, the committee well knew, were already committed to private practice and would make further inroads in this heretofore sacrosanct domain in the years ahead. Expressions like "*independent* private practice" and "*adequate* psychiatric

---

Comment: Can We Meet the Formidable Demand for Psychological Services?" *Am. Psychol.*, 1:179–180, 1946; Robert R. Sears, "Clinical Training Facilities: 1947 – A Report from the Committee on Graduate and Professional Training," *Am. Psychol.*, 2:199–205, 1947; Committee on Training in Clinical Psychology of the American Psychological Association, "Recommended Graduate Training Program in Clinical Psychology," *Am. Psychol.*, 2:539–558, 1947.

34. Karl A. Menninger, "Psychology and Psychiatry," *Am. Psychol.*, 2:139–140, 1947, quoted at p. 140; Darley & Wolfle, "Editorial Comment" (n. 33), p. 179; Laurance F. Shaffer, "The Problem of Psychotherapy," *Am. Psychol.*, 2:459–467, 1947; APA Committee on Training in Clinical Psychology (headed by David Shakow), "Recommended Graduate Training Program in Clinical Psychology," *Am. Psychol.*, 2:539–558, 1947.

safeguards" give the game away.[35] In 1950, APA President George Stevenson, himself a community psychiatrist, gave a spin to the Committee report that was more synchronous with professional and social realities when, here referring to clinical social workers, he remarked:

> That a few lay persons may assume undue authority for the treatment of the emotionally ill is a small even if irritating thing, compared to the great gains that have come through strengthening the social workers' proper skills. Psychiatry has to its credit that it has sensed the danger of proprietorship of its knowledge and has fostered the assumption of responsibility for problems of human behavior in those who are not patients, but are instead clients or pupils, parishioners or probationers.[36]

Despite the fact that members of the APsaA were with very few exceptions members of the APA, the contrast between the two fields in the decade following World War II is striking and extends beyond the issue of whether or not psychologists should be therapy providers. In the aftermath of the war, American psychiatrists were preoccupied with the social implications of their profession, and they evinced a zeal "to project certain psychiatric theories onto a broad range of social troubles." Indeed, this very preoccupation, according to APA President John Whitehorn, distinguished "psychiatric science and practice" in America from most other countries.[37]

---

35. For a different account of these developments, see Grob, *From Asylum to Community* (n. 28), pp. 102–114. Grob gives greater weight to the psychiatrists' continuing resistance to clinical psychologists' incursions into the domain of psychotherapy, which played itself out throughout the 1950s in political opposition to proposed state laws providing for the licensing of clinical psychologists. He concludes, however, that "The debate over psychotherapy was largely symbolic. Neither psychiatrists nor psychologists had ever defined its distinctive attributes or justified their claims to overarching competence. Many groups (including general practitioners), as a matter of fact, were providing psychotherapeutic services to troubled individuals. Above all, there were virtually no adequate evaluations of efficacy, and those that existed generally violated most principles of research design" (p. 114).

36. APA Presidential Address of George S. Stevenson (1950) in *New Directions in American Psychiatry* (n. 16), p. 86.

37. APA Presidential Address of John C. Whitehorn (1951), in *New Directions in American Psychiatry* (n. 16), p. 96.

The preoccupation was a natural extension of lessons learned during the war. If the greatest remediation of combat-related symptoms occurred at battalion aid-stations, with therapeutic success declining as soldiers were moved to rear echelon units, then a "logical corollary," as Gerald Grob has observed, was that "treatment in civilian life as in the military, ha[d] to be provided in a family and community setting rather than in a remote or isolated institution." Similarly optimistic extrapolations followed from wartime innovations that were effective in managing the stress levels of combat soldiers. If "rest periods, rotation policies, and measures directed toward the maintenance of group cohesion and social relationships had reduced psychoneurotic episodes in the military, might not corresponding social and environment changes in the civilian sector optimize mental as well as physical health?" Finally, the simple fact that only 7% of psychiatrically hospitalized GIs were diagnosed psychotic suggested that America's civilian psychiatric focus on psychosis left untouched the vast majority of psychiatric patients—those who, like their military counterparts, suffered from "mild maladjustments and neurotic reactions." Combat fatigue syndrome, when all was said and done, differed from the neuroses of civilian life more in catalyst than in kind. The differences, according to Naval psychiatrist Leon Saul, "resolve themselves into essentially quantitative and statistical ones." For William Menninger, the contrasting patient loads of military and civilian psychiatry pointed to a single, obvious conclusion—"that the practice of psychiatry in civilian life falls far short of its potential contribution to the need."[38]

So reasoned a generation of war-tested psychiatrists, whose leaders— William and Karl Menninger, Henry Brosin, John Appel, Daniel Blain, Franklin Ebaugh, and Roy Grinker among them—saw their specialty as uniquely positioned to address the social and political issues before the nation. Aware of the huge clinical-preventive-custodial-cultural

---

38. Grob, *From Asylum to Community* (n. 28), pp. 12–23, quoted at pp. 18, 19. Leon J. Saul, "Psychological Factors in Combat Fatigue: With Special Reference to Hostility and the Nightmares," *Psychosom. Med.*, 7:257–272, 1945, quoted at p. 271; William C. Menninger, "Psychiatric Experience in the War, 1941–1946," *Am. J. Psychiatry*, 103:577–586, 1947, quoted at p. 580. Walter Bromberg, whose stateside duties for the Navy included weeding out sailors whose psychopathy rendered them unfit for service, wrote of psychiatrists "awakened to the presence of a serious neurotic potential in our population as they witnessed the breaking point in ostensibly stable individuals under wartime stresses." Bromberg, *Psychiatry Between the Wars, 1918–1945* (Westport, CT: Greenwood, 1982), p. 163.

agenda before them, these psychiatrists articulated an activist social ideology that put civilian mental health in the crosshairs of postwar challenges to democracy. Safeguarding civilian mental health would, among other things, oblige postwar psychiatrists to embrace a new psychoeducational role. The very kind of "active ego re-education" that enabled military psychiatrists to return thousands of wartime casualties to active duty would have to be transposed to civilian practice. "In civilian life," wrote Roy Grinker and John Spiegel in the penultimate chapter of *Men Under Stress*, "motivations should have been instilled in early years at home and in school. Since this is not yet sufficiently understood by our educators, it often becomes the psychiatrist's responsibility to stimulate his patient's motivations, set his goals, and direct his sublimations."[39]

Psychiatric training would have to enlarge its purview accordingly. Good training, wrote Karl Menninger, "must of necessity be on a broad base." It must provide the resident "some information about the relations of psychiatry to various facets of life in our world— religious, political, literary, artistic. Certainly it should introduce the student to psychiatric aspects of the social issues and problems of the day."[40] Keeping clinical psychologists out of private practice—the

39. Roy R. Grinker & John P. Spiegel, *Men Under Stress* (Philadelphia: Blakiston, 1945), p. 438.

40. W. Menninger, *Psychiatry in a Troubled World*, (n. 28), p. 461. During the final years of the war and the years immediately thereafter, the *American Journal of Psychiatry* offered abundant avowals of psychiatry's transformative social mission. Among the more grandiloquent is Alan Gregg's "Critique of Psychiatry," presented at the Centenary Meeting of the American Psychiatric Association in Philadelphia in May, 1944. "There will be applications far beyond your offices and your hospitals of the further knowledge you will gain," intoned the Rockefeller Foundation's Director of the Division of Medical Sciences. And he continued: "applications not only to patients with functional and organic disease, but to the human relations of normal people—in politics, national and international, between races, between capital and labor, in government, in family life, in education, in every form of human relationship, whether between individuals or between groups. You will be concerned with optimum performance of human beings as civilized creatures." William Menninger addressed the more pedestrian aspect of the postwar mission in suggesting that "psychiatry might contribute to the common weal through the development of selection methods of public school teachers, and could this be adopted, it might avail more benefit than all our treatment efforts put together." Alan Gregg, "A Critique of Psychiatry," *Am. J. Psychiatry*, 101:285–291, 1944, quoted at p. 291; W. Menninger, "Psychiatric Experience in the War" (n. 38), p. 585.

party line—was a rearguard action that had more to do with postwar politics than therapeutics. In truth, APA members, numbering all of 4,000 at the war's end, needed all the help they could get. "There is enough material to keep all groups busy," remarked Karl Bowman in his Presidential Address of 1946. "There is at least one thing the psychiatrist does not have to worry about: Since he always has more cases than he can possibly handle he will undoubtedly have to avail himself constantly of help from all these different fields."[41]

A superfluity of patients was not the quandary of postwar American psychoanalysts, for whom the influx of European refugees, many with impeccable Freudian credentials, posed a considerable threat to the prewar equilibrium between psychoanalytic providers and their always limited clientele. Whereas the experience of the war years, as it gained expression in military and community psychiatry, pushed the APA outward toward a social agenda that embraced, albeit hesitantly, the "vibrantly, rapidly growing mental health professions" (Wallerstein) outside of medicine, this same experience pulled the APsaA inward toward a medicalized introversion. Community involvement, in the narrowed purview of postwar analysis, signified nothing more than an outreach to psychiatry in which medical analysts would participate in psychiatry residency training, accept hospital appointments and psychiatry department professorships, and assume supervisory roles in state mental hospitals.[42]

41. APA Presidential Addresses of John C. Whitehorn (1951) and Karl M. Bowman (1946) in *New Directions in American Psychiatry* (n. 16), pp. 96, 27. Actually, beginning in 1945, the perception grew that psychiatrists would be grossly inadequate to the postwar needs of veterans with psychiatric disabilities, and that "The only hope, therefore, for adequate treatment of these war-created emergency disabilities, entirely aside from the large numbers of psychoneurotically disabled civilians, lay with the 185,000 practicing doctors in America." The fear of being overwhelmed with veterans led the Commonwealth Fund to finance an experimental two-week course at the University of Minnesota in April 1945 to train primary physicians to conduct psychiatric interviews and implement basic forms of treatment. See Thomas A. C. Rennie, "Psychotherapy for the General Practitioner: A Program for Training," *Am. J. Psychiatry*, 103:653–660, 1947, quoted at p. 653. On the inability of American psychiatrists to meet the postwar demand for psychotherapy, see also Grob, *From Asylum to Community* (n. 28), p. 112 and below, pp. 298–300.

42. See "The Psychoanalyst in the Community," *Bull. Amer. Psychoanal. Assn.*, 5(3):4–10, 1949; M. Ralph Kaufman, "The Role of Psychoanalysis in American Psychiatry," *Bull. Amer. Psychoanal. Assn.*, 6(1):1–4, 1950; M. Ralph Kaufman,

Outside the realm of psychiatric education and inpatient supervision, analysts might accept faculty appointment to schools of social work but were otherwise urged to proceed with due diffidence. Owing to their "long years of highly specialized training," cautioned Lawrence Kubie, analysts "do not often know enough about the technical aspects of social or political or economic or international policy to justify an active espousal of one side or another." Furthermore, the time devoted to activities outside the consulting room invited the possibility of shortchanging patients "in various insidious ways." To be sure, analytic knowledge could be usefully brought to bear on the great issues before the public, but forays into practical community affairs would ipso facto impair the analyst's value as an analyst. Participation in social psychiatry was all but proscribed. "For all the neglect of modern biological psychiatry," Melvin Sabshin recollects of postwar American analysis, "the attitudes of analysts toward social and community psychiatry were even more negative. . . . To be involved in social psychiatry was seen as diluting the basic concentration."[43]

Worse still for the APsaA was clinical collaboration with nonmedical therapists, and worst of all, indeed utterly out of the question, was analytic training of psychologists and social workers who aspired to practice clinical analysis. In point of fact, the analysts' attitude toward lay analysis mimicked the psychiatrists' attitude toward clinical psychology early in the century, when the psychologists' inroads in school

---

"Psychoanalysis in Medicine," *Bull. Amer. Psychoanal. Assn.*, 7(1):1–12, 1951; "The Psychoanalyst and the State Mental Hospital," *Bull. Am. Psychoanal. Assn.*, 8(2):201–204, 1952. Still earlier, in 1944, Leo Bartemeier singled out psychiatric institutions as the central arena for the collaboration of psychiatry and psychoanalysis and noted "that some psychoanalysts have been sought as such for additions to mental hospital staffs to apply their knowledge and skills to the problems of the psychoses." Leo Bartemeier, "The Contribution of Psychiatry to Psychoanalysis," *Am. J. Psychiatry*, 101:205–209, 1944, quoted at p. 207.

43. Lawrence S. Kubie, "The Dilemma of the Analyst in a Troubled World," *Bull. Am. Psychoanal. Assn.*, 6(4):1–4, 1950. Kubie's cautionary remarks drew a spirited rejoinder from members of the APsaA's Committee for the Study of Social Issues, "The Dilemma of the Analyst in a Troubled World – A Reply," *Bull. Am. Psychoanal. Assn.*, 7(1):70–72, 1951 and a final riposte from Kubie, "A Reply to a Reply," *Bull. Am. Psychoanal. Assn.*, 7(2):146–147, 1951. Melvin Sabshin's recollections of this period are in "Turning Points in Twentieth-Century American Psychiatry," *Am. J. Psychiatry*, 14:1267–1274, 1990, quoted at p. 1270.

psychology, which included establishment of psychological clinics and child guidance centers, aroused a knee-jerk repudiation of psychologists' prerogative to evaluate and work remedially with disturbed schoolchildren.[44]

But American psychiatry had matured over the following three decades and come of age during the war. Newly secure in its medical specialty status and beset with the enormity of the postwar agenda, it could afford to be tolerant of nonmedical colleagues. This was not the case for psychoanalysis, whose tenuous claim to subspecialty status made it cling to medicine all the more tenaciously. Absent medical credentials, American analysts of the postwar era could not ride on the coattails of American psychiatry and claim their own small piece of hegemonic American medicine. Nor could they shore up their identification with American medicine in legislative eyes by demonstrating responsiveness to the problem of quackery. Nor could they regulate the supply of clinical analysts in the interest of their own economic well-being. Nor could they prevent senior European lay analysts from exerting undue influence within their small training institutes and professional societies. The relative weighting of these several factors, both regionally and nationally, is difficult to determine,

44. In 1916, the New York Psychiatric Society established a committee to investigate the activities of educational psychologists. The committee's report, which was adopted by the Society, began with the recommendation "that the sick, whether in mind or body, should be cared for only by those with medical training who are authorized by the state to assume the responsibility for diagnosis and treatment." It proceeded to "urge upon thoughtful psychologists and the medical profession in general an expression of disapproval of the application of psychology to responsible clinical work except when made by or under the direct supervision of physicians qualified to deal with abnormal mental conditions." Four years later, when the National Research Council sponsored a three-day conference on the relations between psychology and psychiatry, Carl Seashore, recipient of Yale's first Ph.D. in psychology in 1895 and a recognized authority on the psychology of speech, hearing, and music, recalled the atmosphere of the conference as incorporating "every element of an intensive war. Both sides were contesting for 'living space.' Each considered the other an intruder." See Thomas Verner Moore, "A Century of Psychology in Its Relationship to American Psychiatry," in J. K. Hall et al., eds., *One Hundred Years of American Psychiatry* (NY: Columbia University Press [for the American Psychiatric Association], 1944), pp. 443–477, quoted at p. 472; Carl E. Seashore, *Pioneering in Psychology* (Iowa City: University of Iowa Press, 1942), p. 124; and Gerald N. Grob, *Mental Illness and American Society, 1875–1940* (Princeton: Princeton University Press, 1983), pp. 260–265.

but their collective import is clear. The exclusionary impulse, which gathered together all these trends, trumped the readiness—even the ambivalent and patronizing readiness of American psychiatry—to adopt collegial and training relationships with lay colleagues.

Three years after the Zurich Congress of 1949, the exclusionary impulse of American medical analysts gained expression in the launching of the *Journal of the American Psychoanalytic Association. JAPA* was very much a journal by and for the members of its parent organization; indeed, it would shortly incorporate the Association's *Bulletin*, its newsletter for APsaA members.[45] And these members, with but a handful of exceptions,[46] were physicians who had specialized in psychiatry and gone on to receive psychoanalytic training at one of the APsaA's member institutes. In December, 1951, as the condition of endorsing the proposed publication agreement with International Universities Press, the APsaA's Executive Council insisted on formalizing the principle that "This publication [viz., *JAPA*] should be representative of the viewpoint of the psychoanalytic philosophy of the American Psychoanalytic Association." And then, as if the proviso alone would not suffice, the Council added that "Suitable provisions, methods and means must at all times be made available to the association to see that the journal does function as a true representative of the Association's psychoanalytic philosophy."[47]

And what exactly was this "psychoanalytic philosophy" that *JAPA* was to represent truly and unshakably? The APsaA Executive Council saw no need to spell it out, but it clearly contained the Association's opposition to lay analysis as a central element. Robert

45. John Frosch, *JAPA*'s first editor, comments on the discussions pursuant to absorbing the APsaA's *Bulletin* into its newly launched journal in *"Journal of the American Psychoanalytic Association*: A Retrospective (1953–1972)," *JAPA*, 35:303–336, 1987, quoted at pp. 329–330.

46. Literally a handful. In his presidential address of December, 1952, Robert Knight recorded that at present seven lay analysts were members of the APsaA and some 25 others had been given "some kind of membership status in an affiliate society." In 1955, Ives Hendrick noted that the APsaA membership of 600 or so included six lay analysts and two honorary members. Knight, "Present Status of Organized Psychoanalysis" (n. 18), p. 212; Hendrick, "Presidential Address" (n. 18), pp. 561, 580.

47. Quoted in Frosch, *"Journal of the American Psychoanalytic Association*: A Retrospective" (n. 45), p. 311.

Knight's Presidential Address to the APsaA of December, 1952, which was published in the debut issue of *JAPA* in early 1953, made the point all too clearly. The great majority of APsaA members, observed Knight, were "strongly of the opinion that therapy of sick patients is a medical function and must have medical safeguards. All rediscussions of this issue in the Association have resulted in overwhelming affirmation of the policy against accepting nonphysicians for official training."[48] Two years later, Ives Hendrick, who assumed the APsaA presidency in 1953, made the point more strongly still by giving it a historical trajectory. The APsaA's univocal opposition to lay analysis, he intoned in the pages of *JAPA*, had been asserted at the Association's meetings of 1922 and 1925 and then codified in bylaws of 1932; in a Joint Resolution of 1938; in new bylaws of 1946; and in a Joint Resolution of the Executive Council of 1953. "If one critically surveys our history," he concluded, "it becomes apparent that for over thirty years, whenever the tantrum-like uproar on this matter [of lay analysis] comes to a decisive vote, the principle of medical preparation for therapeutic analysis has always been sustained, and by very large majorities, in the critical votes of this Association."[49] Excluded from the training establishment of the APsaA, denied the cachet of APsaA membership, and able to enlist APsaA members as teachers and mentors only on the sly, the growing contingent of mental health professionals who found their way to psychoanalysis via clinical psychology and clinical social work in the 50s and 60s was no friend of *JAPA*.

The exclusionary impulse that guided the APsaA and its official publication, *JAPA*, through the 1970s ranged across institutional, theoretical, and educational domains. In 1958, the APsaA sought to cement a dictatorship over psychoanalytic training and practice in the United States by requesting subspecialty board status under the aegis of the American Medical Association's Board of Psychiatry and Neurology. Through the proposed Board of Psychoanalysis, the APsaA alone would be empowered to designate who might "be certified as a qualified Psychoanalyst." When the American Board of Psychiatry and Neurology, under its secretary David Boyd, counterproposed a more eclectic Board of Psychoanalysis, of which only three of seven members

48. Knight, "Present Status of Organized Psychoanalysis" (n. 18), pp. 212–213.

49. Hendrick, "Presidential Address" (n. 18), pp. 581–582.

would be appointed by the APsaA, and then appealed to the executive council of the recently established Academy of Psychoanalysis,[50] through its past president Jules Masserman, for nominees to the proposed subspecialty board, the APsaA leadership recoiled in horror. As Masserman recollects, the leadership responded to news of the Board's overture to the Academy "with various mixtures of incredulity, indignation, and panic."[51] Following the APsaA's spring conference of May, 1959, its leadership vainly petitioned the American Board of Psychiatry and Neurology for an APsaA-controlled subspecialty board a second time. By year end, having made no headway with the Board and having failed to forge a consensus among its own divided membership about the desirability of subspecialty board status, the APsaA withdrew its petition and let the matter die.[52]

In the realm of theory, *JAPA*'s continuing identification with the medicalized APsaA gained expression in journal issues that expounded and elaborated Freud's "conflict psychology," its postwar American derivative, ego psychology, and the treatment issues that followed from strict application of what Americans took to be standard psychoana-

---

50. The American Academy of Psychoanalysis was founded in 1956 by a group of medical analysts, most of whom were members of the APsaA. They were "weary of that body's [the APsaA's] reactionary policies, isolationism from the mainstreams of psychiatry and medicine, and arbitrary presumptions that it was the sole arbiter of psychoanalytic certification and practice" (Jules Masserman, *A Psychiatric Odyssey* [NY: Science House, 1971], p. 173). A smaller and more eclectic organization than the APsaA, the Academy, now the American Academy of Psychoanalysis and Psychodynamic Psychiatry, has a current membership of around 550.

51. Masserman, *Psychiatric Odyssey* (n. 50), p. 185.

52. According to Masserman, a member of both the APsaA and the rival American Academy of Psychoanalysis and a key figure in the conversations with the American Board of Psychiatry and Neurology, the APsaA's "deliberate intent" in proposing an APsaA-controlled subspecialty board was "to bolster its threatened stranglehold on psychoanalytic training and practice by extending its control to the proposed subspecialty board in psychoanalysis." The APsaA's vision of the board included the assumption among most of its members that they would receive "automatic certification merely on the basis of membership in the Association and without examination by an unbiased Board as to their actual competence in either psychoanalysis or the parent specialties of psychiatry and medicine" (Masserman, *Psychiatric Odyssey* [n. 50], p. 190). The prospect of a subspecialty board not controlled by the APsaA and therefore capable of becoming "less friendly" to the APsaA in the future was utterly anathema to it.

lytic technique. The links between medicalization and classical psychoanalytic theory and technique are not my concern here, but it is
reasonable to suggest that the kind of psychoanalysis that gained expression in the pages of *JAPA* in the 1950s, 1960s, and 1970s reflected
the continuing need to make psychoanalysis something Freud never
intended it to be: A psychiatric subspecialty grounded in exacting
procedure, a psychiatric subspecialty in search of its own medical-like
instrument. Whatever the underlying reasons for the linkage, the historical reality is clear enough: *JAPA*'s commitment to the APsaA's
vision of psychoanalysis rendered it indifferent, if not antagonistic,
to arguably progressive theoretical departures, such as Heinz Kohut's
psychoanalytic self psychology, which appeared on the scene in the
mid-1970s. Kohut, a past president of the American Psychoanalytic
Association, sought to disseminate his increasingly post-Freudian vision of psychoanalysis only in the pages of the *International Journal
of Psycho-Analysis.*[53] None of the foundational papers delineating his
"psychoanalytic self psychology" was, to my knowledge, submitted
to *JAPA*. Nor was Kohut alone in his well-considered skepticism about
gaining a constructive hearing in the pages of the official journal of
American psychoanalysis. Prominent psychoanalytic theorists who,
into the early 1980s, had to content themselves with publication in
the field's burgeoning part-journals include representatives of other
influential viewpoints, among them interpersonal psychoanalysis, feminist psychoanalysis, and Kleinian psychoanalysis.

On March 1, 1985, four psychologist plaintiffs, with the support
of the Psychoanalysis Division of the American Psychological Association established six years earlier, filed a class-action lawsuit on
behalf of several thousand psychologist-psychoanalysts against the
American Psychoanalytic Association, two of the APsaA's member
societies, and, secondarily, against the International Psychoanalytical
Association. The suit, legally framed as a violation of the Sherman
Antitrust Act of 1890, alleged "that the American [Psychoanalytic

---

53. Arnold Goldberg, personal communication. I hasten to add that Kohut's important methodological paper, "Introspection, Empathy, and Psychoanalysis," which a
later generation would view as a preamble to psychoanalytic self psychology, *was*
published in *JAPA*. See Heinz Kohut, "Introspection, Empathy, and Psychoanalysis:
An Examination of the Relationship Between Mode of Observation and Theory,"
JAPA, 7:459–483, 1959.

Association] had illegally conspired to restrain and monopolize the training of psychoanalysts and the delivery of psychoanalytic services to the public, and that this had deprived qualified psychologists of proper access to this way of earning a livelihood."[54] Following a series of legal setbacks, the APsaA accepted settlement terms in the spring of 1989 that conceded the force of the suit and finally opened the doors of APsaA training institutes to qualified nonmedical practitioners. And, beginning in the mid-1980s, *JAPA* underwent a political-cum-editorial repositioning with the express goal of becoming a forum for the "theoretical pluralism" that was fast becoming a fact of professional life. To this end, it espoused a rhetoric of inclusiveness and became newly receptive to contributions by representatives of all psychoanalytic schools of thought.

Fueled by the four-year lawsuit with the psychologist-psychoanalysts, the rhetoric of inclusiveness translated into practice—but only to a limited extent. *JAPA* did indeed widen its purview and accept contributions by analysts who thought and worked outside the ego-psychological paradigm most congenial to its editors, its editorial board, and the majority of its APsaA-member readers. Well and good. But the journal's new practice of inclusiveness, an a posteriori response to the political clout of psychologist-psychoanalysts and the institutional entrenchment of emergent, postclassical psychoanalytic perspectives, is belied both by the historical circumstances attendant to *JAPA*'s establishment and the political role it played in the life of the profession for more than three decades. As with the *Psychoanalytic Quarterly*, so with *JAPA*. A well-intended policy of editorial ecumenicism can lighten but not erase stigmata that bear the impress of decades of institutional history. Contemporary journal editors, however broad-minded in their pursuit of inclusiveness, cannot control who decides to submit papers for publication in their journals in the first place. Liberal editorial policy, that is, cannot ensure the diversity in top-drawer submissions that is a precondition of diversity in published content. Nor can editors and editorial boards control the historically shaped composition of their journals' respective subscriberships. With respect to these latter two considerations, the *Quarterly* and *JAPA* continue to be part-journals that serve, and are *primarily* read by, a skewed segment of the professional community.

54. Wallerstein, *Lay Analysis* (n. 14), p. 136.

During my two decades as managing director of The Analytic Press, I received anecdotal evidence of this skewing at many of the non-APsaA conferences attended by TAP. I have not conducted survey research, but my impression is that most members of the Psychoanalysis Division of the American Psychological Association (who outnumber members of the APsaA), the International Association of Relational Psychoanalysis and Psychotherapy, and the International Association of Psychoanalytic Self Psychology tend neither to read nor even to care about the *Psychoanalytic Quarterly* or *JAPA*. I do know that many of these analysts—especially the older generation for whom the lawsuit of 1985 remains alive in memory—continue to express bitter feelings toward *JAPA* and its parent organization. In the professional lives of American psychoanalysts, journal-reading habits no less than book-buying proclivities are shaped by particular institutional allegiances and theoretical affiliations. The kinds of journals to which analysts subscribe, no less than the kinds of books they buy, suggest that the will to inclusiveness, belatedly mobilized, cannot reverse a fractionation sustained by the narcissism of not-so-small professional differences that has become institutionally entrenched. *Umbra historiae praesentia infuscat.* Psychoanalytic publishing has become an impossible profession because contemporary psychoanalysts, like the rest of us, are political animals for whom the shadow of history darkens the present.

Chapter 4

Psychoanalytic Journals and the Road to Fractionation: II. The Turn to Pluralism

Prima facie the world is a pluralism; as we find it, its unity seems to be that of any collection; and our higher thinking consists chiefly of an effort to redeem it from that first crude form.[1]

Historically grounded fractionation gains expression in the very concepts that journal editors invoke to counter this state of affairs and to resurrect a vision of their field able to encompass its disparate fragments. Journals such as *JAPA* and *Psychoanalytic Quarterly* now accept the reality of theoretical pluralism and take it as a warrant to publish articles by analysts who espouse disparate theories of mentation, development, psychopathology, and therapeutic action. Since the 1980s, diversity has been the watchword of their faith.[2]

"The Editor's job," wrote Theodore Shapiro on assuming *JAPA*'s editorship in 1984, "is to protect us from poor presentations of ideas—not ideas themselves." Three years into his editorship, Shapiro acknowledged that *JAPA* readers had recently "become accustomed to

1. William James, "Preface," in *The Will to Believe and Other Essays* (NY: Longmans, Green, 1897), p. viii.

2. By which I mean the watchword of their faith as journal editors. As theorists, these same analysts tend to be ambivalent about pluralism, and they have contributed their own thoughtful commentaries about its grounds, its desirability, and the way or ways to overcome it. See, for example, Arnold D. Richards, "The Future of Psychoanalysis: The Past, Present, and Future of Psychoanalytic Theory," *Psychoanal. Quart.*, 59:347–369, 1990; David Tuckett, "Theoretical Pluralism and the Construction of Psychoanalytic Knowledge," in Joseph Sandler, Robert Michels, & Peter Fonagy, eds., *Changing Ideas in a Changing World: The Revolution in Psychoanalysis. Essays in Honour of Arnold Cooper* (London: Karnac Books, 2000), pp. 237–248; and Henry F. Smith, "Obstacles to Integration: Another Look at Why We Talk Past Each Other," *Psychoanal. Psychol.*, 18:485–514, 2001.

terms such as self psychology, empathy, hermeneutics, and narratives," which was no different than the obligation to "become accustomed to new technologies and new ways of understanding." And then, alluding more directly to theoretical pluralism, Shapiro opined that "Even within analysis 'not-so-complementary explanations' abound. We may now be said to variously espouse ego psychology, self psychology, separation-individuation, and object-relations psychology. Many say that these are simply viewpoints, but too often they seem to be alternative explanations."[3] Arnold Richards, who succeeded Shapiro as *JAPA*'s editor in 1997, made the accommodation of pluralism an overarching imperative. Throughout his tenure, he periodically lauded *JAPA*'s participation in the APsaA's "efforts to move from policies of exclusion to a greater inclusivity," and his final statement as editor was an encomium to JAPA's "new diversity of approach."[4]

The Psychoanalytic Quarterly's acceptance of pluralism blossomed under the editorship of Owen Renik in 1993 and has continued with the current editor, Henry Smith.[5] On assuming the *Quarterly*'s editorship in 2002, Smith noted that the journal's traditional editorial goals of encouraging and publishing "the best papers available from all psychoanalytic perspectives, adult and child, in North America and abroad" remained firmly in place; they had, however, been "updated for the contemporary psychoanalytic climate." Immediately thereafter, he instituted a new section of the *Quarterly* devoted to the presentation

3. Theodore Shapiro, "Editor's Introduction," *JAPA*, 32:1–2, 1984, quoted at p. 2; "Editor's Introductory Remarks," *JAPA*, 35:299–301, 1987, quoted at p. 300; "Editorial: Our Changing Science," *JAPA*, 37:3–6, 1989, quoted at p. 4.

4. For example, Arnold Richards, "Politics and Paradigms," *JAPA*, 46:357–360, 1998; "*JAPA* on the Cutting Edge," *JAPA*, 49-5-8, 2001, quoted at p. 8; and "*JAPA*: Ten Years," *JAPA*, 41:1115–1118, 2003, quoted at p. 1117.

5. See, e.g., Owen Renik, "Editor's Introduction," *Psychoanal. Quart.*, 70:1–2, 2001: "Perhaps we do not need a consensus concerning the goals of clinical analysis. Our heterogeneity may be, at least for the present, useful to the development of psychoanalytic understanding" (p. 1). Cf. Renik, "Standards and Standardization," *JAPA*, 51S:43–55, 2003, where he discusses the "dangerous myth" of a "nonpartisan standard of psychoanalytic excellence." "Because our various conceptions of psychoanalytic excellence, deriving as they do from our individual assumptions about psychoanalysis, are often incompatible," he remarks, "much of the formulation and maintenance of psychoanalytic standards is inherently political" (p. 44).

of clinical material of varying lengths and formats, one purpose of which was to enable readers to "explore systematically, within the *Quarterly*'s pages, how different analysts from a variety of perspectives develop hypotheses, and how they evaluate them." This philosophy gained expression in a special 2003 issue on the relationship of theory and practice. The issue, initially conceived by Sander Abend, exemplified Smith's belief "that only as we develop a capacity to study the work of others more dispassionately can we begin to determine what separates 'us' from 'them,' and what might lead toward a degree of reconciliation."[6]

Such liberalization of editorial policy attests to the tacit acceptance of pluralism as an acceptable state of affairs for psychoanalysis, at least for the foreseeable future. In reading and thinking about different theories and technical preferences, journal subscribers are implicitly encouraged to embrace pluralism as some kind of epistemic antidote to the reality of disparate psychoanalytic communities with equally disparate theories of mentation, development, psychopathology, and therapeutic action. Liberalized editorial policy is ipso facto a good thing, but it has had very little impact on the fractionation of the field. And this is hardly surprising. For the new editorial mandate amounts to little more than a willingness to publish, and thereby to juxtapose, contributions by proponents of one or another psychoanalytic school of thought. And, in truth, a strategy of juxtaposition and *proto-dialogue* among proponents of these theories is really all that psychoanalytic journals can offer. Why is this the case? It is because the very concept of theoretical pluralism as used by psychoanalysts is linguistically muddled and epistemologically incoherent and allows nothing more.

Consider the expression *theoretical pluralism*. Linguistically, it conveys the sense that the pluralism in question is only theoretical, i.e., that it operates only in the realm of theory, not in the realm of practice. Yet, the pluralism of which analysts speak is embedded in the real-world activities (both clinical and organizational) of different communities of analysts. So in theoretical pluralism the word

6. H. F. Smith, "Introduction," *Psychoanal. Quart.*, 71:1–3, 2002, quoted at pp. 1–2; "Editor's Note," *Psychoanal. Quart.*, 71:545–547, 2002, quoted at p. 546; "Editor's Introduction: Theory and Practice: Intimate Partnership or False Connection," *Psychoanal. Quart.*, 72:1–12, 2003, quoted at p. 11.

"theoretical" is a misplaced adjective. It makes better sense, semantically, to speak of a "plurality of theories." But this banal phrase lacks the scientistic panache of theoretical pluralism. It sounds better to say that one's discipline embraces theoretical pluralism than to say that it consists of a plurality of rival theories.

The universe of pluralisms is broad and tends to be partitioned along disciplinary lines. Political scientists trace pluralism back to the concept of toleration in early modern Europe and to the British political parties through which toleration gained expression. They equate the modern concept, variously, with an interest-group theory of politics, multiculturalism, and diversity as a political value.[7] Among American sociologists, the concept of pluralism, which arose in reaction to the dominant ethos of assimilationism, was formulated in the 1920s but only gained popularity after World War II. According to Berbrier, the paired concepts (viz., assimilationism and pluralism) are "antithetical master-frames" that guide social discourse about race, ethnicity, and various minority groups. Within the sociology of religion, the notion of "religious pluralism" has posed a discrete set of historical, ethnographic, and empirical questions, with scholars paying special attention to the relationship of what is now termed the "new religious pluralism" to traditional religious diversity of American life and gauging the impact of this pluralism on religious participation.[8]

Philosophers have traditionally invoked notions of óntological pluralism (the idea that there are many "real" things) and epistemic pluralism (the idea that there are many kinds of knowledge and/or ways of knowing). Historians, social scientists, and more recently, psychiatrists,

7. The political science literature on pluralism is vast, but for helpful orientations, see John Gunnell, "The Genealogy of American Pluralism: From Madison to Behavioralism," *Int. Pol. Sci. Rev.*, 17:253–265, 1996 and Giovanni Sartori, "Understanding Pluralism," *J. Democracy*, 8:58–69, 1997. Sartori is especially persuasive on the impoverishment of the concept that followed its explosion into prominence in the 1960s, when "it quickly became a noble and ennobling word with little if any substance" (p. 61).

8. David W. Machacek, "The Problem of Pluralism," *Soc. Rel.*, 64:145–161, 2003; Mark Chaves & Philip S. Gorski, "Religious Pluralism and Religious Participation," *Ann. Rev. Sociol.*, 27:261–281, 2001; Mitch Berbrier, "Assimilationism and Pluralism as Cultural Tools," *Soc. Forum*, 19:29–61, 2004. The original racialist philosophy of cultural pluralism was propounded by Horace Kallen in *Culture and Democracy in the United States* (NY: Boni & Liveright, 1924).

have made extensive use of the notion of explanatory pluralism.[9] The philosopher of science Sandra Mitchell, who explores scientific explanations of complex behavior, has invoked notions of competitive pluralism, compatible pluralism, and integrative pluralism in considering the relations among theories in biology and the social sciences.[10]

In the history of science, there are countless examples of operational and explanatory pluralism of one kind or another. But in science "theoretical pluralism," as psychoanalysts use the term, is not a conceptual resting point that can be theoretically grounded. The only way to ground such pluralism is to embrace a Feyerabendian view of science as "an endless questioning of fundamentals which one associates with pre-Socratic natural physiology: nothing is taken as given, everything can reasonably be denied or affirmed." It is a vision of science that deems it undesirable that scientists should ever reach consensus about anything, a view in which "anything goes."[11] In normal science, *tolerance* of a plurality of grand, paradigm-like theories—which is what "theoretical pluralism" actually denotes—is a temporary way-station

9. On the use of pluralism in philosophy, see Scott L. Pratt, "The Experience of Pluralism," *J. Spec. Phil.,* 21:106–114, 2007 and the references cited therein. On recent conceptions of explanatory pluralism in history and the social sciences, see Jeroen Van Bouwel & Erik Weber, "A Pragmatist Defense of Non-Relativistic Explanatory Pluralism in History and Social Science," *Hist. Theory,* 47:168–182, 2008 and Caterina Marchionni, "Explanatory Pluralism and Complementarity: From Autonomy to Integration," *Phil. Soc. Sci.,* 38:314–333, 2008. On explanatory pluralism in psychiatry, see S. Nassir Ghaemi, *The Concepts of Psychiatry: A Pluralistic Approach to the Mind and Mental Illness* (Baltimore: Johns Hopkins University Press, 2003), especially pp. 3–22, 283–287, 299–308 and Kenneth S. Kendler, "Toward a Philosophical Structure for Psychiatry," *Am. J. Psychiatry,* 162:433–440. I return to these various meanings of pluralism at pp. 245–250, below.

10. Sandra D. Mitchell, Lorraine Daston, Gerd Gigerenzer, et al., "The Whys and Hows of Interdisciplinarity," in Peter Weingart, Sandra D. Mitchell, Peter J. Richerson, et al., *Human by Nature: Between Biology and the Social Sciences* (Mahwah, NJ: Erlbaum, 1997), pp. 103–156. I am citing a section of this chapter written by Sandra Mitchell (pp. 114–125).

11. See Paul Feyerabend, *Against Method* (NY: Schocken, 1978), and the lucid summary of Feyerabend's position in Larry Lauden, *Science and Values: The Aims of Science and Their Role in Scientific Debate* (Berkeley: University of California Press, 1984), p. 20, from which the quoted passage is taken.

in the early history of sciences-in-the-making.[12] We would be in bad shape if medical progress had frozen in the mid-nineteenth century with competing allopathic and homeopathic theories of treatment,[13] so that mainstream internists of the present day could only stay current by embracing the "plurality" of insights—and the incommensurable

12. Of course, analysts, leading TAP authors among them, who espouse the viewpoint that psychoanalysis is a subspecies of interpretive hermeneutics will reject the very attempt to criticize the field's "theoretical pluralism" from the standpoint of normal science. But the theoretical vision of psychoanalysis as hermeneutics is one vision among many and, as such, underscores the very point I am making. The fact that a subcommunity of analysts regards psychoanalysis as a hermeneutic discipline exempt from the strictures of empirical scientific inquiry only underscores the fragmentation of the field. If the hermeneutic vision of analysis emerged triumphant from debates growing out of theoretical pluralism, then the field might achieve disciplinary coherence on its own nonscientific terms. But this vision has not so triumphed, and powerful critiques of psychoanalytic hermeneutics have run hand in hand with the elaboration of the hermeneuticist position. See especially Michael Sherwood's *The Logic Explanation in Psychoanalysis* (NY: Academic Press, 1969); Adolf Grünbaum, *The Foundations of Psychoanalysis: A Philosophical Critique* (Berkeley: University of California Press, 1984); Marshall Edelson, *Psychoanalysis: A Theory in Crisis* (Chicago: University of Chicago Press, 1988); and Adolf Grünbaum, *Validation in the Clinical Theory of Psychoanalysis: A Study in the Philosophy of Psychoanalysis* (Madison, CT: IUP, 1993). Grünbaum remains outspoken in his vision of psychoanalysis as science. In "The Hermeneutic Versus the Scientific Conception of Psychoanalysis" (1999), he characterizes the psychoanalytic hermeneutists as "buying absolution for psychoanalytic motivational hypotheses from the criteria of validation that are applied to causal hypotheses in the empirical sciences. In short they want to escape critical accountability." The paper is reprinted in Jon Mills, ed., *Psychoanalysis at the Limit: Epistemology, Mind, and the Question of Science* (Albany, NY: SUNY Press, 2004), pp. 139–160, quoted at p. 146. See also Adolf Grünbaum, "Is Sigmund Freud's Psychoanalytic Edifice Relevant to the 21st Century?" *Psychoanal. Psychol.*, 23:257–284, 2006 at pp. 277–279.

13. "Allopathic" and "homeopathic" were terms coined by Samuel Hahnemann, the founder of homeopathic medicine, to differentiate ordinary medical practice (which employed drugs that produced effects different from the effects caused by the disease) from homeopathy (which followed the principle of *similia similibus curantur*, according to which cure followed the use of minute quantities of drugs that produced a similar albeit artificial form of the disease itself). Hahnemann elaborated the twin principles of the curative action of similars and the effectiveness of minute doses of drugs (since in illness, he held, the body is enormously more sensitive to drugs than in health) in his *Organon of the Homeopathic Art* (1810), the bible of nineteenth-century homeopathy. Excellent brief accounts of Hahnemann and homeopathy are provided by Lester King, *The Medical World of the Eighteenth Century* (NY: Krieger, 1971 [1958]), chap. 6, and Joseph F. Kett, *The Formation of the American Medical Profession: The Role of Institutions, 1780–1860* (New Haven: Yale University Press, 1968), chap. 5.

languages through which these insights were conveyed—of an official "Journal of Allopathic Medicine" and an official "Journal of Homeopathic Medicine."[14]

We would be no better off if the spirited debate of the late 1880s between phagocytotic (cellular) and humoral theories of immunity—each of which laid claim to an important aspect of the "truth"—had culminated in a benign theoretical pluralism, so that immunologists from the 1890s on could only stay abreast of their emerging specialty by gleaning insights from a "Journal of Cellular Immunity" and a rival "Journal of Serum Therapy," each of which retained its own community of principled, impassioned advocates. The fact that the editors of each journal, in a well-intended spirit of ecumenicism, might welcome contributions by members of the opposite camp, even encourage dialogue among them, would not alter the fact that immunology had not advanced to the status of normal science in which an emergent paradigm, grounded in replicable research findings and shared clinical experience, subsumed the insights of both camps in a consensually agreed-upon language acceptable to everyone who claimed to be an immunologist.[15]

14. Historically, the AMA's efforts to regulate its members' contacts (as to fee-splitting, consultation, and teaching) with homeopaths, which is remarkably anticipatory of the APsaA's efforts prior to the 1985 lawsuit to regulate its members' involvement with the training and clinical practice of lay analysts, gave way to changes in both allopathic and homeopathic practice that, from the 1880s on, "tended to dissolve differences and provide for more peaceful coexistence." By the end of the nineteenth century, homeopathy's dominant liberal wing had embraced bacteriology, microscopy, and serum therapy, in recognition of which the AMA revised its Code of Ethics in 1903 to allow consultation between M.D.s and homeopaths. Indeed, in 1903 the AMA went a step further and elected to admit to membership homeopaths and eclectics willing to relinquish further use of their respective sectarian designations. As a result, "by 1904 the medical profession became unified in a broader orthodoxy." See John S. Haller, Jr., *American Medicine in Transition, 1840–1910* (Urbana: University of Illinois Press, 1981), quoted at p. 266 and John S. Haller, Jr., *The History of American Homeopathy: The Academic Years, 1820–1935* (NY: Haworth, 2005), pp. 272–275. I recur to the normalizing of homeopathy and other varieties of alternative medicine in the late nineteenth and early twentieth centuries in chap. 9, pp. 287–290.

15. In immunology, the critical research that advanced the field beyond "theoretical pluralism" was conducted by Emil von Behring and Shibasaburo Kitasato who, working with Robert Koch, introduced the antitoxin concept in "The Establishment of Diphtheria Immunity and Tetanus Immunity in Animals" (1890). "The discovery

The same may be said of the clashing viewpoints about neural transmission that also peaked during the late 1880s. We would be ill-served by a theoretical pluralism that kept in place (and in play) the reticular theory of neural transmission of Camillo Golgi and Joseph von Gerlach and the synaptic theory of Santiago Ramón y Cajal.[16] Modern neuroscientists and neurologists do not rely on a "Journal of Synaptic Transmission" for their basic understanding of the nervous system but then turn to a rival "Journal of Reticular Transmission" to understand nerve cell communication within dense neural networks or at synaptic gap junctions where pre- and postsynaptic membranes are so close that chemical synaptic transmission yields to direct electrical stimulation of one cell by another.[17]

---

of antibody in 1890 reinforced the trend toward humoral theories of immunity, and interest in cellular immunity declined, not to be seriously revived for almost 60 years. After the work of Emil von Behring and his collaborators, the central theoretical questions in immunology involved how antibodies were formed and how they acquire and exercise their specificity" (Arthur M. Silverstein, *A History of Immunology* [San Diego, CA: Academic Press, 1989], pp. 94–95; see also Ernst Bäumler, *Paul Ehrlich: Scientist for Life*, trans. Grant Edwards [NY: Holmes & Meier, 1984], pp. 52–53) and Harry F. Dowling, *Fighting Infection: Conquests of the Twentieth Century* [Cambridge: Harvard University Press, 1977], pp. 36ff). The fact that the paradigm of mainstream immunology revived the concept of phagocytosis 60 years after the debate of the 1880s alters my point not a single iota. The fact is that, at any single point in the post-1890 history of immunology, immunologists consensually agreed upon a single explanatory paradigm, a single language, and a primary set of questions to be addressed through theories formulated within that paradigm. This is normal science in action.

16. Beginning in 1888, Cajal's evidence of the *correctness* of the synaptic theory came in the form of data that *refuted* reticularist claims. Evidence of synaptic space from the axon side of the neuron came from microscopic data of synaptic boutons, the slight swelling in termination of axons where they conform to the dendrites of the neighboring neuron. Evidence of synaptic space from the dendritic side came from microscopic studies of receptor cells (rods and cones) of the mammalian retina, with axons of rods and cones conforming to the shape of the dendrites of the underlying cells. For Cajal's own graceful account of these discoveries, see his autobiography, initially published in 1937 by the American Philosophical Society and now available as Santiago Ramón y Cajal, *Recollections of My Life*, trans. E. H. Craigie (Cambridge: MIT Press, 1966), Part II, chaps. 4 & 5. For a recent review of these discoveries, see Richard Rapport, *Nerve Endings: The Discovery of the Synapse* (NY: Norton, 2005), especially pp. 122–126.

17. Rapport, *Nerve Endings* (n. 16), pp. 181–183.

Nor do we expect modern epidemiologists to ally themselves, respectively, with one or another school of thought—serology, vaccination, or environmentalism—despite the coexistence of all three currents of epidemic explanation and management during the polio epidemic of 1916 and the influenza pandemic of 1918. Twenty-first-century epidemiologists do not subscribe to separate journals of serological epidemiology, bacteriological epidemiology, vaccinational epidemiology, and environmental epidemiology—each proffering a self-contained, holistic perspective on the causes of, and responses to, modern epidemics—in order to keep up to date in their specialty.

By contrast, from early in the twentieth century American psychoanalytic journal editors set out on the path of fractionation and then turned in the 1980s to what they awkwardly termed "theoretical pluralism." Their various journals, taken together, never cohered conceptually; they never circumscribed and ordered the subject matter of a discipline in the manner of normal science. Rather they contented themselves with the status of part-journals, and their very existence helped deflect psychoanalysis from the progressive evolution of conventional disciplines.

This is a strong claim, and it may be rightly asked, "What makes psychoanalytic journals different from the journals of other professional literatures? After all, any discipline—certainly any scientific field—gives rise to a succession of journals. New journals are continuously coming into being; they often split off from old journals and give expression to new interests, new agendas, new priorities. Different journals in any field have different theoretical, applied, and/or clinical emphases. Are psychoanalytic journals really all that different in this regard?"

I would argue that they are, especially if we understand psychoanalysis as a clinical specialty, viz., as a particular therapeutic modality that belongs to a particular community of professionally trained and licensed health care providers. The uniqueness of psychoanalytic journals emerges all the more clearly through historical comparison with the development of medical specialty journals in the late nineteenth and early twentieth centuries. In all the medical specialties, psychiatry included, journal publishing has been progressive in character. It has an evolutionary trajectory that charts the delineation of the specialty: Its purview, its interrelationships with other specialties, and its domain of specialist procedures, techniques, and interventional modalities.

When medical specialists come together and form journals, they are intent on elevating their specialty by providing a venue for scientific and clinical advance. Specialty journals help create a shared language with which to address an agreed-upon range of professional problems and issues on the basis of a shared, if continuously evolving, knowledge base. To be sure, specific assumptions, explanations, and interventions are always subject to dispute, qualification, and, over time, repudiation. But such disputes do not as a rule focus on those epistemic and operational a prioris that are foundational to the specialty as it has come into existence through praxis. Specialty journals catalyze professional consolidation by providing a forum for professional communication among clinicians whose self-identification falls back on just those paradigmatic assumptions that brought them together in the first place.

In American medicine, it has long been a matter of groups of specialists petitioning the trustees of their parent organization, the American Medical Association, and requesting sponsorship of a new journal as an official mouthpiece of specialty interests. The founders of the *Archives of Internal Medicine* so petitioned in 1907, seeking a journal comparable to Germany's *Zeitschrift für Klinische Medizin* and *Deutsches Archiv für Klinische Medizin*. Pediatricians followed three years later, invoking the model of Germany's *Jahrbuch für Kinderheilkunde* and appealing to "the amount of creditable work in pediatrics which is being done in this country, and of the abundance of material which is available for such a publication as we propose." The surgeons petitioned in 1910 and again in 1911, but the AMA refused sponsorship owing to the fact that "two excellent publications devoted to the surgical specialty" (*Annals of Surgery* and *Surgery, Gynecology and Obstetrics*) were already available to American surgeons; the AMA gave way only in 1912, and it was only in 1920 that the *Archives of Surgery* finally saw the light of day.[18]

18. N. C. Gilberg, "Archives of Internal Medicine," in Morris Fishbein, ed., *A History of the American Medical Association, 1847–1947* (Philadelphia: Saunders, 1947), pp. 1111–1117, quoted at p. 1111; Clifford G. Grulee, "The American Journal of Diseases of Children," in Fishbein, pp. 1118–1128, quoted at p. 1118; Waltman Walters & Morris Fishbein, "Archives of Surgery," in Fishbein, pp. 1154–1159, quoted at p. 1159.

Historically, specialists sought AMA sponsorship in order to upgrade both their knowledge base and their professional image in the face of privately owned publications of uneven quality and questionable advertising practices. In the early twentieth century, advertisements of patent medicines and popular devices, widespread in the professional literature, were anathema to many orthodox practitioners.[19] The founders of the *Archives of Internal Medicine* were explicit in calling for a journal with "no abstracts, no editorials and no advertising." The founders of the *Archives of Otolaryngology*, for their part, petitioned the AMA in 1923 for "a new journal, not privately owned, in which advertising should be strictly ethical according to the standards of the American Medical Association, in which only council accepted products could be advertised and the pages of which should be open especially to research reports."[20]

Certainly, new journals split off from old ones, but others consolidate preexisting and overlapping publications. In 1928, for example, the editors of the original *Archives of Ophthalmology* (founded in 1879), the *American Journal of Ophthalmology*, and the *Ophthalmic Yearbook*, along with representatives of the various ophthalmologic societies and academies, petitioned the AMA trustees for a new journal that would integrate these three publications. The new *Archives of Ophthalmology* was the result.[21] Within an emerging specialty, rival journals will on occasion align themselves with previously established specialties. In late nineteenth-century Germany, for example, the two major neurology journals, Wilhelm Griesinger's *Archiv für Psychiatrie und Nervenkrankheiten* (*Archives of Psychiatry and Neuropsychiatry*), founded in 1868, and Wilhelm Erb's *Deutsche Zeitschrift für*

---

19. See, for example, James Harvey Young, *The Toadstool Millionaires: A Social History of Patent Medicine in America Before Federal Regulation* (Princeton: Princeton University Press, 1962); James Harvey Young, *The Medical Messiahs: A Social History of Health Quackery in Twentieth-Century America* (Princeton: Princeton University Press, 1967); and Sarah Stage, *Female Complaints: Lydia Pinkham and the Business of Women's Medicine* (NY: Norton, 1979).

20. Gilbert, "Archives of Internal Medicine," p. 1113; George M. Coates, "Archives of Otolaryngology," in Fishbein, *History of AMA* (n. 18) pp. 1129–1137, quoted at p. 1129.

21. Frances H. Adler, "Archives of Ophthalmology," in Fishbein, *History of AMA* (n. 18), pp. 1160–1163.

Nervenheilkunde (*German Journal of the Neurosciences*), founded in 1891, appealed to those for whom neurology was wed to psychiatry and internal medicine, respectively. In France and England, on the other hand, neurology had institutional moorings that rendered the specialty autonomous from the outset and yielded journals that were not ancillary to other specialties.[22]

Whether specialty journals grow by fission or fusion, and whether they initially align themselves with one or another established specialty, commonality of interest resides in the specialty per se, not in a particular theoretical rendering of the subject matter of the specialty. Contra psychoanalysis, new journals tend not to arise from fractious differences *within* the specialty. Often they grow out of rivalries *between* disciplines or specialties that lay claim to the same biomedical, clinical, or administrative issues and to the same patient population. Consider, by way of exemplification, the history of psychiatric journals in the United States, which for a time intersects with the history of psychoanalytic journals.

Amariah Brigham, Superintendent of the New York State Lunatic Asylum at Utica, founded and funded the *American Journal of Insanity* in 1844 as a vehicle for the practical concerns of 13 institutional psychiatrists ("alienists") who devoted themselves to managing America's asylums. Articles on hospital construction and administration had pride of place in early volumes, with essays on medical jurisprudence—what we would now term forensic psychiatry—not far behind. Brigham died in 1849, but his brief tenure as editor sufficed to establish *AJI* as the Utica Asylum's house organ. Its editorship passed successively to the next three Asylum superintendents and, beginning with its second editor, T. Romeyn Beck, journal-related

---

22. In France, the *Société de Neurologie de Paris* was founded by Charcot's students in 1899 and immediately aligned itself with the *Revue Neurologique*, which they had established six years earlier "under Charcot's own watchful and approving eye." In Britain, the National Hospital for the Paralyzed and Epileptic, founded in 1860, "officially institutionalized neurological studies and treatments." The Neurological Society of London was founded in 1885 and made *Brain* its official publication two years later. See Christopher G. Goetz, Teresa A. Chmura, & Douglas Lanska, "Part I: The History of 19th Century Neurology and the American Neurological Association," *Ann. Neurol.*, 53(suppl):2–26, 2003, cited at pp. 19–20.

expenses were borne by the Asylum, which was renamed the Utica State Hospital in the late 1880s. This arrangement lasted until 1894, when New York State's newly formed Lunacy Commission attempted to wrest control of the journal from the Utica facility. Rather than hand the journal over to the state, Utica's managers sold it to the American Medico-Psychological Association, forerunner of the American Psychiatric Association, for the sum of $944.50.[23]

Mid-nineteenth-century American alienists were not the only professionals preoccupied with the construction and management of facilities for the incarcerated. No sooner was *AJI* founded than a rift developed between the asylum superintendents and prison reformers, who founded the *Journal of Prison Discipline and Philanthropy* a year later to convey their own viewpoint.[24] As American "psychiatry" broadened its purview in the second half of the nineteenth century, the field bifurcated into public asylum practice on the one hand and private practice with a bourgeois clientele on the other. The emergence of neurology as a specialty in the decade following the Civil War fed into this divide.

Through the end of the Civil War, American physicians treating nervous diseases, whether generalists or alienists operating outside asylum walls, lacked any mouthpiece at all. Only in 1867, when William Hammond launched his *Quarterly Journal of Psychological Medicine and Medical Jurisprudence*, did a publication devoted to mind and nervous system come into being. It was very much a one-man affair, largely given to Hammond's own musings on, inter alia, the nature of instinct, infantile paralysis, medical electricity, and insanity. Three years later Hammond renamed his publication the *Journal of Psychological Medicine: A Quarterly Review of Diseases of the Nervous System* and made a more systematic effort to provide meaningful coverage of clinical issues in neurology and psychiatry. The

---

23. The centennial issue of the *American Journal of Psychiatry* (volume 100, issue 6, 1944) includes informative articles on the early and later history of the journal and its editors. See Richard H. Hutchings, "The First Four Editors," *Am. J. Psychiatry*, 100:29–40, 1944; William Rush Dunton, "The Second Half-Century of the Journal," *Am. J. Psychiatry*, 100:41–44, 1944; and William Rush Dunton, "The American Journal of Psychiatry, 1844–1944," *Am. J. Psychiatry*, 100:45–60, 1944.

24. The journal was launched by the Pennsylvania Prison Society in 1845 as the *Pennsylvania Journal of Prison Discipline and Philanthropy*. It ceased publication in 1919, but a successor journal, *The Prison Journal*, followed in 1921 and remains in publication today.

journal lapsed in 1872, only to be revived in 1874 as *The Psychological and Medico-Legal Journal*, recentered now on Hammond's heightened involvement in the relationship between law and medicine. Following the founding of the American Neurological Association in June, 1875, Hammond abandoned this final version of his journal, which mercifully resisted any further efforts at reincarnation.[25]

Only with the founding of the *Journal of Nervous and Mental Disease* in 1874 was the *American Journal of Insanity*, ever preoccupied with asylum construction and management, given an effective counterpoise. *JNMD* too was a private publication, the brainchild of the Chicago neurologist J. S. Jewell. But, far more effectively than Hammond's journal, it gave voice to psychological medicine in both its neurological and psychotherapeutic dimensions.[26] Jewell launched his quarterly journal, published for its first two years as the *Chicago Journal of Nervous and Mental Diseases*, with this statement of editorial policy:

> The field we have especially in view is that of the nervous system, not only on its own account, but that of its relations to the body of which it forms a part, on the one hand, and to the mind and mental action on the other. It is not our intention to produce a Journal of Insanity. We leave this more restricted and important field to other journals. In our own country it is already occupied, with marked ability, by the *American Journal of Insanity*, now so well known, not alone to the profession in the United States but also in other lands. But we do not expect to neglect mental disease, clearly arising out of organic nervous disease.[27]

25. My account of Hammond's ill-fated journal ventures follows Bonnie Ellen Blustein, *Preserve Your Love for Science: Life of William A. Hammond, American Neurologist* (Cambridge: Cambridge University Press, 1991), pp. 107–111.

26. In Britain, the same divide occurred but the sequence was reversed. Forbes Winslow's *Journal of Psychological Medicine and Mental Pathology*, which espoused a broad medical approach to mental disorder, was launched in 1848 and was of little interest to asylum superintendents. The latter countered in 1855 with their own *Asylum Journal*, the official organ of Britain's Association of Medical Officers of Asylums and Hospitals for the Insane. See Michael Shepherd, "Psychiatric Journals and the Evolution of Psychological Medicine," in W. F. Bynum, et al., *Medical Journals and Medical Knowledge: Historical Essays* (London: Routledge, 1992), pp. 188–206, cited at pp. 191–194.

27. J. S. Jewell, "Editorials," *J. Nerv. Ment. Dis.*, 1:70–73, 224–225, 1874, quoted at p. 225.

The journal, in the manner of most start-up publications, interpreted its mandate flexibly. From the outset, it allocated pages to pragmatic psychiatric concerns, especially asylum reform and criminal responsibility of the insane.[28] But the preponderance of contributions, under its founding editor and especially under his four successors, fell within clinical neurology, neuropathology, and neuroanatomy.[29] Jewell was far more ecumenical in outlook than his immediate successor William Morton, who rededicated *JNMD* to "the teaching of neurological art and science, and the diffusing of a knowledge of diseases of the brain and other nervous systems."[30] Under Morton and the next three editors, the number of psychiatric contributions published in the journal declined precipitously. Between 1894 and 1901, by Eugene Brody's reckoning, only 13% of *JNMD* pages were devoted to psychiatry.[31] In 1895, 20 years after the journal's founding, the *JNMD*

28. Even more eclectic than Jewell's *JNMD* was Charles Hughes's *Alienist and Neurologist*, which Hughes launched out of his native St. Louis in 1880 and continuously published until 1920. A Civil War surgeon who superintended the Missouri State Lunatic Asylum from 1866 to 1872 and served thereafter as expert witness in a number of well-publicized medico-legal trials, Hughes intended his journal to serve as a forum for new, largely biological psychiatric theories being developed in Europe and America. In point of fact, the journal was a hodgepodge of second- and third-tier articles on all manner of topics, biological, neurological, psychiatric, and forensic. It was commercially successful, though, with a circulation comprising nearly 2,000 American and European physicians and one hundred hospitals and libraries. I located these circulation figures at www.aneuroa.org/html/c19html/007-journals.htm.

29. In 1974, Eugene Brody actually analyzed the content of *JNMD* articles during Jewell's tenure (1874–1881) and reported the following: 70 papers (totaling 869 pages) dealt with clinical neurology and neuropathology; 54 papers (totaling 771 pages) dealt with anatomy and physiology; and 41 papers (totaling 692 pages) dealt with "unequivocally psychiatric matters." Eugene B. Brody, "The Journal of Nervous and Mental Disease: The First 100 Years – I. 1874–1881. Setting the Course, the Editorship of J. S. Jewell, M.D.," *J. Nerv. Ment. Dis.*, 158:6–17, 1974, cited at pp. 8–9.

30. William J. Morton, "Editorial Department," *J. Nerv. Ment. Dis.*, 9:196–203, 1882, quoted at p. 197.

31. Eugene B. Brody, "The Journal of Nervous and Mental Disease: The First 100 Years – II. 1882–1901. Persisting Psychiatric Themes and the Renewed Dominance of Neurology," *J. Nerv. Ment. Dis.*, 159:1–11, 1974, cited at pp. 2–3. The four editors who followed J. S. Jewell (William Morton, Bernard Sachs, Charles H. Brown, and William Hammond) never expressly commented on the decline in psychiatric publications in *JNMD*, but Brody surmises that Jewell's successors probably "did

became the official organ of the American Neurological Association, the New York Neurological Society, and the Philadelphia Neurological Society.

And then Smith Ely Jelliffe purchased the journal in 1902, and it underwent a sea change coordinate with Jelliffe's own professional interests and commitments. A polymath who preceded medical training with a degree in engineering and followed it with a degree in classics and a Ph.D. in botany, Jelliffe wrote book reviews for *JNMD* as early as 1896 and joined the editorial staff no later than 1899, when he assumed responsibility for abstracting articles from the French, German, and British literatures for inclusion in the journal's regular "Periscope" section. As new owner of *JNMD*, Jelliffe retained his previous title of "Managing Editor," but within three years he set the journal on a new editorial course—away from organicism, neuropathology, and clinical neurology and toward psychotherapy and psychoanalysis. The process began around 1905, when Jelliffe began writing about the psychotherapy of Paul Dubois and citing psychoanalytic references, and was well along by 1910, by which time "psychoanalytic ideas had lodged themselves firmly in Jelliffe's mind."[32] The new priorities, Jelliffe later recollected, antagonized "older organic neurologists" who, from 1910 on, were especially irritated by his inclusion of psychoanalytic material in *JNMD*.[33]

---

not regard the prevalent psychiatric writing of the period as sufficiently informative to warrant the allocation of Journal space which might be more profitably devoted to other subjects." A second factor, adduced en passant, is that the "accelerating tempo of neuroanatomical and neuropathological research" simply crowded out the psychiatric literature. But Brody ignores the more obvious and salient factor: That Jewell's successors were simply more neurologically committed than Jewell and took the *JNMD*'s editorial raison d'etre, as articulated by Jewell in the first issue, more literally than Jewell himself.

32. Lawrence S. Kubie, "The Journal of Nervous and Mental Disease: The First 100 Years – III. 1902–1944. Smith Ely Jelliffe," *J. Nerv. Ment. Dis.*, 159:77–80, 1974; James B. Mackie, "The Journal of Nervous and Mental Disease: The First 100 Years – III. 1902–1944. The 42-Year Editorship of Smith Ely Jelliffe, a Practical Mystic," *J. Nerv. Ment. Dis.*, 159: 305–317, 1974, quoted at p. 306.

33. Smith Ely Jelliffe, "The Editor Himself and His Adopted Child," *J. Nerv. Ment. Dis.*, 89:545–589, 1939, cited at pp. 572–573.

Matters came to a head in the decade to follow, as Jelliffe's commitment to psychoanalysis became increasingly repugnant to leaders of American neurology and psychiatry alike. Neurologists, in particular, were greatly in need of publication outlets following World War I, and Jelliffe's preference for psychodynamic material made it all the harder for them (and for nonanalytic psychiatrists as well) to find space within *JNMD*.

Jelliffe, it was held, had supplanted the organicist raison d'etre of the *JNMD* with a personal agenda at some distance from mainstream neurology and neuropsychiatry. So claimed the hundred or so psychiatrists and neurologists, mobilized by the Chicago neurologist Hugh T. Patrick, who petitioned the Board of Trustees of the American Medical Association in 1919 to sponsor a new journal to replace *JNMD* as the official organ of the American Neurological Association. The AMA-sponsored *Archives of Neurology and Psychiatry*, whose first issue appeared within the year, was the outcome of the petition.[34] A final fissure occurred four decades later, when the AMA divided its specialty grouping on neurology and psychiatry into separate sections devoted to each specialty. The *Archives of Neurology and Psychiatry*, which had been preponderantly neurological in tone, tenor, and content since its inception, followed suit. In 1959, it bifur-

---

34. John Burnham provides an excellent review and discussion of the course of events that eventuated in the founding of the *Archives of Neurology and Psychiatry* in 1919. Incidentally, as Burnham perceptively observes, opposition to psychoanalysis, however important, was not the only issue that mobilized sentiment in support of a new journal. Two other salient factors were Jelliffe's refusal to screen journal advertising in a manner consonant with reform sensibilities—his refusal, in particular, to reject ads from makers of proprietary medicines—and *JNMD*'s sloppy editing and delayed publication of the American Neurological Association's annual *Transactions*. See Burnham, "The Founding of the *Archives of Neurology and Psychiatry*; or, What Was Wrong with the *Journal of Nervous and Mental Disease?*" *J. Hist. Med. Allied Sci*, 36:310–324, 1981. Though not focusing on the founding of journals per se, two excellent articles by Bonnie Blustein explore the collateral issue of the late nineteenth-century professionalization of American neurologists. It was the neurologists' scientific aspirations and claim to specialty status that fueled their unhappiness with the psychoanalytic content of Jelliffe's *JNMD* and insistence on a new journal. See Bonnie Ellen Blustein, "New York Neurologists and the Specialization of American Medicine," *Bull. Hist. Med.*, 53:170–183, 1979 and "'A Hollow Square of Psychological Science': American Neurologists and Psychiatrists in Conflict," in Andrew Scull, ed., *Madhouses, Mad-Doctors, and Madmen: The Social History of Psychiatry in the Victorian Era* (Philadelphia: University of Pennsylvania Press, 1981), pp. 241–270.

cated into separate *Archives of Neurology* and *Archives of General Psychiatry*, the latter under the editorship of Roy R. Grinker, Sr.[35]

But this coming and going of new journals never impugned the disciplinary integrity of psychiatry or neurology—or, for that matter, of the hybrid neuropsychiatry. Rather, the new journals conveyed with increasing specificity the clinical trajectory of specialties-in-the-making. In the process, they charted the historical evolution of the clinical domains and treatment modalities specific to one or another specialty. The succession of journals within specialties such as neurology and psychiatry underscores the fact that these domains and these modalities are not static over time; they evolve, and the successive journals in which specialists record their theories and practices chart the evolution. But this *kind* of evolution operates within a normal science framework and is progressive within that framework. Medical specialties do not at any historical moment yield a plethora of journals that, in a manner analogous to psychoanalysis, proffer different paradigmatic readings of the anatomy, physiology, and pathology that are foundational to the specialty as a domain of inquiry and locus of clinical intervention. To access alternate readings of early development and its vicissitudes commensurate with the paradigms of, say, Lacanian, Kleinian, and self-psychological psychoanalysis, one must leave medicine altogether and compare a medical specialty with an alternative healing modality: Internal medicine with Christian Science; pharmacotherapy with homeopathy; orthopedics with chiropractic.

Psychoanalytic journals that, beginning in the 1930s, aspired to represent the field, to become its publishing mainstream, never succeeded in charting the evolution of anything approaching a psychiatric subspecialty. For all the talk of method, of procedure, of technique, and (eventually) of "analyzing instruments" in their pages, *Psychoanalytic Quarterly* and *JAPA* failed to make the field what Freud never

---

35. Grinker, who had served on the editorial board of the *Archives of Neurology and Psychiatry* since 1951, envisioned the new *Archives of General Psychiatry* as an eclectic, multidisciplinary journal that would "extend and expand the psychiatric field, without sacrificing the dynamic point of view or alienating or losing its teachers." But an ecumenicism that encompassed biomedical and social science perspectives on psychiatric disorder was ipso facto repugnant to many analysts, and Grinker's policy, as he recollected, "created almost insurmountable resistances and brought us into a struggle for greater eclecticism." See Roy R. Grinker, Sr., *Fifty Years in Psychiatry: A Living History* (Springfield, IL: Thomas, 1979), pp. 29–32, quoted at p. 31.

intended it to be: A handmaiden to medicine. The psychiatric journals were successful in the very manner that the psychoanalytic journals were not. They charted the evolution of a specialty that was increasingly absorbed into a medical paradigm.[36] The "psychiatry" encapsulated in the *American Journal of Insanity* is not the "psychiatry" that gained expression in the *Journal of Nervous and Mental Disease*. Nor is the "psychiatry" promulgated by the *JNMD* from 1874 to 1901 the "psychiatry" re-visioned by Jelliffe after he purchased the journal in 1902. Nor, finally, is the psychiatry epitomized by Jelliffe's *JNMD* the "psychiatry" of the *Archives of General Psychiatry*. We discern here a normalizing trajectory that leads us to what we have come to understand—for better and for worse—as contemporary American psychiatry.[37] American psychoanalytic journals, whose respective constituencies were from the start set off from one another

36. And within that medical paradigm, I submit, psychoanalysis was quietly absorbed into the "biopsychosocial model" that emerged in American psychiatry in the 1980s, struggled to gain traction, and shortly gave way to psychopharmacology as psychiatry's superordinate model and interventional modality. The foundational statements of the biopsychosocial model are George L. Engel, "The Need for a New Medical Model: A Challenge for Biomedicine," *Science*, 196:129–136, 1977 and "The Clinical Application of the Biopsychosocial Model," *Am. J. Psychiatry*, 137:535–544, 1980. The best historical study of the biopsychosocial model, especially its role in medical, residency, and fellowship training at Engel's own University of Rochester Medical School, is Theodore M. Brown's "The Historical and Conceptual Foundations of the Rochester Biopsychosocial Model" (2000), www.human-nature.com/free-associations/engel2.html, of which only an abbreviated version has been published as "George Engel and Rochester's Biopsychosocial Tradition: Historical and Developmental Perspectives," in Richard Frankel, Timothy Quill, & Susan McDaniel, eds., *The Biopsychosocial Approach: Past, Present, Future* (Rochester: University of Rochester Press, 2003), pp. 199–219. The expressly psychoanalytic assumptions that inform the biopsychosocial model are examined by Graeme J. Taylor, "Mind-Body-Environment: George Engel's Psychoanalytic Approach to Psychosomatic Medicine," *Aust. N. Zeal. J. Psychiatry*, 36:449–457, 2002. I look at Engel's biopsychosocial model from a different perspective at pp. 297–300, below.

37. In Britain, the trajectory has been straight and narrow. *The British Journal of Psychiatry* has continuously given pride of place to biological explanations and interventions for psychiatric disorders since its founding as the *Asylum Journal* in 1853. Throughout the entire twentieth century, the journal published only five psychoanalytic papers. See Joanna Moncrieff & M. J. Crawford, "British Psychiatry in the 20th Century—Observtions from a Psychiatric Journal," *Soc. Sci. Med.*, 53:349–356, 2001.

by basic differences in self-understanding, take us only to contemporary fractionation.

The growth of the psychoanalytic journals in the United States bears little relationship to the growth of medical specialty literature. There are, however, interesting areas of convergence between psychoanalytic journals and early twentieth-century journals in clinical and consulting psychology. No less than psychoanalysis, clinical psychology generated journals that were the brainchildren of gifted individuals— individuals who, if not the field's founders (in the sense that Freud founded psychoanalysis) were among its pioneering spirits. In 1906, Morton Prince, himself a psychiatrist, founded the *Journal of Abnormal Psychology* to give expression to his belief that the same learning principles that governed normal development could explain, and provide remedial strategies for addressing, behavioral disorders and psychoneuroses. Lightning Witmer's *Psychological Clinic*, founded a year later, was the first American journal in what would evolve into child psychology. It grew out of Witmer's psychoeducational clinic at the University of Pennsylvania where, beginning in 1896, he developed and applied a clinical method of evaluating and treating Philadelphia-area schoolchildren with mental disabilities and behavioral disorders. By the 1920s, the germinal focus of "clinical psychology," the diagnostic testing and mental evaluation of retarded and learning-disordered schoolchildren, no longer organized the field. Increasingly, clinical psychology bifurcated into professional communities guided by psychoanalysis on the one hand and behaviorism on the other, with Gestalt formulations challenging both camps. "Representatives of each school," the historian John Reisman wryly observes, "seldom neglected an opportunity to criticize their rivals."[38]

But the rival schools of American clinical psychology never fractionated in the manner of psychoanalytic schools. Until the late 1940s, clinical psychology was simply too small and too fragile in its claims of professionalism to allow fragmentation. The clinical psychologists' parent organization, the American Psychological Association (APA), which only incorporated in 1925, dedicated itself to the advancement

38. John M. Reisman, *A History of Clinical Psychology*, 2nd ed. (NY: Brunner-Routledge, 1991 [1980]), p. 163.

of psychology as a science, not as a profession. It was therefore disinclined to intercede on behalf of its small contingent of proto-clinicians. And the proto-clinicians themselves were too weak to organize on their own behalf. At the APA convention of 1917, a group of disgruntled clinical psychologists felt their interests would be better served by their own organization and formed the American Association of Clinical Psychologists (AACP). But the experiment was short-lived and the AACP dissolved itself in 1919, at which time the APA pledged to represent clinical psychologist interests more effectively.

In the quarter century to follow, the APA's promise of involvement proved empty, and clinical psychologists had neither the numbers nor the professional clout to sustain a robust program of journal publication, much less a program that elaborated competing visions of their field in the manner of psychoanalysis. When in 1924 the APA's Section on Clinical Psychology undertook its own formulation of standards, it fell back, unsurprisingly, on generic criteria: A Ph.D. from an approved graduate school followed by four years of professional training that included one year of supervised work in psychological diagnosis. In 1935, the APA's Committee on Standards of Training simply recommended that anyone laying claim to the title "clinical psychologist" should have a Ph.D. and a year of supervised experience. It was left to Columbia University's department of psychology to develop a three-year graduate curriculum for clinical psychology in 1936; this program of graduate work and internship was endorsed by the Boston Society of Clinical Psychologists a year later. That same year, the APA's own Clinical Section disbanded out of frustration. It was replaced by the self-standing American Association of Applied Psychology (AAAP), which sought to provide a home for APA members identified, respectively, with consulting psychology, clinical psychology, educational psychology, and industrial psychology. Pride of place went to the self-designated consultants, and the AAAP began publishing its *Journal of Consulting Psychology* in 1938.[39]

This early effort at organizational reform notwithstanding, the fact remains that, throughout the 1930s, consulting psychologists, whether or not they donned the "clinical" appellation, continued to be identi-

---

39. Reisman, *History of Clinical Psychology* (n. 38), pp. 160–161, 210–214.

fied in the marketplace as professional examiners whose diagnostic testing skills were foundational to their work. As late as 1931, there were only some 800 psychologists in the U.S. engaged in this kind of broadly clinical work, and the work itself—diagnostic testing and interviewing in psychiatric clinics and state hospitals; diagnostic testing and remedial teaching in child guidance clinics and university-affiliated psychoeducational clinics—rarely included psychotherapy. Small wonder that, as the decade progressed, clinical psychologists became increasingly exasperated with a parent organization that made only token efforts to establish clinical training standards and a medical establishment that consigned them to second-class status in the clinics and bureaus in which they found employment.[40]

The medical psychoanalysts, all of whom were licensed physicians, showed no such exasperation, even if Freud did. Rather, from the 1920s on, they basked in an empowering Freudian glow. A decade later, they had become leading members of a "Cinderella" medical specialty (viz., psychiatry) that had stepped into the spotlight, and their psychoanalytic bona fides derived from a training system that bore the imprimatur of Freud himself.[41] The requisite Freudian lineage meant that psychoanalysis could not *become* scientific in the way that clinical psychology and psychiatry *aspired* to be. Ipso facto, psycho-

40. See, for example, S. H. Tulchin, "The Psychologist," *Am. J. Orthopsy.*, 1:39–47, 1930 and J. E. W. Wallin, "Shall We Continue to Train Clinical Psychologists for Second String Jobs?" *Psychol. Clinic*, 18:242–245, 1929/30.

41. It was Karl Menninger who enshrined psychoanalytic psychiatry as a "Cinderella specialty" throughout the 30s. See, for example, Karl Menninger, "Polysurgery and Polysurgical Addiction," *Psychoanal. Quart.*, 3:173–199, 1934 and "The Cinderella of Medicine," *NY State J. Med.*, 38:922–925, 1938, reprinted in *A Psychiatrist's World: The Selected Papers of Karl Menninger, M.D.*, ed. B. H. Hall (NY: Viking, 1959), pp. 646–654. In the latter paper, Menninger credited Thomas Salmon with the first use of the Cinderella figure in relation to psychiatry, though he provided no source (p. 651). Even Menninger's grandiloquence was surpassed by that of Edward Strecker, clinical director of the Institute of Pennsylvania Hospital, who predicted in 1940 that "the day will come when [the] Cinderella of Medicine, Psychiatry, will be honored as a wise and bountiful Social Princess dispensing a largess of culture." See Strecker, *Beyond the Clinical Frontiers: A Psychiatrist Views Crowd Behavior* (NY: Norton, 1940), p. 199. For a general discussion of the manner in which American psychoanalysts and psychoanalytic psychiatrists of this time sought to subordinate aspects of medicosurgical treatment planning to psychoanalytic-psychiatric assessment, see Paul E. Stepansky, *Freud, Surgery, and the Surgeons* (Hillsdale, NJ: Analytic Press, 1999), pp. 172–186.

analysis *was* scientific, but only in the idiomatic manner Freud deemed it so ab initio. Keeping in mind the definitional, nomenclatural, and institutional prerogatives reserved for Freud the founder, psychoanalytic journals were never in a position to delineate a disciplinary domain that, over time, would be filled in by a community of like-minded clinical investigators and practitioners. A clinical discipline—say a discipline whose domain encompasses the investigation of unconscious mental processes and their transpositions and transformations as revealed by the method of free association—would have allowed the possibility of employing that method to generate clinical findings and theoretical understandings different from, even antithetical to, those of the method's inventor.

This was not the case with psychoanalysis, whose early journals and serials were vehicles for conveying the founder's approval and disapproval and the followers' filial allegiance. Maneuvering Jung into the contours of conventional discipleship, Freud selected him to be the editor of the first such publication, the *Jahrbuch für psychoanalytische und psychopathologische Forschungen*. This relegation of authority, so Freud believed, provided an institutional roadblock to disaffiliation: ". . . he [Jung] can hardly back out, he could not repudiate his past even if he wanted to, and the *Jahrbuch*, of which he is the editor, is a tie not to be broken," Freud intoned to Karl Abraham in the summer of 1908. And then, as if to underscore the obvious, he added, "I hope that he has no intention of breaking the tie with me."[42]

But psychoanalytic journals, to a disheartening degree, have always been about the forging of alliances, the exacting of fealty, and, yes, the breaking of ties. "Things are quite lively in Vienna: I am being treated very tenderly," a mollified Freud wrote Jung in the spring of 1910. "The two editors [Alfred Adler and Wilhelm Stekel] have agreed to discuss each number of the *Zentralblatt* [*für Psychoanalyse*] with me in advance, and I am to have full veto power." And in the fall of 1911, anticipating the maiden issue of a third psychoanalytic journal, the *Imago*, Freud admonished Jung that "the *Jahrbuch*, the

42. Freud to Abraham, July 23, 1908, in Hilda C. Abraham & Ernst L. Freud, eds., *A Psycho-Analytic Dialogue: The Letters of Sigmund Freud and Karl Abraham, 1907–1926*, trans. B. Marsh & H. C. Abraham (NY: Basic Books, 1965), p. 47.

Zentralblatt and the newborn child [*Imago*] must not be three individuals, but three organs of a single biological unit."[43]

The metaphor is apt. Early psychoanalytic journals were intended to be appendages of a common torso, with Freud literally and figuratively at the head. These journals were never intended to disseminate findings—including disparate findings—that followed from the application of a common method of inquiry. Rather, they were united ab initio around a body of doctrine, with Freud's approval the ultimate source of legitimation. This project failed. As demonstrations of fealty fell short, as political loyalties wore thin, as the burdens of discipleship became oppressive, as what Freud's early followers construed as the psychoanalytic method led to theories and therapies not in conformity with Freud's own, Freud played out the politics of affiliation and disaffiliation through journals. In his correspondence, the journals are continuously absorbed into tactical maneuvering on behalf of the cause. The *Zentralblatt* was part of Freud's "war plan" for countering Jung's tendentious use of the *Jahrbuch*; later it became the prize out of which the treasonous Stekel had "cheated" him.[44] The *Imago* was yet "another of the possessions" that Freud hoped to pass on to Jung. The founding of the *International Zeitschrift für ärztliche Psychoanalyse* in the fall of 1912 sealed Freud's effort to "lure[d] away as many as we could from Stekel." And finally, the *Jahrbuch* was "booty" that Jung sought to wrest from Freud.[45]

The so-called dissidents played their part in this fissiparous dynamic by retaining, at least for a time, the "psychoanalytic" appellation. They

43. Freud to Jung, May 2, 1910; Freud to Jung, November 16, 1911, in William McGuire, ed., *The Freud-Jung Letters*, trans. R. Manheim & R. F. C. Hull (Princeton: Princeton University Press, 1974), pp. 315, 464.

44. Freud to Ferenczi, October 2, 1912, in Eva Brabant et al., *Correspondence of Sigmund Freud and Sándor Ferenczi*, vol. 1, trans. P. T. Hoffer (Cambridge: Harvard University Press, 1993), p. 409; Freud to Jones, November 13, 1913; Freud to Jones, November 22, 1913, in R. Andrew Paskauskas, ed., *The Complete Correspondence of Sigmund Freud and Ernest Jones, 1908–1939* (Cambridge: Harvard University Press, 1993), pp. 238, 242. On Freud's view of Stekel's editorial intentions apropos the *Zentralblatt* as treasonous, see Freud to Ferenczi, October 27, 1912, in *Correspondence of Freud and Ferenczi*, vol. 1, p. 418.

45. Freud to Jung, November 14, 1911, in *Freud-Jung Letters*, (n. 43), p. 463; Freud to Ferenczi, November 14, 1912, in *Correspondence of Freud and Ferenczi*, vol. 1 (n. 44), p. 431.

created their own journals, which, to return to Freud's metaphor, became new analytic "biological units" existing alongside one another. Over time, these units developed organs of their own in the form of additional publications, training establishments, clinics, conferences, and membership organizations. In the United States, the outcome would be the fractionation of the field into a plurality of paradigmatically discordant psychoanalyses.[46]

In both Europe and America, many newly launched journals served the particular psychoanalytic vision of yet other founders. We see this development over the course of the past century in journals aligned with Adler, Jung, Stekel, Reich, Horney, Reik, Klein, Menninger, Lacan, Sullivan, Spotnitz, and Kohut, among others. Nor, within the realm of psychoanalytic journals, is there even a consensus on what fealty to Freud's *own* vision of psychoanalysis consists of. A return to Freud; loyalty to Freud; loyalty to Freud's method of inquiry; loyalty to the Freudian method as refracted through the lens of contemporary epistemology; loyalty to Freudian theories as amended by contemporary developmental and psychotherapy research—journals aligned with Kleinian analysis, Lacanian analysis, ego-psychological analysis, relational psychoanalysis, psychoanalytic self psychology, conflict-psychology psychoanalysis, infancy research, and neuropsychoanalysis all make one or more such claims. This is because each such journal, no less than the institute or society out of which it arose, provides anchorage for a particular kind of psychoanalytic identity that, for institutional, economic, and "social defensive" reasons, has come to be conflated with a psychoanalytic identity writ large.[47] Psychoana-

---

46. "Freud alone is not responsible for this history [of fractionation], of course, though by insisting on his proprietorship of psychoanalysis and establishing shibboleths of orthodoxy he set it firmly on this path." Kenneth Eisold, "The Profession of Psychoanalysis: Past Failure and Future Possibilities," *Contemp. Psychoanal.*, 39:557–582, 2003, quoted at pp. 561–562.

47. For discerning consideration of why such conflation became an institutional and personal necessity, see the various articles of Kenneth Eisold, especially "The Intolerance of Diversity in Psychoanalytic Institutes," *Int. J. Psycho-Anal.*, 75:785–800, 1994; "The Splitting of the New York Psychoanalytic Society and the Construction of Psychoanalytic Authority," *Int. J. Psycho-Anal.*, 79:871–885, 1998; and "The Profession of Psychoanalysis" (n. 46). See also César Garza-Guerrero, "'The Crisis in Psychoanalysis': What Crisis Are We Talking About," *Int. J. Psycho-Anal.*, 83:57–83, 2002, especially p. 78: "Our professional identity is chiefly defined by the schools, groups, societies and the international organization to which we belong."

lytic identity has always had this metonymic quality: The particular part-identity established (and internalized) in the course of one's training, and exemplified by the journals aligned with that training, comes to stand for the psychoanalytic whole.

Throughout the psychoanalytic world, and especially in the United States and Western Europe, the metonymic dynamic has fueled the creation of part-journals wed to one or another normative claim about what loyalty to Freud, a return to Freud, or a contemporary appreciation of Freud looks like. For most of the twentieth century, journal editors, self-professed Freudians no less than dissidents, embraced an exclusionism more typical of religious sects than scientific communities. In 1932, the infant *Psychoanalytic Quarterly* clung to Freud's words with a tenacity that unsettled no less a luminary than Franz Alexander. He was concerned the *Quarterly* would reject his submitted paper, he wrote Jelliffe, because one member of the editorial board found it "extremely revolutionary and in contradiction to certain 'sentences' in one of Freud's early writings."[48]

But the seeds that sprouted into the luxuriant garden of American psychoanalytic journals, as we initially observed, were not indigenous to America. They were imported from Vienna. The incipient fractionation of the field was apparent to the publisher of the first psychoanalytic serial, the *Jahrbuch für psychoanalytische und psychopathologische Forschungen*, in the statement of editorial intent that began the very first issue of 1909. "[Franz] Deuticke telephoned me yesterday," Freud wrote Jung, the *Jahrbuch*'s editor. "He has doubts about one or two passages in your draft, and now I am reminded of them by his question marks in the manuscript. His first objection is that your [word] *ferner* [also, as well as] seems to create an opposition, or at least a dividing line between my school and the Zurich Clinic." And Freud continued:

> To tell the truth, I would rather you did not identify any particular school with me, because if you do I shall soon be obliged to confess that my pseudo-students or non-students are closer to me than my

48. Alexander to Jelliffe, May 6, 1932, cited in Nathan Hale, *The Rise and Crisis of Psychoanalysis in the United States* (NY: Oxford University Press, 1995), p. 120. Kenneth Eisold illuminates the historical context in which the "young professionals" within the New York Psychoanalytic Society—including those aligned with the *Psychoanalytic Quarterly*—sought to establish a rigidly orthodox hegemony at the expense of their more eclectic forebears during the 30s and early 40s. See Eisold, "Splitting of the New York Psychoanalytic Society" (n. 47).

students *sensu strictiori*. Also, I should not like to be held more directly responsible for the *work* of Stekel, Adler, Sadger, etc. than for my *influence* on you, Binswanger, Abraham, Maeder, etc.[49]

This remarkable testimony suggests the very opposite of what Freud intends: That psychoanalysis has always been schoolish in the manner of sects.[50] In America, the field has come to comprise many Freuds, many teachers, and endless varieties of pupilage. Now, early in the twenty-first century, despite well-intentioned efforts among analysts to achieve common ground, the field gives the appearance of a melee of brother bands who raise the same banner, claim the same high ground, make war among themselves, and then declare a truce. The truce is the state of "theoretical pluralism" that we touched on in the opening pages of this chapter and will explore more fully in the chapter to follow.

49. Freud to Jung, January 22, 1909, in *Freud-Jung Letters* (n. 42), pp. 200–201, emphasis in the original.

50. "The isolation and monastic nature (with all of its homogenizing regressive tendencies for primitive idealizations and paranoid anxieties) of the original circle of the Viennese master and his disciples sealed our fate: we have placed ourselves in charge of perpetuating this very same organizational and pseudo-educational structure, with a quasi-religious fidelity that is surprising in that it has not yet surprised us—we have ecumenically preserved it as ego-syntonic." Garza-Guerrero, "'Crisis in Psychoanalysis'" (n. 47), p. 78.

Chapter 5

Theoretical Pluralism and Its Discontents

There are very few psychoanalysts around these days, only Freudians, or Kleinians, or Lacanians, or self psychologists.[1]

Through the second half of the nineteenth century, the disturbing frequency of chloroform death led European surgeons to back away from the drug and revert to ether as the general anesthetic of choice in major operations.[2] Chloroform death remained a puzzle. What caused it? By the 1880s, European opinion converged on the drug's depressant action on the heart. But a vocal minority, led by Edward Lawrie, a British surgeon who joined the Indian Medical Service in 1872, continued to follow the dictates of the mid-century Scottish surgeon James Syme, according to whom chloroform endangered only respiration. The Hyderabad Chloroform Commission of 1888, funded by Lawrie's employer and benefactor, Nizam Mir Mahboob Ali Khan, ruler of the State of Hyderabad, set out to provide a definitive answer to this problem. In a scientific protocol impressive for its time, 128 fully grown pariah dogs were repeatedly administered chloroform in overdose. After cessation of breathing, each dog was revived by artificial respiration until the final test, at which point it was permitted to expire. The observational findings, to Lawrie's delight, "confirmed" his sense that chloroform death always occurred by failure of respiration, not by cardiac-related syncope.

1. Jay Greenberg, "The Analyst's Participation: A New Look," *JAPA*, 49:359–381, 2001, quoted at p. 361.

2. My account of the two Hyderabad Commissions and their sequelae follows Linda Stratmann, *Chloroform: The Quest for Oblivion* (Stroud: Sutton, 2003), pp. 201–217. See also A. H. B. Masson et al., "Edward Lawrie of the Hyderabad Chloroform Commission," *Brit. J. Anaes.*, 41:1002–1011, 1969.

The British medical establishment took note and was unimpressed. In response to the *Lancet*'s skepticism about Lawrie's findings, the Nizam funded a second chloroform commission at which the *Lancet*'s own representative would journey to India to repeat the experiment. And so in the fall of 1889 Thomas Lauder Brunton, an internationally recognized pharmacologist with a teaching appointment at London's St. Bartholomew's Hospital, set out for India to lead the second commission. Trained at Edinburgh in the most advanced experimental techniques of the time, Brunton began his career by investigating the action of digitalis and achieved professional acclaim for using the vasodilator amyl nitrate to treat angina pectoris. By the time of the second chloroform commission, he was well-published in cardiovascular and respiratory physiology and pathology.[3] He arrived with modern instrumentation—a sphygmograph, or blood pressure recording apparatus, modified to show pulse-beats as tracings on soot-blackened paper—to make doubly sure that the commission's findings would be free of bias. To the astonishment of the European medical establishment, the findings of the Second Hyderabad Chloroform Commission confirmed those of the first. In the case of each and every dog, Brunton reported, respiration had stopped before the heart. This finding was verified by the instrumentally recorded tracings. In an astonishing reversal of accepted wisdom, the second commission reported that chloroform-induced heart failure, to the extent it occurred, was not a danger but a safeguard that prevented further absorption of respiration-threatening chloroform. The full report that gave expression to these findings was published at the Nizam's expense in 1891.

The problem is that the findings of both commissions, we now know, were specious. In the four decades following James Young Simpson's introduction of chloroform in 1847, European and American surgeons had reported hundreds of cases in which chloroform-

3. On Brunton, see W. Bruce Fye, "T. Lauder Brunton and Amyl Nitrite: A Victorian Vasodilator," *Circ.*, 74:222–229, 1986 and Christopher Lawrence, "Physiological Apparatus in The Wellcome Museum. 2. The Dudgeon Sphygmograph and Its Descendants," *Med. Hist.*, 23:96–101, 1979. Thirteen years after he journeyed to India, in 1902, Brunton published a remarkable paper on the possible surgical treatment of mitral stenosis that outlined the technique for mitral commisurotomy developed in the late 1940s. See Harris B. Shumacker, *The Evolution of Cardiac Surgery* (Bloomington: Indiana University Press, 1992), pp. 31–34.

induced cardiac arrest occurred with stunning suddenness. In point of fact, chloroform *does* depress cardiac function; chloroform death *is* frequently a result of sudden cardiac arrest. How were the findings of both Hyderabad Commissions, scientifically credible in their time and place, ultimately falsified? It was a matter of pulling apart Lawrie's experimental design, reinterpreting the findings it generated, and making distinctions that were masked either by the design or by the inattentiveness of the experimenters.

Did none of the Indian dogs die of cardiac arrest? Well, in nine cases, animals did indeed expire in their sealed boxes after initial induction of chloroform. But these animals died before the experiment proper began, so their deaths were excluded from the experimental results; it was simply assumed these nine dogs died from failure of respiration. And what of the blood-pressure tracings that presumably sustained the Second Commission's findings? In 1890, Lawrie asked the Cambridge physiologists W. H. Gaskell and L. E. Shore to review the Second Commission's prized tracings; to Lawrie's chagrin, they found that the curves not only failed to sustain the Commission's findings but actually supported the opposite conclusion as to cardiac syncope. Gaskell and Shore then devised a series of ingenious cross-circulation experiments in which a single administration of chloroform reached the body and brain, respectively, of two connected dogs. This design, which enabled the effects of chloroform on the brain and heart to be studied separately, confirmed that chloroform directly affected the heart.

And then there was the disconfirming role of new evidence that invalidated the Hyderabad Commission's experimental assumptions about the unitary nature of chloroform-induced syncope, i.e., its assumptions about what exactly it was investigating. In 1891, the same year that Gaskell and Shore reinterpreted the Second Commission's blood-pressure tracings and performed their cross-circulation experiments, the Geneva surgeon Gustave Julliard differentiated between "primary syncope," which followed the initial inhalations of chloroform and was cardiac-induced, and "secondary syncope," which occurred during deeper anesthesia and was characterized by respiratory failure. A year later H. A. Hare and E. Q. Thornton of Jefferson Medical College in Philadelphia ascribed the Second Commission's failure to observe cardiac paralysis following injection of chloroform into the jugular veins to poor experimental method. And five years later, in 1897, the London Hospital physiologist Leonard Hill attested to the Commission's "ignorance of precise physiological methods" and seconded Julliard's distinction between primary and secondary syncope.

By 1897, then, a consensus had emerged as to the speciousness of the findings of both Hyderabad Commissions. In this same year, Freud abandoned his early seduction theory, viz., his belief that early childhood seductions—acts of sexual molestation or assault by mothers, fathers, brothers, nursemaids, nannies, and the like—were the necessary and sufficient cause of hysterical and obsessional neurotic symptoms in adulthood. Freud's belief in this theory was grounded in the verbal reports of his female patients. His skepticism and eventual repudiation of the theory was grounded in doubts about the veracity of these selfsame reports. Freud simply lost confidence in the theory and replaced it with another theory; he no longer believed it to be "true." In an oft-cited letter to his confidant Wilhelm Fliess of September 21, 1897, Freud adduced the "reasons for disbelief," a portion of which is given here:

> The continual disappointment in my efforts to bring a single analysis to a real conclusion; the running away of people who for a period of time had been most gripped [by analysis]; the absence of the complete successes on which I had counted; the possibility of explaining to myself the partial successes in other ways, in the usual fashion—this was the first group. Then the surprise that in all cases, the father, not excluding my own, had to be accused of being perverse—the realization of the unexpected frequency of hysteria, with precisely the same conditions prevailing in each, whereas surely such widespread perversions against children are not very probable. The [incidence] of perversion would have to be immeasurably more frequent than the [resulting] hysteria because the illness, after all, occurs only where there has been an accumulation of events and there is a contributory factor that weakens the defense. Then, third, the certain insight that there are no indications of reality in the unconscious, so that one cannot distinguish between truth and fiction that has been cathected with affect. . . . Fourth, the consideration that in the most deep-reaching psychosis the unconscious memory does not break through, so that the secret of childhood experiences is not disclosed even in the most confused delirium.[4]

4. Freud to Fliess, September 21, 1897, in Jeffrey Moussaieff Masson, trans. & ed., *The Complete Letters of Sigmund Freud to Wilhelm Fliess, 1887–1904* (Cambridge: Harvard University Press, 1985), pp. 164–165.

Do hysterical and obsessional patients bear the mark of premature sexual seductions and premature acts of sexual aggression, respectively, or do they suffer from ego-dystonic fantasies that gain expression in their various hysterical and obsessional-neurotic symptoms? Which is it, and on what basis do we make the determination? Freud abandoned one theory and adopted another because his personal musings culminated in disbelief. *He* could not bring a single analysis that incorporated the belief in literal seductions to what *he himself* thought to be a "real conclusion." Relying on the seduction hypothesis as his interpretive handle, *he* could not keep patients in treatment, much less achieve the degree of clinical success that *he himself* relied on. *He* could not accept the incidence of perversion that the seduction theory presupposed; *he* could not believe that quite so many fathers, his own included, had committed acts of rank perversity.

The third and fourth reasons given in Freud's letter are not merely self-referential but theoretically loaded in ways that simply cannot be scientifically unpacked. A theory is being repudiated on the basis of new permutations of the selfsame mindset that gave rise to the theory in the first place. It is, Freud believes, a matter of the nature of unconscious experience, which gives "no indications of reality" (reason 3) and does not yield up unconscious memories of actual events even in cases of "deep-reaching psychosis" (reason 4). The childhood etiology of neurosis, Freud declares, now directs him to "a theoretical understanding of repression and its interplay of forces." In place of unsolved problems and anomalies that cannot be brought within the explanatory purview of the seduction hypothesis, we are given inferences about unconscious experience that suggest a new line of theoretical inquiry. Freud retains his conviction that he has detected something unconscious, but the something is no longer a forgotten memory of actual abuse but a repressed fantasy of the same. Freud continues to place his trust in the finely tuned manner in which he hears his patients, in the receptiveness of what a later generation of analysts would term his "analyzing instrument." But for all the aforementioned reasons, he has come to hear differently.

In exploring the action of chloroform on the body, there was a universally accepted baseline, a ne plus ultra, of its poisoning effect: The death of the patient, usually within minutes of administration of the drug.[5] And the effect of chloroform induction—the circumstances attendant to this baseline (as to dosage, method of induction, initial and delayed reactions to induction, and the like)—could be clinically observed and experimentally recorded anywhere the drug was administered. Not so the repudiated seduction theory. In what I believe to be a prototypical example of psychoanalytic theory change, there is no *consensual* baseline of clinically salient "real conclusions" and expectant "complete successes" attendant to the clinical approach Freud is employing with the particular patients he is treating. Still less is there a consensually agreed on *method* that enables independent observers to confirm the extent to which the seduction hypothesis obviates the possibility of reaching such conclusions and successes. There are simply no public criteria for adjudging notions of clinical success and failure. A year earlier, in one of his published defenses of the seduction hypothesis, Freud wrote that the seduction hypothesis had been supported in some 18 cases of hysteria, in each of which he had been able "to discover this connection [between actual seduction and hysteria] in every single symptom, and, where the circumstances allowed, to confirm it by therapeutic success."[6] In 1896, we have therapeutic success (albeit where unspecified "circumstances" permit); in 1897 we have the absence of real conclusions and complete successes. What is the difference between the *therapeutic* success of 1896 and the elusive *complete* success of 1897? In point of fact, what do terms like "therapeutic success," "real conclusion," and "complete success" actually denote? Self-evidently, we are worlds removed from the kind of publicly scrutinized instrumental findings that eventuated in a widely accepted explanation of chloroform death.

5. In the universe of psychotherapy, only work with suicidal patients provides an analogous ne plus ultra: "Working with chronically suicidal patients was exciting, since it drew on my medical background as well as my psychotherapy training. Therapy turned on life-or-death issues. At the very least, I could determine the outcome: the patient would either be alive or dead." Joel Paris, *The Fall of an Icon: Psychoanalysis and Academic Psychiatry* (Toronto: University of Toronto Press, 2005), p. 146.

6. Sigmund Freud, "The Aetiology of Hysteria." In James Strachey ed., *Standard Edition of the Complete Psychological Works of Sigmund Freud*, 3:191–221 (London: Hogarth Press, 1962), quoted at p. 199.

To put the matter differently, we may say that there are no external or even intersubjective referents[7] for assessing the shift from the seduction hypothesis to the theory of fantasy-induced neurosogenesis as a *progressive* change from the standpoint of science or medicine or even of psychological caregiving. The replacement of one theory with another is theory change by fiat. Its justification is ex cathedra; it is a matter of what Freud the clinical observer of particular patients (not Freud the scientist) deems believable at a particular point in time. The shift in belief systems, seemingly *commonsensical*, is *only* common-sensical; it is a matter of what Freud chooses to infer or not to infer commonsensically from what his patients tell him. It does not convey a sense of progress because Freud's personal grounds of belief and disbelief cannot be scientifically unpacked.

These grounds can be explored psychologically and historically, to be sure. Following Jeffrey Masson, we can enlarge on the historical and biographical circumstances attendant to Freud's adoption of the seduction theory and offer historically grounded speculations about the psychological and adventitious reasons he relinquished it.[8] But there matters end. When all is said and done, we are left with two theories and no clinically or scientifically salient criteria for comparing them. That is, Freud's shift from the seduction theory to the theory of fantasy-induced neurosogenesis is not accompanied by any kind of data that allow us to compare and assess the clinical course of

7. In the language of the philosophy of science, there are no agreed-upon coherence conditions.

8. As to Freud's adoption of the seduction hypothesis, Masson records Freud's exposure, during his study trip to Paris in 1885, to a substantial French literature on the frequency of sexual abuse in early childhood and his attendance at Paul Brouardel's autopsies of physically, and presumably sexually, abused children. As to Freud's abandonment of the seduction hypothesis, Masson develops both a psychological explanation (the "suppression" of the seduction hypothesis and recourse to fantasy was necessary to preserve Freud's relationship to Wilhelm Fliess in the aftermath of Fliess's botched operation on Freud's patient Emma Eckstein) and an opportunistic one (the "suppression" of the seduction hypothesis and recourse to fantasy was an adventitious strategy of reconciliation with the German-speaking psychiatric establishment that had marginalized him on account of this hypothesis). See Jeffrey Moussaieff Masson, *The Assault on Truth: Freud's Suppression of the Seduction Theory* (NY: Farrar, Straus, and Giroux, 1984), pp. 14–54 on the historical context of Freud's adoption of the seduction hypothesis and pp. 55–144 on the psychological and opportunistic reasons for Freud's repudiation of the seduction hypothesis.

comparably "hysterical" or "obsessional neurotic" patients treated from the vantage point of the seduction theory on the one hand and the successor theory of fantasy-induced neurosogenesis on the other. We complete the process of theory change where we began it: With Freud's necessarily time-bound and impressionistic vision of real conclusions and complete successes.

As to chloroform poisoning, matters did not end with the consensus of 1897. More black boxes appeared; more black boxes were opened. Chloroform was indeed capable of inducing cardiac arrest, but what was the mechanism of its depressant action? In a classic paper of 1902, the Australian anesthetist Edward Embley argued that chloroform-induced cardiac arrest resulted from the drug's overstimulation of the vagal nerve center of the brain. A decade later, in laboratory work conducted between 1911 and 1913, London University College Hospital's A. G. Levy, working collaboratively with Thomas Lewis in a study of cardiac arrhythmias during anesthesia, picked up the chloroform-induced ventricular fibrillation that Embley had missed.[9] The latter, he argued, was the mechanism of cardiac arrest. Who was right and who was wrong? A new instrument, the electrocardiograph, provided the answer. This instrument had not been available to either man; it was a rarity in British laboratories in the period Levy conducted his studies and only reached Australia in 1912, a decade after Embley's paper. But subsequent electrocardiograph studies unequivocally bore out Levy's conclusion. The vagal nerve theory was wrong; the ventricular fibrillation theory was right. The latter marked a progressive advance in understanding the mechanism of chloroform-induced cardiac arrest and the fatalities attendant to it.

In the case of psychoanalytic theory change, one searches in vain for black boxes that can be opened up and whose contents can be subjected to scientifically, or even intersubjectively, meaningful scru-

9. On Embley, see Geoffrey Kay, "Embley, Edward Henry (1861–1924)," in *Australian Dictionary of Biography*, vol. 8 (Melbourne: Melbourne University Press, 1981), pp. 436–437. A. G. Levy's finding was reported in "The Relation Between Successive Responses of the Ventricle to Electric Stimuli and Ventricular Fibrillation," *J. Physiol.*, 49:54–66, 1914. For a discussion of Levy and his research, see W. Bruce Fye, "Ventricular Fibrillation and Defibrillation: Historical Perspectives with Emphasis on the Contributions of John MacWilliam, Carl Wiggers, and William Kouwenhoven," *Circ.*, 71:858–865, 1985, at p. 862 and P. M. E. Drury, "Anaesthesia in the 1920s," *Brit. J. Anaes.*, 80:96–103, 1998.

tiny. Absent an "analyzing instrument" that produces data open to public inspection, how do we go about collecting evidence that serves as an epistemic guarantor that the replacement of one theory with another is in fact progressive? Indeed, what do we even *mean* by progressive theory change in psychoanalysis? What are the consensually agreed-upon coherence conditions that anchor a unitary understanding of psychoanalytic progress? If we understand analytic progress teleologically as theory- and practice-related shifts that moved toward Freud's mature, final theories, then the shift from the seduction hypothesis to the theory of fantasy-driven neurosogenesis is unquestionably progressive. But if we frame progress outside the box encapsulated by Freud's historically contingent psychoanalysis, if we stipulate a different set of coherence conditions, then the question becomes more interesting and admits of dialogue and debate. If we look at the theory change from the standpoint of contemporary understandings of trauma, posttraumatic stress, and dissociation, for example, then its progressive character becomes arguable. If we look at it sociologically in terms of the documentable prevalence of childhood sexual abuse and its devastating clinical sequelae, then the progressive character of the change becomes arguable. If we look at it in terms of a societal commitment to child welfare and a collateral obligation to identify and incarcerate sexual offenders, then the progressive nature of the change becomes arguable.

Does the so-called "analyzing instrument" offer a way out of the morass? Is it simply a matter of "refining" and "purifying" the instrument so that the data it gathers will be consistent across the population of analysts who employ it? For Freud, writing in 1912, the analyst was the tool of the analytic method and as such was enjoined to "turn his own unconscious like a receptive organ towards the transmitting unconscious of the patient." Freud elaborated the simile in this manner:

> He must adjust himself to the patient as a telephone receiver is adjusted to the transmitting microphone. Just as the receiver converts back into soundwaves the electric oscillations in the telephone which were set up by sound waves, so the doctor's unconscious is able, from the derivatives of the unconscious which are communicated to him,

to reconstruct that unconscious, which has determined the patient's free associations.[10]

In the hands of Otto Isakower, a popular and controversial teacher at the New York Psychoanalytic Institute in the 1950s and 60s, and of his students, who taught and wrote a generation later, the analyzing instrument that emerged from Freud's simile signified the state of mind attendant to the deployment of Freud's psychoanalytic method. Isakower elaborated the concept of the analyzing instrument in a pedagogical context. Specifically, he sought to cultivate in his students a capacity for self-observation that would insinuate itself into the way they listened to their patients. The analyst's unconscious, drained of theoretical ideas and tuned to the unconscious of the patient, acquired the valence of Freud's "receptive organ"; it was tantamount to an instrument-like receiver.[11]

Beginning in 1980, several of Isakower's students returned to the analyzing instrument in order to underscore the interactive, reciprocal processes embedded in the expression. For Zvi Lothane, in particular, the analyzing instrument more properly denoted the coordinate states of mind of analyst and analysand—what he referred to as their "conjoint interpersonal team activity"—as the analyst listens with "evenly hovering attention" to the analysand's stream of free associations. When the analyst turns his unconscious to the unconscious of the patient in the manner of a receptive organ, he enters a dreamlike state of consciousness, fraught with visual imagery, that conduces to an understanding of the patient's unconscious meanings. In this interactive sense, the instrument signifies the mobilization of what Lothane terms "reciprocal free association." One may broaden the plane of contact between the patient's transmitting organ and the analyst's receptive organ, and so argue that the reciprocal illuminating of unconscious meanings pertains not only to verbal messages but to visual stimuli, movement patterns, and autonomic nervous system

10. Sigmund Freud, "Recommendations to Physicians Practicing Psycho-Analysis." In James Strachey, ed., *Standard Edition of the Complete Psychological Works of Sigmund Freud*, 12:109–120 (London: Hogarth Press, 1958), quoted at pp. 115–116.

11. Isakower's lectures on the analyzing instrument, along with contemporary commentaries, were finally gathered and published in the *Journal of Clinical Psychoanalysis*, vol. 1, 1992.

responses as well. In this manner the analyzing instrument becomes a "multichannel system" consisting of various sensory components.[12]

These writings underscore the analyzing instrument as a trope that subsumes—one might say condenses—the interpersonal and communicative skills (verbal and nonverbal) that subtend the ability to listen to another, to process what the other says (or intimates or communicates gesturally or denies), and to comment on what the other says (or intimates or communicates gesturally or denies) in analytically appropriate ways.[13] But if the analyzing instrument metonymically stands for the psychoanalytic method, how can it serve as an *instrumental* means of evaluating the method or the results of the method's deployment in any conventional scientific sense? Instruments, even the simplest of them, do more than attest to the method that *theorizes* their existence.

In the realm of medicine, instruments can be simple amplifiers of physiological processes, in which case they enlarge the physician's sensorium in a manner that aids evaluation and diagnosis. The stethoscope is one such amplifier; one can listen to lung and heart sounds with the naked ear, but the stethoscope, in amplifying what one hears, renders audible signs and symptoms of disease that elude the former. So mediate auscultation, which René Laënnec discovered in 1816, has an instrumental valence and, derivatively, a diagnostic power, that direct auscultation—listening with the ear on the patient's chest or back—does not. Sometimes the sensory feedback provided by one or another type of instrument is subject to individual preference. One can percuss or tap the chest, back, and abdomen with the fingers drawn together or spread apart, with the tapping hand gloved or not.[14] Or, as was the practice throughout the second half of the nineteenth

12. Leon Balter, Zvi Lothane, & James Spencer, "On the Analyzing Instrument," *Psychoanal. Quart.*, 43:474–504, 1980; Zvi Lothane, "The Analyzing Instrument and Reciprocal Free Association," *J. Clin. Psychoanal.*, 3:61–82, 1994; Theodore J. Jacobs, "The Use of the Self: The Analyst and the Analytic Instrument in the Clinical Situation," in Joseph Reppen, ed., *Analysts at Work: Practice, Principles, and Techniques* (Hillsdale, NJ: Analytic Press, 1985), pp. 43–58, quoted at p. 46.

13. Balter et al., "On the Analyzing Instrument" (n. 12), p. 475.

14. Leopold Auenbrugger, who discovered the diagnostic value of percussion in Vienna in 1754 and published his findings in his *Inventum Novum ex Percussione Thoracis Humani, ut Signo, Abstrusos Interni Pectoris Morbos Detegendi* [*A New Discovery that Enables the Physician to Detect Hidden Diseases of the Chest from*

century, one can tap with a percussion hammer. One can percuss directly onto the chest, back, and abdomen of the patient or tap onto another mediating instrument, the pleximeter (a small ivory, metal, or rubber disk that serves as resonator), to hear and "process" diagnostically meaningful sounds about the organs lying beneath the percussive tap. One can substitute the left index finger for the pleximeter in order to supplement sound with tactile resistance during percussion. It matters not. The percussing tool, whether the finger or the hammer, whether striking the chest or the pleximeter or the examiner's left index finger, is the conduit of instrumentally acquired information that transcends any one preferred *method* of percussing. It conveys sounds that any and all may hear in clinically meaningful ways.

Leopold Auenbrugger, who discovered the clinical value of thorax percussion in Vienna in the 1750s, differentiated among the *sonus altior* (high tympanic sound), the *sonus carnis* (dull sound), and the *sonus obscurior* (sound of indistinct quality). Diagnostically, these sounds were found to convey *objective* information about collections of fluid in the chest and, as Auenbrugger discovered, this information was of great value in detecting pleurisy and empyema in his patients. Of course, one can construe the pathological sounds however one wishes. One can understand the underlying organ pathology—what collateral and convergent "instrumental" findings found to be, then and now, pleurisy and empyema—in whatever way one chooses. One can treat or not treat the organ pathology of which sounds are signs

---

the Percussion of the Human Thorax] of 1761, "practiced percussion with the tips of all the fingers of one hand, over a thin shirt and with a soft leather glove on his hand." Whereas Auenbrugger tapped with fingertips tightly drawn together, Jean Corvisart, who introduced chest percussion in Paris after 1797 and translated Auenbrugger's work into French in 1808, "used the palmar surfaces of the extended and approximated fingers—'à main ouverte'—to percuss the chest." Herman L. Blumgart, "Leopold Auenbrugger. His 'Inventum Novum' – 1761," *Circ.*, 24:1–4, 1961, quoted at p. 2; Guenter B. Risse, "Pierre A. Piorry (1794–1879), the French 'Master of Percussion,'" *Chest*, 60:484–488, 1971, quoted at p. 484. For additional brief accounts, see R. G. Rate, "Leopold Auenbrugger and 'The Inventum Novum,'" *J. Kan. Med. Soc.*, 67:30–33, 1966 and D. E. Bedford, "Auenbrugger's Contribution to Cardiology: History of Percussion of the Heart," *Brit. Heart J.*, 33:817–821, 1971. S. Weir Mitchell took up Auenbrugger, his invention of percussion, and his rescue from obscurity through Corvisart's French translation near the end of his famous address of 1891 to the Second Congress of American Physicians, *The Early History of Instrumental Precision in Medicine* (New Haven: Tuttle, Morehouse & Taylor, 1892), p. 24.

according to whatever theory one subscribes to. It matters not. The fact is that the chest or back tap of the patient with pleurisy-like or empyema-like disease simply does not sound like the chest or back tap of the healthy person. It conveys the sound of disease, as borne out by the localized pathologic changes observed during postmortem dissection. The percussor's state of mind has nothing to do with it; his instrument and trained ear have everything to do with it.

In 1875, two German neurologists, Heinrich Erb and Carl Westphal, publishing independently and simultaneously in Westphal's own *Archiv für Psychiatrie und Nervenkrankheiten* [*Archives of Psychiatry and Nervous Diseases*], described the phenomena that Erb, but not Westphal, understood to be tendon or "muscle stretch" reflexes. Erb described how a reflex hammer applied to the patellar tendon elicited the patellar (i.e., knee-jerk) reflex, and went on to explain the diagnostic utility of the latter. He used a percussion hammer to elicit this and other tendon reflexes, and for several decades thereafter physicians followed him in tapping tendons with preexisting instruments that had been designed to percuss. But lightweight percussion hammers were ultimately found inadequate to elicit tendon reflexes reliably, so beginning in 1888 and continuing into the 1920s, various function-specific reflex hammers were designed and manufactured in the United States and Europe. The first reflex hammer was designed in 1888 by the Philadelphia neurologist John Madison Taylor, an assistant to S. Weir Mitchell at the Philadelphia Orthopedic Hospital and Infirmary for Nervous Disease.

Mitchell took avuncular pride in his assistant's invention. Both he and his neurological colleague C. K. Mills praised and popularized it, the latter proclaiming it "the best hammer for tapping the much-abused patellar ligament."[15] Many alternative designs followed: the Kraus hammer, the Troemner hammer, the Berliner hammer, the Babinski/Rabiner hammer, and the Queen Square hammer, among the best known. Each design had its advocates and critics; each did the same thing—it elicited tendon reflexes.[16] As simple as the instrument was,

15. Quoted in Douglas J. Lanska, "The History of Reflex Hammers," *Neurol.*, 39:1542–1549, 1989 at p. 1545.

16. The chronology of, and rationale for, these successive designs are ably reviewed by Lanska, "History of Reflex Hammers" (n. 15) and Francisco Pinto, "A Short History of the Reflex Hammer," *Pract. Neurol.*, 3:366–371, 2003.

it did more than ratify the existence and elicit-ability of tendon reflexes. To wit, it revealed and carried knowledge beyond the neurology that gave rise to it. Put differently, the lowly reflex hammer had a shaping impact on the field of inquiry within which it was diagnostically deployed. In the words of Francis Schiller, "while neither reflexes nor hammers were much newer than pitchforks, they helped in the construction of a new edifice: the functioning nervous system as an assembly of interdependent and hence variably active reflexes."[17]

What can we say about the analyzing instrument as the *instrumentality* of psychoanalytic listening and conduit of psychoanalytic information? A half-century ago, Isakower thought that his trainees could learn to enter into a state of mind in which their theoretical ideas and personal idiosyncrasies were extruded from their analytic listening. The static idea of an instrument underscored the force of his pedagogical injunction to keep the analytic field free of unwanted intrusions. But the mindset associated with this injunction—which may well entail a set of teachable psychological skills—is not an *objectifying* aid to observation. The "listening" mindset cannot, in the manner of the simple reflex hammer, help construct an edifice that transcends the grounds of its creation. For the analyzing instrument is locked in tautological embrace with *Freud's* analytic method, which makes specific theoretical assumptions about the nature of analytic listening, processing, and talking (or not talking). The analyzing instrument offers no way of amplifying and thereby transforming clinical "sounds" (in the form of the patient's free associations, self-reports, replies to analytic queries, body language, and the like) in ways that push the method (and the theories that underwrite it) into uncharted terrain. In point of fact, it is difficult to see how so paradoxical an instrument can lead to new insights that challenge the method for which the instrument stands.

Contemporary psychoanalysis, which, inter alia, devalues the classical psychoanalytic method as the conduit for *objective* understanding of one isolated mind by another, makes a shambles of Isakower's admirable but quixotic supervisory quest. Yes, the analyst may mimic a kind of purified instrumental receptiveness by *trying* to extrude subjective, personality-based contaminants from his mode of listening to

17. Francis Schiller, "The Reflex Hammer," *Med. Hist.*, 11:75–85, 1967, quoted at p. 84.

and processing another's communications. But the disproof is in the trying. To suggest that the analyzing analyst can *become* his own instrument is to impute to a willfully engaged (or willfully inculcated) state of mind the objectifying *power* of instruments as *external* aids to observations. Anyone, after all, can claim to be an analyzing instrument who, following Freud's precepts, concentrates attention on inner psychic processes and suspends critical attitudes toward the ideas, images, and fantasies that derive from such concentration. "The technique," Freud observed in 1912, "is a very simple one."[18] To be sure, the psychological foundation that undergirds the technique is not so simple. The analyzing state of mind may well imply, as Lothane suggests, a capacity for controlled regression coordinate with the regression of the freely associating analysand, and this capacity, in turn, may well implicate a special set of interpersonal and communicative skills that rely on native psychological endowment.[19] But a skill set is not tantamount to an instrument, and it is a category mistake to suggest otherwise.

And, in point of fact, psychoanalysis revolves around the exploration of just those unwanted intrusions that, for Isakower, contaminated the analyzing instrument. As William Grossman wisely observed in 1995, the personal intrusions that Isakower sought to banish from the analyst's purified listening instrument are the very stuff of any human encounter in its psychodynamic aspects. Such intrusions, he wrote, "are an expression of unconscious fantasies the analysis of which, in both analyst and patient, is an integral part of analysis," and Isakower's effort to ward off rather than to explore them simply led "to an artificial objectivity that must distort observations." Once the analyzing instrument was treated as anything more than a didactic metaphor, Grossman continued, "Isakower's formulations seemed to lose touch with the inevitable multi-level functioning, the ongoing conflict that characterizes mental activity of the analyst and that of the patient." Inevitably, the re-visioning of human listening activity

18. Sigmund Freud, "Recommendations to Physicians Practicing Psycho-Analysis" (n. 10), p. 111.

19. ". . . the use of the analyzing instrument presupposes not only previous adequate analysis of the analyst but also his adequate self-analytic capacities." Balter et al., "On the Analyzing Instrument" (n. 12), p. 494.

as the deployment of an instrument was tantamount to a distorting filter, an anti-instrument that impeded rather than purified observation, and this because "inevitably, the effort to *focus on and isolate* the process of keeping the mind in an open and uncritical state with respect to regressive thinking led to a *critical* attitude and exclusion of other thoughts."[20] The very subjectivity that humanizes the analyst's listening and imparts empathic resonance to what is heard nullifies the claim that such listening elicits information in the manner of an instrument.

Even if we allow for a different *kind* of postclassical analytic instrument that aids the analyst in engaging, and working through dyadically, those personally charged attitudes Isakower sought to exclude summarily from the analytic field, we are left in a quandary. To speak of the refinement of the analyzing instrument in this latter sense is simply to elide the quandary of theoretical pluralism, since refinement is necessarily pegged to one or another perceptual sensitivity that corresponds to one or another interpretive orientation.[21] To equate the analyzing instrument more globally with the "broad range of internal experiences" through which the analyst refracts the analysand's experience is to fall back on tautology.[22] In either case, the analyzing instrument at most functions heuristically; it helps the individual ana-

20. William I. Grossman, "Psychological Vicissitudes of Theory in Clinical Work," *Int. J. Psycho-Anal.*, 76:885–899, 1995, quoted at pp. 894–895 with emphases in the original.

21. As in the "most refined instrument" that enables the analyst "to register the workings of the ego defenses" (Richard Sterba, "Clinical and Therapeutic Aspects of Character Resistance," *Psychoanal. Quart.*, 22:1–20, 1953, quoted at pp. 17, 18). For enlargement of the claim and its technical implications, see Paul Gray, "'Developmental Lag' in the Evolution of Technique," in *The Ego and Analysis of Defense*, 2nd ed. (Lanham, MD: Aronson, 2005), pp. 27–61.

22. See Richard Lasky, "Countertransference and the Analytic Instrument," *Psychoanal. Psychol.*, 19:65–94, 2002. Lasky's differentiation of the "analytic instrument" from countertransference only underscores the manner in which discussions of the "instrument" give way to tautology: E.g., "I think the analyst's entire personality serves as the basis for the analytic instrument—conscious, unconscious, conflicted and unconflicted—and feel under no obligation, theoretically, to separate out the analyst's 'healthy' and 'unhealthy' characteristics in positing the suggestion that everything that occurs in the analyst's inner life either is, or has the potential to become, part of the 'analytic instrument'" (p. 70). If everything about the analyst is potentially in the service of his or her "analytic instrument," then the very concept of instrument is emptied of any "instrumental" meaning; it means nothing.

lyst conceptualize what he or she does with the individual patient that may (or may not) redound to the patient's benefit.

This heuristic helpfulness is not to be underestimated. It is like the trained finger that, in late nineteenth-century British and American medicine, was commonly extolled as a more reliable measure of radial pulse than the arcane tracings of the sphygmograph.[23] But neither the trained finger nor the analyzing instrument can function as a vehicle of progress, for neither provides an invariant finding that can be shared with others and then compared with later findings.[24] They are nothing like the instrumentation that provides pulse or ECG tracings. The latter are supraindividual tools that accompany the movement of knowledge from the private realm to the public realm and ensure that the knowledge being moved about remains constant through its various transformations.[25] These tracings can be correlated with other findings, with pulse rate, temperature, and symptomatology, for example, thereby rendering visible patterns obscure to subjective assessment. The instruments that yield these tracings serve "to make diagnosis more uniform and therapeutics more rational"; they provide "useful teaching and consulting tools."[26] And most impor-

23. We have two superb articles on the debates surrounding the introduction of medical instrumentation, especially the sphygmometer (or sphygmomanometer), in the second half of the nineteenth century. For the situation in Britain, see Christopher Lawrence, "Incommunicable Knowledge: Science, Technology and the Clinical Art in Britain, 1850–1914," *J. Contemp. Hist.*, 20:503–520, 1985. For the situation in the United States, see Hughes Evans, "Losing Touch: The Controversy Over the Introduction of Blood Pressure Instruments in Medicine," *Tech. Cult.*, 34:784–807, 1993.

24. And this was the very argument set forth by Julius Hérisson, whose sphygmometer of 1835 was the first noninvasive device to measure and graphically render the pulse beat via a column of mercury. Whereas the tactile sensations revealed by pulse-feeling were too imprecise to allow exact comparison with later findings, the sphygmometer "produced numerical results that gave the physician a description of the pulse he could easily compare with later observations." Thus, the instrument was eminently suited to instructing students and also permitted long-distance consultations by letter. See Stanley Joel Reiser, *Medicine and the Reign of Technology* (Cambridge: Cambridge University Press, 1978), pp. 98–99.

25. I am using "instrument" and "tool" in the conceptual sense of Latour. See Bruno Latour, *Pandora's Hope: Essays on the Reality of Science Studies* (Cambridge: Harvard University Press, 1999), especially pp. 24–79.

26. Evans, "Losing Touch" (n. 23), pp. 797–798.

tantly, they provide a consensually agreed-upon basis for mediating among rival explanatory claims.

To be sure, we must theorize about the behavior of sphygmographs and electrocardiographs; their tracings too are subject to interpretation. Indeed, as late as 1900, British physicians were cautioned away from the sphygmograph, since the reading of its tracings could "twist facts in the desired direction."[27] But with instruments such as syphygmographs and electrocardiographs, we at least have facts to twist; we are no longer in the realm of direct sensory data that can only be transposed into words and communicated to colleagues with great difficulty. This was the quandary of the great clinical pulse readers of the late nineteenth century. As the pioneering British physiologist John Burden-Sanderson observed in 1867, the physician learned "the habit of discriminating pulses instinctively" and thence learned "valuable truths from it, which he can apply to practice." But absent an agreed-upon yardstick for evaluating the meaning of different pulse sounds, such clinical knowledge virtually died with the individual clinician: "How difficult—how impossible—is it for the skilled physician to impart his knowledge to his less experienced junior!" In the manner of psychoanalysts of different theoretical persuasions who come together to analyze case material, experienced nineteenth-century pulse readers who "gathered together to examine the same pulse and to describe their impressions would give different accounts of what they felt." In America, George Oliver, one of Harvey Cushing's house officers in 1903, reported that even experienced, Harvard-based pulse readers could not agree on the strength of pulses, and each described what his fingers told him using a different vocabulary.[28]

Of course differences among pulse readers and analyzing instruments alike may be instructive. A quarter century ago, the British analyst Joseph Sandler suggested that the analyst "can be regarded as an instrument, a sort of probe into the psychoanalytic situation, that organizes the experience the analyst has in interaction with his pa-

27. W. H. Broadbent, *The Pulse* (London, 1890), p. 33, quoted in Lawrence, "Incommunicable Knowledge" (n. 23), p. 516.

28. George Oliver, "The Pulse and Blood Pressure," *Clin. J.*, 13:243, 1898, cited in Evans (n. 23), p. 800.

tients through the formulation of unconscious theoretical structures."
Sandler was a clinical pragmatist who believed that practicing analysts routinely devised personal solutions to the "discrepancies and
incongruities" in the "official" or "public" psychoanalytic theories
they had been taught. The instrumental use of the analyst as a research
tool, he held, would reveal the misalignment between these public
psychoanalytic theories and the private, idiosyncratic theories that
individual analysts fell back on in their day-to-day work. "The probe,"
he wrote "can be withdrawn from the situation and the theories which
have been formed can be examined."[29]

But what exactly is the point of such examination? At best it underscores the failure of official theory to guide the practices of individual analysts in personally satisfying ways. At worst, it underscores
the nonexistence of any *conventionally* instrumental basis for arriving at a public theory that pulls together, and makes conceptual sense
of, the diverse private theories that working analysts devise and rely
on. There may be a point to the exercise, but absent an instrument
that is superordinate to the unofficial theories brought to light, it is a
point that goes nowhere, scientifically speaking.

Nineteenth-century pulse instrumentation, by way of contrast, provided a basis for comparing, contrasting, and integrating the variable
accounts of individual pulse readers. As instruments of precision,
however imperfect, they "render[ed] the comparison of individual
labor possible" and "lift[ed] the general level of acuteness of observation." So Silas Weir Mitchell intoned in his address to the Second
Congress of American Physicians and Surgeons in 1891. The lesson
was well in hand a generation earlier, when eminent instrumentalists
such as Edouard Seguin and Austin Flint realized that quantifying the
pulse would enable physicians to stipulate in a general way the relationship between normal and abnormal pulse and thereby pave the
way for diagnostic accuracy across the population of individual pulse
readers. The trained finger, however sensitive, was not adequate to
the evaluation of pulse in its several diagnostically salient components.
Seguin argued this point as early as 1867, as did Flint, for whom "It
is evident that few of the characters of a pulsation, occupying as it

29. Joseph Sandler, "Reflections on Some Relations Between Psychoanalytic Concepts and Psychoanalytic Practice," *Int. J. Psycho-Anal.*, 64:35–45, 1983, quoted at
p. 38.

does but a seventieth part of a minute, can be ascertained by the sense of touch alone."[30]

The sphygmograph came to the rescue. It provided qualitative and quantitative information that individually trained fingers could not, since it discerned and recorded pulse in "its frequency, strength, rhythm, volume, and the shape of the curve it produced when permitted to trace a path on paper through the use of amplifying instruments."[31] Like the microscope, the stethoscope, the thermometer, and the percussion hammer, it amplified human sensory endowment in ways that transcended the vagaries of individual instances of such endowment. In this sense, to recur to Weir Mitchell's address of 1891, it not only increased the acuteness of observation but also gave birth to "new standards in observation."[32] It permitted a consensus about the *reality* of patterns and indices, the discernment and recording of which fell to the instrument and not to the trained ear, eye, or finger.

The graphic rendering of pulse provides one such set of patterns, the graphic rendering of tremor yet another. In 1887, Charcot, using various pneumatic, tambour-like instruments, produced tremor recordings that sustained the differentiation of multiple sclerosis from Parkinson's disorder that he and Edmé Vulpian had proposed 20 years earlier. A year later, the New York neurologist Fredrick Peterson used the Edward sphygmograph to make estimates of tremor frequency that remain consistent with contemporary estimates.[33]

To be sure, consensus about the reality of graphically rendered patterns of pulse and tremor activity is not tantamount to agreement about

30. S. Weir Mitchell, *Early History of Instrumental Precision in Medicine* (n. 14), p. 8. Edouard Seguin, "Sphygmometry," *Med. Rev.*, 2 (1867), at pp. 248, 251, cited and quoted by Audrey B. Davis, *Medicine and Its Technology: An Introduction to the History of Medical Instrumentation* (Westport, CT: Greenwood Press, 1981), p. 125. The same point was elaborated in America a generation later by clinicians of comparable stature, Richard C. Cabot, Theodore Janeway, George W. Crile, and Harvey Cushing among them. See Evans, "Losing Touch" (n. 23), passim.

31. Davis, *Medicine and Its Technology* (n. 30), p. 125.

32. Mitchell, *Early History of Instrumental Precision* (n. 14), p. 8.

33. Douglas Lanska, "Nineteenth-Century American Contributions to the Recording of Tremors," *Move. Dis.*, 15:720–729, 2000; Douglas J. Lanska, Christopher G. Goetz, & Teresa A. Chmura, "Development of Instruments for Abnormal Movements: Dynamometers, the Dynamograph, and Tremor Recorders," *Move. Dis.*, 16:736–741, 2001.

the diagnostic meaning (if any) of these selfsame data. Late nineteenth-century clinicians typically questioned whether the information provided by sphygmographs was of any clinical utility at all. After all, Karl Vierordt invented the first usable sphygmograph in 1853, but Theodore Janeway only introduced the concept of essential hypertension in 1913. Throughout the second half of the nineteenth century and into the early twentieth century, through the successive refinements of pulse-recording instrumentation by Marey (1860), Dudgeon (1881), and Riva-Rocci (1896), British and American physicians continued to attach little if any meaning to moderately elevated blood pressure. Indeed, some clinicians, the American internist Allen G. Rice among them, deemed it a protective physiological response to disease.[34]

Similarly, one may dispute Charcot's and Vulpian's use of tambour-generated tracings to sustain their differentiation of Parkinson's and multiple sclerosis.[35] Perhaps the tracings only signify different permutations of one or the other condition. Perhaps they point to a third type of degenerative pathology that undergirds the symptomatology of Parkinson's and MS alike. The point is this: Any such disputing must still account for Charcot's differentiating "myographic curves." With the graphic rendering of pulse and tremor activity, that is, we at least have tracings that stand apart from rival theories that interpret them in different ways and to different ends. In the realm of medical instrumentation, we can ordinarily distinguish between the dependable observational theories involved in the construction of instruments and the generation of data on one hand, and the target theories tested by the instruments on the other.[36] The well-known limitations of nineteenth-century pulse and tremor recording apparatuses, most of

34. Evans, "Losing Touch" (n. 23), pp. 794–797. Rice argued this point in an essay on hypertension that won the Fiske Fund Prize of 1916 and was published as *The Value of Blood Pressure in the Diagnosis and Prognosis of Disease* (Providence, RI: Snow & Farnham, 1916).

35. The clinical and histoanatomical findings that led Charcot to differentiate multiple sclerosis from Parkinson's disorder (prior to Charcot, "paralysis agitans") in the period 1868–1870 are ably reviewed by Colin L. Talley, "The Emergence of Multiple Sclerosis as a Nosological Category in France, 1838–1868," *J. Hist. Neurosci.*, 12:250–265, 2003.

36. See Larry Lauden, *Science and Relativism: Some Key Controversies in the Philosophy of Science* (Chicago: University of Chicago Press, 1990), pp. 47–48.

which were clinically abandoned early in the twentieth century, do not call into question the normal science assumptions that sustained the construction of these mechanically ingenious instruments. Indeed, these assumptions led to data whose relative inutility does not compromise their basic validity.[37]

Consider another example from the very period of Freud's early theorizing. In the emergent technologies of blood monitoring, we can differentiate between the public data provided by hemocytometers (as to the quantity of red blood corpuscles) and hemoglobinometers (as to the amount of hemoglobin within these corpuscles) and the tendentious employment of these data to sustain socially constructed disease categories, such as chlorosis (a cluster of vague symptoms that included lethargy, nervousness, gastric disturbance, and faint green pallor) and splenic anemia (an anemia, or lowered red blood count, allegedly caused by a damaged, enlarged spleen). In the former, hemoglobin analysis provided a medical rationale for a theory that mandated the moral supervision of adolescent girls; in the latter, it enabled early twentieth-century operators to construct a theory consistent with their newly emergent identity as surgeon-scientists empowered to explore the abdomen.[38]

Neurological evaluation in late nineteenth-century neurology provides a final example. Neurologists of Freud's era employed a host of anthropometric measuring devices—dynamometers (to measure muscle strength), dynamographs (to record the duration of tonic contractions), aesthesiometers (to measure sensitivity to touch)—of questionable clinical utility but sound design.[39] These instruments recorded

37. Late nineteenth-century tambours and sphygmographs could measure the amplitude and frequency of gross tremors but were limited in their ability to record fine or very large amplitude tremors. Further, their use "required contact of the apparatus with the measured body part, and both added to the inertia of the latter, altering somewhat the characteristics of the tremor. In addition, such instruments measure tremor in only one plane." Yet, these limitations notwithstanding, "nineteenth-century measurements of tremor frequency were generally consistent with modern estimates." Lanska, "Nineteenth-Century American Contributions to the Recording of Tremors" (n. 33), p. 728.

38. See Keith Wailoo, *Drawing Blood: Technology and Disease Identity in Twentieth-Century America* (Baltimore: Johns Hopkins University Press, 1997), chaps. 1 & 2.

39. See Douglas J. Lanska, "William Hammond, the Dynamometer, the Dynamograph," *Arch. Neurol.*, 57:1649–1653, 2000; Davis, *Medicine and Its Technology* (n. 30), pp. 169–176. Hammond's *Treatise on the Diseases of the Nervous System*

data that could be used tendentiously in court proceedings;[40] their clinical utility rarely extended beyond "proving" muscle and nerve injury among litigating victims of railway and industrial accidents. But all such instruments produced anatomic and physiological data subject to public inspection, data that provided a common ground for theorizing about normality and abnormality, neurologically understood. Psychoanalytic theory appraisal, for its part, admits no such distinction between public data and theories tested with the data, since the analyzing instrument that gathers data can only be employed in a theory-laden manner by theory-burdened individuals. Some analysts question the degree to which such data, in the form of clinical facts pertaining to "the intimate sphere," can be rendered public at all.[41] Here the point is methodological: The analyzing instrument (viz., the trained listener who follows the method of psychoanalysis) simply does not provide a means for standing outside, and mediating among, the theoretical and clinical commitments of individual psychoanalytic instrumentalists. It does not satisfy the requirement of scientific (or medical) instrumentation from Galileo's use of the telescope to the present: To provide new ways of probing nature and to increase the precision of the results of such probes. It therefore stands outside any account of progress that relies on instrumentation.[42]

(1871), the first American textbook of neurology, begins with a 30-page introduction on neurologic instruments. See Bonnie Ellen Blustein, *Preserve Your Love for Science: Life of William A. Hammond, American Neurologist* (NY: Cambridge University Press, 1991), pp. 118–119.

40. A. Patten & B. M. Patten, "William A. Hammond, the Dynamograph, and Bogus Neurologic Testimony in Old New York," *J. Hist. Neurosci.*, 6:257–263, 1997.

41. ". . . it seems intrinsically evident that clinical facts in psychoanalysis are not duplicable in the same way that experiments are in physics. These clinical facts are restricted, in their character of social fact, to the time and space in which they took place. However, they can be published through their communication by means of language, just as a dream is made public through its verbal communication. Psychoanalytic clinical facts share with the dream the property of pertaining to the intimate sphere." Juan Francisco Jordan-Moore, "Intimacy and Science: The Publication of Clinical Facts in Psychoanalysis," *Int. J. Psycho-Anal.*, 75:1251–1266, 1994, quoted at p. 1252.

42. Harold I. Brown, "Incommensurability Reconsidered," *Stud. Hist. Phil. Sci.*, 36:149–169, 2005, at pp. 163–165.

And so we circle back to theoretical pluralism and the manner in which it militates against the very idea of psychoanalytic progress. What is the *instrumentality* of progress in a pluralistic era? Consider this prosaic question: What is a psychoanalytic fact? I frame the question not in terms of the well-rehearsed objectivist-subjectivist debate but in terms of science as an activity. In his classic *Science in Action*, Bruno Latour observes that "a fact is what is collectively stabilized from the midst of controversies when the activity of later [published] papers does not consist only of criticism or deformation but also of confirmation. The strength of the original statement does not lie in itself, but is derived from any of the papers that incorporate it."[43]

Latour's point of view underscores the degree to which scientific progress ultimately falls back on social knowledge. All scientific facts, not just "intimate" psychoanalytic facts, are transpersonal (or "social") in this sociological sense. Put differently, facts and the hypotheses into which facts are incorporated are not the property (or findings or discoveries) of individuals; rather, in the words of the philosopher Helen Longino, they emerge "through a process of critical emendation and modification of those individual products by the rest of the scientific community."[44] In the day-to-day workings of normal science, members of a cohesive and bounded scientific community undertake activities (especially as to the "critical emendation and modification" that occur in writing and publishing) that elevate individual products to consensually agreed-upon facts.

What are the agreed upon psychoanalytic facts in this action-related sense of the term? Is the Oedipus complex as Freud understood it (viz., as the fons et origo of neurosogenesis) a psychoanalytic fact? Is intrapsychic conflict a fact? Is the self-psychological notion of selfobject a fact? Is Melanie Klein's "paranoid-schizoid position" a fact? Is Lacan's notion of the imaginary a fact? Relying on the published journal literature, one would have to say that for one part of the psychoanalytic world each of these concepts is a consensually agreed-upon fact (in this sociological sense) and for another part it is not. What we lack

43. Bruno Latour, *Science in Action* (Cambridge: Harvard University Press, 1987), p. 42.

44. Helen E. Longino, *Science as Social Knowledge: Values and Objectivity in Scientific Inquiry* (Princeton: Princeton University Press, 1990), p. 68.

are agreed-upon coherence conditions that link the analysand's words and behaviors to the analyst's explanatory models and thereby facilitate dialogue among Freudian analysts, self-psychological analysts, Kleinian analysts, and Lacanian analysts. Secure psychoanalytic knowledge should be the property of the entire community of psychoanalysts; it should transcend "the contributions of any individual or even of any subcommunity within the larger community."[45] But the reality is that psychoanalytic knowledge has for over a century been distributed among various subcommunities with different background assumptions. Theoretical pluralism, which differs radically from the explanatory pluralism espoused by social scientists, historians, and psychiatrists,[46] formalizes the reality that different psychoanalytic facts are the preserve of different psychoanalytic subcommunities.[47]

Where does theoretical pluralism leave the field? It is formidably difficult to have dialogue when basic facts are not agreed upon in the manner of normal scientific discourse. Theoretical pluralism, in rejecting a stable observation language, is akin to a scientific conventionalism that embraces a number of acceptable theories that are inconsistent with one another, but whose respective truth-values cannot be empirically decided. Psychoanalytic facts, or at least *many* psychoanalytic facts, exist only within specific psychoanalytic theories; indeed, the epistemic thrust of pluralism is to show how any theoretical system so permeates what is observed as to make the observables—the "facts"—necessarily true. An Oedipus complex, an intrapsychic conflict, a self-selfobject relationship, a relational matrix, an attachment bond, a

45. Longino, *Science as Social Knowledge* (n. 44), p. 69.

46. I comment further on the nature of explanatory pluralism, in contradistinction to theoretical pluralism, in chapter 7, pp. 245–250.

47. Cf. Steven Cooper, "Facts All Come with a Point of View," *Int. J. Psycho-Anal.*, 77:255–273, 1996: ". . . what we currently have is something akin to a set of Kleinian facts, Winnicottian facts, Kohutian facts, Interpersonal facts, Intersubjective facts and the like" (p. 259). Cooper raises the possibility that analysts simply dispense with the concept of "fact" altogether and replace it with "observation," which better captures, he believes, the "constructive process of observation between analyst and patient. I believe that the word 'observation' implies more readily that what we observe is never theory-free" (p. 260). It is a difference without a point, since "observation" by definition denotes something out there (viz., facts) learned by observing. The issue is epistemic, not linguistic.

paranoid-schizoid position—they are all facts, equally salient and equally true within the theories that impart meaning to them. Claims that incorporate these facts can never be disproved, because every such claim is true by virtue of the meaning it derives from the parent theory. Conversely, facts (and the claims that organize them) that appear to contradict a theory are necessarily outside the theory and, as such, are not false but meaningless.[48]

At the very end of 1897, Freud, in his letters to Fliess, continued to wrestle with the tenability of the seduction hypothesis (which he had come to refer to as the "father-etiology") based on what he heard and did not hear from his patients. A full three months after his ostensible rejection of the seduction hypothesis, Freud continued to attest to the reality of the "scenes" remembered by his patients. On December 12, he announced that his "confidence in the father-etiology has risen greatly," and 10 days later, he recurred to "the intrinsic authenticity of infantile trauma."[49] In point of fact, Freud could not be sure; he ricocheted between theories of actual and fantasized seductions, and with good reason. Both theories not only explained the same set of clinical issues but also invited anomalies of a complementary nature.[50] The hysteric whose reports of literal abuse were accepted as fact had, as her counterpart, the sexually abused trauma victim whose reports of abuse were dismissed as fantasy. Finally, both theories reinforced trenchant bodies of scientific literature to which Freud was equally

48. Here I follow (and paraphrase) Mary Hesse, "Models of Theory-Change," in *Revolutions and Reconstructions in the Philosophy of Science* (Bloomington: Indiana University Press, 1980), pp. 125–139, especially p. 136. Where Hesse speaks of "observational sentences," I substitute "claims"; where she speaks of "system," I speak of "theory." Among analysts who have thoughtfully explored these epistemic issues of facticity, communicability, and publishability, see Jordan-Moore, "Intimacy and Science" (n. 41); Daniel Widlöcher, "A Case Is not a Fact," *Int. J. Psychoanal.*, 75:1233–1244, 1994; Roy Schafer, "The Conceptualization of Clinical Facts," *Int. J. Psychoanal.*, 75:1023–1030, 1994; David Tuckett, "The Conceptualization and Communication of Clinical Facts in Psychoanalysis," *Int. J. Psychoanal.*, 76:653–662, 1995; and Steven Cooper, "Facts All Come with a Point of View" (n. 47).

49. Freud to Fliess, December 12, 1897 and December 22, 1897, in *Letters of Freud to Fliess* (n. 4), pp. 286, 288.

50. This manner of comparing the seduction hypothesis and the theory of fantasy-driven neurosogenesis adopts the pragmatic framework of Larry Lauden, *Progress and Its Problems* (Berkeley: University of California Press, 1978), especially pp. 45–69.

well exposed during his year of study in Paris. The seduction hypothesis reinforced the writings of Tardieu, Bernard, and Brouardel that attested to the frequency of early childhood sexual abuse within the family. The theory of fantasy-driven neurosogenesis, on the other hand, reinforced the complementary literature, found in the writings of Fournier, Brouardel, and Bourdin, that attested to children's predictable recourse to pseudologica phantastica, to their tendency to simulate when it came to early sexual experience. To be sure, Freud's intuitive sense, probably abetted by adventitious factors, drew him to fantasy over actual seduction. But in 1897 his treatment *method* provided no appraisal measure for determining which theory was potentially more effective at explaining and resolving the treatment issues of his patients.

At the very time Freud ricocheted between the seduction hypothesis and the theory of fantasy-driven neurosogenesis, the Scottish physician James Mackenzie, utilizing an 81-year-old instrument, the stethoscope, examined a desperately ill 50-year-old patient who had been under his care since 1880.[51] During this period, the patient had suffered recurrent attacks of rheumatic fever, with attendant inflammation and contraction of the mitral valve that regulates blood flow between the left auricle and left ventricle. For 18 years Mackenzie had heard the presystolic murmur attendant to the progressive narrowing

51. My account of Mackenzie's discovery of auricular (atrial) fibrillation draws on R. McNair Wilson, *The Beloved Physician: Sir James Mackenzie* (NY: Macmillan, 1926), pp. 120–125 and Alex Mair, *Sir James Mackenzie MD, 1853–1925: General Practitioner* (London: Royal College of General Practitioners, 1986), pp. 144–147. On Mackenzie's development and use of the clinical polygraph and his attitude toward medical instrumentation more generally, see Audrey B. Davis, *Medicine and Its Technology* (n. 30), pp. 128–131. There is no small irony in the fact that Mackenzie, whose use of the clinical polygraph led to his discovery of atrial fibrillation, feared that reliance on instruments would impair the clinician's judgment and "unfit" him for clinical work. He eventually abandoned the clinical polygraph for more traditional methods of clinical observation and was skeptical of electrocardiography from the outset. See Gerald L. Geison, "Divided We Stand: Physiologists and Clinicians in the American Context," in Morris J. Vogel & Charles E. Rosenberg, eds., *The Therapeutic Revolution: Essays in the Social History of American Medicine* (Philadelphia: University of Pennsylvania Press, 1979), pp. 67–90 at pp. 83–84 and Joel D. Howell, "Early Perceptions of the Electrocardiogram: From Arrhythmia to Infarction," *Bull. Hist. Med.*, 58:83–98, 1984, at p. 96.

of the patient's mitral valve, her worsening mitral deficiency. But in early 1898, auscultation no longer revealed this onerous heart sound; the presystolic murmur that Mackenzie had listened to and monitored for 18 years simply vanished. Teamed with this perplexing development was a dramatic change in the patient's pulse tracings, as recorded by Mackenzie's ink polygraph, a refinement of the Dudgeon sphygmograph that permitted simultaneous recording, via separate receivers, of the heartbeat, venous pulse, and arterial pulse. Coincident with the disappearance of the presystolic murmur, the patient's pulse had become persistently irregular; the ink polygraph showed that a negative (or auricular) pulse had been replaced by a positive (or ventricular) pulse.

What did all this mean? Mackenzie theorized that, because the disappearance of the presystolic murmur accompanied a cardiovascular deterioration that signaled impending death, the patient's auricles had ceased to function entirely; thus the disappearance of the long-heard presystolic murmur. More than a century later, we say that Mackenzie, the father of modern cardiology, "discovered" auricular (or atrial) fibrillation, which he initially termed auricular paralysis. What he did was interpret an absence of sound through the stethoscope that correlated with changes in his patient's pulse tracings.

What was the mechanism of this life-threatening rhythmic aberration? MacKenzie himself had no idea how to open this black box and suggested that his colleague, Thomas Lewis, explore the phenomenon experimentally. Lewis's research established beyond doubt that the condition which Mackenzie had not heard through his stethoscope—the absence of presystolic murmur—corresponded with the rapid, independent contractions of the muscular fibers of the left auricle; Mackenzie's "auricular paralysis" was renamed "auricular fibrillation." In 1920 Lewis theorized that the latter was caused by a wave of electrical stimulation (a "circus movement") traveling continuously around the base of the great veins of the auricle. Here was a credible theory consistent with Mackenzie's interpretation of what he had not heard through his stethoscope and seen through his sphygmograph in 1898. But it was wrong. More than three decades later, in 1952, Myron Prinzmetal and his colleagues, making use of refined instrumentation in the form of high-speed cine-electrocardiography and cathode-ray oscillography, demonstrated that auricular fibrillation originated from a single rapidly discharging "ectopic focus"[52] rather than from a complete circle of movement around the great heart veins. Another black box was opened via instrumentation; the result was another instance of progressive theory change that rested on an agreed-upon methodology for rendering graphic representations of heart sounds meaningful indices of cardiovascular functioning.

Analysts, no less than cardiologists, are guided by what they hear and what they do not hear. The silence of the analysand, the momentary pause, the resistive interlude, the affective implosion for which words fail—they are all pregnant with meaning.[53] But heart sounds—however interpretable—have the salience of publicly inspectable data. The same sounds are available to anyone who puts stethoscope to chest at the same point in time. The relationship of these sounds to cardiac functioning is guided by theory, to be sure, but at any moment in medical history it is a reliable theory that recruits empirical evidence generated by the best instrumentation of the day. Explanatory differences at the level of this theory may exist, but they are potentially resolvable, whether through new data captured by more refined instrumentation or by appeal to superordinate methodologies for inspecting and interpreting these data. Excepting ambiguous periods of transition, where methods of theory appraisal and evaluations of new kinds of data are in dispute, often in *lively* dispute, the theory that connects heart sounds to cardiac functioning will be embraced by the entire community of cardiologists.

The sounds heard by the analyst are very different: They are verbal expressions of complex mental "productions," which are themselves

52. In the human heart, the sinoatrial (SA) node is a specialized group of cells in the right atrium that produces a small electrical stimulus approximately 72 times per minute; this stimulus regulates the rate and timing of heartbeats. An ectopic focus, also called an ectopic pacemaker, is an excitable group of cells that causes a premature heartbeat outside the normally functioning SA node.

53. Of course, the meaning of silence in psychoanalytic treatment is woven into a vast literature dealing with both theory and clinical process issues. For reviews of earlier literature on the topic, see Leo S. Loomie, "Some Ego Considerations in the Silent Patient," *JAPA*, 9:56–78, 1961 and Roy C. Calogeras, "Silence as a Technical Parameter in Psycho-Analysis," *Int. J. Psycho-Anal.* 48:536–558, 1967. More contemporary, focal considerations of silence include Fred Busch, "The Silent Patient: Issues of Separation-Individuation and Its Relationship to Speech Development," *Int. Rev. Psycho-Anal.*, 5:491–499, 1978 and Nina Coltart, "The Silent Patient," *Psychoanal. Dial.*, 1:439–453, 1991.

embedded in dense life narratives. How does the analyst hear these sounds? He listens through a theoretical filter that translates sounds into meaningful, narratively embedded utterances. This filter, following the mind-set of many contemporary analysts, comprises not only a theory (or a theoretical sensibility) but also the analyst's own subjective person-hood, his or her own unique subjectivity. The extreme version of this sensibility is intersubjectivity theory, which holds that what the analyst hears in the treatment, the meanings that he imputes to the patient's talking and not talking, are not even attributes of the patient. Rather, the meanings captured by these auditory data are specific to the "inter-subjective field" that arises from the "intersection" of the analyst's sub-jectivity and the patient's subjectivity, respectively.[54]

One need not go as far as the intersubjectivists to recognize that analytic sounds, far more than heart sounds, only become meaningful when they are infused with the analytic listener's subjectivity, which is itself a product of the analyst's own dense life narrative. In this man-ner, analytic "listening" is analogous to "seeing" in Wittgenstein's ordinary-language sense: Just as seeing presupposes something beyond retinal stimulation or visual sense-datum that we then infer to be some-thing other than what we are visually aware of, so analytic listening presupposes something beyond aural stimulation to which meanings are simply added.[55] Analytic listening is not merely theory-laden; it is theory-enabled. The analyst's theoretical commitments and therapeu-tic values *inhere* in the act of listening; he cannot hear at all absent a conceptual organization that derives from his unique amalgam of theo-retical commitments and theory-filtered knowledge and experience.

---

54. This viewpoint is associated with the work of Robert Stolorow and his colleagues. At The Analytic Press, I published several of their expositions of intersubjectivity theory: Robert Stolorow, Bernard Brandchaft, & George Atwood, *Psychoanalytic Treatment: An Intersubjective Approach* (Hillsdale, NJ: Analytic Press, 1987); Rob-ert Stolorow & George Atwood, *Contexts of Being: The Intersubjective Foundations of Psychological Life* (Hillsdale, NJ: Analytic Press, 1992); Donna Orange, George Atwood, & Robert Stolorow, *Working Intersubjectivity: Contextualism in Psycho-analytic Practice* (Hillsdale, NJ: Analytic Press, 1997).

55. One of the best expositors of "seeing" in Wittgenstein's ordinary-language sense is N. R. Hanson. See his *Patterns of Discovery: An Inquiry into the Conceptual Foun-dations of Science* (Cambridge: Cambridge University Press, 1961) and *Percep-tion and Discovery: An Introduction to Scientific Inquiry* (San Francisco: Freeman, Cooper, 1969).

Further, the very sensibility (or "analytic attitude") that renders the analyst critically self-reflective about the grounds of his listening militates against the privileging of one kind of listening over and against another. As noted above, what the analyst hears, the "facts" he gleans from his patient's utterances—as infused with, perhaps even transformed by, his own subjectivity—grow out of specific psychoanalytic theories. These facts—the fact of an object-libidinal transference, an internal object, a self-selfobject relationship, an intersubjective field, a relational matrix, an internal working model, a paranoid-schizoid position, a realm of the imaginary—exist only because of theories that structure analytic listening. There are no readily apparent grounds, either empirical or epistemological, for favoring one theory over another. And so there are no readily apparent grounds, either empirical or epistemological, for privileging one analyzing instrument over another. Absent such grounds, there is no method of theory appraisal consistent with the idea of progress, even a pragmatic notion of progress that focuses, per Laudan, on comparative problem-solving efficacy.

For what, after all, is the *locus* of psychoanalytic problem-solving? It is the individual patient, who comes to treatment with problems, however they are characterized, to be illuminated, attenuated, and hopefully resolved. To be sure, a small percentage of patients will have experienced treatment with analysts of different persuasions and will be quick with comparative judgments on the degree of success with which their "problems" or "issues" were addressed by their respective analysts. But such judgments (no less than each analyst's listening) are surely unique to such patients; they are shaped by individual subjectivity and of little probative force.[56] How do we get outside the

---

56. This is not to say it would be pointless to canvas analysands on their analytic experiences, especially analysands in treatment with analysts strongly identified with one or another theoretical approach. Robust data from a statistically significant universe of analytic patients would be invaluable. But analysts have never incorporated patient reports into their comparative assessments of theory, technique, and therapeutic efficacy. To be sure, ethical and legal constraints complicate the use of patient records and patient self-reports, but, as historians of medicine have been demonstrating since the 1980s, such constraints do not rule out their use completely. I am not aware of any systematic effort to use patient "data" to illuminate differences among different schools of analysts or differences between what analysts say (and write about) and what they actually do. The salience of the patient's point of view was brought to professional attention by the late Roy Porter more than two decades ago in his classic essay, "The Patient's View: Doing Medical History from Below," *Theory Soc.,*

succession of individual analyst-patient dyads in a manner that sustains comparative claims—a manner which lets us claim that, under specifiable conditions and with certain kinds of patients, the self psychologist is more effective than the Freudian analyst? The Lacanian more effective than the relationalist? Or vice versa.[57]

The fact is that we cannot. Theory appraisal is tainted by theory-enabled listening. Theoretical pluralism, when it becomes an epistemic status quo, *disables* the very capacity for comparative theory appraisal that enables medical specialties and their adjunctive healing modalities (nursing, dentistry, optometry, podiatry) to move forward. Over the past decade, analysts have increasingly accepted pluralism as a fact of contemporary psychoanalytic life, but such acceptance has not been accompanied by understanding of the epistemic quandary that follows such acceptance. Pluralism, in this scheme of things, is a tolerable way-station that enables constructive dialogue among proponents of different theories and treatment strategies. Put Freudians, Lacanians, self psychologists, object relationalists, neuropsychoanalysts, interpersonalists, relationalists, and dynamic systems approach analysts together in a room, insist that they address one another respectfully and engage one another constructively, and good things are bound to happen.

What exactly *are* these good things? Historically, exchanges among proponents of different psychoanalytic schools of thought have searched in vain for honest brokers. Typically, dialogue is sponsored by a representative of one such school, so that the good things tend to be framed

---

14:175–198, 1985. Flurin Condrau has recently revisited the issues raised by Porter and clarified the methodological and epistemological difficulty of writing medical history "from below" in "The Patient's View Meets the Clinical Gaze," *Soc. Hist. Med.*, 20:525–540, 2007. For an analytically astute overview of the use of patient records in understanding physician behavior, see Guenter B. Risse & John Harley Warner, "Reconstructing Clinical Activities: Patient Records in Medical History," *Soc. Hist. Med.*, 5:183–205, 1992. Edward Shorter's *Doctors and Their Patients: A Social History* (New Brunswick, NJ: Transaction, 1991 [1987]) retains its usefulness as a broadly informative and entertaining survey of the patient's viewpoint throughout history.

57. To make such claims would move psychoanalysis away from "theoretical pluralism" and toward "explanatory pluralism" as it is used by social scientists and psychiatrists. See below, pp. 245–247.

in terms of persuading representatives of different schools of thought to see the error of their ways, or at least to cease and desist in their criticism of the sponsoring school's viewpoint. Thus, Arnold Richards, a self-avowed "contemporary Freudian conflict theorist," urges his "conflict theorist" colleagues to "be proactive in explaining and defending our viewpoint to the public, to other mental health professionals, and now, no less important [sic], to psychoanalysts who see things differently." If he and theoretically like-minded colleagues are "to advance psychoanalysis as a science and not simply to defend our hegemony, the effort to represent our interests to other psychoanalysts—including self psychologists, relational psychoanalysts, and interpersonalists—must engage these colleagues constructively."[58]

What does the effort to represent one set of psychoanalytic interests to colleagues with competing sets of interests have to do with pluralism? What Richards really proffers is a kind of tactical *toleration* for purposes of dialogic persuasion. The concept of pluralism, which emerged in the aftermath of the sixteenth- and seventeenth-century wars of religion, begins where toleration leaves off. For toleration only accepts diverse beliefs, whereas pluralism takes the existence of diverse beliefs as a guiding value. The Italian political scientist Giovanni Sartori puts it thusly: "Pluralism affirms the belief that diversity and dissent are values that enrich individuals as well as their polities and societies." When Richards, the Freudian conflict theorist, welcomes non-Freudian colleagues to the table so that he and like-minded colleagues can represent their interests and defend their viewpoint, he is not advocating a pluralistic psychoanalytic culture. He is asking only for toleration, which, in Sartori's words, means "that we do have beliefs that we believe to be the right ones, and yet concede to others the right to have wrong beliefs."[59]

Richards refers to colleagues who "see things differently." Quite so. In the face of self-justifying theories whose "seen things" fall back on different mentalistic world views and are framed in partially incommensurable languages, what exactly does "constructive engagement" look

58. Arnold D. Richards, " A. A. Brill and the Politics of Exclusion," *JAPA*, 47:9–28, 1999, quoted at pp. 21–22.

59. Giovanni Sartori, "Understanding Pluralism," *J. Dem.*, 8:58–69, 1997, quoted at pp. 58, 64–65.

like? One is hard-pressed to see it as other than a strategy of persuasion, pure and simple. Richards, perhaps unwittingly, is explicit about this fact. If contemporary Freudians refuse to enter into dialogue with proponents of other viewpoints, he opines, "we [viz., contemporary Freudians] cannot hope to persuade colleagues that rival systems, regardless of their merits, incorporate serious misconstruals of contemporary Freudianism." When all else fails, let us bury our respective hatchets, come in peace, and try to persuade one another. In Richards's benign vision of a psychoanalytic coming together, theory appraisal in any rationalistic sense has given way to what Donald Spence pejoratively termed "the rhetorical voice of psychoanalysis."[60] In point of fact, the call to dialogue, absent methodological and axiological ground rules framed in a shared language, amounts to an enshrining of the rhetorical voice. The latter gains expression in even so well-intended a gesture as Richards's subsequent "plea for a measure of humility" in psychoanalytic discourse.[61] Civil discourse and graceful acceptance of criticism may promote peaceful coexistence in an era of pluralism, but they are not responsive to what Richards terms "the challenges of pluralism." The latter are epistemic, not attitudinal.[62]

Nor can these challenges be met through summary pronouncements about what is central and what peripheral to some paradigm-free generic version of psychoanalysis. Consider the American ego psychologist Leo Rangell. Rangell's vision of a "total composite" psychoanalytic theory—essentially Freudian conflict theory enlarged by the insights of American ego psychology—is the ultimate expression of the rhetorical voice. Satisfied that his version of Freudian psycho-

---

60. Donald P. Spence, *The Rhetorical Voice of Psychoanalysis: Displacement of Evidence by Theory* (Cambridge: Harvard University Press, 1994).

61. Arnold D. Richards, "Psychoanalytic Discourse at the Turn of Our Century: A Plea for a Measure of Humility," *JAPA*, 51(suppl): 73–89, 2003.

62. And these epistemic challenges, in turn, are rooted in the "deeply flawed authority" of American psychoanalytic institutes and societies that, beginning in the early 1940s, imposed theoretical conformity, neglected the scientific need to test psychoanalytic claims, and evinced "bad faith and corruption in the attitude towards lay analysts." See Kenneth Eisold, "The Splitting of the New York Psychoanalytic Society and the Construction of Psychoanalytic Authority," *Int. J. Psycho-Anal.*, 79:871–885, 1998, quoted at p. 881 and "The Profession of Psychoanalysis: Past Failures and Future Possibilities," *Contemp. Psychoanal.*, 39:557–582, 2003, esp. pp. 564–567.

analysis contains all the ingredients of a unified theory of psychoanalysis, Rangell arrogates to himself and those analysts who think like him the task of identifying the "nonexpendable elements" of traditional theory and those accretions to traditional theory that are "valid," with validity being a function of compatibility with the preexisting Freudian/ego-psychological totality.

There is a vicious circularity in such reasoning, since anyone can claim that his or her personal amalgamation of concepts and therapeutic strategies is the "totality" that best represents his or her experience, and then proceed to judge the validity of new ideas in terms of their compatibility with this individually time-tested totality. But one man's totality is another's abridgement. Rangell's psychoanalytic core—the constellation of writings that are foundational to "his" psychoanalysis—follows a path from Freud to Heinz Hartmann to Otto Fenichel to David Rapaport.[63] A contemporary Kleinian core might go from Freud to Karl Abraham to Melanie Klein to Betty Joseph. A self-psychological core might go from Freud to Sándor Ferenczi to D. W. Winnicott to Heinz Kohut to motivational systems theorists such as Joseph Lichtenberg (or, alternatively, from Freud to D. W. Winnicott, to Heinz Kohut to intersubjectivity theorists such as Robert Stolorow). Every theoretically minded, school-affiliated psychoanalyst can reconstruct a trajectory of growth to theoretical wholeness.

63. Interview of Leo and Anita Rangell by Susan Rosbrow-Reich and Laurie W. Raymond, in Raymond & Rosbrow-Reich, eds., *The Inward Eye: Psychoanalysts Reflect on Their Lives and Work* (Hillsdale, NJ: Analytic Press, 1997), pp. 139–180 at pp. 164–165. In this interview of May, 1991, Rangell remarked that Otto Fenichel's *Psychoanalytic Theory of Neurosis*, published in 1945, "to me is still a bible." Rangell claims that the "collective consensus" will determine which ideas are part of the "generally held theoretical system" of psychoanalysis, but the claim is tendentious because Rangell unilaterally eliminates concepts (such as the selfobject) that are essential to particular analytic communities. The fact is, there *is* no cohesive psychoanalytic community within which consensus can be sought. If psychoanalysts were capable of a "reasonable consensus" about essential and inessential concepts, the field would never have fractionated into separate schools of thought with their own training establishments. To argue, as Rangell does, that attachment research "and its accompanying issues" are "an intrinsic part of composite theory" or that Kohut's notion of selfobject "is already in main theory under different guises" is simply to underscore his rhetorical insistence that the paradigm of American ego psychology that emerged in the 1950s and 1960s has proven more adequate to psychoanalytic theory and practice than any of the rival totalities that arose in its wake. See Leo Rangell, *The Road to Unity in Psychoanalytic Theory* (Lanham, MD: Aronson, 2007), pp. 85–96, quoted at pp. 87, 89.

Rangell's "total composite theory" falls back on a notion of "inclusion" grounded in his own paradigmatic (viz., ego-psychological) assumptions. In much the same way, Richards's embeddedness in the American ego-psychological tradition frames his call for dialogue; analogous calls for dialogue by Kleinians, relationalists, self psychologists, and Lacanians would have very different, but no less salient, narrative scaffoldings. All such calls for dialogue, however well-intended, obscure the disheartening degree to which psychoanalytic theories have congealed into paradigm-like worldviews that make specific ontological claims about the kinds of entities[64] that constitute the mental domain of human experience. Thomas Kuhn clearly overstated the case in his original insistence that rationality only pertains to choices within a paradigm and not to choices between paradigms. But his remarks about the inherent difficulty of dialogue among proponents of different paradigms remain apropos and help explain why the kind of dialogue called for by Richards and others has been so unavailing in reversing the fractionation of the field:

> To the extent, as significant as it is incomplete, that two scientific schools disagree about what is a problem and what a solution, they will inevitably talk through each other when debating the merits of their respective paradigms. In the partially circular arguments that regularly result, each paradigm will be shown to satisfy more or less the criteria that it dictates for itself and to fall short of those dictated by its opponent.[65]

---

64. I intend "entities" to comprise not only structures but also forces, tendencies, proclivities, desires, wishes, and the like.

65. Thomas Kuhn, *The Structure of Scientific Revolutions*, 2nd ed. (Chicago: University of Chicago Press, 1970), pp. 108–109. Apropos Richards's aforementioned plea for "a measure of humility," Greenberg makes the relevant Kuhnian point in noting that "the abstract ideas that we apply to the material do not simply give shape to our findings; they define what will become the data of observation in the first place. . . . Which of these is seen as salient, and how the various pieces fit together, is always a function of the observer's preconceptions" (Jay Greenberg, "Commentary on Richards," *JAPA*, 51[suppl]: 89–98, 2003, quoted at p. 90). Wallerstein, in his prefatory remarks to the *JAPA* supplement, observes that Greenberg's argument "is based on the undeniable truth that we all approach phenomena with preconceptions that shape what we regard as observable data (and what we ignore as inconsequential, or preclude entirely from our vision), and that we can never fully shake ourselves free of our preconceptions about how things hang together." See Robert S.

It is not that dialogue among proponents of different psychoanalytic theories is pointless. Dialogue, especially when accompanied by examination of differences and efforts at intertheory interpretation, can be of considerable clarifying benefit.[66] But clarification per se is not tantamount to integration or synthesis or even to critical comparison. The fact is that, given the holistic character of psychoanalytic theories, dialogue is necessarily inconclusive. The kind of dialogue promoted by Richards and others does not tend to rational closure; it cannot overcome power differentials and attitudinal barriers that are the product of decades of institutional history; it cannot move the field forward.

Or at least it has not evinced an ability to move the field forward to date. When analysts of different theoretical persuasions come together to discuss a single case presentation, the comparative yield is little more than an underscoring of theoretical pluralism. Consider the 1987 issue of the journal *Psychoanalytic Inquiry* entitled "How Theory Shapes Technique: Perspectives on a Clinical Study," in which Martin Silverman, a Freudian psychoanalyst, presented a clinical case that elicited commentary by many analysts, a leading self psychologist (Arnold Goldberg) and interpersonalist (Edgar Levenson), among them. Summarizing the wildly divergent rereadings of the case, Estelle Shane was led to remark that "the diversity of opinions regarding the diagnosis and dynamics of Silverman's patient [would] suggest that one's theoretical stance takes precedence over other considerations." And Sydney Pulver, in his epilogue to the issue, was led to conclude that "Facts, per se, do not exist. The very idea of what constitutes data and is thus worth recording is determined by the analyst's theoretical bent."[67]

Wallerstein, "The Intertwining of Politics and Science in Psychoanalytic History," *JAPA*, 51(suppl): 7–21, 2003, quoted at p. 11.

66. Of course, it is arguable whether such dialogue among psychoanalysts of different schools of thought has ever taken place. The French analyst André Green, for one, believes it has not, and he offers the expression "pluralistic pseudo-thought" to describe what typically passes as comparative psychoanalytic discussion, particularly on the Internet. See André Green, "The Illusion of Common Ground and Mythical Pluralism," *Int. J. Psycho-Anal.*, 86:627–632, 2005, at p. 629.

67. Estelle Shane, "Varieties of Psychoanalytic Experience," *Psychoanal. Inq.*, 7:199–206, 1987; Sydney Pulver, "Epilogue," *Psychoanal. Inq.*, 7:292, 1987.

This lesson was reinforced three years later in a second issue of *Psychoanalytic Inquiry* given to multiple theoretical commentaries on a case history, this time a self-psychological presentation by James Fosshage. Faced with another series of theory-driven reformulations so disjunctive as to preclude dialogue, the issue editors, Jule Miller and Stephen Post, put the best face on interpretive incommensurabilities and lauded the exercise simply for underscoring "The necessary and inevitable role that theory plays in clinical analysis—in data selection, in understanding, in analytic technique, and even in clinical perception."[68] But surely there is more to common ground than the hortatory call to dialogue. In the world of contemporary psychoanalysis, a united front must be forged; it cannot be willed into existence by good intentions or linguistic legerdemain. "Psychoanalysis today is under siege. We are fighting for survival—the survival of our profession and of our ability to deliver quality care to our patients." Nothing has changed since Robert Pyles, then immediate past president of the American Psychoanalytic Association, offered this assessment to the APsaA membership in his plenary address of November 25, 2000.[69] How can a field captured by so many entrenched subcom-

---

68. Jule Miller & Stephen L. Post, "Epilogue," *Psychoanal. Inq.*, 10:623, 1990. I am not aware that the comparative exercise has progressed beyond the scholasticism of the case commentary issues of *Psychoanalytic Inquiry*. Indeed, I am uncertain that such exercises *can* progress beyond school-based reformulations of clinical material that attempt to persuade the reader to inhabit a different psychoanalytic world. Certainly the 2003 issue of *JAPA* given to psychoanalytic politics, with its succession of tendentious, school-based accounts, does not suggest that anything has changed. I am of a mind with Frank Summers, who recently observed, "The fact that multiple theories are competing for the psychoanalytic stage should not be confused with dialogue. One need only peruse the 2003 supplemental issue of *JAPA* on psychoanalytic politics to see this attitude in action. Charges of distortion from theorists of each school of the other's views prevailed over substantive discussion of ideas. Such charges and countercharges are typical when theorists do confront each other's ideas. There is no indication in any of the articles in that issue that a single writer was in any way influenced by the arguments of any other. One can scan the psychoanalytic landscape long and hard without finding evidence that any theoretical paradigm has been significantly modified by the ideas of another." Frank Summers, "Theoretical Insularity and the Crisis of Psychoanalysis," *Psychoanal. Psychol.*, 25:413–424, 2008, quoted at p. 417.

69. Robert L. Pyles, "The Good Fight: Psychoanalysis in the Age of Managed Care," *JAPA*, 51(suppl): 23–41, 2003, quoted at p. 23.

munities defend its disciplinary bulwark and move forward in politically, socially, and clinically responsible ways? What are the conceptual and clinical metals out of which a united front may be forged? Are there strategies of collective renewal that analysts may pursue in an era of theoretical pluralism?

Chapter 6

Whence Progress?

... there are really no good empirical grounds for supposing that the efficacy of psychoanalysis is best explained in terms of psychoanalytic theory, or that the efficacy of alternative forms of professional psychotherapy [is] best explained in terms of their conventionally associated theories (behaviorist, cognitive, gestalt, and the like). With respect to theoretical accounts of the efficacy of professional psychotherapies, the situation is epistemically wide open.[1]

If well-meaning dialogue among proponents of different schools of thought cannot pull psychoanalysis onto a normal science trajectory, then what can? Is there another pathway to common ground and the kind of sustained evolutionary growth that issues from it? Perhaps, as many leading analysts believe, the field can progress in the manner of normal science if its theory and practice are brought into conformity with the more robust findings of other fields of inquiry. It is a matter of mapping psychoanalytic hypotheses onto the more robust findings of another discipline or disciplines in order to achieve congruence or at least compatibility among the several fields. As David Olds has recently observed, until such time as psychoanalytic research devises credible measures of clinical efficacy, "an important support for psychoanalysis will be its credibility derived from parallel sciences." Information derived from these sciences, he continues, may have an evidential valence. It provides fodder for already active controversies within the field; it enters into deliberations about clinical theory and

1. John D. Greenwood, "Freud's 'Tally' Argument, Placebo Control Treatments, and the Evaluation of Psychotherapy," *Phil. Sci.*, 63:605–621, 1996, quoted at p. 610.

technique; and it may eventually promote "a corralling of analytic theory into a more consistent and less fragmented discipline."[2]

Perhaps, then, we can speak of psychoanalytic progress if the term signals a willingness to opt for a version of psychoanalytic theory that best aligns with "parallel sciences." Such a psychoanalytic theory, in the language of philosophy of science, would stand up to tests in diverse domains of application. In so doing, it would be more reliable and yield more tenable clinical approaches than competing psychoanalytic theories that met clinical-heuristic tests only in the psychoanalytic domain. But what sounds like a promising line of advance has its own pluralistic problems. To wit, it runs up against the sheer multiplicity of nonclinical domains in which psychoanalytic theories are currently being mapped; the incommensurabilities among some of these domains; and the inability of psychoanalysis to rank order these nonclinical domains in ways that may eventually precipitate "better" and "worse" mapping strategies.

What nonclinical domains are relevant to evolution of a progressive psychoanalysis? Over the past quarter century, the mapping project has embraced information theory, observational infancy research, neuroscience, systems theory, connectionism, attachment theory, complexity theory and chaos theory (sometimes under the umbrella of nonlinear dynamic systems theory), semiotics, and metaphor theory. Historically, the mapping in question has aimed at establishing compatibility rather than entailment. With respect to neuroscience, the compatibility may be sketched in such broad brush strokes as to be virtually generic in character. For example, the psychophysiology of stress allows us to speculate about a possible neuroanatomical basis for the "transduction" of nonphysical symbolic stimuli into physical events in the brain, and of physical changes in the body into psychological phenomena with mental meanings.[3] More typically, it is a matter of

2. David D. Olds, "Interdisciplinary Studies and Our Practice," *JAPA*, 54:857–876, 2006, quoted at p. 873.

3. Morton Reiser, *Mind, Brain, Body: Toward a Convergence of Psychoanalysis and Neurobiology* (NY: Basic Books, 1984), pp. 165–166, 198. Two decades ago, Reiser was appropriately circumspect about the nature of such "convergence": "The data indicate how such things could happen, not actually how they do happen" (p. 166). Convergence, from his standpoint, merely signified "the search . . . for a clinical perspective and for a useful way of approaching data from the two widely disparate

analogical reasoning that posits a "convergence" or "intersection" between a particular psychoanalytic concept and a neuroscientific finding. The psychoanalytic concept of defense is theorized to be "related" to the notion of interhemispheric communication, or the mutative impact of psychoanalytic interpretations is found compatible with concepts of "brain plasticity" and the priming of "learning readiness" within the CNS, or the psychoanalytic concept of adaptation is found compatible with the neuroscientific concept of neural control.[4] Such convergences have, in the hands of specific authors, generally been keyed to one kind of psychoanalytic theory or another. The literature recruiting brain science to the support of traditional psychoanalytic hypotheses about mental functioning is punctuated by the books of Morton Reiser (1984), Fred Levin (1991), and Arnold Modell (1993), respectively.[5] Modell was among the first analysts to utilize the neurophysiological model of Gerald Edelman, a Nobel prize winner, as biological scaffolding of a psychoanalytic theory that revolved around a self-generating "private" self. He found Edelman's work especially resonant with Winnicottian object relations theory.[6]

Over the past decade, neurophysiological and neurobiological findings and concepts have continued to be appropriated by exponents of traditional ego psychology, "modern" Freudian psychoanalysis, self psychology, and relational/interpersonal psychoanalysis. The search for "consiliences" between psychoanalysis and neuroscience led to the formation of the Neuroscience Study Group of the New York

---

realms of mind and brain" (p. 186). The fact that "data from the psychoanalytic method cannot be meaningfully linked directly to data from biological methods of studying the physiologic motor or effector aspects of the stress response" led to his espousal of a dual-track approach, according to which meanings do not explain physiology and physiology does not explain meanings (p. 210). Movement toward a "convergence of psychoanalysis and neurobiology," within so modest a venue, lay simply in coming closer "to specifying some modest but heuristically worthwhile details and working hypotheses" (p. 197).

4. Fred M. Levin, *Mapping the Mind: The Intersection of Psychoanalysis and Neuroscience* (Hillsdale, NJ: Analytic Press, 1991), chaps. 2, 3, & 4, respectively.

5. Morton Reiser, *Mind, Brain, Body* (n. 3); Levin *Mapping the Mind* (n. 4); Arnold Modell, *The Private Self* (Cambridge: Harvard University Press, 1993).

6. Modell, *The Private Self* (n. 5), pp. 55–58, 72 and passim.

Psychoanalytic Institute in the early 90s, and this group has grown into the Arnold Pfeffer Center for Neuro-Psychoanalysis and the International Neuro-Psychoanalysis Society, with the latter launching the interdisciplinary journal *Neuropsychoanalysis* in 1999.[7] One early signpost of the maturing analytic use of neuroscience was Karen Kaplan-Solms and Mark Solms's *Clinical Studies in Neuro-Psychoanalysis: Introduction to a Depth Neuropsychology*, published in 2000. Relying on a series of neuropsychological/psychoanalytic case studies of patients with localized brain lesions, the authors employed a neuro-dynamic variant of the classical *clinico-anatomical method* as a vehicle for establishing consiliences between complex mental processes, psychoanalytically rendered—and cast entirely in the language of Freud's own metapsychology and its ego-psychological elaboration in America—and specific brain centers.

What exactly is the clinico-anatomical method that Kaplan-Solms and Solms employ in their search for consiliences? In the first half of the nineteenth century, French pathologists of the Paris clinical school performed postmortem dissections to identify at the tissular level the anatomical lesions associated with patients' symptomatology and clinical course.[8] In the great institutions linked together in the municipal

---

7. On these developments, see Mark Solms & Oliver Turnbull, *The Brain and the Inner World: An Introduction to the Neuroscience of Subjective Experience* (NY: Other Press, 2002), pp. 300–304.

8. We associate the development of pathological anatomy with the pioneering research of Xavier Bichat and his gifted students, among them René Laënnec, Gaspard Bayle, Guillaume Dupuytren, Pierre Louis, and Gabriel Andral. But "in a way," as Erwin Ackerknecht has observed, "almost every Paris clinician was a pathological anatomist" during this half century. The standard work on the Paris clinical school and its innovations is Ackerknecht's *Medicine at the Paris Hospital, 1794–1848* (Baltimore: Johns Hopkins Press, 1967), quoted here at p. 164. For examples of revisionist historiography arguing against the singular role of Paris clinical researchers in the epistemological and clinical shift of the early nineteenth century, including the emergence of pathological anatomy, see the essays by L. W. B. Brockliss, Othmar Keel, and Ann La Berge in Caroline Hannaway & Ann F. La Berge, eds., *Constructing Paris Medicine*, Clio Medica, vol. 50 (Amsterdam: Rodopi, 1998). For a balanced assessment of the aforementioned volume that reemphasizes the uniqueness of Paris as birthplace to "a new kind of medical research community, different from anything that had existed until then," see George Weisz's masterful review essay, "Reconstructing Paris Medicine: Essay Review," *Bull. Hist. Med.*, 75:105–119, 2001, quoted at p. 114.

hospital system of Paris, active therapies yielded to the "expectant method": French clinicians typically allowed disease to run its course; for the many patients who never recovered, autopsy would hopefully bear out diagnosis. "The triumph with these [French] physicians," observed an American student studying in Paris in the mid-1850s, "is in the dead-room."[9] This correlative clinico-anatomical method, in turn, was adopted by mid-nineteenth-century German neurology, which refined the method of the Paris school to the point of identifying the brain centers associated with specific kinds of neurological dysfunction.[10] Kaplan-Solms and Solms, while following Freud in rejecting a "narrow localizationist neurology," propose an inversion of the classical clinico-anatomical approach: They suggest we *begin* with neurological patients whose brain lesions have been diagnostically confirmed and work with them analytically to grasp clinically the degradation of "complex mental processes" associated with their damaged brain centers. In this manner, modified psychoanalytic therapy of neurologically impaired patients acquires an *evidential valence* commensurate with the postmortem findings of nineteenth-century French and German pathologists. To wit, psychoanalytic illumination of the functional impairment of patients with specific brain lesions—again, rendered exclusively in the language of ego functions and ego deficits—circumscribes the contribution of individual brain centers to the anatomically distributed "functional systems" that underlie complex mental processes. In this manner, the neurodynamic method, employed comparatively over a range of neurological cases, provides the "dynamic neurological representation" of complex mental processes.[11]

9. Quoted in John Harley Warner, *The Therapeutic Perspective: Medical Practice, Knowledge, and Identity in America, 1820–1885* (Princeton: Princeton University Press, 1986), p. 191.

10. Paul Broca's and Carl Wernicke's discoveries, in 1865 and 1874 respectively, of the localized brain lesions that correspond to the two varieties of aphasia that bear their names, the loss of the power of speech (Broca's amnesia) and the loss of the capacity to understand spoken language (Wernicke's amnesia) are among the crowning "correlative" achievements of the localizing tradition.

11. Karen Kaplan-Solms & Mark Solms, *Clinical Studies in Neuro-Psychoanalysis: Introduction to a Depth Neuropsychology*, 2nd ed. (NY: Guilford, 2002 [2000]), p. 43. Kaplan-Solms & Solms illustrate what they mean by "dynamic neurological

Observational infancy research has an even older lineage and has been invoked to support classical psychoanalytic theory (in the guise, for example, of Anna Freud's and René Spitz's studies of mother-infant separation during World War II or Margaret Mahler's observations of the separation-individuation process). More recently, it has achieved special salience among proponents of nonlinear systems theory approaches, motivational systems theory, and relational theory.[12] Modern infancy research sustains the research program of the Boston Change Process Study Group (BCPSG), which relies on findings about early mother-infant negotiations that subserve mutual regulation and the implicit, enactive nature of the infant's "relational knowing" to anchor a vision of analytic process as the progressive development of "implicit relational knowing." Such knowing—which comprises, inter alia, a shared subjective sense of dyadic "coherence" and therapeutic "fittedness"; co-created therapeutic intentions; and a co-created direction of therapeutic inquiry—emerges out of the moment-by-moment unpredictability of discrete "relational moves" by analyst and analysand. This approach, as BCPSG members have acknowledged, falls back on research findings that are convergent with "central tenets" of relational psychoanalysis.[13]

---

representation" by considering the "neurodynamics" of dreaming. They identify and describe six separate disturbances of dreaming associated with lesions (and their associated syndromes) in six different brain regions. Dreaming cannot be localized in any one of these brain regions; rather, dreaming, a complex mental process, draws on the elementary component functions associated with each of these regions. The process of dreaming thereby "unfolds over a functional system that has six fundamental component parts: the left inferior parietal region, the right inferior parietal region, the deep ventromesial frontal region, the ventromesial occipito-temporal region, the frontal limbic region, and the temporal limbic region, . . . the function of dreaming cannot be localized within any of these regions; rather, it must be thought of as a dynamic process that unfolds between [sic] these different component parts of the functional system as a whole." See pp. 44–57, quoted at p. 52.

12. Among many noteworthy works of the past quarter century, I single out Joseph Lichtenberg, *Psychoanalysis and Infant Research* (Hillsdale, NJ: Analytic Press, 1983); Daniel Stern, *The Interpersonal World of the Infant: A View from Psychoanalysis and Developmental Psychology* (NY: Basic Books, 1985); and Beatrice Beebe & Frank Lachmann, *Infant Research and Adult Treatment: Co-constructing Interactions* (Hillsdale, NJ: Analytic Press, 1995).

13. Daniel N. Stern, et al., "Non-Interpretive Mechanisms in Psychoanalytic Therapy: The 'Something More' Than Interpretation," *Int. J. Psycho-Anal.*, 79:903–921, 1998;

Information theory was first mapped onto psychoanalysis in two influential books of the 70s; beginning in the 80s, it reemerged in the form of Bucci's sophisticated multiple-code theory, with its parsing of analytic transactions into subsymbolic, nonverbal symbolic, and verbal symbolic categories of information processing and associated research protocol for assessing analytic transcripts in terms of "computerized referential activity."[14] Metaphor theory has been recruited in defense of classical psychoanalytic notions of transference, defense, and the defended against.[15]

In Olds's work of the mid-90s, the connectionist model (the activation of neural network systems) was adduced in support of free association, repression, and "higher-level modulating defenses"—it sustained a kind of cranialized ego psychology. This path to integration was subsequently pursued by Westen and Gabbard, for whom the connectionist model, with its notion of "parallel constraint

J. P. Nahum & The Boston Change Process Study Group (BCPSG), "Explicating the Implicit: The Local Level and the Microprocess of Change in the Analytic Situation," *Int. J. Psycho-Anal.*, 83:1051–1062, 2002; BCPSG, "The 'Something More' than Interpretation Revisited: Sloppiness and Co-Creativity in the Psychoanalytic Encounter," *JAPA*, 53:693–729, 2005; BCPSG, "The Foundational Level of Psychodynamic Meaning: Implicit Process in Relation to Conflict, Defense, and the Dynamic Unconscious," *Int. J. Psycho-Anal.*, 88:1–16, 2007 (reference to "central tenets" at p. 7); BCPSG, "Forms of Relational Meaning: Issues in the Relations Between the Implicit and Reflective-Verbal Domains," *Psychoanal. Dial.*, 18:125–148, 2008; BCPSG, "Forms of Relational Meaning: Reply to Commentaries," *Psychoanal. Dial.*, 18:197–202, 2008.

14. Emmanuel Peterfreund, *Information, Systems, and Psychoanalysis: An Evolutionary Biological Approach to Psychoanalytic Theory.* (Psychological Issues Monograph 25/26; NY: International Universities Press, 1971); A. D. Rosenblatt & J. T. Thickstun, *Modern Psychoanalytic Concepts in a General Psychology* (Psychological Issues Monograph 42/43; NY: International Universities Press, 1977); Wilma Bucci, "Dual Coding: A Cognitive Model for Psychoanalytic Research," *JAPA*, 33:571–607, 1985; Wilma Bucci, *Psychoanalysis and Cognitive Science: A Multiple Code Theory* (NY: Guilford, 1997).

15. Antal F. Borbely, "Toward a Temporal Theory of the Mind," *Psychoanal. Contemp. Th.*, 10:459–487, 1987 and "A Psychoanalytic Concept of Metaphor," *Int. J. Psycho-Anal.*, 79:923–936, 1998.

satisfaction,"[16] could be mapped onto ego-psychological concepts of conflict, defense, and compromise formation; used to break down such "overinclusive concepts" as projective identification and enactment; and worked into a cognitive-neuroscientific elucidation of the phenomena of transference-countertransference.[17]

Semiotics, with its concepts of sign and sign systems, has been proffered as foundational to a new metapsychology that locates mental process in the same conceptual world as all other biological processes. In the sophisticated rendering of Olds, semiotics not only helps to resolve "certain antinomies within the [psychoanalytic] theory, particularly between biological reductionism and hermeneutics," but also leads to clinically useful reformulations of transference, enactment, drive, and especially affect.[18] Dynamic systems theory (aka complexity theory, chaos theory), as we shall see below, has been utilized by analysts all over the theoretical spectrum to markedly different ends; different variants of it have proven especially congenial to contemporary ego psychology and to relational psychoanalysis/intersubjectivity theory, respectively.[19]

16. According to connectionism, "perception, memory, and cognition involve processes of parallel constraint satisfaction, in which the brain simultaneously and unconsciously processes various features of a stimulus or situation (called constraints because they limit the conclusions that can be drawn). The mind then draws the best tentative conclusion it can based on the available data. In other words, it equilibrates to the solution that provides the best 'fit,' given current conditions and the person's chronically and recently activated networks." Drew Westen & Glen O. Gabbard, "Developments in Cognitive Neuroscience: I. Conflict, Compromise, and Connectionism," *JAPA*, 50:53–98, 2002, quoted at p. 75.

17. David D. Olds, "Connectionism and Psychoanalysis," *JAPA*, 42:581–611, 1994. See especially p. 596: "We are, in effect, equating the ego with the brain, and making consciousness one of the brain's output vectors." Westen has published extensively in both psychological and psychoanalytic journals on the impact of cognitive neuroscience on psychodynamic understanding. Here I have relied on his two overview essays with Gabbard: Westen & Gabbard: "Developments in Cognitive Neuroscience" (n. 16) and Drew Westen & Glen O. Gabbard, "Developments in Cognitive Neuroscience: II. Implications for Theories of Transference," *JAPA*, 60:99–134, 2002.

18. David D. Olds, "A Semiotic Model of Mind," *JAPA*, 48:497–529, 2000 (quoted at p. 525), and "Affects as a Sign System," *Neuro-Psychoanal.*, 5:81–95, 2003.

19. See Estelle Shane & William J. Coburn, issue eds., "Contemporary Dynamic Systems Theories: Innovative Contributions to Psychoanalysis," *Psychoanal. Inq.* 22(5),

Attachment theory has been in vogue since the early 90s and has been recruited in support of motivational-systems approaches to psychoanalysis, object relations theories, aspects of classical psychoanalysis, and especially relational psychoanalysis.[20] It has also yielded its own re-visioning of psychoanalytic developmental theory, replete with attachment-supported concepts, such as Fonagy's notion of "mentalization," that attempt to bridge the divide between intrapsychic and interpersonal experience via an interactive model of the manner in which young children come to an understanding of psychic reality. According to the theory of mentalization, the young child's reflective understanding of his own mental states, his "core sense of mental selfhood," grows out of playful interactions in which the child experiences his own mental states being reflected on by a parent or older playmate. Empirical studies cited by Fonagy and his coworker Mary Target suggest that the attachment system and the "reflective system" are interrelated, so that "security of attachment is related to mentalizing capacity."[21] Reciprocally, developmental research suggests that the caregiver's "mindfulness" about the child's mental status predicts

---

2002; "Nonlinear Systems Theory and Psychoanalysis: Symposium in Honor of Emmanuel Ghent" (Introduced by David D. Olds), *Psychoanal. Dial.*, 15:223–319, 2005. For a provocative relational rendering of gender informed by dynamic systems theory, see Adrienne Harris, *Gender as Soft Assembly* (Hillsdale, NJ: Analytic Press, 2005).

20. See Joseph Lichtenberg, *Psychoanalysis and Motivation* (Hillsdale, NJ: Analytic Press, 1989) and Joseph Lichtenberg, Frank Lachmann, & James Fosshage, *Self and Motivational Systems: Toward a Theory of Psychoanalytic Technique* (Hillsdale, NJ: Analytic Press, 2001). On the special affinity of relational/interpersonal psychoanalysis to attachment theory, see Peter Fonagy, *Attachment Theory and Psychoanalysis* (NY: Other Press, 2001), pp. 123–134.

21. The theory of mentalization was set forth in two major papers published in 1996: Peter Fonagy & Mary Target, "Playing with Reality: I. Theory of Mind and the Normal Development of Psychic Reality," *Int. J. Psycho-Anal.*, 77: 217–233 and Mary Target & Peter Fonagy, "Playing with Reality: II. The Development of Psychic Reality from a Theoretical Perspective," *Int. J. Psycho-Anal.*, 77:459–479. Quoted phrases are at II, pp. 461, 466. For more recent examinations of mentalization in relation to attachment issues, see Fonagy, *Attachment Theory and Psychoanalysis* (n. 20), pp. 168–179, and Peter Fonagy et al., *Affect Regulation, Mentalization, and the Development of the Self* (NY: Other Press, 2002).

the likelihood of secure attachment.[22] The Boston Change Process Study Group has made ample use of attachment research in providing examples of the kinds of early relational transactions in which meanings (e.g., of conflict or defense) are enactively encoded; such research sustains the Group's foundational concept of "implicit relational knowing."[23]

Taken in its totality, the mapping literature is something to behold. It is evocative, suggestive, and conducive to many novel insights. But to date it has failed utterly to provide a basis for psychoanalytic common ground. For when all is said and done, we are left with a plethora of integrative strategies, each of which has its own proponents and critics. There are surprisingly few lines of communication among the integrators, much less a profession-wide consensus about how to prioritize the various integrative projects in the interest of promoting common ground. So we are left to ponder: Who will integrate the integrators? Is a psychoanalysis that is "consilient" with modern neuroscience more important than a psychoanalysis convergent with certain central tenets of modern infancy research? Is the quest for a flexibly postclassical relational theory that embraces the range and multiplicity of self states (as per complexity theory) superordinate to the quest for a comprehensive motivational theory consistent with the findings of modern neuroscience? Is the search for new metapsychological grounding principles, such as the concept of the sign, that wed psychoanalysis to all other biological processes, more important than hermeneutic exegesis of psychoanalytic inquiry as a singularly human science in the spirit of Dilthey's *Geisteswissenschaften*?

Even proponents of specific integrative approaches have difficulty ascertaining what kind of psychoanalysis their mapping strategies speak to. In the case of attachment theory, the difficulty is augmented

22. Peter Fonagy & Mary Target, "Early Intervention and the Development of Self-Regulation," *Psychoanal. Inq.*, 22:307–335, 2002, cited at p. 321. Fonagy & Target cite Arietta Slade et al., "Mothers' Representation of Their Relationships with Their Toddlers: Links to Adult Attachment and Observed Mothering," *Develop. Psychol.*, 35:611–619 in support of the claim that parental "mindfulness" is a "significant predictor" of secure attachment.

23. BCPSG, "Foundational Level of Psychodynamic Meaning" (n. 13), pp. 8, 10–11.

by the fact that attachment research has not only been mapped onto aspects of different psychoanalytic theories but has also given rise to an analytically oriented, attachment-based psychotherapy modality. Indeed, analytic theorists have played no small role in delineating this modality and specifying the manner in which it intersects with, and differs from, psychoanalytic treatment approaches. Arietta Slade, among others, has used Fonagy's theory of mentalization as the basis of a new "hybrid" approach to child psychotherapy that involves concomitant treatment of child and mother. At the community level, this type of "mentalization-based therapy" has gained expression in "reflective parenting programs" in which therapists "model the reflective stance" in an effort to make difficult babies and children more "sensible" to their parents.[24]

The relationship between attachment-based psychotherapy and psychoanalysis is conceptually ambiguous. Analytic theorists, as noted, have formulated the modality, but they are equivocal on whether they are offering an empirically sustained variant of psychoanalysis or a new genre of psychotherapy. Slade has been in the front ranks of integrators expatiating on the implications of attachment research for clinical work; her examination of how attachment findings shape clinical listening, clinical formulations, and clinical goals has been published in two venues, once in the *Handbook of Attachment* under the heading "Implications for the Theory and Practice of Individual Psychotherapy with Adults" and once in the *Journal of the American Psychoanalytic Association* under the heading "Implications for Psychoanalysis."[25]

One need not quibble with the distinction between "individual psychotherapy with adults" and "psychoanalysis" at the level of clini-

---

24. Arietta Slade, "Representation, Symbolization, and Affect Regulation in the Concomitant Treatment of a Mother and Child: Attachment Theory and Child Psychotherapy," *Psychoanal. Inq.*, 19:797–830, 1999. Arietta Slade, "Reflective Parenting Programs: Theory and Development," *Psychoanal. Inq.*, 26:640–657, 2007.

25. Arietta Slade, "Attachment Theory and Research: Implications for the Theory and Practice of Individual Psychotherapy with Adults," in Jude Cassidy & Phillip R. Shaver, eds., *Handbook of Attachment: Theory, Research, and Clinical Applications* (NY: Guilford Press, 1999), pp. 575–595. A portion of this essay was republished a year later as "The Development and Organization of Attachment: Implications for Psychoanalysis," *JAPA*, 48:1147–1174, 2000.

cal heuristics. But the heuristic value of Slade's undertaking does not make it ipso facto a tenable integrative strategy. It may well be, as she avers, that "it is possible to develop an ear for attachment themes and attachment patterns" without falling prey to the "categorical ways of thinking" associated with rigid attachment classification. In this manner, attachment classifications become "metaphors for qualities of psychological organization and internalized object representations." Understood thusly, the classifications can "directly affect both how the clinician understands the dynamics underlying the patient's psychic organization, and how she speaks to such dynamics in the clinical situation." Alluding to "dismissing" and "preoccupied" patterns of attachment behavior, Slade observes that "One has only to be frozen out by a patient's detachment, ensnared in a patient's enmeshment, or lost in a patient's disorientation to appreciate the implications of these patterns for understanding aspects of clinical process."[26]

Well and good. There is much to admire in Slade's sensitive rendering of the way different attachment organizations shape here-and-now therapeutic relationships. But as a psychoanalytic mapping strategy, her approach involves a conceptual sleight of hand. After all, psychodynamically speaking, one can only make sense of being "frozen," "ensnared," or "lost" in theory-specific ways. As a vehicle for getting at the dynamics underlying psychic organization—as opposed to broadening clinicians' sensitivity to such dynamics—attachment categories either remain anaclitic on one or another psychoanalytic theory or supplant psychoanalytic theory altogether. Absent a guiding psychoanalytic theory to make sense of such consulting-room behaviors, that is, we are left with explanations framed in terms of an attachment-category typology that can be fitted to the here-and-now phenomenology of clinical work with patients with primitive pathology, often trauma victims, who were heretofore understood variously and *differently* by specific psychoanalytic theories. Further, the attachment typology yields its own psychotherapeutic roadmap, since attachment classifications implicate attachment-based explanations of different affect-regulatory strategies and the dynamic representational models that grow out of them. In attachment-based psychotherapy, in contradistinction to psychoanalysis, "notions of attachment organization

26. Slade, "Development and Organization of Attachment" (n. 25), pp. 1159, 1161; Slade, "Attachment Theory and Research" (n. 25), p. 585.

provide a therapist with metaphors for thinking about early patterns of affect regulation and defense, and of imagining and speaking to a patient's experience." By listening for attachment themes, therapists come to hear narratives that "emerge as a function of attachment organization" and devise interventions responsive to this organization.[27]

Slade's use of attachment theory is tantamount to a *heuristic* mapping approach: It finesses the issue of just which psychoanalytic theory (or which parts of which theories) will be called on to explain the consulting-room phenomenology of disordered attachment. A complementary mapping approach that involves attachment theory is more properly termed *holistic*: It finesses the fact that specific attachment findings can only align with specific psychoanalytic claims. According to the latter strategy, attachment research, along with its associated neurobiological claims, is adduced in support of psychoanalytic therapy in some generic sense of the term. The same researchers who dedicate themselves to establishing the relevance of attachment theory to the clinical endeavor are generally disinclined to appeal to attachment findings to mediate among the rival theoretical claims of different schools of analysis. Slade, Fonagy, and Target all evince this tendency, as does Allan Schore, an avowed integrationist for whom "psychoanalytic therapeutic relationships" per se can alter the psychoneurobiological deficits that arise from traumatic attachments owing to the "lifelong plastic capacity of the prefrontal limbic cortex." The precise character of such relationships, the theoretical assumptions that shape them and posit their clinical trajectory, is of far less moment to him. A decade ago, he simply observed that a rapprochement between psychoanalysis and neurobiology would necessarily involve, inter alia, the field's "reintegration of its own internal theoretical divisions." Five years later, this prerequisite gave way to a less constraining proviso, as Schore simply admonished that "self-psychological, relational, and intersubjective psychoanalytic clinicians now need to integrate updated

---

27. Slade continues: "Thus the nature of a therapist's efforts to transform and enter into a patient's narrative will be profoundly shaped by the individual's attachment security. How therapists talk to patients and what they endeavor to do in their talking and in their listening will vary as a function of the patients' predominant (at a given point in treatment) attachment organization." Slade, "Attachment Theory and Research" (n. 25), p. 585.

developmental and neurobiological information into their conceptions of psychopathogenesis."[28]

Juxtaposed with both the heuristic and holistic approaches to "attachment" integration is what I will term the *piecemeal* approach: Here it is simply a matter of itemizing points of contact between attachment research and various psychoanalytic schools of thought. Certain theorists enter the game with a priori theoretical preferences; others simply strive for ecumenical inclusiveness. Attachment research has been adduced in support of the Oedipus complex, even when the latter is reframed in terms of attachment-derived insights.[29] But it has led others to jettison the Freudian concept of infantile sexuality that grounds oedipal dynamics and to supplant it with attachment-mediated bridge concepts such as "hedonic capacity" and "hedonic intersubjectivity."[30] Fonagy and Target, while defending the saliency of attachment research to oedipal conflict, have linked their attachment-supported theory of mentalization to British object relations theory, interpersonalism, and self psychology, all of which explain self development in terms of an interpersonal process that requires "interaction with the minds of others." The four-year-old child's emerging

28. Allan N. Schore, "A Century After Freud's Project: Is a Rapprochement Between Psychoanalysis and Neurobiology at Hand?" *JAPA*, 45:807–840, 1997, quoted at pp. 830, 833; Allan N. Schore, "Advances in Neuropsychoanalysis, Attachment Theory, and Trauma Research: Implications for Self Psychology," *Psychoanal. Inq.*, 22:433–484, 2002, quoted at p. 472.

29. In addition to the aforementioned papers by Fonagy & Target, see Diana Diamond & Frank Yeomans, "Oedipal Love and Conflict in the Transference/Countertransference Matrix: Its Impact on Attachment Security and Mentalization," in Diana Diamond, Sidney Blatt, & Joseph Lichtenberg, eds., *Attachment and Sexuality* (NY: Analytic Press, 2007), pp. 201–236; Lisa Weinstein, "When Sexuality Reaches Beyond the Pleasure Principle: Attachment, Repetition, and Infantile Sexuality," in *Attachment and Sexuality*, pp. 107–136, and Daniel Morehead, "Oedipus, Darwin, and Freud: One Big, Happy, Family?" *Psychoanal. Quart.*, 68:347–375, 1999. Morehead's claims about the "sexual elements in early attachments" (p. 368) are contested by Morris Eagle, "Attachment and Sexuality," in *Attachment and Sexuality*, pp. 27–50 at pp. 41–43.

30. Jeremy Holmes, "Sense and Sensuality: Hedonic Intersubjectivity and the Erotic Imagination," in *Attachment and Sexuality* (n. 29), pp. 137–160; Daniel Widlöcher, "Primary Love and Infantile Sexuality: An Eternal Debate," in Daniel Widlöcher, ed., *Infantile Sexuality and Attachment*, trans. Susan Fairfield (NY: Other Press, 2001), pp. 1–35.

ability to mentalize, they hold, resonates with Winnicottian, Kleinian, and Bionion views of the "oscillation or equilibrium" between paranoid-schizoid and depressive positions in the face of new experience at this same developmental juncture. Nor is self psychology left out of the picture. They convey appreciation of the self-psychological concept of selfobject but offer a new construal of selfobject functioning from the standpoint of mentalization: "The empathic behavior of early objects" is to be understood as enhancing self-esteem "through facilitating a sense of mental agency, an intentional stance[,] to use Dennett's terminology (1978), which the child experiences as deriving directly from his experience of his own mental states."[31]

Allan Schore also gravitates to self psychology, albeit through an alternate reading of the relationships among early selfobject provision, attachment experience, and adult psychopathology. For him, "deficiencies in the provision of selfobject experiences of affect synchrony and interactive repair" are the very stuff of "dysregulating traumatic attachments." And this "ambient relational trauma of disorganized-disoriented-insecure attachments" compromises the "experience-dependent maturation of the right [cerebral] hemisphere," which, in turn, generates the severe self-pathologies described by Kohut.[32] Here deficient selfobject provision retains a phenomenologically self-psychological cast, but the self pathologies that result from it are mediated by arrested neurobiological maturation. Citing and drawing inferences from a large body of neuroscientific research reports, Schore argues that insecure attachments have specifiable, lifelong neuroanatomical sequelae, so that attachment research per se ultimately becomes subsumed within the broader integrative project that links psychoanalysis to neuroscience. Specifically, traumatic attachment experiences "skew the developmental trajectory of the right brain over the rest of the life span." The resulting "self" deficits, the dissociative phenomena of PTSD among them, "are the expression of a malfunctioning orbitofrontal cortical-subcortical system, the senior executive of the right brain."[33]

31. Target & Fonagy, "Playing with Reality: II. Development of Psychic Reality" (n. 21), pp. 470, 475.

32. Schore, "Advances in Neuropsychoanalysis, Attachment Theory, and Trauma Research" (n. 28), quoted at pp. 460–461, 469–470.

33. Schore has argued for the consiliences among right-brain development (especially apropos the orbitofrontal cortex), insecure attachments, early relational trauma, and

A more fine-tuned variant of the piecemeal approach involves theorizing multiple points of contact between attachment findings and individual strands of divergent psychoanalytic theories. Consider Fonagy's *Attachment Theory and Psychoanalysis* (2001), lauded on its cover as "a unique and remarkable contribution to our understanding of the meaningful relationship that has evolved between psychoanalytic and attachment theories."[34] This endorsement by Joy Osofsky, in my view, misleadingly suggests that the book adumbrates a relationship between a unitary attachment theory and a unitary psychoanalytic theory. In point of fact, Fonagy's project is informed by his admission that "psychoanalytic theory cannot, at its current stage of evolution, be reduced to a singular coherent set of propositions." It follows that the search for commonalities between attachment theory and psychoanalysis becomes ab initio the simple stipulating, in additive fashion, of "points of contact" and "points of divergence" between attachment theory and each major psychoanalytic school of thought.[35] When, in his penultimate chapter, Fonagy is finally led to consider more globally "the rediscov-

---

a family of self pathologies in a series of publications over the past 15 years. Representative overviews aimed at different professional readerships include "A Century After Freud's Project" (n. 28); "The Effects of a Secure Attachment Relationship on Right Brain Development, Affect Regulation, and Infant Mental Health," *Infant J. Ment. Health*, 22:7–66, 2001; "The Effects of Early Relational Trauma on Right Brain Development, Affect Regulation, and Infant Mental Health," *Infant J. Ment. Health*, 22:201–269, 2001; "Dysregulation of the Right Brain: A Fundamental Mechanism of Traumatic Attachment and the Psychopathogenesis of Posttraumatic Stress Disorder," *Austral. N. Zeal. J. Psychiatry*, 36:9–30, 2002. Quoted phrases are from this last paper.

34. Fonagy's book is an outgrowth of his contribution to Cassidy & Shaver, eds., *Handbook of Attachment* (n. 25). See Peter Fonagy, "Psychoanalytic Theory from the Viewpoint of Attachment Theory and Research," in *Handbook of Attachment*, pp. 595–624.

35. Fonagy, *Attachment Theory and Psychoanalysis* (n. 20), p. 157. The psychoanalytic schools to which "points of contact" and "points of divergence" are successively adduced are North American structural theory; the Klein-Bion Model; the "Independent School" of British psychoanalysis; North American object relations theory; modern psychoanalytic infant psychiatry; and American interpersonal-relational psychoanalysis. In a separate chapter that supplements this school-specific "points of contact"/"points of divergence" approach, Fonagy reviews the contributions of four major "psychoanalytic attachment theorists": Karlen Lyons-Ruth, Morris Eagle, Jeremy Holmes, and Arietta Slade. Several years earlier, Eagle was much clearer in

ery of psychoanalytic ideas in attachment theory," he can do no better than identify a single correspondence between attachment behaviors and Erik Erikson's more than half-century-old notion of "basic trust" and then elaborate an admittedly "quite contentious analogy" between insecure attachment and Melanie Klein's three-quarter-century-old concept of a paranoid-schizoid position.[36] Herein apparently is the locus of "the meaningful relationship . . . between psychoanalytic and attachment theories" as of 2001.

The additive mentality—the belief that isolated points of contact between attachment theory and specific theory-based psychoanalytic claims *add up to* theoretical convergence—has dominated the integrative agenda in the years following Fonagy's *Attachment and Psychoanalysis* (2001). New points of contact have been posited, and they have been elucidated with increasing depth and subtlety. But the strategy remains the same, and the outcome of the project is the integration of attachment theory with a "virtual" psychoanalysis that exists in the mind of the integrator. Two recent papers provide sophisticated variants of this pathway to integration, Diana Diamond's "Attachment Disorganization: The Reunion of Attachment Theory and Psychoanalysis" (2004) and Peter Fonagy and Mary Target's "The Rooting of the Mind in the Body" (2007).

Diamond (2004) homes in on the fourth attachment category, "disorganized-disoriented," and its adult analogue on the Adult Attach-

---

delineating convergences between attachment theory and "contemporary psychoanalysis," which he understood as an amalgam of object relations theory and self psychology. See Morris Eagle, "The Developmental Perspectives of Attachment and Psychoanalytic Theory," in Susan Goldberg, Roy Muir, & John Kerr, eds., *Attachment Theory: Social, Developmental, and Clinical Perspectives* (Hillsdale, NJ: Analytic Press, 1995), pp. 123–150.

36. Fonagy, *Attachment Theory and Psychoanalysis* (n. 20), pp. 180–182. Erikson's schema of psychosocial development, of which "basic trust" was the first developmental achievement, was never integrated into psychoanalytic discourse and rates only very occasional mention in contemporary journal literature. Klein's "paranoid-schizoid position" is of course integral to Klein's original theory of early development. Contemporary relational thinkers occasionally make analogical use of the Kleinian "positions," but the positions retain explanatory currency principally among a numerically small community of Kleinian analysts in Klein's native Britain and in South America. Is this, then, what the "meaningful relationship" between psychoanalytic and attachment theories (per Joy Osofsky's jacket endorsement) finally comes down to?

ment Interview (AAI), "unresolved for trauma and loss." Within the recent attachment literature, she argues, microanalysis of parent–child transactions has identified specific parental behaviors that mediate between parents' own unresolved experiences of trauma and loss and the emergence of disorganized attachment in their infants. These mediating factors, in turn, are illuminated by four specific psychoanalytic concepts, "both classic and contemporary": Freud's theory of traumatic anxiety (1926); Melanie Klein's theory of paranoid-schizoid and depressive positions (1935); Ernst Kris's theory of strain trauma (1956); and, moving into our own time, Sidney Blatt's object-relational theory of personality development as the dialectical interplay of an anaclitic line of relatedness and an introjective line of self-definition.

With each of these particulars, it is simply a matter of mapping the behaviors of the "unresolved" parent and the "disorganized" infant onto the targeted psychoanalytic concepts; the attachment behaviors "are illuminated by and in turn illuminate" the psychoanalytic concepts. Ernst Kris's half-century-old notion of "strain trauma," for example, links up with "the chaotic and contradictory response of the disorganized infant who resorts to stilling or freezing behavior, to crying and turning in circles, or to dropping silently to the floor upon reunion with the parent." Klein's theory of paranoid-schizoid and depressive positions also links up with disorganized attachment, because the disorganized infant's behavior evinces defenses such as splitting and projective identification "in their most rudimentary forms as represented as action schemata." Parents whose AAIs designate them "unresolved with respect to trauma and loss" provide evidence for the intrapsychic registration and repetition of traumatic anxiety as Freud understood it. Equally, their AAI narratives suggest that they have failed to complete the central task of Klein's depressive position, i.e., mourning the lost object and relinquishing the illusion of control over it. The successive alignment of psychoanalytic concepts taken from Freud, Klein, Kris, and Blatt with the "indirect behavioral and affective cues" associated with parentally unresolved trauma and loss and its transmission to infants achieves an additive weight that mutates into integration; these four points of alignment *are* the "reunion" of attachment theory and psychoanalysis.[37]

---

37. Diana Diamond, "Attachment Disorganization: The Reunion of Attachment Theory and Psychoanalysis," *Psychoanal. Psychol.*, 21:276–299, 2004, quoted at pp. 283, 287.

Fonagy and Target's (2007) more ambitious effort links the promise of integration with a re-visioning of attachment theory per se. In its original formulation, they hold, attachment theory relied on a first-generation cognitive psychology that revolved around the computer metaphor and gained expression in Bowlby's abstractive notion of the Internal Working Model. Now, the authors enjoin, attachment theory must couple with a second-generation cognitive science that allows for the bodily and environmental contexts of attachment experiences and sustains "neurologically plausible" accounts of those experiences. In short, it is a matter of embracing recent formulations of "embodied cognition" (or "enactive mind") and using them to align attachment theory with a modern, "embodied," affect-oriented psychoanalysis.[38]

Fonagy and Target's purchase on attachment theory, no less than Diamond's, evokes a tradition of classical psychoanalytic writings. For Diamond the rapprochement between attachment theory and psychoanalysis is rooted in classical writings on trauma and loss (including traumatic anxiety, strain trauma, and paranoid-schizoid mentation) that, in turn, segue into the modern object-relational perspective of Blatt. For Fonagy and Target, the relevant "classical contributions to psychoanalysis" are contributions that anticipate modern cognitive understanding of the physical origins of thought; papers by Isaacs (1943), Hoffer (1950), and Greenacre (1960) are signposts of this literature.[39] These writings blossom into contemporary analytic under-

---

38. Peter Fonagy & Mary Target, "The Rooting of the Mind in the Body," *JAPA*, 55:411–456, 2007. In published commentary that immediately followed the publication of this paper, Robbins and Zacks, both cognitive scientists, cogently challenged Fonagy and Target's two guiding assumptions, viz., that Bowlby's attachment theory derives from a first-generation, disembodied cognitive science, and that contemporary cognitive science aligns with "embodied cognition" as Fonagy and Target understand and use the term. According to Robbins and Zacks, Fonagy and Target speciously conflate "embodied cognition" with cognitive neuroscience and social-affective neuroscience, three "quite different" trends in recent cognitive science. And more tellingly still, "not all social-affective neuroscience theories assign a significant role to the body, and relatively few cognitive neuroscience theories do." Here my primary interest is not with the accuracy of Fonagy and Target's claims but rather with the kind of integrative strategy that derives from these claims. See Philip Robbins & Jeffrey M. Zacks, "Attachment Theory and Cognitive Science: Commentary on Fonagy and Target," *JAPA*, 55:457–467, quoted at p. 464.

39. Susan Isaacs, "The Nature and Function of Phantasy," *Int. J. Psycho-Anal.*, 29:73–97, 1948; Willi Hoffer "The Development of the Body Ego," *Psychoanal. Study*

standing of affect and metaphor, both of which organize the mind in ways that "offer us the opportunity to forge powerful links between psychoanalysis and attachment theory."[40]

For Diamond, the "reunion" of attachment theory and psychoanalysis is signaled by research that sustains extrapolation from attachment behaviors to attachment representations that mediate between the parent's experience of trauma and loss and the infant's experience of disorganized attachment. For Fonagy and Target, a different kind of representation bridges the gap between attachment research and treatment dynamics. They focus on "symbolic representations" of attachment experiences that retain "vestiges of sensations and predispositions that make the unconscious emergence of attachment experiences an immediate reality for most psychoanalytic patients in relation to their analyst." The sensations and predispositions in question hearken back to bodily rooted behaviors, affects, gestures, and preverbal communications, all of which, via procedural coding, link language to early bodily analogues (e.g., "holding on to an idea," "grasping an idea") and thereby achieve psychoanalytic relevance as an alternative language system for communicating unconscious fantasy.[41]

For Fonagy and Target no less than for Diamond, the integrative project is not intended to mediate among different psychoanalytic theories. Mediation gives way to addition, with the integration of attachment theory to psychoanalysis arising, Athena-like, from successive instances of mutual illumination between one or another attachment finding and one or another psychoanalytic concept or insight. Theirs is a cornucopia-like response to fractionation in which all the psychoanalytic schools, with their respective part-theories, are invited to bring their conceptual fruit. With such disparate ingredients at hand, it is no wonder that their global integrative claims necessarily fall back on a generic psychoanalysis, a "virtual" psychoanalysis, that bears little relationship to the reality of discrete, paradigm-like psychoanalytic theories in competition with one another.

Child, 5:18–24, 1950; Phyllis Greenacre, "Regression and Fixation: Considerations Concerning the Development of the Ego," *JAPA*, 8:703–723, 1960.

40. Fonagy & Target, "Rooting of the Mind in the Body" (n. 38), pp. 425, 431.

41. Fonagy & Target, "Rooting of the Mind in the Body" (n. 38), p. 431.

And it is this latter fact that eludes such integrative projects. To return to Fonagy and Target, the notion of "embodied cognition" has no centripetal impact on entrenched psychoanalytic schools of thought. It aligns attachment theory to psychoanalysis through bodily derived and gesturally (and prosaically and syntactically) conveyed "feelings" and "concerns" that make contact, variously, with libido theory, attachment theory, relationality, object relations, affect theory, and self experience. As such, "embodied cognition" is less an instrument of theoretical unification than a new multidisciplinary thread that reinforces the fragile weave of the cornucopia that holds together psychoanalytic part-theories and part-identities in an era of theoretical pluralism.

In the case of attachment theory, there is at least a coherent body of observational research to which the integrators may appeal. That is, psychoanalytic cartographers understand attachment research findings in essentially the same way, even if they disagree among themselves on whether the mapping project should be approached heuristically, holistically, or piecemeal—and, among those who adopt the piecemeal approach, on which specific attachment findings should be mapped onto which specific psychoanalytic ideas. In the case of nonlinear dynamic systems theory (complexity theory, chaos theory) there is more fundamental disagreement about what the "theory" or "model" or "approach" actually presages in terms of a psychoanalytic theory of mind and theory of therapeutic action. More classically oriented analysts, such as Galatzer-Levy, have seen aspects of the theory (e.g., fractal patterns, attractors) as compatible with the empirical exploration of specific psychoanalytic hypotheses. In two well-wrought papers, Piers has argued that dynamic systems theory actually revivifies traditional concepts of character and character pathology, as elaborated by David Shapiro in particular. In so doing, it aligns itself with modern ego psychology, which attends simultaneously to the individual's continuity and self-similarity across time and to his "context-dependent fluidity or variability in response to contextual and intersubjective influences."[42]

42. Robert M. Galatzer-Levy, "Psychoanalysis and Dynamical Systems Theory: Prediction and Self Similarity," *JAPA*, 43:1085–1113, 1995; Craig Piers, "Character as Self-Organizing Complexity," *Psychoanal. Contemp. Th.*, 23:3–34, 2000; Craig Piers, "The Mind's Multiplicity and Continuity," *Psychoanal. Dial.*, 15:229–254, 2005.

Certain aspects of dynamic systems theory, such as the phenomenon of emergence, have yielded different mapping perspectives, even among commentators at the more conservative end of the spectrum. Galatzer-Levy believes emergence provides an alternate view of the meaning of dramatic and abrupt therapeutic change. Palombo, in the first book-length effort to map complexity theory onto psychoanalysis, explored such clinically unanticipated "phase transitions" as analogues to the emergence of new structures at "the edge of chaos" in complex systems. He offers complexity-framed explanations of such "emergent" phenomena in support of traditional psychoanalytic technique, whereas Galatzer-Levy believes these same phenomena encourage modifications of technique to facilitate such change. Piers, for his part, is less concerned with the implications of emergence for abrupt therapeutic change than for the analytic understanding of stable symptomatology. Whereas conventional psychoanalysis, with its linear developmental assumptions, equates symptoms with "preserved mental content," dynamic systems theory leads us to reconceive them as emergent phenomena arising from a psychological context that manifestly lacks the "necessary ingredients to explain their arrival" and leads the symptom carrier to feel a "loss of volitional self-direction." A shift in therapeutic focus follows, as the effort to discern unconsciously preserved mental content gives way to a "zero[ing] in on the transition rules that characterize the way an individual organizes subjective experience, including mental contents."[43]

Whether the focus is on abrupt phase transitions or the restrictive transition rules that inhere in consciously nonsensical symptoms, dynamic systems theory, for commentators such as Galatzer-Levy, Palombo, and Piers, does not wipe out the operation of "prescribed developmental sequences" in select domains; indeed, "there are clear indications that many aspects of development are programmed in this fashion."

43. Robert M. Galatzer-Levy, "Psychoanalysis and Dynamical Systems Theory" (n. 42); Robert M. Galatzer-Levy, "Emergence," *Psychoanal. Inq.*, 22:708–727, 2002, quoted at p. 719; Stanley Palombo, *The Emergent Ego: Complexity and Coevolution in the Psychoanalytic Process* (Madison, CT: International Universities Press, 1999); Craig Piers, "Emergence: When a Difference in Degree Becomes a Difference in Kind," in Craig Piers, John P. Muller, & Joseph Brent, eds., *Self-Organizing Complexity in Psychological Systems* (Lanham, MD: Jason Aronson, 2007), pp. 83–110, quoted at p. 102.

Olds, another classically oriented cartographer, understands systems theory in much the same way. He allows that it has effected a "loosening" of the epigenetic model and thereby "opened the way to relational theories emphasizing that one's behavior is often influenced by another, that in a dyad there may be mutual influence, making the behavior of either person less predictable and more interactive." But he stops well short of any sort of complexity-driven re-visioning of the theoretical structure that sustains the analyst's traditional modus operandi: Complexity theory, he observes, "does not mean that all bets are off; we do indeed make fairly reliable predictions about people, but we are more modest." He is joined in this estimation by Piers, for whom understanding the mind as a nonlinear system *means* discerning continuity in the mind's coherent pattern of varied and multiple states. Construed as a nonlinear dynamic system, mind arranges, co-ordinates, and organizes subjective experience, "but always does so from a set of predisposing attitudes," by which Piers means that mind "has a particular perspective or vantage point in relation to the flow of subjective experience, leaving it poised in a state of biased readiness to perceive, organize, interpret, respond to, and remember experience in a distinctive and recognizable manner."[44]

Commentators such as Olds, Piers, Galatzer-Levy, and Palombo approach dynamic systems theory in a spirit of what I will term progressive conventionalism. To wit, they use systems theory to loosen the relationship between psychoanalytic theory and practice and to allow for a more flexible, even creative kind of "psychoanalytic technique," all the while leaving existing theory in place. This approach, especially as exemplified in the work of Olds and Piers, is consonant with the viewpoint of the late Emmanuel Ghent, for whom dynamic systems theory and Gerald Edelman's theory of "neuronal group selection" played off one another in theoretically complementary (and constraining) ways. Neuronal group selection, according to Ghent, with its provision of "innately organized primitive values that prepared the organism, in our case the human infant, to prefer certain types of stimulation over others," provided a kind of biological anchorage for the nonlinear properties of dynamic systems. Human motivational systems, he held, are "highly complex derivatives" of these primitive

---

44. David D. Olds, "Interdisciplinary Studies and Our Practice" (n. 2), p. 869; Piers, "Mind's Multiplicity and Continuity" (n. 42), p. 251.

values or preferences; the complexity in question derives from "emergent creative neural synthetic activity," and the ensuing nonprogrammed development ensures the unique qualities of individual motivational needs. Herein is Ghent's warrant for what Olds terms the "loosening" of the epigenetic model. But this emergent, blueprintless process necessarily falls back on the evolutionary a prioris of neuronal selection, further "amplified and modulated by hormonal influence and primitive reflexes." So Ghent, with Olds, does not see dynamic systems theory as sustaining a clinical approach anathema to traditional clinical theory in its cautiously predictive aspects. And Ghent, no less than Olds, assigns developmental research an important role in mediating among the field's current medley of "competing organizational systems."[45] Both theorists understand that dynamic systems theory paves the way to more provisional, relationally grounded psychoanalytic "knowing." But neither finds in this *tendency* the coup de grace of psychoanalysis in its conventionally predictive aspects, an epistemic state of affairs in which, to recur to Olds, "all bets are off."

And yet recent relationally and intersubjectively oriented commentators, such as Stolorow, Seligman, Sucharov, and Weisel-Barth, do indeed convey the sense that in fundamental ways all bets *are* off. For these theorists, complexity theory, in the clinical domain no less than the biological, is understood to supplant the epigenetic model of development and linear cause-and-effect structure elaborated by Freud more than a century ago. As such, it provides a warrant for questioning and even repudiating the field's theoretical infrastructure. Weisel-Barth edges toward this position in her pragmatic construal of the complexity model as clinical justification for considering multiple theoretical frames and for cultivating humility about the explanatory adequacy of any one psychoanalytic theory. Clinical sensitivity to complexity simply means that psychoanalytic theories, however "suggestive and useful," are necessarily "provisional and instrumental." Complexity theory, she observes, renders illusory the very ideas of absolute truth and essential reality as they pertain to the clinical interaction. Stolorow takes the argument one step further, since he believes systems theory renders obsolete the very notion of "preestablished developmen-

45. Emmanuel Ghent, "Wish, Need, Drive: Motive in the Light of Dynamic Systems Theory and Edelman's Selectionist Theory," *Psychoanal. Dial.*, 12:763–808, 2002, quoted at pp. 784, 800.

tal programs" and psychological phenomena understandable in terms of "fixed intrapsychic structures." Seligman, for his part, suggests that the experiential immediacy captured by systems theory obviates the need for theory choice, conventionally understood, since "the organized chaos in analytic theory could be seen as a reflection of the multifaceted nature of the analytic field of study, rather than as a symptom or an impediment." In this vision of things, systems theory is an emergent psychoanalytic metatheory that, at one fell swoop, undercuts the kind of empirical hypothesis-testing program Galatzer-Levy has in mind and renders suspect even the "fairly reliable predictions about people" Olds falls back on.

And then there is Stolorow, who believes that dynamic systems theory obviates the need for any *further* theory choice by designating a clear winner in the here and now. To wit, systems theory provides scientific anchorage for the "unremitting contextualism" of his particular purchase on psychoanalysis: Intersubjectivity theory. Stolorow's "invocation" of modern structuralism in his early work of the 1980s, according to Coburn, "anticipated the spirit of nonlinear dynamic systems theory." Indeed, intersubjectivity theory has evolved into "intersubjective systems theory" which, in recent formulations, has been equated with a "quantum relational holism" that replaces conventional notions of "intrapsychic space" and "intrapsychic representation" with a vision of mental life as distributed across a series of interpenetrating relational fields. It is not only the individual's "personal world of experience" that is reframed as a "field event." The analyst has no greater claim to a structurally bounded individual psyche than the patient. And so, when either one speaks, "he or she speaks not only for him or herself, but, at a deeper level, for the dyad, for one's social network, community, culture, world, and universe."[46]

46. Robert D. Stolorow, "Dynamic, Dyadic, Intersubjective Systems: An Evolving Paradigm for Psychoanalysis," *Psychoanal. Psychol.*, 14:337–346, 1997; William J. Coburn, "A World of Systems: The Role of Systemic Patterns of Experience in the Therapeutic Process," *Psychoanal. Inq.*, 22:655–677, 2002; Maxwell S. Sucharov, "Representation and the Intrapsychic: Cartesian Barriers to Empathic Contact," *Psychoanal. Inq.*, 22:686–707, 2002; Stephen Seligman, "Dynamic Systems Theories as a Metaframework for Psychoanalysis," *Psychoanal. Dial.*, 15:285–319, 2005; Joye Weisel-Barth, "Thinking and Writing about Complexity Theory in the Clinical Setting," *Int. J. Psychoanal. Self Psychol.*, 1:365–388, 2006. Stolorow, Seligman, Coburn, and Sucharov are quoted at p. 338, p. 312, p. 659, and p. 698 of their respective articles.

The dynamic systems theory of some relationalists and all inter-subjectivists bears little resemblance to the dynamic systems theory of conventionalists such as Galatzer-Levy, Ghent, Palombo, Piers, and Olds. For the latter, systems theory hardly mandates the kind of "un-remitting contextualism" that replaces the notion of bounded individual psyches with something tantamount to a "quantum relational holism." The contextualization associated with developmental non-linearity is indeed hemmed in—by the evolutionary a prioris of neuronal selection, by innately organized primitive values, by the "biased readiness" to perceive, organize, and remember experience in certain ways that is the stuff of character. Piers speaks for this latter cohort of integrators in balancing the contextualism inherent in varied and multiple states with the boundedness of the individual mind. Absent severe pathology, he writes, mind is

> an instable chaotic system, acutely sensitive and responsive to internal fluctuations and external perturbations. This allows the mind to make qualitative state changes, giving rise to a rich variability and multiplicity of states. At the same time, a strange attractor with its infinitely deep, self-similar packing structure represents the mind's overall organization, coherence and continuity. That is, in health we have individuals who are recognizable in the midst of their multiplicity.[47]

The radical relationalists and intersubjectivists, on the other hand, do *not* understand dynamic systems theory as a framework for locating the multiplicity of self states within a mental organization that, absent severe pathology, evinces the coherence and continuity associated with "character." In their hands, dynamic systems theory veers toward an ontological twilight zone in which the very "meaning, ownership, and location" of mental experience is called into question. The radical relationalists and intersubjectivists share little enough with conventionalist colleagues who believe that dynamic systems theory, while loosening "linear" genetic thinking, permits cautious predictions about conventionally "boundaried" individuals and even encourages empirical tests of the developmental and clinical hypotheses that sustain such predictions. They make for stranger bedfellows still with attachment theory integrators, whose closed-system, linear thinking

47. Piers, "Mind's Multiplicity and Continuity" (n. 42), p. 252.

(in the former's view) leads them to equate specific patterns of mother-infant interaction with invariant attachment categories, however "metaphorically" (Slade) the categories are clinically understood.

But the radical relationalists and intersubjectivists stand in an antipodal relationship to the neurobiological cartographers who believe modern biology is a stimulus for testing specific psychoanalytic ideas about how the mind works. The expansive supra-individual "contextualism" of the former gives way to the intensive sub-individual "contextualism" of the latter, where the mental life of thoroughly boundaried individuals implicates indwelling (and inter-penetrating) systems framed in terms of brain morphology, neuro-physiology, and molecular biology. Here we are in the world of cell-biological insights capable of illuminating "the elementary mechanism of psychic determinism"; of selective atrophy of brain tissue (e.g., of the hippocampus) locking in pathological reactions to early stress by impairing the development of declarative memory; of psychotropic, drug-induced changes in brain function "alter[ing] the dynamic formulations we can make, and the kinds of interpretations we might venture."

According to the neuropsychoanalysts, a medley of biologically reductionist approaches to these and other aspects of mentation should enable us to differentiate empirically among the different types of unconscious process; inevitably, we will be led to "a deeper understanding of human behavior."[48] More recently still, we are in the realm of prefrontal and parietal-lobe mirror neurons, which, according to Olds, "may have evolved as a brain mechanism for the recognition of actions, in a complex sense including the goals and intentions of the actors." As such, mirror neurons are understood to subtend the psychoanalytic concept of identification and may also help to demystify the concept of projective identification. In a more far-reaching formulation, Gallese, Eagle, and Migone argue that the goal-specific firings of mirror neurons invite the hypothesis of an "embodied simu-

---

48. See Eric R. Kandel, "Biology and the Future of Psychoanalysis: A New Intellectual Framework for Psychiatry Revisited," *Am. J. Psychiatry*, 156:505–524, 1999; Eric R. Kandel, *In Search of Memory: The Emergence of a New Science of Mind* (NY: Norton, 2006), pp. 372–375, quoted at p. 372; Olds, "Interdisciplinary Studies and Our Practice" (n. 2), p. 866.

lation mechanism"[49] that operates automatically (i.e., prereflectively and nonconsciously) and sustains neurally grounded reframings of, inter alia, unconscious communication, interaction, attunement, projective identification, mirroring, empathic understanding, and therapeutic action.[50]

In all such theorizing, we are securely ensconced in what intersubjectivists apprehend as the Cartesian realm of isolated mind/brains, however stretched to accommodate mirror-neural networks whose "shared" activation in observer and observed is hard-wired. Here we bring the instrumentalities of normal science to bear on the understanding of *researchably* isolated mind/brains. And the research program of neuropsychoanalysis is normatively driven. Mind, Solms and Turnbull tell us, is an aspect of nature that can be observed and studied scientifically, but it is also that part of nature that we ourselves occupy. Neuroscientists have finally begun investigating the inner workings of mind, but their "neuroscience of subjective experience" has yet to be integrated with psychoanalytic descriptions. And this, they continue, "is neither a happy nor a healthy situation. Clearly, there is only one thing to be done about it: *the two perspectives have to be integrated and combined, and thereby reconciled with one another.*"[51]

How do we bring together such ontologically incongruous frames of reference? The integrative potential of neuroscience, according to its proponents, resides in ever-advancing brain-imaging techniques that hold the promise "not only for diagnosing various neurotic illnesses

49. "Embodied simulation mechanism" is defined as a neural "modeling" mechanism that establishes a direct (neural) link between an agent who engages in certain types of purposive action or evinces certain emotions or sensations and the observer of such actions, emotions, and/or sensations. According to Gallese, the mirror neuron system "is likely a neural correlate of this mechanism." Vittorio Gallese, "Embodied Simulation: From Neurons to Phenomenal Experience," *Phenom. Cog. Sci.*, 4:23–48, 2005 and "Mirror Neurons and Intentional Attunement: Commentary on Olds," *JAPA*, 54:47–57, 2006, quoted at p. 54.

50. David D. Olds, "Identification: Psychoanalytic and Biological Perspectives," *JAPA*, 54:17–46, 2006, quoted at pp. 36, 40; Vittorio Gallese, Morris N. Eagle, & Paolo Migone, "Intentional Attunement: Mirror Neurons and the Neural Underpinnings of Interpersonal Relations," *JAPA*, 55:131–176, 2007.

51. Solms & Turnbull, *Brain and Inner World* (n. 7), p. 294, emphasis in the original.

but also for monitoring the progress of psychotherapy." Neuropsychoanalysts can point to very recent imaging findings that are demonstrably relevant to diagnosis, treatment selection, and treatment outcome.[52] For these analysts, the dialogue between neuroscientists and psychoanalytic clinicians must embrace the language, the methodology, and the overarching axiology of normal science. "In the dialogue between neuroscientists and psychoanalysts," observe Beutel, Stern, and Silbersweig in a recent issue of *JAPA*, "it must be realized that psychoanalytic models are not solely either the starting or the end point, but rather are part of an entire spectrum of mind-brain models, any of which may turn out to be more valid in the light of conjoint investigations."[53]

And this is precisely the point: Psychoanalysis can only enter into conversation with neuroscience to the extent that, in the manner of normal science, it brings its own indigenously psychoanalytic "models" to the table. Already, it has been argued, basic psychoanalytic tenets, such as unconscious processing and the developmental impact of early experience have been "substantiated by recent neuroscience findings." Recent imaging findings provide a basis for refining psychoanalytic understanding of affect, self-regulatory functioning, and transference in a manner that moves them in the direction of affective neuroscience.[54] Turnbull looks to recent research on multiple emotion systems, confabulation, and anosognosia for neurobiological grounding of basic *Freudian* claims about the role of instinctual mechanisms and the pleasure principle in mental life. Neuroscience allows the recrudescence of the Freudian concept of drive, now subsumed within a family of appetitive states and mapped onto Panksepp's SEEK-

52. See Amit Etkin, Christopher Pittenger, H. Jonathan Polan, & Eric R. Kandel, "Toward a Neurobiology of Psychotherapy: Basic Science and Clinical Applications," *J. Neuropsy. Clin. Neurosci.*, 17:145–148, 2005 and Bradley S. Peterson, "Clinical Neuroscience and Imaging Studies of Core Psychoanalytic Constructs," *Clin. Neurosci. Res.*, 4:349–365, 2005. I take up the relevance of recent imaging studies to psychoanalysis and provide additional references in chapter 7, pp. 222–225.

53. Manfred E. Beutel, Emily Stern, & David A. Silbersweig, "The Emerging Dialogue Between Psychoanalysis and Neuroscience: Neuroimaging Perspectives," *JAPA*, 51:773–801, 2003, quoted at p. 794.

54. See Peterson, "Clinical Neuroscience and Imaging Studies" (n. 52).

ING basic-emotion command system.[55] Can we isolate a part of the brain that has the properties Freud imputed to the "system Ucs."? Indeed we can, reply Solms and Turnbull:

> The *ventromesial quadrant of the frontal lobes*, more than any other brain region, meets these criteria. Bilateral damage to this part of the brain does indeed produce a state of mind that shows several properties reminiscent of what Freud (1915) described as "the special characteristics of the system Ucs." These functional characteristics were listed as follows: "exemption from mutual contradiction, primary process (mobility of cathexis), timelessness, and replacement of external by psychical reality." [p. 187][56]

Neuroanalytic claims, especially when adduced by analysts, may be grander in both synthetic and comparative ways. Beyond providing global support for axioms of classical psychoanalysis, the "major relevance of neuroscience to psychoanalysis," according to Pulver, "is that it helps us choose between competing psychoanalytic theories." It lends support to a comprehensive motivational systems approach, Pulver continues, as developed, for example, by Lichtenberg. It sustains a developmental affect theory grounded in biologically given basic affects. It even signals the rebirth of psychoanalytic structural theory which, long under attack, "shows promise of rising from the ashes in a form congruent with current concepts in neuroscience."[57] The mirror-neuron

55. Solms & Turnbull, *Brain and Inner World* (n. 7), pp. 115–119. Jaak Panksepp's functional anatomy of emotion, which assigns brain locations to four basic-emotion command systems (SEEKING, RAGE, FEAR, and PANIC) is spelled out in his highly influential *Affective Neuroscience: The Foundations of Human and Animal Emotions* (NY: Oxford University Press, 1998). Panksepp's theory is highly valued by contemporary neuropsychoanalysts. On the neuroscientific revitalization of the drive concept, see also Allan Schore, "A Century After Freud's Project" (n. 28), p. 827: "Recent psychobiological and neurobiological studies thus strongly indicate that the concept of drive, devalued over the last twenty years, must be reintroduced as a central construct of psychoanalytic theory."

56. Solms & Turnbull, *Brain and Inner World* (n. 7), p. 101 (emphasis in the original).

57. Sydney E. Pulver, "On the Astonishing Clinical Irrelevance of Neuroscience," *JAPA*, 51:755–772, 2003, quoted at pp. 763, 764; Oliver Turnbull, "Was Freud Right? Psychoanalysis in the Light of Modern Brain Research." Introductory Remarks at "Neuro2005: Brain, Mind, Psyche," Congress of the Wissenschaftszentrums NRW

supported hypothesis of "automatic embodied stimulation" conduces to specific theoretical choices and underwrites departures from the traditional psychoanalytic method. Among the former is replacing the self-psychological notion of "mirroring" with the more empirically robust notion of a therapeutically congruent response; among the latter is the reasonableness of dispensing with the analytic couch to increase the patient's opportunities for reflecting on transference reactions "in the light of cues emitted by the analyst and to understand and internalize various aspects of the analyst's reactions and the effects these reactions have on him or her."[58] Connectionism underscores the salience of just such clues by insisting that analytic anonymity, the analyst as a Freudian "blank screen," is a cognitive impossibility. As soon as patient and analyst engage one another, neural networks involving, inter alia, authority and intimacy relationships, are reciprocally activated.[59]

In short, we are back in a world of psychoanalytic models, theories, theory choice, preestablished developmental programs, and neurobiologically grounded (and hence potentially "fixed") intrapsychic structures. It is a world of normal science in which the "meaning, ownership, and location" of mental experience are amenable to neuro-

---

and the Kompetenznetzwerkes NeuroNRW, 30 November 2005, available online at http://www.wz.nrw.de/Neuro2005/Dokumentationen/TURNBULL%20FORMATIERT.pdf. Pulver's surmise about the neuroscientific rebirth of psychoanalytic structural theory seems to be in the process of being borne out. See, for example, Solms & Turnbull, *Brain and Inner World* (n. 7), pp. 97, 137, 286–287.

58. Gallese, Eagle, & Migone, "Intentional Attunement" (n. 50), pp. 131–176; quoted at p. 163. Cf. Olds, "Interdisciplinary Studies and Our Practice" (n. 2), p. 863.

59. "From a connectionist perspective, the act of presenting for treatment evokes a set of highly specific wishes, fears, affects, and cognitive constructions, including expectations about helping relationships, doctors, confiding intimate material, confiding shameful material, and so on. Every early contact the patient has with the analyst—the initial referral, the first telephone contact, the way the analyst greets the patient in the waiting room—will be processed in light of these wishes, fears, and expectations. . . . No matter how anonymous and nonintrusive the analyst attempts to be, he or she can create nothing resembling a 'blank screen' for the patient's transference projections, because no situation is free from interpretation of the situation in light of prior experiences." Westen & Gabbard, "Developments in Cognitive Neuroscience: II. Implications for Theories of Transference" (n. 17), p. 123.

scientific specification and, as such, are not subject to a "radical con-textualism" that diffuses them across inter- and transpersonal systems and makes it exceedingly difficult even to write about them within the narrative framework of conventional clinical discourse.[60] Indeed, it is a world comfortably at home with a neurobiologically anchored "pri-vate" self that is "the locus of personal value and personal meaning" and, as such, must be protected from intrusion.[61] It is difficult to en-vision routes to integration more paradigmatically disjunctive than the mapping strategies of the neuropsychoanalysts on the one hand and the relational-intersubjective proponents of dynamic systems theory on the other.

With the radical incommensurability of neurobiological mapping and the kind of systems-theory mapping proffered by relationalists and intersubjectivists, we circle back to our point ab initio: The map-ping of psychoanalytic theory onto new disciplines, the effort to re-fashion psychoanalytic theory so that it stands up to tests in diverse domains of application, has not countered the centrifugal forces that have pulled the field apart and left increasingly self-contained part-fields in their wake. Only within the past several years have we seen the emergence of a metaintegrative literature that explores the coa-lescence of different mapping strategies and provides suggestions for the kind of research program that can move the field forward. Will the cartographers prevail? It is an open question. To date, they have failed to reverse the fractionation of the field and have all too often contributed to it. That is, the various theoretical orientations have been mapped onto divergent integrative strategies, so that the fractionation of the field has almost been displaced onto the preferential appropria-

60. See Weisel-Barth, "Thinking and Writing About Complexity Theory" (n. 46), p. 383: "Take the term 'self,' for example. Denotatively and connotatively the word describes a discrete and bounded entity. How, then, can we use this word 'self' in clinical descriptions of diffuse relational states? How can we incorporate its current meaning with our understanding of the fluidity of self-experience, the porosity of boundaries, and the blending of self-experiences in intersubjective meetings?" Con-trast this position with that of Modell, for whom the inner core of the self is biologi-cally "discrete and bounded" in a way that removes the individual, per Edelman, from the inputs of real time. For Modell, analytic work privileges the "privacy" of the self, which must be guarded against intrusion and pathogenic decentering. See Modell, *Private Self* (n. 5), pp. 75–96.

61. Modell, *Private Self* (n. 5), p. 75.

tion of one or another disciplinary domain by different groups of psychoanalytic cartographers.

I say "almost" because—alluding once more to the small band of knowledgeable metaintegrators—there are obvious exceptions. Certain analytic exponents of attachment theory have successfully resisted the blandishments of the psychoanalytic schools and opted instead to explore open-mindedly the emergent (and therapeutically relevant) research agenda and derivative clinical sensibility that follow from empirical attachment research.[62] Less frequently, one encounters papers that are genuinely metaintegrative, i.e., that pull together fundamental insights from several nonanalytic domains in re-visioning clinical process material.[63]

---

62. From a large and continuously expanding integrative literature on attachment theory, I single out studies by Fonagy & Target, Holmes, Eagle, and Gullestad as exemplifying a broad-minded, nontendentious use of attachment research. Their perspectives differ, but they share an ecumenical appreciation of the strengths and limitations of attachment theory that resists alignment with any one psychoanalytic tradition. We have considered the important work of Fonagy & Target above. Holmes views attachment theory as sustaining its own interpretive framework as a genre of psychodynamic therapy; Eagle sees it as supplementing and deepening a pragmatic psychoanalytic orientation that incorporates various emphases of classical analysis, object relations theory, relational theory, and self psychology; whereas Gullestad believes attachment theory provides a useful counterpoise to psychoanalytic assumptions about development, pathogenesis, and treatment but has very minimal implications for psychoanalytic technique. See Jeremy Holmes, "'Something There Is That Doesn't Love a Wall': John Bowlby, Attachment Theory and Psychoanalysis," in Goldberg et al., *Attachment Theory* (n. 35), pp. 19–43; Jeremy Holmes, "Defensive and Creative Uses of Narrative in Psychotherapy: An Attachment Perspective," in Glenn Roberts & Jeremy Holmes, eds., *Healing Stories: Narrative in Psychiatry and Psychotherapy* (NY: Oxford University Press, 1999), pp. 49–66; Morris Eagle, "Clinical Implications of Attachment Theory," *Psychoanal. Inq.*, 23:27–53, 2002; Siri Erika Gullestad, "Attachment Theory and Psychoanalysis: Controversial Issues," *Scand. Psychoanal. Rev.*, 24:3–16, 2001.

63. I have cited what I consider noteworthy recent efforts at metaintegration in the foregoing but will give the full references once more: Emmanuel Ghent, "Wish, Need, Drive: Motive in the Light of Dynamic Systems Theory and Edelman's Selectionist Theory," *Psychoanal. Dial.*, 12:763–808, 2002; David D. Olds, "A Semiotic Model of Mind," *JAPA*, 48:497–529, 2000; David D. Olds, "Affects as a Sign System," *Neuro-Psychoanal.*, 5:81–95, 2003; David D. Olds, "Identification: Psychoanalytic and Biological Perspectives," *JAPA*, 54:17–46, 2006; Vittorio Gallese, Morris N. Eagle, & Paolo Migone, "Intentional Attunement: Mirror Neurons and the Neural Underpinnings of Interpersonal Relations," *JAPA*, 55:131–176, 2007. To this brief list, I would add the four publications by the Boston Change Process Study Group given

The Boston Change Process Study Group exemplifies the metainte-grative approach in its various published papers, all of which fuse together elements of cognitive science (as to procedural memory), infancy research (as to mother-infant mutual regulation and the implicit, enactive ground of "relational knowing"), and dynamic systems theory (as to the self-organizing properties of the analyst-analysand dyad and the emergent properties of interactive and dialogic "sloppiness" within that dyad) in a re-visioning of therapeutic action. In this metaintegrative view of things, micro units of analyst-analysand exchange yield incremental changes in implicit relational knowing that gradually coalesce into shared relational intentions with emergent properties. The analogue of this meeting of minds is an increased sense of interactive coherence (or analyst-analysand "fittedness") which, according to BCPSG members, the patient experiences as increased vitalization or well-being, i.e., as "getting better."[64]

---

above (n. 13) and two additional papers: Scott M. Davis, "The Relevance of Gerald Edelman's Theory of Neuronal Group Selection and Nonlinear Dynamic Systems for Psychoanalysis," *Psychoanal. Inq.*, 22:814–840, 2002 and E. Virginia Demos, "The Dynamics of Development," in Piers et al., *Self-Organizing Complexity in Psychological Systems* (n. 43), pp. 135–163. Davis pulls together, and then exemplifies with an excellent case presentation, notions of primary and higher-order consciousness (and the categorization mappings that sustain these notions) associated with Edelman's theory of neuronal group selection; the notion of deep attractor states (and the fluctuations that give rise to new patterns) associated with dynamic systems theory; and the suboptimal attachment experiences associated with attachment theory. Demos reviews contemporary understandings of early childhood development from the standpoint of a "bio-psycho-social approach" that makes pragmatic use of attachment research, dynamic systems theory, and neuroscientific findings relevant to the biological bases of development. In terms of the book literature, Joseph Lichtenberg, *Psychoanalysis and Motivation* (Hillsdale, NJ: Analytic Press, 1989) and Joseph Lichtenberg, Frank Lachmann, & James Fosshage, *Self and Motivational Systems: Toward a Theory of Psychoanalytic Technique* (Hillsdale, NJ: Analytic Press, 1992) not only epitomize the metaintegrative sensibility, but also expound a clinical approach that is metaintegrative in synthesizing a range of research findings available at the time of writing. Wilma Bucci's multiple-code theory is an outstanding example of a metaintegrative research program that seeks to integrate psychoanalysis with research findings from various fields within the cognitive sciences. See especially Wilma Bucci, *Psychoanalysis and Cognitive Science: A Multiple Code Theory* (NY: Guilford, 1997).

64. See references in n. 13, especially BCPSG, "The 'Something More' than Interpretation Revisited," pp. 695, 709, 714ff., and BCPSG, "Explicating the Implicit," pp. 1057–1059.

Finally, there are a very few cartographers, such as Olds, who are able to comment knowledgeably on multiple mapping enterprises and discern incipient convergences among them, if only at the level of procedural knowledge tending to slow shifts in psychoanalytic praxis over time. Olds's thoughtful assessment of converging research findings that provide multidisciplinary anchorage for the psychoanalytic concept of identification exemplifies the promise and limitations of contemporary metaintegration as it pertains to traditional explanatory constructs.[65]

But isolated examples of metaintegrative sensibility will be of little avail if they do not give rise to some kind of consensual agreement about the need for metaintegration and the direction it should take. The metaintegrators are themselves a minuscule subset of a tiny subfield of integrators. To date they have had, as best I can determine, no cumulative impact on the entrenched psychoanalytic part-fields. And this failure—this absence of a centripetal pull growing out of their various mapping strategies—derives from the fact that psychoanalytic part-fields, the institutionalization of "dissidence," have typified the entire history of the field and were securely in place long before the integrative efforts of the current generation.

Most psychoanalysts have not sought a true modus vivendi with science. Rather, they begin with theoretical and institutional commitments and deploy scientific language of one sort or another to shore up those commitments. The *rhetoric* of science, which is what the community of analysts (including the analytic cartographers) has in common, bolsters sagging professional self-esteem and conveys a credible "scientific" front to a skeptical public that now includes insurers, legislators, and health care managers. But the rhetoric of science bespeaks neither a consensual understanding of science nor a commonality of scientific interest. Observational infancy researchers, attachment theorists, neuropsychoanalysts, proponents of metaphor theory, connectionist theory, semiotics, multiple code theory, and dynamic systems theory—they all have one or another purchase on

---

65. "At this point it is too early to put these various scientific findings together into a coherent theory. I hope that my project here, of bringing these strands together in one train of thought, might in time lead to new models, and to hypotheses as to their possible integration." Olds, "Identification" (n. 50), p. 36; cf. Olds, "Interdisciplinary Studies and Our Practice" (n. 2).

science and, derivatively, on the nature and clinical operation of a scientific psychoanalysis.

Early twenty-first-century psychoanalysis, for all its postclassical progressiveness and postmodern leanings, is very much in the position of Anglo-American medicine in the second half of the nineteenth century, when professional legitimation resulted from the manner in which physicians deployed the rhetoric of science (in one form or another), not from their ability to apply the content of science to their clinical work. If we look at the variegated ways in which nineteenth-century British and American physicians deployed science—invoking everything from pre-Listerian "sanitary science," to phrenology, to empirically "validated" remedies such as bloodletting, to homeopathy and naturopathy, to experimental physiology, to bacteriology, to a sui generis clinical science—it is quickly apparent "that the nineteenth-century profession, though outwardly demonstrating increasing homogeneity, must be resolved into a series of distinct and frequently competing subgroups. Each of these fragments invoked a definition of biomedical knowledge designed to accord with its particular aspirations. In effect, science, mirroring the profession itself, must be seen not as a fixed entity but as a collage of discrete and malleable constituents."[66]

And these constituents, no less than the constituent schools of contemporary psychoanalysis, were often in lively conflict. Virtually

66. See the justly influential article of S. E. D. Shortt, "Physicians, Science, and Status: Issues in the Professionalization of Anglo-American Medicine in the Nineteenth Century," *Med. Hist.*, 27:51–68, 1983, quoted at p. 60. No less discerning is John Harley Warner's "Science in Medicine," *Osiris*, 2nd ser., 1:37–58, 1985. Warner stresses, inter alia, that throughout the nineteenth century, science had diverse meanings even for those physicians who formed the orthodox mainstream at any one time: "Orthodox physicians' disagreements about medical science went far deeper than disputes over each other's theories. They often disagreed fundamentally about what kinds of natural knowledge were and were not legitimate and desirable in medicine" (p. 52). He notes further that for nineteenth-century physicians, the meanings of science ranged beyond universal knowledge to observations by American practitioners of correlations among local meteorology, fluctuating disease conditions, and other changes in the natural environment. Seen in historical context, "physicians' environmental and epidemiological investigations must be regarded as in substantial measure basic research by any categorization applicable to a field like medicine" (p. 56).

all of the nineteenth-century professional communities proclaimed their scientific bona fides, but heated and prolonged conflicts arose among *differently* scientific constituencies. Between the late 1860s and the early 1890s, to give one well-known example, medical proponents of experimental physiology (also referred to as physiological therapeutics) as the scientific guide to clinical practice locked horns with equally principled defenders of a strict empiricism that gave scientific pride of place to clinical observation and the individual peculiarities of sick patients. Two different ideals of science subtended these positions— medicine as an applied science aspiring to the precision and exactitude of experimental science versus medicine as a sui generis clinical science drawing on, but not mechanically constrained by, the findings of the laboratory.[67] Yet a third ideal—the vision of a specialist medical science at the interstices of laboratory and clinic—reflected the ongoing, irresolvable tension between the first two ideals.[68]

The situation in contemporary psychoanalysis is not far different. Like their forebears in nineteenth-century medicine, early twenty-first-century analysts reach out to science through diverse epistemological and ideological commitments.[69] The ethnographically conceived and observationally grounded "science" of attachment research is not the "science" of neurobiology, with its stress on discrete consiliences based

---

67. See John Harley Warner, "Ideals of Science and Their Discontents in Late Nineteenth-Century American Medicine," *Isis,* 82:454–478, 1991, for an illuminating account of this debate, which involved differing visions of scientific medicine and differing notions of professional responsibility and integrity. On analogous tensions in England, see Christopher Lawrence, "Incommunicable Knowledge: Science, Technology and the Clinical Art in Britain, 1850–1914," *J. Contemp. Hist.,* 20:503–520, 1985.

68. This was the vision of the Interurban Clinical Club (William Osler, Rufus Cole, et al.). In the early twentieth century, it became the vision of Samuel Meltzer and Alfred Cohn, Rockefeller Institute research clinicians. Meltzer founded the American Society of Clinical Investigation in 1908; Cohn was the first editor of the *Journal of Clinical Investigation* in 1924. See Russell C. Maulitz, "'Physician Versus Bacteriologist': The Ideology of Science in Clinical Medicine," in Morris J. Vogel & Charles E. Rosenberg, eds., *The Therapeutic Revolution: Essays in the Social History of American Medicine* (Philadelphia: University of Pennsylvania Press, 1979), pp. 91–107.

69. Warner, "Science in Medicine" (n. 66), p. 57; Maulitz, "'Physician versus Bacteriologist'" (n. 68), p. 104.

on imaging-guided localization or, at the very least, per Solms, on the *circumscribing* of brain centers that form the functional networks of complex mental processes. The "science" of biologically open dynamic systems is neither the science of observable and recordable attachment findings nor the science of imaging-guided neuroanatomical con-siliences. The sciences of semiotics and linguistics, notwithstanding intriguing points of contact with dynamic systems theory, occupy their own very different conceptual domains. Proponents of each integra-tive strategy invoke their own definition of psychoanalytic knowledge and bolster it by rhetorical deployment of one or another *kind* of sci-ence. And there matters tend to rest.

The absence of convergence among discrete integrative approaches to psychoanalytic knowledge takes us back to theoretical pluralism, now transmuted into a pluralism of disciplinary mapping strategies, each proffering its own scientific vision and, to a large extent, its own theory-driven set of clinical priorities. We are left with four options. We can wait patiently for the "field" to evolve beyond "integrative pluralism" as it becomes clearer over time which mapping strategies are more and which less clinically salient and clinically implementable. Alternatively, we can wait patiently for one or more of the meta-integrators (or, in the future, schools of metaintegrators) to transcend the integrative "schools" in a compelling grand synthesis that subsumes the local insights captured by proponents of attachment theory, dy-namic systems theory, neurobiology, cognitive neuroscience, semiotics, and the like.

A third option has different, perhaps more modest, goals and takes us back to the publications of the Boston Change Process Study Group, about which further comment is in order. Here it is a matter of pursu-ing a metaintegrative synthesis that reframes psychoanalysis in a way that renders conventional theory of secondary importance, even epiphenomenal, to an understanding of analytic process and cure. For the BCPSG, notions of dyadic coherence and "fittedness" are not theory-bound, at least not in the conventional sense of theory. Rather, they fall back on developmental a prioris with implicit evolutionary moorings, viz., that human beings are designed to co-create with oth-ers meanings that are relational in character. Such meanings, accord-ing to the BCPSG and their allied infancy researchers, are erected on a foundation of tiny "intention units" that, from the beginning of life, are grasped implicitly and represented nonsymbolically. In these units, and not in instinctual drives, one arrives at the "basic structure" of motivated human behavior in its interactive and psychodynamic dimensions.[70]

The problem with the BCPSG group project—if it is a problem—is that its vision of analytic process and cure contains little that is recognizably analytic. One can construe most any kind of talking therapy as a dialogic journey in which communicative ambiguity and "fuzzy intentionalizing" slowly and haltingly give way to a clarity of co-created intentions that alters the domain of "implicit relational knowing" and leads to a feeling of "getting better." The BCPSG's argument, as I grasp it, is that the moment-by-moment unpredictability of *any* therapeutic process—the fact that the process cannot prescribe particular "relational moves" much less be constrained by "consistent narrative structure at the local level"—coexists with dyadic movement toward a superordinate therapeutic endpoint, as guaranteed by the principle of equifinality.[71] In a nutshell: Therapeutic interaction, informed by developmental "relational" imperatives and played out on a grid opened up by dynamic systems theory, allows different and equally effective pathways to a final therapeutic destination.[72]

---

70. BCPSG, "Foundational Level of Psychodynamic Meaning" (n. 13), p. 6. Of course, for BCPSG members, intention units themselves have a subjectively drivelike quality: "Subjectively, intentions are felt to have a thrust or a leaning forward of the intention itself towards its felt or to-be-discovered goal" (p. 6; cf. "Forms of Relational Meaning" [n. 13], p. 131). In their most recent publication, BCPSG members refine their notion of "intention units" by positing an "intention unfolding process." This process is "meant to include all the phases of an intention: its pre-execution phase while it is forming, its execution, and its aim. Taken together, we call this the 'intention unfolding process.' The intention unfolding process arises from a fundamental psychological process that chunks the flow of motivated human behavior into intentions. The mental process of parsing human behavior into intentions and motives is considered a mental primitive, in the sense that it appears to be an innate mental tendency necessary for adaptation in a social world of other motivated beings." BCPSC, "Forms of Relational Meaning" (n. 13), p. 129.

71. "There are many equally valid and effective pathways for the dyad, many of which might arrive at roughly the same destination. In biology and developmental psychology, this equivalence of diverse and idiosyncratic pathways is called the principle of equifinality." BCPSG, "'Something More' than Interpretation Revisited" (n. 13), p. 711.

72. BCPSG, "Explicating the Implicit" (n. 13), p. 1059; "'Something More' than Interpretation Revisited" (n. 13), pp. 701, 711. The developmental principle of equifinality is one legacy of late-nineteenth-century embryology, specifically, Hans Driesch's

I am hard-pressed to apprehend how a feeling of coherence or "fittedness"—continuously recalibrated, punctuated by catalytic "now moments" and occasional "moments of meeting," and ultimately progressive in character—speaks to the specifically *psychoanalytic* character of a psychoanalytic treatment process. In its astute micro-analysis of relational moves as the elemental bits and pieces of an interactive process that leads to a reframing of psychodynamic categories of explanation, the BCPSG project is consonant with one of three pathways proffered by Kenneth Eisold for a "reconsidered psychoanalytic project." This pathway obliges psychoanalysis to relinquish its claim to be a discrete treatment modality and to partner with the psychotherapies, in which capacity it would offer the latter "the benefits of insight and inquiry in the treatment of psychiatric disorders." The special contribution of psychoanalysis to psychotherapeutic process, understood thusly, would reside in a sophisticated model of therapeutic communication that revolved around the relationship of "implicit" and "reflective-verbal" domains in what therapists and patients hear from, and then say to, the other. Such an "analytic" grasp of the nature of therapeutic communication would sustain a fine-grained analysis of the continuously interdigitating intentions of both therapist and patient "to make and adjust the state of the[ir] relationship." Psy-

---

experiments demonstrating that sea urchin half-embryos developed into whole organisms. The principle posits (a) that in open or complex systems, developing organisms with different initial or early conditions can reach the same endpoint; and (b) that in open or complex systems, organisms that share the same initial conditions can reach the same endpoint by different pathways. The principle has been evinced in various microgenetic studies of human development involving, e.g., skill acquisition and language development. The principle was popularized by Ludwig von Bertalanffy, whose *General Systems Theory* (NY: Braziller, 1969/1976 rev. ed.) extended it from organisms to all manner of complex groups, including societies. Following Bertalanffy's own usage of the term "teleology" in describing the common end states achieved by living organisms, groups, and societies, we may say that the BCPSG's notion of a superordinate therapeutic endpoint following from the transformation of implicit relational knowing (via any number of dyadic pathways) is teleologically mandated. For succinct summaries of the principle of equifinality and its disciplinary applications, see Gilbert Gottlieb, "The Relevance of Developmental-Psychobiological Metatheory to Developmental Neuropsychology," *Develop. Neuropsych.*, 19:1–9, 2001 and Gilbert Gottlieb, "Probabilistic Epigenesis of Development," in Jaan Valsiner & Kevin J. Connolly, eds., *Handbook of Developmental Psychology* (London: Sage, 2003), pp. 3–17.

choanalysis would also bring to psychotherapy a nuanced understanding, undergirded by analytically oriented infancy research, of the richly variegated ways that defensive behavior, conflict, and the psychodynamic unconscious may all be "conveyed and transacted in the implicitly represented relational processes."[73]

Finally, in contradiction to the first three options, the fourth option circles back to the heuristic, intuitionist criteria posited by Wallerstein two decades ago. For Wallerstein, we recall, the common ground linking analysts of various stripes and persuasions came down to the "everyday commonplace feeling that somehow all of us, adherents of whatever theoretical position within psychoanalysis, seem to do reasonably comparable clinical work and bring about reasonably comparable changes in the comparable enough patients that we deal with." This feeling, in turn, fell back on what Wallerstein believed to be a "commonality of the clinical observational data of our consulting rooms" along with the experience-near clinical theory that refracted these data through the prism of "transference and resistance, of conflict and compromise, actually of course the original fundamental elements of Freud's famous 1914 definition of psychoanalysis."[74]

Would that an everyday feeling, wed to commensurate observational data and universally accepted experience-near clinical theory, could promote disciplinary cohesiveness through a meeting of analytic minds. Sadly, Wallerstein's meliorative assumptions about com-

---

73. Kenneth Eisold, "The Profession of Psychoanalysis: Past Failures and Future Possibilities," *Contemp. Psychoanal.*, 39:557–582, 2003, at p. 579; BCPSG, "Foundational Level of Psychodynamic Meaning" (n. 13), pp. 6–7; BCPSG, "Forms of Relational Meaning" (n. 13), p. 144. I recur to Eisold's "reconsidered psychoanalytic project" in chapter 9, p. 312.

74. Robert S. Wallerstein, "Psychoanalysis: The Common Ground," *Int. J. Psycho-Anal.*, 71:3–20, 1990, quoted at p. 4. In "On the History of the Psycho-Analytic Movement" (1914), Freud wrote that "the theory of psycho-analysis is an attempt to account for two striking and unexpected facts of observation which emerge whenever an attempt is made to trace the symptoms of a neurotic back to their sources in his past life: the facts of transference and of resistance. Any line of investigation which recognizes these two facts and takes them as the starting-point of its work has a right to call itself psycho-analysis, even though it arrives at results other than my own." Sigmund Freud, "On the History of the Psycho-Analytic Movement." In James Strachey, ed., *Standard Edition of the Complete Psychological Works of Sigmund Freud* 14:7–66 (London: Hogarth Press, 1957), quoted at p. 16.

mon ground have had little impact on the field; indeed they have stimulated a further round of animated controversy.[75] They have not, in
any ascertainable institutional or organizational sense, spurred belated
recognition of the commonalities that subtend analytic part-identities
and moved the profession forward. They have not made the peace. If
anything, the centrifugal forces pulling the field apart into institutionally entrenched part-fields have only intensified in the two decades
following Wallerstein's pronouncement. This is because the very concepts Wallerstein invokes to convey commonality—observational data,
transference and resistance, conflict and compromise—have long since
acquired distributed meanings among proponents of the various psychoanalytic schools.[76] How can one lodge common ground in the very
concepts that gave rise to theoretical pluralism in the first place?

75. Critical reactions to the notion of clinical common ground were coterminous
with Wallerstein's espousal of the concept at the International Psychoanalytical
Association's Montreal (1987) and Rome (1989) Congresses and have been a staple
of the literature ever since. One of the early critics of the notion was Arnold Richards,
whose comments first appeared in his "Programme Notes, 36th IPA Congress, Rome,
1989, the Search for Common Ground: Clinical Aims and Processes" (*Int. J. Psycho-
Anal.* 72:45–56, 1991) and were reprinted as "The Search for Common Ground" in
Robert S. Wallerstein, ed., *The Common Ground of Psychoanalysis* (Northvale, NJ:
Aronson, 1992). Leo Rangell, who has long understood his preferred theory—American ego psychology—as inclusive of the selective (in his view) emphases of other major
psychoanalytic theories, criticized Wallerstein's notion of common ground at the time
of its promulgation and in many publications over the following 20 years. For representative examples, see Leo Rangell, "The Future of Psychoanalysis: The Scientific
Crossroads," *Psychoanal. Quart.*, 57:313–340, 1988; "The Theory of Psychoanalysis: Vicissitudes of Its Evolution," *JAPA*, 55:1109–1137, 2002; and "An Analysis of
the Course of Psychoanalysis: The Case for a Unitary Theory," *Psychoanal. Psychol.*,
23:217–238, 2006. Among the many critical reactions to Wallerstein's notion of
common ground, the following are especially illuminating: Roy Schafer, "The Search
for Common Ground," *Int. J. Psycho-Anal.*, 71:49–52, 1990; André Lussier, "The
Search for Common Ground: A Critique," *Int. J. Psycho-Anal.*, 72:57–62, 1991;
Arnold Modell, "Common Ground or Divided Ground?" *Psychoanal. Inq.*, 14:201–
211, 1994; Cecilio Paniagua, "Common Ground, Uncommon Methods," *Int. J.
Psycho-Anal.*, 76:357–371, 1995; and André Green, "The Illusion of Common Ground
and Mythical Pluralism," *Int. J. Psycho-Anal.*, 86:627–632, 2005.

76. And of course the very notion of shared "observational data" is epistemologically suspect, as Wallerstein among others has more recently acknowledged. See
Robert S. Wallerstein, "The Intertwining of Politics and Science in Psychoanalytic
History," *JAPA*, 51(suppl): 7–21, 2003, at p. 11, and the discussion at pp. 247–250,
below.

Various notions of transference, to take one example, have long taken root in the autochthonous soil of different psychoanalytic schools. Does the notion of transference that binds analysts in shared endeavor fall back on drive theory, self development, interpersonal schemas, emotion schemas (per Bucci), early object relationships, here-and-now interaction, nested interpersonal/transpersonal fields, semiotic transformations, or the activation thresholds of neural networks? This is tantamount to asking *whose* vision of transference effects common ground. Classical object-libidinal transference framed in terms of oedipal dynamics? Archaic preoedipal transferences? Primitive part-object transferences of the Kleinian variety? Self-selfobject transferences in the manner of psychoanalytic self psychology? Imaginary and symbolic transferences evoked by the analytic setting in the manner of Lacan?

Is the transference that binds analysts of different persuasions to be apprehended within a historical, one-person frame of reference or within a modernist two-person "interactive" paradigm? Is it to be understood via connectionism as a network of mutually activating (and inhibiting) transference paradigms, each of which implicates a specific object-relational constellation? Is it to be reframed, in accord with dynamic systems theory, as an intersubjective field concept? Or, in accord with another version of dynamic systems theory, is the concept of transference to be jettisoned completely, since transference phenomena arise within an unstable nonlinear system in which backward and forward prediction are equally impossible?[77] Just as each psychoanalytic school—which includes the proponents of each integrative approach—proffers its own version of "valid" science, so each psychoanalytic school has its own purchase on the concept of transference, and each purchase falls back on quasi-paradigmatic theories of mental development, psychopathology, therapeutic action, and cure. To be sure, there are points of contact among the various theories but, to this point in time, the intersections have been outweighed by paradigm-like incommensurabilities among the theories in toto.

The same observations hold with respect to each and every item in Wallerstein's, which is to say Freud's, list of common-ground-

---

77. Joseph Schachter, *Transference: Shibboleth or Albatross?* (Hillsdale, NJ: Analytic Press, 2002), pp. 91–104.

promoting particulars. The concept of resistance, to take one further example, has long been robbed of any collective theoretical significance. The very usefulness of the concept has been cogently challenged from various perspectives, mainstream Freudian psychoanalysis and psychoanalytic self psychology among them.[78] To the extent that the concept retains valence, it has come to mean radically different things to different analysts, and these differences refer back to paradigmatic incommensurabilities among the respective theories out of which the meanings arise. Freudian, self-psychological, and Lacanian notions of resistance, for example, do not occupy different points along the self-same continuum; rather, they fall back on fundamentally different understandings of what is being resisted, why it is being resisted, in what ways the resistance is adaptive or maladaptive (and the criteria according to which adaptation and maladaptation are to be understood), and how interactive, transactional, and/or co-constructed such resistant phenomena are. In brief, we have various notions of resistance and its role in therapeutic work, and each notion tends to its own conceptual orbit.

One could easily discourse on the widely distributed, and often incompatible, meanings of "conflict and compromise" in contemporary psychoanalysis, but my point is by now clear. If psychoanalysts of various stripes and persuasions are to achieve common ground in

78. According to Roy Schafer, "the idea of resistance is diffuse and superfluous, too focused on relatively manifest content, and too dependent on theoretical propositions about the therapeutic process that no longer dominate sound Freudian analytic practice. Consequently, I consider the idea of resistance to be technically confusing." Schafer, while allowing for the continued descriptive use of a word (viz., resistance) that is "so well established in the clinical lexicon," drains it of any explanatory value: ". . . in the most appropriate analytic approach, we as analysts hardly give any weight to the idea of resistance. Instead, we think in the general terms of transference and defensive operations. Specifically, we think in terms of enactments within the analytic relationships that are about the analytic relationship itself." Kohut's radical re-visioning of "defense and resistance" as adaptive strategies in the service of psychological survival has shaped self-psychological discourse over the past two decades and exerted considerable influence on proponents of intersubjectivity theory and relational/interpersonal psychoanalysis. See Roy Schafer, *Retelling a Life: Narration and Dialogue in Psychoanalysis* (NY: Basic Books, 1992), pp. 219–247, quoted at pp. 221, 227; Heinz Kohut, *How Does Analysis Cure?*, edited by Arnold Goldberg with the collaboration of Paul E. Stepansky (Chicago: University of Chicago Press, 1984), pp. 111–151.

the interest of cultural and scientific legitimacy, if they are to move forward as a cohesive discipline with the specialized knowledge that is the hallmark of any profession, it cannot be on the basis of psychoanalytic concepts formulated by Freud in 1914. There must be a different route to common ground. What might that route be?

Chapter 7

Science Matters

The therapeutic "test" is no test at all; witness chiropractic and Eddyism.[1]

The various integrative approaches reviewed in the preceding chapter leave unanswered the overarching normative question: *Should* psychoanalysis aspire to become more scientific by enlisting the aid of one or more of these strategies? The question really means: Will psychoanalysts, individually or collectively, choose to pursue the path of one or another variant of normal science, in which case they will likely become less psychoanalytic and more eclectically psychotherapeutic in orientation. The fractionation of the field inveighs against the possibility of a single pathway to scientific assimilation. As we have seen, the various integrative strategies have too often been mapped onto the divergent theories and clinical sensibilities of one or another psychoanalytic school of thought. Paradoxically, the progressive marginalization of psychoanalysis over the past 40 years has not pushed the field toward consensus on key matters. On the contrary, marginalization from without has run in tandem with fragmentation from within. During the same period that psychoanalysis was progressively relegated to the margins by psychiatry, clinical psychology, and health care providers, the field underwent fission; it became dispersed among the various psychoanalytic schools.

Historically, this is an anomalous development, since attacks from without typically promote cohesiveness and unity of purpose among marginalized professional groups. In early nineteenth-century America, regular medical practitioners were a beleaguered lot whose recourse to excessive bleeding and administration of "heroic" doses of toxic

1. Harry Stack Sullivan, "The Common Field of Research and Clinical Psychiatry," *Psychiat. Quart.*, 1:267–291, 1927, reprinted in Harry Stack Sullivan, *Schizophrenia as a Human Process* (NY: Norton, 1974 [1962]), pp. 140–156, quoted at p. 141.

mercury compounds (especially calomel) literally drove patients to their graves. Their "regularity"—the fact that they had apprenticed with "regular" physicians and attended lectures at one or another medical institution—did not prevent them from being socially ostracized and occupationally marginalized. Yet, by mid-century, they came together in response to the encroachment of medical sects. Regular practice, that is, became Orthodox Medicine partly in response to the sectarian challenge of hydropaths, eclectics, Thomsonians, and homeopaths. The failure of American psychoanalysts to cohere into something tantamount to American Psychoanalysis in reply to its critics and detractors has compromised the field's ability to follow the historical example of other successful revitalization movements in accommodating itself to key special interest groups—organized medicine, health policy decision-makers, government elites, and potential client groups—in the interest of moving the entire field toward mainstream acceptance.[2]

Is it possible that one or another kind of integrative strategy will win out over the others? Is such a prospect even desirable? Analysts themselves must decide. I myself hope that researchers will continue to delineate the interrelationships between psychoanalysis and neuroscience, because I believe this integrative approach holds the greatest promise of bringing psychoanalysis into the scientific mainstream in a manner that comprehends and grants dignity to nonanalytic mechanisms of therapeutic action in realms as disparate as psychotropic medication and cognitive-behavioral interventions. Of course, it has been a central argument of this work that psychoanalysts of various stripes and persuasions have not agreed—and perhaps *cannot* agree—on "core constructs" that typify psychoanalysis as a discipline and provide a basis for a common ground program of neurobiological assessment. What is left to analysts if they cannot agree on core constructs and appropriate methodologies to test them? School-based partisan claims as to the nature of contemporary psychoanalysis make

2. John Harley Warner, "Medical Sectarianism, Therapeutic Conflict, and the Shaping of Orthodox Professional Identity in Antebellum American Medicine," in W. F. Bynum & Roy Porter, eds., *Medical Fringes and Medical Orthodoxy, 1750–1850* (London: Croom Helm, 1987), pp. 234–260; Hans A. Baer, "Divergence and Convergence in Two Systems of Manual Medicine: Osteopathy and Chiropractic in the United States," *Med. Anthro. Quart.*, 1:176–193, 1987; Anthony F. C. Wallace, "Revitalization Movements," *Am. Anthro.*, 58:264–281, 1956.

it difficult even to enter into dialogue with Adolf Grünbaum, whose philosophical critique of the scientific standing of psychoanalytic hypotheses was issued a full quarter-century ago. How do analytically trained researchers go about devising uncontaminated empirical tests to validate or invalidate specific psychoanalytic claims, per Grünbaum, if psychoanalysts themselves cannot agree on those claims specific to psychoanalysis—specific, that is, to psychoanalysis in its disciplinary entirety?

Grünbaum's critique of the field's scientific bona fides centered on Freud's *own* evidential claims, and its most searching rejoinder came from a classical Freudian analyst, Marshall Edelson. The aspect of Grünbaum's critical inquiry that elicited the greatest analytic attention was what he termed Freud's "tally argument"—*Freud's* belief that psychoanalytic treatment only provides durable cure when the analyst's interpretations (which include their suggestive impact at the time they are made) convey insight that conforms to the patient's actual experience; interpretive insight *tallies* with what is "real" in the patient.[3]

The Tally Argument, as Grünbaum named it and framed it, was not the basis of Freud's specific explanatory claims (as to, for example, the mechanism of repression). Rather, it represented his attempt to justify the psychoanalytic method of inquiry and the data it generated in the face of the common criticism, which Freud himself enunciated in devil's advocate fashion in the last of his *Introductory Lectures*, that the analyst's suggestive impact on the patient and the patient's positive transference to the analyst eroded the "objective certainty" of the clinical findings. Grünbaum argued that Freud failed to prove the Tally Argument, and further, that its major premise about the probative value of data obtained within the psychoanalytic situation

3. Adolf Grünbaum, *The Foundations of Psychoanalysis: A Philosophical Critique* (Berkeley: University of California Press, 1984), pp. 130ff. Grünbaum identified and explicated the "Tally Argument" five years prior to the publication of his book in "Epistemological Liabilities of the Clinical Appraisal of Psychoanalytic Theory," *Psychoanal. Contemp. Th.*, 2:451–526, 1979, an expanded version of which appeared in *Noûs*, 14:307–385, 1980. Morris Eagle was among the few analysts who accepted Grünbaum's critique of Freud's Tally Argument and wrestled with its implications. See Morris N. Eagle, *Recent Developments in Psychoanalysis: A Critical Evaluation* (NY: McGraw-Hill, 1984), chaps. 14 & 16. The range of responses to Grünbaum's book is well represented in the 41 "open peer commentaries" gathered in *Brain Behav. Sci.*, 9(2), 1986.

was "well-nigh empirically untenable." And absent a replacement for Freud's Tally Argument, with its specious assumption that "clinical data" are uncontaminated by the analyst's suggestive influence, there was "woefully insufficient ground to vindicate the intraclinical test-ability of the cardinal tenets of psychoanalysis."[4]

Edelson, in turn, formulated a reply to Grünbaum by invoking a "nonstatement"[5] view of scientific theory. The treating analyst, he held, begins with a patient to whom he assigns the predicate "[so-and-so] is a Freudian system" and then formulates and tests hypotheses about the patient that derive from the various law-like relationships that obtain within a Freudian system. If, over the course of analysis, the hypotheses were borne out, then the analyst had added confirming instances to the scientific truthfulness, the "veridicality," of a Freudian system, which, for Edelson, was tantamount to psychoanalysis.

By defining the domain of psychoanalysis as the set of psychological entities (wishes, beliefs, memories, thoughts, perceptions, etc.) that belongs to a single subject (i.e., the analysand), Edelson sought to meet the evidential burden of eliminative inductivism in the single-subject

---

4. Grünbaum, *Foundations of Psychoanalysis* (n. 3), p. 128. Freud's formulation of what Grünbaum terms the Tally Argument is in his lecture on "Analytic Therapy" in Part III of his *Introductory Lectures*. See Sigmund Freud, *Introductory Lectures on Psycho-Analysis: Part III. General Theory of Neuroses* (1917). In James Strachey, ed., *Standard Edition of the Complete Psychological Works of Sigmund Freud*, 16: 452–453 (London: Hogarth Press, 1963). Grünbaum clarified the meaning of the Tally Argument in his "Author's Response" to the commentaries in *Brain and Behavioral Sciences* (n. 3), pp. 266–281 at p. 271 and two decades later in "The Reception of My Freud-Critique in the Psychoanalytic Literature," *Psychoanal. Psychol.*, 24:545–576, 2007.

5. The nonstatement view of theory of the 1970s was anticipated by Frederick Suppe in his *Introduction to Logic* (NY: Van Nostrand, 1957), and then elaborated in the 1970s by Joseph Sneed (*The Logical Structure of Mathematical Physics* [Dordrecht: Reidel, 1971]); Wolfgang Stegmüller (*The Structure and Dynamics of Theory* [NY: Springer-Verlag, 1976]); and Ronald Giere (*Understanding Scientific Reasoning* [NY: Holt, 1979]). It held that an empirical scientific theory does not consist of a class of sentences or propositions, but rather of a set-theoretic predicate, in the manner Edelson uses the expression ". . . is a Freudian system." Heir in spirit to the logical positivism of the early twentieth century, the nonstatement view provided a structuralist account of science according to which a scientific theory comprised a "core" that could be mathematically formalized along with a set of structures that represented all the physical situations to which the theory was intended to apply (Stegmüller).

setting of a psychoanalytic treatment. In simple terms, he believed that psychoanalytic hypotheses consistent with "a Freudian system" could be formulated and tested with each and every treatment situation, patient by patient, analyst by analyst.[6] To the extent that individual psychoanalytic treatments provided supportive evidence for these hypotheses, they attested to the "truthfulness" of a Freudian explanatory model relative to competing models (such as behaviorism) whose claims were incompatible with "a Freudian system." This is what eliminative inductivism means: The collecting of "evidential instances" that support one explanatory model but not rival models that fall within the same domain and thereby increase the credibility of the former model at the expense of the latter. The weight of cumulative evidence that supports the credibility of one model (or theory) simultaneously eliminates the credibility of rival models.[7]

It is not my intent to revisit Edelson's vision of "scientific" psychoanalysis beyond noting that it was very much the successor to efforts by analysts of the postwar generation to systematize psychoanalytic theory by applying formal logic to Freudian metapsychology,[8] and that it gained no real traction within an American psychoanalytic community that was already transitioning to theoretical pluralism at the time of his writing. More than a quarter century after the publication of *Hypothesis and Evidence in Psychoanalysis* (1984) and *Psychoanalysis: A Theory in Crisis* (1988), Edelson's metapsychological outline of "a Freudian system"[9] has become quaintly archaic for all but a

6. Marshall Edelson, *Hypothesis and Evidence in Psychoanalysis* (Chicago: University of Chicago Press, 1984), pp. 77–108.

7. For a particularly clear definition of eliminative inductivism, see Friedel Weinert, "The Construction of Atom Models: Eliminative Inductivism and Its Relation to Falsificationism," *Found. Sci.,* 5:491–531, 2000 at p. 502.

8. Edelson lists works by Arlow and Brenner, Fenichel, Gill, Klein, Rapaport, Rubinstein, Schur, and Waelder as "notable efforts to systematize psychoanalytic theory" that preceded his own. (*Hypothesis and Evidence* [n. 6], p. 79). In point of fact, his abstractive approach to psychoanalytic theory, with its reliance on formal logic and absence of clinical material, is closely aligned with David Rapaport's writing from the 1950s, which culminated in *The Structure of Psychoanalytic Theory* (*Psychological Issues,* Monograph 6; NY: International Universities Press, 1960).

9. Edelson, *Hypothesis and Evidence* (n. 6), pp. 78–83.

handful of American analysts. His notion of analysis as a "procedure" that generates data, the evidential value of which depends on the success with which the procedure is implemented, is more in line with Freud's surgical metaphor than with contemporary discussions of technique, which emphasize the role of the analyst's subjectivity in the very creation of analytic data.[10] Nor, finally, did Edelson's insistence that efforts to provide a neurobiological foundation for psychoanalysis "should be resisted as expressions of logical confusion" prefigure the quarter century to follow.[11] It did not allow for advances in neuroscience, including the dramatic refinement of neuroimaging technologies. And it seriously misread the evolving sensibilities of neuroscientific

10. Marshall Edelson, *Psychoanalysis: A Theory in Crisis* (Chicago: University of Chicago Press, 1988), p. 272. On the vision of psychoanalytic method encapsulated in Freud's surgical metaphor, see Paul E. Stepansky, *Freud, Surgery, and the Surgeon* (Hillsdale, NJ: Analytic Press, 1999). Edelson's scientific vision of psychoanalysis as a "procedure" that, depending on the instrumental precision with which it is performed, could generate more or less robust data, is worlds removed from contemporary "postclassical" analysis, which stresses the analyst's subjective participation, even co-construction, of the data that emerge through an "analytic process." Edelson was of a mind with James Strachey, who argued during the Controversial Discussions of 1943 of the British Psychoanalytic Society that analytic "fitness" was a matter of "valid technique," not of views on etiology or theory. "I am prepared to insist," he wrote, "that upon the whole a valid technique is not necessarily or even chiefly the *product* of our scientific findings and theories, but that it is rather the most efficient instrument by which they can be reached. And I suggest that the essential criterion of whether a person is fit to conduct a training analysis is not whether his views on etiology or theory are true, but whether his technique is valid." See Strachey's "Discussion Memorandum" of February 24, 1943, in Pearl King & Riccardo Steiner, eds., *The Freud-Klein Controversies, 1941–45* (London: Routledge, 1991), pp. 602–610, quoted at p. 607, emphasis in the original.

11. Edelson, *Hypothesis and Evidence* (n. 6), p. 110. In his autobiography, Eric Kandel recollects a 1986 symposium at Yale honoring Morton Reiser at which he and Edelson both presented papers. Following Kandel's paper on learning and memory in the snail, in which he observed that "all mental illness, regardless of symptoms, must be associated with distinctive alterations in the brain," Edelson rose during the discussion "and said that, while he agreed that psychotic illnesses were disorders of brain function, the disorders that Freud described and that are seen in practice by psychoanalysts, such as obsessive-compulsive neurosis and anxiety states, could not be explained on the basis of brain function." For Kandel, Edelson's insular viewpoint was emblematic of "the unwillingness to think about psychoanalysis in the broader context of neural science [that] hindered the growth of psychoanalysis during biology's recent golden age." See Eric R. Kandel, *In Search of Memory: The Emergence of a New Science of Mind* (NY: Norton, 2006), pp. 420–421.

researchers and psychoanalytic clinicians alike with respect to the *kind* of questions (regarding, for example, the conscious and unconscious components of anxiety; aspects of self-regulatory functioning; identification; transference; the "emotional brain" and the "synaptic self") amenable to neurobiological specification.

Neurobiologists have known for more than three decades that different types of psychopathology reflect specific alterations in neuronal and synaptic function, and that "insofar as psychotherapy works, it works by acting on brain, not on single synapses, but on synapses nevertheless." It is only within the past decade, however, that neuroimaging resolution has advanced to the point of becoming consequential to therapists and analysts. Imaging now allows researchers to ascertain basal metabolic and stimulus-responsive brain changes subsequent to successful psychotherapy, and then to show how such changes both align with, and differ from, brain changes that follow successful pharmacotherapy. A landmark study of the pharmacotherapy of unipolar depression found, through imaging, a basis to differentiate treatment responders from nonresponders; the study design "can be at least conceptually extended to psychotherapy." And preliminary imaging studies of obsessive-compulsive disorder suggest that orbitofrontal cortex (OFC) activity levels predict treatment response and, more intriguingly still, provide a basis for differentiating among different treatments, viz., lower pretreatment OFC metabolism predicted better response to medication than psychotherapy, whereas higher OFC metabolism predicted the opposite. In the near future, multivariate analysis of neuroimaging findings may enable researchers to dissolve the global concept of "major depression" into distinct etiologies on the basis of imaging findings that reveal why some patients improve with particular therapies and others do not. In this vision of things to come, choice of therapy and treatment outcome prediction may come to "depend more on the functional characteristics of that individual's brain than on how the patient is diagnosed."[12]

---

12. Eric Kandel, "Psychotherapy and the Single Synapse: The Impact of Psychiatric Thought on Neurobiological Research," *New Eng. J. Med.*, 301:1028–1037, 1979, reprinted as a "neuropsychiatry classic" in *J. Neuropsy. Clin. Neurosci.*, 13:290–300, 2001 quoted at p. 291; Amit Etkin, Christopher Pittenger, H. Jonathan Polan, & Eric R. Kandel, "Toward a Neurobiology of Psychotherapy: Basic Science and Clinical Applications," *J. Neuropsy. Clin. Neurosci.*, 17:145–148, 2005, quoted at pp. 149, 148.

Neuroimaging findings bearing on diagnosis, treatment selection, and treatment outcome are relevant to psychoanalysis but are not focally "neuropsychoanalytic." Within this later domain, neuroimaging studies are useful because they oblige analytic researchers to formulate a list of core constructs amenable to scanning methodologies—and, to be sure, a list of constructs not so amenable. And there is the credible hope that neuroimaging findings themselves may be able to refine certain psychoanalytic assumptions in scientifically progressive ways. Already, we have studies that push the psychoanalytic understanding of affect toward a bipartite model of separate systems of affect valence and affect arousal consistent with affective neuroscience and recent infancy research. And we have imaging studies that have enlarged the analytic purview on self-regulatory functioning in terms of the dynamic interplay of bottom-up and top-down neural processing of sensory input.[13] Only a short remove in psychoanalytic relevance is the use of imaging to differentiate the conscious and unconscious processing of anxiety-inducing stimuli and to examine the failure of conscious processes to regulate unconscious biases among patients with posttraumatic stress disorder (PTSD).[14]

Many, perhaps most, analysts will demur from this vision of things to come, but they do so at their own peril. There is something profoundly antitherapeutic, not to say anti-Freudian, about indifference to postpsychotherapy changes in brain function detectable with neuroimaging. The analytic salience of neuroimaging findings will only increase in the years ahead. Even if such findings are not adequate to the testing of "experience-near" clinical constructs, even if they cannot underwrite a new kind of common ground, even then they may come to the aid of psychoanalysis. Neuroimaging, in its ability to group

13. For a discerning synthesis of neuroimaging findings in relation to psychoanalytic concepts of pleasure and unpleasure, self-regulatory functioning, and transference, see Bradley S. Peterson, "Clinical Neuroscience and Imaging Studies of Core Psychoanalytic Constructs," *Clin. Neurosci. Res.*, 4:349–365, 2005.

14. A. Etkin, K. C. Klemenhagen, J. T. Dudman, et al., "Individual Differences in Trait Anxiety Predict the Response of the Basolateral Amygdala to Unconsciously Processed Fearful Face," *Neuron*, 44:1043–1055, 2004; L. M. Shin, C. I. Wright, P. A. Cannistraro, et al., "A Functional Magnetic Resonance Imaging Study of Amygdala and Medial Prefrontal Cortex Responses to Overtly Presented Fearful Faces in Posttraumatic Stress Disorder," *Arch. Gen. Psychiatry*, 62:273–281, 2005.

patients on the basis of biological variables that are linked to type of treatment, may normalize the determination of "analyzability," i.e., it may help identify the kind of patient who, with or without medication, is more likely to profit from extended psychodynamic treatment. Of course it is for analysts to help researchers understand more fully and more subtly what it means to "profit from extended psychodynamic treatment." Influential neuroscientists at the forefront of this research have long welcomed psychoanalysis to the table. As Eric Kandel observed three decades ago, "psychiatry [by which he clearly meant psychoanalytic psychiatry] must pose the questions" that neurobiology "need answer."[15] Peterson concludes his review of recent imaging studies of core psychoanalytic constructs by observing that "Progress in further defining the neural bases of these core constructs will require the close collaboration of neuroscientists and psychoanalysts in the development of experimental paradigms that simplify the analytic field for systematic study while maintaining reliability and ecological validity." It is for analysts to decide whether, and in what fashion, they will participate in a collaborative undertaking that, for Peterson, "merely defines the hard work of empirical research."[16]

Psychoanalysts who reject the neuroscientific pathway to progress look elsewhere for a remedy to fractionation. Perhaps psychoanalysis can be revivified by adopting a "comparative" or "comparative-integrative" approach to training that focuses on the theoretical and clinical differences among the various psychoanalytic schools rather than teaching students psychoanalysis from the standpoint of one or another such school. The Swiss analyst Paul Parin who, with his wife

15. Kandel, "Psychotherapy and the Single Synapse" (n. 12), p. 291. Kandel made this point more forcefully still two decades later in his reply to commentaries elicited by his "A New Intellectual Framework for Psychiatry," *Am. J. Psychiatry*, 155:457–469, 1998. There, by way of underscoring his appreciation of psychoanalysis, he wrote that ". . . those aspects of biology that aspire to contribute to the science of the human mind must take the insights of psychoanalysis into consideration. . . . If biology is to explore the mind, biologists will need all the guidance they can get from students of mental processes." Eric R. Kandel, "Letter to the Editor," *Am. J. Psychiatry*, 156:665–666, 1999.

16. Peterson, "Clinical Neuroscience and Imaging Studies" (n. 13), p. 361.

Goldy Parin-Matthey and Fritz Morgenthaler, founded the German school of ethnopsychoanalysis, introduced the idea of "comparative psychoanalysis" in a paper of 1976, but his concern was anthropological, i.e., with the application of psychoanalysis to nonwestern subjects, in whom inner conflicts had to be understood in the context of nonwestern social conditions and historical processes. In 1985, the American analyst Roy Schafer recurred to the term as a conceptual vehicle for examining the divergent technical approaches and embedded "moral positions" of Melanie Klein, Heinz Kohut, and Merton Gill in relation to (then) mainstream Freudian psychoanalysis. Over the past decade, the term has come into vogue in a pedagogical context: It has been proffered as a constructive, harmony-promoting alternative to the training of analysts in the conventional school-based training institute.[17]

Candidates instructed through the comparative-psychoanalytic approach, it is held, will emerge with a respectful and open-minded appreciation of the strengths and limitations of each psychoanalytic school of thought. Optimally, they will be equipped to transcend the part-theories of the present and embrace a higher-order "dialectical synthesis" of currently segregated explanatory models. So holds the Canadian analyst Brent Willock, who announces in a recent work that "If psychoanalysis is or was dying, the comparative-integrative perspective predicts a rousing resurrection." According to Willock, the comparative-integrative approach is the only way to overcome the "Napoleonic tendencies" evinced by the various psychoanalytic schools of thought. Teaching psychoanalysis comparatively aims to supplant these tendencies with an ecumenical receptiveness to the insights and clinical strategies of different psychoanalytic schools. Students so taught will learn about their field in an educational environment characterized by "Socratic humility and commitment to continuing learning." They will not be indoctrinated into the constricted mind-set of one or another kind of psychoanalysis. Instead, their free-floating attention will be "at liberty to roam and resonate with insights from

---

17. Paul Parin, "Das Mikroskop der vergleichenden Psychoanalyse und die Makrosocieta," *Psyche*, 30:1–25, 1976, translated into English as "The Microscope of Comparative Psychoanalysis and the Macrosociety," *J. Psychol. Anthro.*, 1:141–164, 1978; Roy Schafer, "Wild Analysis," *JAPA*, 33:275–299, 1985.

a wide range of contributors from diverse geographical locations and historical epochs."[18]

Willock's vision of comparative-integrative training has been implemented at his own Toronto Institute of Contemporary Psychoanalysis. In the United States, Stuart Pizer and Steven Cooper, whom I interviewed in 2007, have played prominent roles in establishing comparative-psychoanalytic curricula at the Massachusetts Institute for Psychoanalysis (MIP) and the Boston Psychoanalytic Society and Institute (BPSI), respectively.[19] They echo Willock's sense of the concept as an attitude that gives rise to both a pedagogical perspective and a nontraditional curriculum.[20] For Pizer, the attitude "strives to be inclusive, doing justice to distinction while avoiding polarizing,

18. Brent Willock, *Comparative-Integrative Psychoanalysis: A Relational Perspective for the Discipline's Second Century* (NY: Analytic Press, 2007), pp. 169, 168, 136.

19. The Columbia Center for Psychoanalytic Training and Research too has added a comparative dimension to its training curriculum, though it differs from the BPSI and MIP programs in its systematic focus on the epistemological implications of a discipline whose knowledge base derives from "a conglomerate of partial theories and theoretical models." Ellen Rees explains the rationale of the Columbia Center's Methodology Sequence thusly: ". . . since we rely on a pluralistic perspective to encompass diverse and diverging models and theories, we have to contend with contradictory ideas and concepts that represent different meanings. It is important that candidates be able to recognize contradictory ideas and be able to think about the advantages and disadvantages of maintaining them in their current state. It is important that they understand that we are struggling with the question of whether a multiplicity of theoretical meanings is inherent in the development of our thinking, and/or is a transitional phase as we strive for a different integration in our thinking." This approach, which seeks to enable candidates to "mak[e] sense of current controversy and debate" rather than simply to devise a pragmatic approach to theory choice and application, strikes me as more challenging than either the BPSI or MIP program. See Ellen Rees, "Thinking About Psychoanalytic Curricula: An Epistemological Perspective," *Psychoanal. Quart.*, 76:891–942, 2007, quoted at pp. 894, 895, 898.

20. These interviews were conducted via email and formed a unit of an online symposium I led from April 15 to July 15, 2007. The symposium, sponsored and hosted by The Psychoanalytic Connection, was titled, "Uncommon Ground and the Possibilities for Our Psychoanalytic Future: An Online Symposium with Paul Stepansky and Invited Guests." My electronic exchanges with Stuart Pizer and Steven Cooper, which led off the unit entitled "Comparative Psychoanalysis: To What End?", took place in May, and were presented to symposium participants on June 8, 2007. All quoted remarks attributed to Pizer and Cooper in the following paragraphs are taken from these interviews and reproduced here with their kind permission.

dichotomizing, foreclosing assumptions. Comparative psychoanalysis seeks to avoid privileging one 'school' over others. It values respectful dialogue, including vigorous disagreement, in the discourse of the community." For Cooper, whose curricular revisions at BPSI followed his successful teaching experiences at MIP, the comparative approach falls back on clinical pragmatism: By learning to examine the same "clinical data" from the viewpoints of different analytic schools of thought, students work toward a complementarity of vision that helps them grasp the conceptual lacunae and work through the clinical blind spots associated with any one school of thought. "My primary reason for valuing comparative psychoanalysis," Cooper told me,

> is that I deeply believe that each theory valorizes particular illusory concepts that are helpful but that we do well to be able to question. Freud emphasized drive as the mythological frontier between psyche and soma. Self psychologists rely on the selfobject concept. Relational theorists rely on concepts such as enactment and countertransference expressiveness. Each theory has its focus, whether it is the understanding of mind, the understanding of a particular diagnostic group, or the illumination of specific elements of the clinical encounter. These linchpin concepts in each theory provide a central lens on the clinical situation or the understanding of mind, but they are also accompanied by particular potential blind spots. When comparative analysis uses a theory external to the one employed by a particular analyst, it can sometimes provide helpful ways of thinking about these blind spots.[21]

These several comparative training programs ultimately rely on mature students able to "hold" and work with multiple perspectives and special faculty willing to subordinate their own school-bound identities to the comparative project. Pizer stresses that teachers at MIP are typically allied with one or another psychoanalytic school, but the com-

---

21. Cooper made this same point in "Facts All Come with a Point of View," *Int. J. Psycho-Anal.*, 77:255–273, 1996, where he invoked a second useful image to address the blind spots inhering in any one psychoanalytic school of thought. "Our body of theory, we hope, acts as a kind of check and balance system regarding what has been overemphasized or minimized within a particular method of [theoretical] formulation. Each theory probably holds on to some omnipotent fantasies of formulation" (p. 270).

parative framework of instruction encourages them to "entertain the limiting cases, the particular vulnerabilities, the gaps in each school." Students may well perceive certain teachers identified with one or another school of thought as "defending the faith," but the raison d'etre of the training program assures them the freedom to question all their instructors. "Although they may at times face defensiveness," Pizer remarks, "there is no reprisal for challenging any dogma." Cooper who, with several colleagues, undertook the challenge of moving a traditional APsaA institute grounded in American ego psychology in a comparative direction, devised a curriculum that taught specific psychoanalytic concepts (e.g., object, defense, drive, motivation) in a comparative way. This approach, he related, "promotes an integrative way of thinking about psychoanalytic concepts without simultaneously smoothing over differences. It also allows students to appreciate bold and revolutionary revisions in psychoanalytic ideas more fully as well as bridge theorists who attempt to integrate contributions from divergent theories." This curricular innovation was generally well received among students, but it proved less than congenial to later chairpersons of the BPSI curriculum committee, some of whom sought "to reduce some of the comparative focus, stacking the deck with their theoretical preferences. It is not unlike what goes on in congressional committees when one political party takes over chairmanship of the committee— they try to influence things in the direction of their political preferences."

A hint of the limitations of comparative psychoanalysis as a response to theoretical pluralism may be gleaned from the different educational trajectories posited by Cooper, Pizer, and Willock, respectively. What exactly are the goals of comparative psychoanalytic training? Cooper's commitment to the approach is grounded in the pragmatic usefulness of various theories in bringing "outside" perspectives to bear on the kinds of clinical quandaries and impasses that candidates are bound to encounter. He does not see the comparative approach as tending toward any kind of metaintegration. It is not intended to dissolve the differences among the different psychoanalytic schools; at most it promotes a clinically productive complementarity among them. In this sense, it simply accepts and makes the most of theoretical pluralism.[22] Pizer

22. "Comparative psychoanalysis is not a choice, something that we can dispense with at this point. It is what we are left with in the context of fundamentally different ways of working with patients." PES interview of Steven Cooper (n. 20).

adopts a comparable premise. At MIP, he told me, "we neither strive for synthesis nor really believe in it. Each theory needs to be examined, received, and questioned on its own terms. And there are some basic incompatible assumptions that our comparative approach would not want to gloss over." At its best, then, the comparative approach works toward an "adaptive multiplicity" through which students acquire the ability to "hold multiple perspectives, even multiple identifications" as they work toward clinical maturity and commence their analytic careers. Simultaneously, in a more hopeful vein, Pizer acknowledges that the comparative approach espouses "something beyond peaceful coexistence of theories and 'schools,'" if only as an ideal.

> It is more a recognition of the commonalities embedded in disparate schools, without the effort to coerce a false merger. Certainly it seeks to cultivate a more complex knowledge base, as free as possible of resistances to any approach, so that development, attachment, affect, sexuality, the embodied bases of psychic functioning, the growth and integrity of the self, the creative and autonomous agency of each subjectivity, the negotiation of intimacy, passion, self-interest, responsibility and generativity, the construction of meaning, the healing and liberating potential in analytic process can all be held in mind (tacitly) by an analyst immersed in the thicknesses of the analytic moment.

Pizer's ideal of a resistance-free psychoanalytic ecumenicism may be a bit more heartening to proponents of "common ground" than Cooper's realization that comparative psychoanalysis simply reflects, and teaches candidates to make the most of, theoretical pluralism. But, prognostically speaking, both viewpoints pale alongside Willock's utopian vision of the kind of metaintegration destined to grow out of the comparative approach. For Willock, the comparative-integrative approach is far more than a pragmatic means of identifying theory-specific blind spots; it points the way to a new metamodel that "represents a radically different attitude toward all models including those not yet conceived." In this manner, the comparative-integrative perspective functions as "a container for models and a methodology for theory creation," and it only comes to fruition through the "achieved synthesis" that emerges from it. This synthesis, in turn, becomes a new thesis, evoking its own "fresh antithesis."[23]

23. Willock, *Comparative-Integrative Psychoanalysis* (n. 18), pp. 160, 133.

Willock's belief that a comparative approach to existing psycho-analytic theories tends toward a "dialectical synthesis" of these theo-ries into something new and transcendent takes us back to theoretical pluralism and the problems that inhere in it. In Willock's view of things, models, theories, and paradigms are coextensive; the point of the comparative-integrative exercise is to advance the field "from a uniparadigmatic to a multiparadigmatic, dialectical perspective." The troublesome notion of paradigmatic incommensurability, the most provocative and widely debated aspect of Kuhn's philosophy of science, nowhere enters his discussion.[24] More than two decades ago, Schafer prefaced his own foray into comparative psychoanaly-sis by acknowledging that "there can be no theory-free and method-free vantage point from which to assess in some absolute manner competing approaches and the often diverse phenomena to which they give rise or which they require to be emphasized." Twenty-two years later, Steven Cooper defined comparative psychoanalysis as "the examination of various ways that different analysts look at the same clinical data," only to add: "Naturally, the data are not the same clinical data partly by dint of looking at them with different lenses." Stuart Pizer, as noted above, readily conceded "some basic

24. Willock, *Comparative-Integrative Psychoanalysis* (n. 18), pp. 148, 97; For re-cent discussions of incommensurability and a comprehensive bibliography on the topic, see Paul Hoyningen-Huene & Howard Sankey, *Incommensurability and Re-lated Matters* (Dordrecht: Kluwer, 2001). Harold I. Brown ("Incommensurability Re-considered," *Stud. Hist. Phil. Sci.*, 36:149–169, 2005, at pp. 149–153) provides an elegant summary of Kuhn's original conceptualization of incommensurability before proceeding to a discussion of Kuhn's modification of the meaning of the term in his later writings. Ricardo Bernardi ("On Pluralism in Psychoanalysis," *Psychoanal. Inq.*, 12:506–525, 1992 at p. 517) is among the few analysts to acknowledge that incom-mensurability in the sense of Kuhn and Feyerabend limits the ability to compare and contrast psychoanalytic theories. For a recent example of a psychiatric theorist who, while proffering a version of psychiatric "explanatory pluralism," acknowledges and wrestles with Kuhnian incommensurability, see Kenneth S. Kendler, "Toward a Philo-sophical Structure for Psychiatry," *Am. J. Psychiatry*, 162:422–440, 2005 at p. 438: "Kuhn . . . might argue that the competing scientific paradigms within psychiatry are 'incommensurable,' that their advocates have such widely divergent viewpoints that they effectively inhabit different professional worlds. Furthermore, he would assert that data in our field are heavily theory-laden and deeply intertwined with theoreti-cal assumptions. In such circumstances, effective communication across paradigms and finding a common ground on which the various paradigms might fairly compete would be difficult. These arguments have force."

incompatible assumptions that our comparative approach would not want to gloss over."[25]

What Schafer, Cooper, and Pizer implicitly grasp that Willock misses is the difference between theories and paradigms. The former presuppose the latter; they come into being through the broadly conceptual and verbally uncodifiable world visions provided by the latter. Theories that fall within the selfsame paradigm can be compared and contrasted in the hope of finding underlying commonalities and/or achieving new syntheses. But theories that fall within different paradigms, to one degree or another, cannot, since they lack a common language with which to describe observations that rely on (or arise through) the concepts they deploy. In earlier chapters, I have characterized psychoanalytic theories as *theories with paradigm-like features* in order to underscore the serious obstacles—though not the impossibility—of comparing, contrasting, and integrating them.

Willock glosses over these issues because he believes that, for training purposes, all psychoanalytic theories are commensurable or at least commensurable enough; they can be spoken of in a common language and imbibed and critically compared by students who have not learned to function within them. I applaud his resolve to implement an educational "paradigm" that "promote[s] serious study of all models, combining what proves substantial in each into a more comprehensive framework."[26] The serious, comparative study of different mod-

---

25. Schafer, "Wild Analysis" (n. 17), p. 277. PES interviews of Cooper and Pizer (n. 20). Cooper presented his Kuhnian perspective on psychoanalytic data more than a decade earlier in "Facts All Come with a Point of View" (n. 21). There he observed that "Within the method of comparative psychoanalysis, it is necessary and inevitable that facts are not what they seem. Facts, if indeed they are facts, need always be reconceptualized and redefined within each theoretical orientation and context" (p. 270). Only the Columbia Center's "Methodology Sequence" seems to take the "basic incompatible assumptions" of different psychoanalytic theories as the central point of the comparative exercise. Only at Columbia, that is, do the "incompatible assumptions" provide a point of entry to the teaching and learning of an "epistemological perspective" through which candidates can understand the implications of entering a field in which "essential concepts encompass heterogeneous and sometimes contradictory ideas" and then explore various options for living with and/or overcoming tensions associated with the fact that psychoanalysts "have never succeeded in establishing an agreed-upon and reliable methodology for evaluating our derivations of latent content from manifest content." Rees, "Thinking About Psychoanalytic Curricula" (n. 19), quoted at p. 894.

26. Willock, *Comparative-Integrative Psychoanalysis* (n. 18), p. 149.

els is ipso facto a good thing; it promotes critical thinking and intellectual flexibility. But a "comprehensive framework" is not a necessary product of the comparative exercise, much less a *unitary* comprehensive framework shared by all who study different models comparatively. Or, adopting his own terminology, "dialectical synthesis"[27] is not an emergent property of examining and contrasting different theories of the mind, much less different theories that tend toward paradigmatic self-containment. The yield of the comparative exercise runs up against the problem of incommensurability and the inability of trainees to devise a way of reasoning around it or through it.

In making his case for a comparative-integrative approach to psychoanalysis, Willock invokes the authority of a coterie of theorists who developed their own integrative analytic frameworks between two and three decades ago. In Willock's view, their books and papers are "recent" writings that underscore the need for the new approach.[28] I have

27. Throughout his book (n. 18), Willock equates the expressions "dialectical synthesis" and "dialectical resolution" with the triadic progression of thesis-antithesis-synthesis. In this manner, Freud's psychoanalysis gives rise to Kohut's self psychology as its antithesis, with the tension between the two positions still awaiting a "more encompassing integration" or synthesis (p. 60). This mechanical sense of dialectic has nothing to do with Hegel, though Willock introduces his notion of dialectic with a reference to Hegel's first book, *Phenomenology of Spirit* (1807) at p. 59. In point of fact, the triadic dialectic method was introduced into German philosophy by Kant's onetime student, Johann Gottlieb Fichte. Hegel "never once used these three terms [thesis, antithesis, and synthesis] together to designate three stages in an argument or account in any of his books" and actually derided such mechanical formalism in the Preface to the *Phenomenology*. Hegel's dialectic, which he introduced in his *Science of Logic* (1812–1816), is a method of analysis through which the philosopher can make use of determinate and finite categories in order to achieve knowledge of the infinite. For accessible introductions to Hegel's dialectic, which is far removed from Fichte's mechanical three-step, see Walter Kaufmann, *Hegel: A Reinterpretation* (NY: Anchor Books, 1966 [1965]), pp. 153–163, quoted here at p. 154; J. N. Findlay, *The Philosophy of Hegel: An Introduction and Re-Examination* (NY: Collier, 1966 [1958]), pp. 55–79; and Ivan Soll, *An Introduction to Hegel's Metaphysics* (Chicago: University of Chicago Press, 1969), pp. 134–135, 146–150. Hegel's dismissal of mechanical, Fichte-like approaches to dialectic is in the preface to *Phenomenology of Spirit*, trans. A. V. Miller (Oxford: Clarendon Press, 1977), sections 50 & 51, pp. 29–30.

28. Willock quotes from a wide literature criticizing the traditional psychoanalytic training curriculum and justifying a comparative approach that goes back to the contributions of James Strachey and Edward Glover to the British Psychoanalytical Society's "Controversial Discussions" of 1943–1944. Among "recent" anticipations of the comparative-integrative viewpoint, he gives pride of place to John Gedo,

great respect for Willock's exemplars of the comparative-integrative sensibility: Otto Kernberg, John Gedo, and Roy Schafer. But several important facts must be borne in mind. First, these theorists elaborated something tantamount to comparative-integrative frameworks as senior theorists and clinicians who had been trained in one psychoanalytic school of thought. In their respective ways, they worked in and through a single analytic tradition over a period of decades. They pushed that theoretical tradition conceptually and clinically to the breaking point, viz., to a point where theoretical contradictions and clinical limitations led them to a new theory that simultaneously preserved and transcended the insights embodied in the tradition through which they came of age—to something like *Aufhebung* in Hegel's (and not Fichte's) dialectical sense.[29]

Secondly, their respective integrations occupied what we now perceive as a very limited portion of the theoretical spectrum. To oversimplify, Kernberg and Schafer devoted themselves to syntheses of American ego psychology and Kleinian psychoanalysis, and made allowance for non-Kleinian object relations theories. Gedo, whose theoretical palette was larger, devised an intricate "hierarchical model of the mind" (initially, in collaboration with Arnold Goldberg) that represented a unique synthesis of ego psychology, object relations theories, self psychology, and what he understood as the biology of

---

Psychoanalysis and Its Discontents (NY: Guilford, 1984); Otto F. Kernberg, "Institutional Problems of Psychoanalytic Education," *JAPA*, 34:799–834, 1986; Otto F. Kernberg, "The Current Status of Psychoanalysis," *JAPA*, 41:45–62, 1993; and Robert S. Wallerstein & Edward M. Weinshel, "The Future of Psychoanalysis," *Psychoanal. Quart.*, 59:341–373. Willock is hardly alone in compressing analytic time and citing publications 20 or 30 years old as "recent" contributions that sustain a new argument or new position on this or that issue; it is a common practice among analysts. I am reminded of a conversation I had early in my career with a prominent, elderly New York analyst who was more than a year overdue in submitting the final draft of her manuscript. I confronted her at a conference, conveyed some mild frustration, and tried to explain to her the consequences of her dilatoriness, to which she replied good-naturedly: "Honey, in analytic time a year is nothing."

29. *Aufhebung*, literally out- or uplifting, is commonly translated as "sublation" and signifies the simultaneous preservation and destruction of the past that fuels Hegel's dialectic. I use the term here to signify the manner in which theorists such as Kernberg, Gedo, and Schafer strove to preserve insights gleaned from their native theoretical traditions within the integrative framework of their mature theoretical perspectives.

adaptive deficits. Their projects of the 80s made no allowance for, say, the Lacanian and interpersonal traditions, and could not anticipate the rebirth of attachment theory or the relational turn of the 90s, much less the multidisciplinary integrative approaches reviewed in chapter 6. Finally and perhaps most sadly, these integrative projects by three immensely knowledgeable American analysts have not come together; I am aware of no higher-order synthesis that has grown out of their respective integrative agendas that might transcend theoretical pluralism and unify analysts in the face of clinical, social, and political marginalization.

Comparative psychoanalysis, as Cooper pointed out, is less a curricular choice than a pedagogical gloss on "what we are left with in the context of fundamentally different ways of working with patients." Theoretical pluralism is the status quo of American psychoanalysis for better and worse. Comparative approaches to psychoanalytic training and practice, as presently conceived, do more than simply ratify this status quo by striving to maximize the "better" and minimize the "worse" aspects of the pluralistic environment. The better denotes an openness to the interpenetration of theoretical models in clinically useful ways that transcend analytic part-identities.[30] But there is a wishful aspect to these approaches that finesses limitations of lived psychoanalytic experience in the face of incommensurabilities among

---

30. More than a decade ago, Cooper believed just such interpenetration was a fait accompli. He wrote that "Melanie Klein's views on the presentational world have affected all psychoanalytic theory far beyond the reaches of formal Kleinian psychoanalysis. Winnicott's mapping of the relational world and its component parts including the patient, the analyst and the intermediate space between the two has also influenced many branches. While many analysts reject Kohut's formal school of self psychology, his work has influenced all analysts in their augmented attunement to the iatrogenic effects of interpretation in the analytic setting, just as Balint's work emphasized many years earlier" ("Facts All Come with a Point of View" [n. 21], pp. 269–270). Logically, this appeal to tacit knowledge is argument petitio principii, i.e., it presumes what remains to be demonstrated. Analytic knowledge is not public. How can Cooper or anyone know how these or other views have influenced practice within the individual consulting room? Further, even if one allows for the interpenetration of theory in heuristically beneficial ways, there is no evidence that this kind of interpenetration has exerted a centripetal force on the field, which is more fractionated now than at the time of Cooper's writing. To wit, "integration and interpenetration of theoretical models" has not pulled together the segregated psychoanalytic part-fields whose respective theories may be drawn together in any number of individualized approaches to practicing psychoanalysis.

the approaches being compared. Comparative approaches cannot break out of the confines of the status quo by invoking a "drive for unification" that will somehow lead open-minded students out of the densely winding thickets of pluralism to the bright light of a "multi-paradigmatic dialectical perspective." Challenging candidates to adopt a critical, comparative perspective on theory, exhorting them to "contain" disjunctive and/or contradictory viewpoints, to "hold" multiple perspectives, and to understand such containment and such holding as "a vibrant condition of conflict"[31]—these instructional strategies cannot endow psychoanalytic students with the *background knowledge* and *lived experience* that elevate an integrative sensibility to a capacity to theorize and work integratively.

Nor, finally, does the comparative approach, pedagogically conceived, address the research imperative that, in the best of all worlds, would exist alongside the heuristic goal of achieving clinical broad-mindedness. I refer to the task of devising forms of comparative empirical inquiry that correlate the technical stance and interpretive strategy associated with different psychoanalytic theories with treatment outcome for different categories of patients. Such inquiry is not part of the comparative curriculum in America, though Thomä and Kächele, working out of the Ulm University Department of Psychotherapy and Ulm Psychoanalytic Institute in Germany, have developed a methodology for such an approach to "comparative psychoanalysis."[32]

---

31. Willock, *Comparative-Integrative Psychoanalysis* (n. 18), pp. 133, 97.

32. See Helmut Thomä & Horst Kächele, "Comparative Psychoanalysis on the Basis of a New Form of Treatment Report," *Psychoanal. Inq.*, 27:650–689, 2007. Such comparative research will likely never take place in America, but it is methodologically possible. John Greenwood discusses the grounds and methodology of just such comparative empirical inquiry in his effort to reframe Grünbaum's Tally Argument. According to Greenwood's alternate reading of the latter, the empirical challenge bequeathed by Freud is to prove that the efficacy of psychoanalytic therapy, which for Freud was a given, "tallies" with theoretical psychoanalytic explanations of that efficacy. Greenwood tackles this empirical challenge by considering the kinds of placebo control treatments that would have to be devised to establish the relevance of Freudian theory to the efficacy of Freudian therapy. I am suggesting that the empirical project he has in mind can be extended to the empirical comparison of different psychoanalytic theories in relation to agreed-upon outcome criteria. It would be a matter of stipulating naturalistic factors common to all forms of psychoanalytic therapy in order to demonstrate differences in treatment course and outcome (for different kinds of patients) among analysts conducting treatment along different

Yes, the comparative programs are to be commended for doing the best they can with theoretical pluralism and, in the process, for attracting some of the best and brightest psychoanalytic candidates—candidates who well understand the fractionated state of the field and seek more than indoctrination into one or another of the psychoanalytic schools.[33] But such students can only go so far. Cooper acknowledged a major point of resistance to the approach:

> One of the potential pitfalls of a comparative focus from the point of opponents is a concern that the plethora of theories will make contemporary candidates in training feel too adrift. I have heard some candidates say that they want to feel that there is "a way" to practice analysis. For these candidates a comparative focus leaves them feeling that anything goes or, at the very least, confused about too many choices.

Pizer related to me the MIP Curriculum Review Task Force's consideration of potential changes to the comparative curriculum "in order to provide a somewhat more cohesive and comprehensive approach to the various paradigms." And Willock, to his credit, related the following criticism of a first-year student in the Toronto comparative program: "I don't have a grasp of any of the schools, so how can I appreciate how they challenge and oppose each other?"[34]

---

theoretical lines. See John D. Greenwood, "Freud's 'Tally' Argument, Placebo Control Treatments, and the Evaluation of Psychotherapy," *Phil. Sci.*, 63:605–621, 1996.

33. Pizer, Cooper, and Willock all readily concede that their respective comparative training programs are most appealing to a special kind of analytic candidate. The Toronto program, according to Willock, "may initially be less daunting and more appealing to students who already have considerable knowledge of psychoanalysis and are, furthermore, familiar to some extent with the history of ideas, the clash of paradigms, the necessity of viewing phenomena from multiple perspectives, and the desideratum of pulling together diverse bodies of thought." If students of such sensibility and knowledge represent typical psychoanalytic candidates, then we have indeed crossed over to Pangloss's best of all possible worlds. Willock, *Comparative-Integrative Psychoanalysis* (n. 18), p. 157.

34. Willock adds that the candidate in question "did allow that during his second year, he began to get the hang of it." Willock, *Comparative-Integrative Psychoanalysis* (n. 18), p. 172.

In such admirably frank admissions, Cooper, Pizer, and Willock are all anticipated by Edward Glover, who presided over the Training Committee of the British Psycho-Analytic Society during World War II, when the polarizing power struggle between Freudian and Kleinian analysts threatened to paralyze, even to destroy, the Institute. Here there was no pretense of a pedagogically "comparative" approach, as candidates were simply pulled in divergent directions by the assemblage of Freudian, Kleinian, and "Middle Group" training analysts, supervisors, and seminar leaders collectively charged with their analytic education. Glover had long believed that candidates "are not or should not be sucking infants—that they should be able to stand up to differences of opinion and method existing amongst their teachers and that they should learn to form their own opinions on controversial matters." Yet his experience following the exodus of Melanie Klein to Britain belied his belief. Experience had taught him, he reported in May, 1942, that such capacity for independent judgment

> is too much to expect from any but the most superior candidates; but even well-balanced candidates are unfavorably affected by the situation. From recent experiences of taking seminars I should say that our present candidates are in a welter of confusion, bafflement, and bewilderment. Nor is it possible for the candidate to escape— for his transferences once established will handcuff him securely to his analytical father or mother.[35]

Glover's solution was to urge his colleagues to toe the Freudian line, to make psychoanalytic training consistently Freudian in tone, tenor, and substance. Candidates, he held, should only be introduced to "controversial views"—and only to "legitimately" controversial views at that—in an advanced course. And "reasoned" (read: Freudian) criticism of all such legitimately controversial views would have to be an essential part of the course.[36]

35. Cited in King & Stein, *Freud-Klein Controversies* (n. 10), p. 146.

36. *Legitimately* controversial views, according to Glover "were views and methods which though giving rise to differences of opinion *do not appear to contradict* any essential Freudian principles." King & Stein, *Freud-Klein Controversies* (n. 10), p. 597, emphasis in the original.

To be sure, Glover's psychoanalysis is of a different time and place. Comparative training programs in an era of theoretical pluralism, it can be argued, are far different from oppositional training experiences in an era of Freudian orthodoxy and Kleinian challenge. And yet Glover offers salient observations that contemporary psychoanalytic educators might well heed. He was insistent about the singular shaping impact of the training analysis, which fostered identifications and allegiances that could not be easily offset by exposure to different viewpoints. During and after their analyses, he remarked, candidates worked under professional conditions "calculated not only to prevent resolution of [their] transferences but to promote their reactivation. . . . The analysis may stop but the Candidate remains in an extended or displaced analytic situation." Nor could a "balanced curriculum" effect a correction of preexisting biases ingrained during a training analysis, "except in those Candidates who have a temperamental inclination to eclecticism or whose analysts have kept aloof from controversy or have no strong feelings on differences of opinion within the Society." Finally, the intellectual intent of comparative training programs cannot totally offset the intent, whether conscious or unconscious, of school-based teachers and analysts to win converts to their brand of psychoanalysis. This goal may coexist with a concurrent commitment to comparative and integrative training goals. The question is whether it necessarily subverts it. Here too Glover, speaking from the emotionally battered meeting room of the British Psycho-Analytic Society in the midst of physically battered wartime London, makes a point that contemporary educators ignore at their peril: "We must face the fact that so long as important divergences exist in our Society, the immediate aims of training are bound to be influenced by the more distant aim of securing converts to any given set of views."[37]

These historical provisos aside, there is much to admire in comparative training programs although, contra Willock, such programs cannot be a source of institutional cohesion and professional renewal. The comparative approach, as implemented in a scattering of training programs, promises to graduate a small number of critically minded and clinically resourceful analysts. But this approach to training, implemented piecemeal according to the ideals of individual educators and the politics of individual training institutes, will have no impact on

37. King & Steiner, *Freud-Klein Controversies* (n. 10), quoted at pp. 612–613, 614.

the field's fractionation; indeed, the comparative task is predicated on such fractionation. It holds no possibility of a consensually agreed-on integration that transcends pluralism; indeed, according to Pizer and Cooper, such integration is not its goal. Some, but not all,[38] "comparative" graduates may arrive over time at their own syntheses of different schools of thought, but no centrifugal dynamic, no metaphysical dialectic, will bring these self-styled solutions together in a manner that moves the entire field forward. At best, we will end up with individual islands of integrative sensibility, i.e., with a small number of broad-minded, versatile clinicians who have learned to navigate clinically with, through, and around different theories. They will be the exceptions. The comparative programs cannot do anything to dislodge an epistemic reality that has evolved since World War II: The preconscious *fixedness* of analysts in one or another theoretical tradition that Victoria Hamilton documented in her survey research among British and American analysts in the 1990s. Hamilton invoked the term "preconscious" to convey the manner in which notions associated with one or another psychoanalytic school of thought orient clinical work in an a priori manner. That is, they constrain the analyst's understanding of all patients in advance of the encounter with any one patient. This is the psychological anlagen of the professional reality to which Stephen Mitchell and Margaret Black called attention in their text of 1995, the simple fact

---

38. Pizer, Cooper, and Willock all stress the varying end roads of comparative training for different candidates. According to Pizer, most MIP graduates "evolve their own analytic identity, a personal amalgam. Some come in as advocates of a school and leave still advocating or preferring that perspective, but perhaps [are] at least more conversant with a range of theories. Others do find a particular school unappealing. Some dramatically shift in their biases." Willock too acknowledges diverse outcomes, among them the fact that some graduates of the Toronto program begin and end training with a primary identification with one or another psychoanalytic school of thought. The gains of comparative training thereby become heuristic, viz., the enrichment that follows exposure to other schools of thought: "If, for example, a student entered our program devoted almost exclusively to Klein, and continued so, we believe she or he will, nonetheless, be a better, less naïve, more knowledgeable, broadminded, creative Kleinian for having engaged in this challenging discourse. We would prefer that such graduates would also consider themselves self-psychological, egopsychological, interpersonal, and so forth. For some, however, this broadening may only happen to a limited extent." PES interview of Stuart Pizer (n. 20); Willock, *Comparative-Integrative Psychoanalysis* (n. 18), p. 159.

that "It is difficult to find any psychoanalyst who is really deeply conversant with more than one approach."[39]

Perhaps the comparative enterprise will be better served if it concentrates on the background assumptions, both constitutive and contextual, that underlie different psychoanalytic theories, and not on the narratives that these theories direct their proponents to tell. For background assumptions, to the extent that they are psychoanalytic in character, are background assumptions of one type or another. It is not a matter of global psychoanalytic assumptions that are subsequently channeled into one or another theoretical framework.[40] Some kind of theoretical or philosophical framework is embedded in the assumptions. It follows that different background orientations inculcate different ways of seeing. The Lacanian analyst, the self psychologist, the relationalist, and the Kleinian all see different kinds of facts that congeal into their respective background orientations.[41]

---

39. Victoria Hamilton, *The Analyst's Preconscious* (Hillsdale, NJ: Analytic Press, 1996); Stephen Mitchell & Margaret Black, *Freud and Beyond: A History of Modern Psychoanalytic Thought* (NY: Basic Books, 1995), p. 207. The French analyst André Green, an outspoken critic of Wallerstein's notion of psychoanalytic common ground, made the same point more scathingly a decade later: "I am not therefore arguing on my own behalf but in order to underline the absence of true communication between the psychoanalytic movements, which most of the time are isolated within their respective parishes. Most of the time psychoanalysts speak only one language in psychoanalysis, their own, in spite of schematizing attempts." André Green, "The Illusion of Common Ground and Mythical Pluralism," *Int. J. Psycho-Anal.*, 86:627–632, 2005, quoted at p. 631.

40. I differ here from David Tuckett, who believes that analytic "facts" emanate from a "background orientation" that shapes a psychoanalytic sensibility, which sensibility is thereupon lodged within a "consistent theoretical framework." But the background orientation that sensitizes analysts to "occurrences within the session" (Tuckett) is not the gift of an all-knowing psychoanalytic God. It is shaped by the particular psychoanalytic school in which an analyst has been trained and socialized. See David Tuckett, "The Conceptualization and Communication of Clinical Facts in Psychoanalysis," *Int. J. Psycho-Anal.*, 76:653–662, 1994.

41. To stress, as Tuckett ([n. 40], p. 658) does, the importance in clinical communications of expatiating on the "subjective context" through which clinical facts emerge merely transposes the "preconscious" (Hamilton) hold of psychoanalytic part-identities back one level. To wit, "subjective context" no less than "background

Perhaps analysts can have more productive comparative dialogues about who they are and what they do if they bypass official theory and concentrate instead on the philosophical (and latently theoretical) assumptions that underlie their respective theories. Clinical "facts," as Roy Schafer pointed out more than a decade ago, are supremely plastic; they do not exist outside the particular narrative story line in which they are conceptualized and embedded. Schafer is content that there is no way to step outside the resulting hermeneutic circle, that any account of analytic facticity must fall back in circular fashion on later as well as earlier conceptualizations of clinical facts.[42] But there are more and less effective ways of getting at the background assumptions that underlie the continuously evolving story lines. Perhaps, following Mary Hesse and Helen Longino, the theory-ladenness of observation can be mitigated simply by *focusing* on the background assumptions of different theories, which is to say the beliefs that demonstrate the evidential import of certain kinds of data (or "facts") in relation to favored hypotheses.[43] Perhaps analysts can determine what their respective background assumptions have in common and thereby

orientation" falls back on school-based epistemic preferences that heighten subjective responsiveness to the particular facts (contextual and otherwise) gathered in one or another narrative frame. The challenge of intersubjectively meaningful communication cannot be met through a simple injunction to provide subjective context in sufficient detail. For a more nuanced consideration of the various ways in which "subjective context" shapes the analyst's apprehension of "facts" that ground formulation, interpretation, and technique, see Cooper, "Facts All Come with a Point of View" (n. 21).

42. Roy Schafer, "The Conceptualization of Clinical Facts," *Int. J. Psycho-Anal.*, 75:1023–1030, 1994, quoted at p. 1028. Two years later, in a discussion of the analyst's possession of "valid evidence," Schafer fell back on a more conventionalist account of clinical facticity, in which analytic "facts" remained contestable because different schools of thought "determine differential weighting and selective presentation of evidence and differential sensitivity to the varied forms of transference." This viewpoint conveys a weaker constructivism than the claim that analyst and analysand conjointly *construct* evidence by placing the latter's utterances in one or another narrative context. See Roy Schafer, "Authority, Evidence, and Knowledge in the Psychoanalytic Relationship," *Psychoanal. Quart.*, 65:236–253, 1996, quoted at p. 242.

43. Mary Hesse, "Theory and Observation," in *Revolutions and Reconstructions in the Philosophy of Science* (Bloomington: Indiana University Press, 1980), pp. 63–110; Helen E. Longino, *Science as Social Knowledge: Values and Objectivity in Scientific Inquiry* (Princeton: Princeton University Press, 1990), pp. 38–61.

carve out areas of intersection among their theories. At the very least, a focus on background assumptions rather than theory-driven claims might permit neutral description of psychoanalytically salient states of affairs, even absent agreement of the particular hypotheses for which such states of affairs are taken as evidence.

Inviting analysts to have dialogues about the background assumptions that inform their theory-driven clinical inferences is tantamount to asking them to go back to basics, but I think the field has reached a critical juncture from which common ground can only be established from the ground up, not from theory-driven argument down. Analysts have to understand that the evidential relations that sustain their favored theories are not autonomous, eternal truths. Rather, these relations are constituted in the context in which evidence is assessed; they presuppose one or another set of background assumptions. And, as Longino reminds us, implicit background assumptions can be rendered explicit; they can always be articulated.

Of course, it is easy to say that analysts *should* compare and contrast their background assumptions to see what it is about all such assumptions that render them commonly analytic; it is another matter entirely to implement the recommendation. The 2005 publication, with multiple commentaries, of Jon Mills's "A Critique of Relational Psychoanalysis" in the pages of *Psychoanalytic Psychology* provided just such an opportunity for dialogue about a certain class of background assumptions (viz., philosophical ones) that are woven into relational and intersubjective writing and seem to subtend a host of postmodern psychoanalytic approaches. But a penetrating analysis of background assumptions was lost in a series of exchanges characterized by gratuitous judgmentalism, vituperative language, and, on occasion, ad hominem attack. I take no sides in the exchange other than to register profound disappointment that an opportunity for comparative examination of background assumptions (including further differentiation of such assumptions among different postclassical and/or postmodern schools) was utterly wasted. And it is just such comparative examination that the field urgently needs.

Whereas American psychoanalysis has splintered into many schools, American psychiatry has lived for three decades with a single, central split: That between its biomedical wing (which comprises, inter alia, molecular genetics, molecular biology, neurobiology, cognitive neuroscience, and pharmacology) and its psychotherapeutic wing. The anthropologist Teresa Luhrmann, who conducted field research at a number of psychiatric institutions in the mid-90s, discovered a field that was—as she titled her book—"of two minds." She provided a historical perspective on "the growing disorder in American psychiatry" (to quote her subtitle), reviewing the by now familiar story of the remedicalization of psychiatry in the 1970s, which culminated in the publication of the American Psychiatric Association's neo-Kraepelinian third edition of its *Diagnostic and Statistical Manual* (DSM-III) in 1980.[44]

Luhrmann's fieldwork offers compelling first-person accounts of how the growing split between psychoanalysts and "psychiatric scientists" gained expression in psychiatric training. By the early 1980s, entering psychiatric residents guileless enough to believe they had chosen a cohesive medical specialty beheld "a sprawling confrontation between what were then thought of as the 'two camps.'" Psychiatric training programs of the period mirrored the split in "two-tone" psychiatric residencies. But parity among the parties to the split was short-lived if it ever existed at all. By the late-80s, proponents of "psychiatric science" had essentially won the training wars, as psychotherapy training was radically devalued in one hospital-based residency program after another.[45]

What Luhrmann termed the "muting" of psychotherapy was greatly abetted by managed-care policies. Hospital administrators, whose concern with efficiency, cost-effectiveness, and manualized interventions antedated the arrival of managed care, used the financial crisis in health care as leverage in curtailing the psychodynamic component of psychiatric training. By the mid-90s, insurers simply refused to pay for the extended, but still short-term, hospitalizations that made psychotherapy possible. The near-death of psychotherapy training in residency programs, according to Luhrmann, resulted from "a financial crisis in the context of lingering ideological tension."[46]

The crisis extended to psychiatric life outside the hospital, where

44. T. M. Luhrmann, *Of Two Minds: The Growing Disorder in American Psychiatry* (NY: Knopf, 2000). The revolution in American psychiatry heralded by the publication of DSM-III is discussed in chapter 1, p. 6.

45. Luhrmann, *Of Two Minds* (n. 44), pp. 232, 237.

46. Luhrmann, *Of Two Minds* (n. 44), p. 250.

by 1990 consumers confronted "the progressive sharp diminution of coverage for long-term psychotherapy." The phrase comes from Robert Wallerstein, whose plenary address of that year to the California Psychiatric Association painted a despairingly bleak picture. The token time allocated to psychotherapy training in residency programs (which Wallerstein quantified) left newly trained psychiatrists profoundly ill-equipped to practice office psychotherapy. And as if the absence of training were not disincentive enough, it ran in tandem with mounting financial pressure (in the form of drastic insurance caps on reimbursement) to veer away from psychotherapy practice in life after residency. The handwriting was on the wall. "What seems most likely to me, given the way things have been going to this point," Wallerstein ruefully observed, "is that intensive psychotherapy of any kind will be squeezed out of the system, to be relegated to the private market for those more affluent and sophisticated who can afford it and will seek it on their own." Now, almost two decades after Wallerstein's glum assessment, psychiatric educators continue to call for the virtual elimination of psychotherapy from residency programs.[47]

And yet, throughout the tumultuous history of their field over the past three decades, psychiatric educators have never proposed the teaching of "comparative psychiatry." Indeed, the phrase makes no more sense than the idea of teaching "comparative surgery" or "comparative internal medicine." Among diabetologists, there have been conflicting guiding ideals and clinical approaches to diabetes management for a half century,[48] but internists do not take fellowships in "comparative endocrinology." What medical specialties—even psychiatry— retain that psychoanalysis lacks is paradigmatic integrity. In medicine, there is a shared understanding of cellular biology, biochemistry, anatomy, and pathophysiology that subtends different

47. Robert S. Wallerstein, "The Future of Psychotherapy," *Bull. Menn. Clin.*, 55:421–444, 1991, quoted at pp. 435, 436; Eugene H. Rubin & Charles F. Zorumski, "Psychiatric Education in an Era of Rapidly Occurring Scientific Advances," *Acad. Med.*, 78:351–354, 2003, especially at p. 353: "We don't dispute the importance of psychotherapies as therapeutic tools, but we do not believe that the primary role of psychiatrists in the future will be the delivery of formal psychotherapies."

48. These conflicting ideals and clinical approaches are beautifully set forth by Chris Feudtner in *Bittersweet: Diabetes, Insulin, and the Transformation of Illness* (Chapel Hill: University of North Carolina Press, 2003), especially chaps. 5 & 8.

therapeutic values and treatment philosophies. There is a refereed journal literature that has a normal-science *valence* for all members of a specialty, even if any number of published claims and findings are subject to different interpretations and weightings in support of different values and philosophies. Taken together, a shared medical understanding and a commonly held journal literature promote discussion of different philosophies and values and of the treatment preferences to which they give rise. In psychiatry, the offshoot of such discussion, optimally, is an "explanatory pluralism" that signifies the acceptance of interventional perspectives that differ "in their levels of abstraction, use divergent scientific tools, and provide different and complementary kinds of understanding." Receptiveness to such pluralism signifies a willingness to consider "multiple mutually informative perspectives" in determining "the optimal level in the causal processes underlying psychiatric illness at which intervention can be best focused and understanding most easily achieved."[49]

A "principled" psychiatric pluralism also signifies a willingness to accept the limited applicability of any one treatment modality, and to recognize that different kinds of psychotherapy and different mixes of psychotherapy and psychopharmacology may be optimal for patients with different conditions. This kind of "pluralism" is wedded to psychiatric nosology and the empirical research that grows out of it. It might lead a psychiatrist to recommend supportive psychotherapy for a patient with mild anxiety or affective disorders; pharmacotherapy guided by existential (empathy-based) therapy or cognitive-behavioral treatment for a patient with moderate depression; psychodynamic treatment, with or without medication, for a patient with a mild-to-moderate personality disorder; and psychodynamically attuned pharmacotherapy along with supportive care for a patient with major psychiatric illness.[50]

Of such correlations and of their bearing on individual treatment

49. Kendler, "Philosophical Structure for Psychiatry" (n. 24), p. 436.

50. This kind of pragmatic pluralism is thoughtfully espoused by S. Nassir Ghaemi in *The Concepts of Psychiatry: A Pluralistic Approach to the Mind and Mental Illness* (Baltimore: Johns Hopkins University Press, 2003), especially at pp. 3–22, 283–287, 299–308. Ghaemi traces such "principled pluralism" to the philosophy of Karl Jaspers and its application to psychiatry in the work of Leston Havens, Paul McHugh, and Philip Slavney. See pp. 10–15 and passim.

decisions, reasonable men and women will always disagree. But neither the empirical data that support this kind of "pluralism" nor the interlinking "causal processes" within which appropriate levels of intervention are situated typically enter into such disagreements. Since the publication of DSM-III in 1980, American psychiatrists have spoken a common language, however limited that language may be. For everything that language has given up, it has enabled psychiatry "to map its professional jurisdiction" in socially, politically, and clinically useful ways. The "narrowing of the psychiatric gaze" has not been without benefit.[51] Among other things, it has permitted psychiatrists, whatever their differences, to discuss treatment philosophies, therapeutic options, and levels of intervention within the relatively cohesive paradigm of a medical "specialty."

The situation in psychoanalysis is very different. Here we encounter schools of thought that fall back on paradigmatically disjunctive narratives. Such narratives posit entirely different "causal" chains of events to account for human development in its healthy and affiliative aspects and in its arrested, derailed, and conflicted aspects. Certain (though surely not all) core "facts" that arise from and through these narratives are fundamentally different. It is not a matter of different opinions about the "optimal level" of intervention within stories that share overlapping (or even intersecting) chronologies of eventful particulars.

It is therefore quite difficult to discuss the "factual" particulars contained in the developmental narratives of, say, self-psychological, Kleinian, and Lacanian analysts in a paradigmatically coherent manner. It is not a matter of the elasticity or pliability of core concepts that are used in different ways by self-psychological, Kleinian, and Lacanian analysts.[52] The developmental narratives yield concepts that are autochthonous to one or another of the theories. For self psycholo-

---

51. Both quoted phrases belong to Mitchell Wilson, whose history of DSM-III and its impact on American psychiatry concludes with a thoughtful assessment of what psychiatry has gained and lost from the narrowed gaze that followed from the descriptive language of DSM-III. Mitchell Wilson, "DSM-III and the Transformation of American Psychiatry," *Am. J. Psychiatry*, 150:399–410, cited and quoted at p. 408.

52. I am arguing against the meliorative vision of Joseph Sandler, for whom the elasticity of psychoanalytic concepts "play[s] a very important part in holding psychoanalytic theory together. As psychoanalysis is made up of formulations at varying

gists and Lacanians, it is not a matter of how to determine the interpretive possibilities that reside in the good and bad breasts, in the introjective and projective management of primitive envy and rage; such facts simply do not exist within their paradigms of development. For Kleinians and Lacanians, it is not a matter of what clinical use to make of grandiose and idealizing self-selfobject relationships; these very concepts lie outside their developmental ontologies. For self psychologists and Kleinians, it is not a matter of deciding what clinical use to make of the Lacanian Imaginary, Symbolic, and Real Orders; these concepts simply do not exist within their discursive universes.

We can line up these three developmental stories and compare and contrast them, in a manner of speaking, just like we can line up and compare Ptolemaic, Copernican, and Einsteinian narratives of the universe-in-action. But we cannot easily bring them together under a single psychoanalytic tent and draw on their respective "facts" to fashion an "optimal level" of psychoanalytic intervention for this or that problem or deficit or conflict with this or that type of patient. For the problems and deficits and conflicts that arise from each of these narratives are fundamentally different from the problems and deficits and conflicts of the other two narratives, and we lack a theory-neutral set of rules—call it a metapsychology—that permits us to map one set of narrative particulars onto the other two.

To be sure, self psychologists, Kleinians, and Lacanians can, with effort and imagination, understand one another; the absence of translatability among their visions of developmental psychopathology does not foreclose the possibility of communication through interpretation and language acquisition.[53] But, to this point in time, members of these

---

levels of abstraction, and of part-theories which do not integrate well with one another, the existence of pliable, context-dependent concepts allows an overall frame of psychoanalytic theory to be assembled." See Sandler, "Reflections on Some Relations Between Psychoanalytic Concepts and Psychoanalytic Practice," *Int. J. Psycho-Anal.*, 64:35–45, 1983, quoted at p. 36.

53. Kuhn made this point in later writings in revising the incommensurability thesis initially set forth in *The Structure of Scientific Revolutions* (Chicago: University of Chicago Press, 1962). See, for example, Thomas Kuhn, "Commensurability, Comparability, Communicability" (1983) and "Possible Worlds in History of Science" (1989), both reprinted in Thomas Kuhn, *The Road Since Structure* (Chicago: University of Chicago Press, 2000), pp. 33–57 & 58–89, respectively.

schools of thought have evinced little desire to engage in such effortful imaginative activity.[54] After all, their respective developmental ontologies are, from where they sit, true to intrapsychic and interpersonal reality; each provides a sturdy guide to therapeutic intervention according to a specific theory of therapeutic action and cure. Self-psychological, Kleinian, and Lacanian psychoanalyses are paradigmatically disjunctive but ontologically coterminous: They all have a narrative wholeness that encompasses a universe of developmental possibilities and clinical-analytic contingencies. They cannot be differentiated as interventional perspectives that pertain to one or another level of abstraction; each school of thought, according to its proponents, is fully explanatory in relation to *all* psychoanalytically relevant levels of abstraction.

American psychiatrists do not share this peculiarly psychoanalytic quandary, since their underlying epistemic interests are much more convergent. As noted, they are content that any one kind of psychiatric narrative should have a limited range of therapeutic applicability. They enter into lively disputes about the appropriate range of this or that modality (e.g., psychopharmacology) or the applicability of this or that modality to this or that instance or class of instances. But they agree on the *relevance relation* of different kinds of explanatory factors to different clinically observable conditions.[55] This is why, for all its divergence of opinion among dogmatists, eclectics, integrationists,

---

54. Late in my career at TAP, I published Lewis A. Kirshner's *Having a Life: Self Pathology After Lacan* (Hillsdale, NJ: Analytic Press, 2004), which was the first book-length study (to my knowledge) to attempt an integration of self-psychological and Lacanian concepts. Kirshner was unique in having learned both languages, but his colleagues took little notice, and sales of the book were very modest.

55. The notion of relevance relations, which reflects the fact that "verbally the same why-questions may be a request for different types of explanatory factors," comes from Bas van Fraassen, *The Scientific Image* (Oxford: Clarendon Press, 1980), chapter 5, quoted at p. 131. My understanding of the kind of explanatory pluralism adopted by psychiatry, which bears no relation at all to what psychoanalysts understand by "theoretical pluralism," has been influenced by Jeroen Van Bouwel & Erik Weber, "A Pragmatist Defense of Non-Relativistic Explanatory Pluralism in History and Social Science," *Hist. Theory*, 47:168–182, 2008. I also find Caterina Marchionni's brief for the complementarity and integrability of macro- and micro-explanations in the social sciences suggestive of the ways different psychiatric levels of abstraction can be brought together in reaching consensually agreed-upon treatment plans. See Caterina Marchionni, "Explanatory Pluralism and Complementarity: From Autonomy to Integration," *Phil. Soc. Sci.*, 38:314–333, 2008.

and pluralists,[56] American psychiatry remains a single specialty, subject to the standards of the Accreditation Council for Graduate Medical Education (ACGME), which requires that all psychiatry residents receive training in biological and psychological interventions. And it is why we behold programs in "comparative psychoanalysis" that are admirable in intent but symptomatic of fractionation and retreat to the margins.

56. Ghaemi, *Concepts of Psychiatry* (n. 50), pp. 3–23.

Chapter 8

Varieties of Healing, Conventional and Otherwise

Because of the many striking parallels the alternative medical systems have with psychoanalytic ideas (for example, belief in underlying causes, theoretical statements about "meaning," and the constant use of energy metaphors, among others), it is not surprising that a psychoanalytic theory fits them well. . . . One can still ask, however, whether this suggests that psychoanalysis provides an "explanation" of these other traditions or is better viewed as another illustration of alternative medicine, which itself has yet to be adequately "explained."[1]

In 2002 the *Journal of the American Psychoanalytic Association* published a two-page article by Richard Gottlieb titled "A Psychoanalytic Hypothesis Concerning the Therapeutic Action of SSRI Medications." Gottlieb sought to formulate a hypothesis whose psychoanalytic specificity would set it apart from psychiatric, electrochemical, and neuroanatomical explanations of the effectiveness of the family of selective serotonin reuptake inhibitors (Prozac, Paxil, Zoloft, et al.). He began by noting that

Psychoanalysis [has] yet to fulfill the promise that its theory and unique form of listening would contribute to our understanding of some effects of psychotropic medications. Analysts are said to listen to their patient as do no other students of mind/brain, yet we have offered no interpretation of the therapeutic benefits of highly effective SSRI (selective serotonin reuptake inhibitor) medications.[2]

1. David Hufford, "Review of Robert C. Fuller, *Alternative Medicine and American Religious Life*," *J. Am. Hist.*, 77:985, 1990.

2. Richard M. Gottlieb, "A Psychoanalytic Hypothesis Concerning the Therapeutic Action of SSRI Medication," *JAPA*, 50:969–971, 2002, quoted at p. 969, here and in the two paragraphs to follow.

Corroborative support of the perception of a promise unfulfilled was not forthcoming. Who among twenty-first-century neuroscientific, pharmacological, and psychiatric researchers was looking to psychoanalysis for an understanding of "some effects of psychotropic medications"? For that matter, who among Gottlieb's analytic colleagues had sounded the call? Guided by the impressionistic assumption that psychoanalysis was enjoined to address the matter of SSRI effectiveness, Gottlieb took up the interpretive gauntlet in the form of his hypothesis that "*the essential benefits of these medications derive from their capacity to modify aggression.*"

This claim was not elaborated theoretically or developmentally in terms of a particular psychoanalytic perspective on aggression. Gottlieb was content to invoke a range of descriptively "aggressive" behaviors, all of which fell back, ipso facto, on "aggressive conflict . . . involv[ing] unconscious mental functioning, unconscious fantasy, and unconscious modes of defense." This ego-psychological rendering of "aggressive" behaviors was shared by mainstream American psychoanalysts throughout the 1940s, 50s, and 60s. Writing in 2002, Gottlieb took it to be the common property of contemporary analysts, few of whom "can have failed to note the repeated reports of successfully medicated depressives to the effect that 'I am no longer angry in the way I used to be.'" "The details vary," Gottlieb continued,

> but these reports are consistent around the theme of the patient's being less inclined toward rages, less irritable. Events that in the past might have provoked fury are now merely irritating: "They roll off me." Some people do not spontaneously volunteer these reports, but they will speak of the changes if asked. From others one might only hear, "My friends say I'm easier to get along with." And most evident of all is a less hurtful attitude toward the self.

The same was true of childhood depressions, where the behavior of medicated children was "marked by a subsiding of tantrums, a softening of embattled positions, and a decrease in angry posturing and outbursts." To the extent that SSRIs ameliorated obsessional symptoms, Gottlieb held, it was because such symptoms derived from "excessive aggression." Medication-induced relief was "readily understandable as a consequence of modification of the aggression that drives them." Finally, extending his hypothesis to cases of social anxiety and excessive shyness, Gottlieb referred to one of his patients, a woman in whom an SSRI-effected overcoming of an inability "to borrow a kitchen utensil from her neighbor . . . seemed once more a question of aggression, this time unconscious and projected."

Has analytic time stood still? One is struck that in an era of sophisticated integrative and metaintegrative efforts to bring psychoanalysis into conversation with varieties of normal science, *JAPA*'s editors saw fit to publish a "psychoanalytic hypothesis" that pridefully isolated itself from "psychiatric, electrochemical, [and] neuroanatomical" considerations bearing on the effectiveness of one class of psychotropic medication and guilelessly ignored the diffusion of clinical and theoretical insights about a putatively psychoanalytic mechanism of action—aggression—among the various schools of psychoanalytic thought. It was as if a half century of criticism of Freud's metapsychology, which undergirds his theory of sexual and aggressive instinctual drives, never took place.

Spurred by Gottlieb's provocative brief contribution, readers lost no time in submitting letters to the journal, and *JAPA* published a selection of them two years later, in volume 52(2), 2004. Gottlieb's critics observed, variously and repeatedly, that the relation between SSRIs and the attenuation of aggressive behavior was not specific to SSRIs (Ostow; Wolpert); that serotonin was a generally inhibiting chemical that reduced not only aggression but also "libido, enterprise, and energy" (Ostow); that laboratory and clinical research, in demonstrating the cascading precortical and cortical changes wrought by SSRIs, militated against any notion of a "unitary mechanism of action" (Sandberg); and that the "dampening" effect of serotonin on once-adaptive primate behaviors was not tantamount to a reduction of aggression (Levinson).[3]

Gottlieb's heuristic appreciation of psychoanalytic aggression made no allowance for reappraisals of Freudian drive theory dating back to the 1960s and giving rise, in America alone, to the post-Freudian notions of aggression espoused, variously, by interpersonalists, self psychologists, intersubjectivists, relationalists, and

---

3. I am citing and quoting from "Letters: On the Therapeutic Action of SSRI Medications," *JAPA* 52:483–498, 2004, and specifically from the letters of Michael H. Levinson (pp. 483–486); Mortimer Ostow (pp. 486–487); Edward Wolpert (p. 489); and Larry S. Sandberg (pp. 490–491).

attachment researchers. One commentator, Michael H. Levinson, observed that

> His [Gottlieb's] assumption that the effectiveness of SSRIs for such different conditions as OCD, social anxiety, and depression suggests a common mechanism—e.g., aggression—underlying these different pathologies is reductionistic and a throwback to highly disputable metapsychological notions. Not only has the traditional drive formulation of aggression been of questionable value for clinical psychoanalysis, but it is even more dubious to apply such a concept to contemporary psychopharmacology.[4]

Leaving unquestioned the psychoanalytic tenability of Gottlieb's guiding assumptions, *JAPA*'s book review editor prefaced publication of the aforementioned commentaries by simply noting that Gottlieb's brief article had "drawn considerable comment on a topic at the interface of psychoanalysis and psychopharmacology." One ponders what exactly the topic was. Was it the explanatory grounds of psychotropic drug action? Was it the role of "excessive aggression" in the nosologically varied mood disorders amenable to pharmacological intervention? Was it the role of aggression reduction in the reported benefits of SSRI treatment?

Lost in the celebratory gloss that analysts were participating in a debate (however internal to analysis) about psychotropic drug action was any awareness of the historical circularity of the entire interlude. No one—not Gottlieb, not his commentators, and not the *JAPA* editors—appreciated that Gottlieb's hypothesis simply reprised analytic explanations of drug effectiveness that emerged when the first generation of psychotropics—prochlorperazine, chlorpromazine, and reserpine—was introduced in the mid-1950s. In 1956, Nathan Kline, the pioneering researcher who promoted the psychiatric use of the early antidepressant iproniazid, collaborated with Mortimer Ostow, one of Gottlieb's discussants a half century later, in an influential paper that placed psychotropic action within a psychoanalytic framework that revolved around the binding of psychic energy. As David Healy has summarized, the two speculated

4. Letter of Michael H. Levinson (n. 3), p. 483.

that as psychic conflicts all involved the binding of psychic energy in various different ways and as a great deal of ego energy went into binding instinctual (or id) energy down to produce a range of inhibited states, it was conceivable that a drug that took energy away from the ego might lead to liberation of instinctual energy—it might be a psychic energizer. Alternatively, a drug that reduced libidinal energy might release ego energy. Such a drug, Kline suggested, in principle, would increase levels of energy and drive up appetite—both for food and for sex. It would increase responsiveness to stimuli and would leave available supplies of energy, the awareness of which would lead to a sense of joyousness and optimism.[5]

The notion that psychotropics correct an "energetic disequilibrium," an "abnormality in ego energy content or distribution brought about by the pathogenic process," was elaborated at length in Ostow's *Drugs in Psychoanalysis and Psychotherapy* (1962). One is hard-pressed to differentiate Kline and Ostow's psychoenergic construal of the psychotropic action from Edward Wolpert's gloss, 53 years later, on Gottlieb's SSRI-linked hypothesis: "Some mood stabilizers, such as lithium carbonate and depakote, are also able to modify aggression in ways that prevent the recurrence of both mania and depression in bipolar patients. Such observations suggest that affective disorders generally are diseases of dysregulation of energy: too much or too little in the system clinically representing mania on the one hand, or depression on the other."[6] The more focal claim that psychotropics modulate and/or redirect primarily aggressive psychic energies was made by McGill University's Hassan Azima in a series of publications on the action of the tricyclic antidepressant imipramine (Tofranil) beginning in 1959.[7] Earlier still, during World War II, analytically

5. David Healy, *The Antidepressant Era* (Cambridge: Harvard University Press, 1997), p. 55.

6. Mortimer Ostow, *Drugs in Psychoanalysis and Psychotherapy* (NY: Basic Books, 1962), quoted at p. 127. Letter of Edward Wolpert (n. 3), p. 489.

7. H. Azima, "Imipramine (Tofranil): A New Drug for the Depressed," *Can. Med. Assn. J.*, 80:540, 1959; H. Azima, "Psychodynamic Alterations Concomitant with Tofranil Administration," *J. Can. Psychiat. Assn.*, 4:172–181, 1959; H. Azima & R. H. Vispro, "Effects of Imipramine (Tofranil) on Depressive States: A Clinical and

trained military psychiatrists used barbiturates, especially sodium amytal and sodium pentothal—the instruments of narcotherapy—to help traumatized GIs access the "excessive quantities of aggression" that their crippled egos had repressed. Such soldiers, prior to psycho-analytically guided treatment, were "stubborn rigid characters with much reaction formation often of the compulsive type." Under pen-tothal, however, "the release of some of their aggressions often shakes them into violent symbolic gestures or even convulsive spasms."[8] In the realm of psychoanalytic theorizing about drug action, it would seem, what goes around comes around.

Throughout the 1950s, of course, analysts were equally at home bringing their "theory and unique form of listening" (Gottlieb) to bear on frank neurological disorders. Parkinson's disease, as Healy reminds us, "was still seen in many quarters as resulting from anger that indi-viduals could not deal with, which had then been inhibited in a way that resulted in immobility." And psychoanalytic explanations of epilepsy, which came into vogue in Britain and America after World War I, when they gathered around L. Pierce Clark's invidious notion of a neuropathic "epileptic constitution," persisted beyond the half-century mark. Hans Berger's discovery of electroencephalography

Psychodynamic Study," *Arch. Neurol. Psychiatry,* 81:658–664, 1959; H. Azima, "Psychodynamic and Psychotherapeutic Problems in Connection with Imipramine (Tofranil) Intake," *J. Ment. Sci.,* 107:74–82, 1961. Incidentally, Ostow noted that Azima's "interesting observations" corresponded with his own, but held that the reported "shifts of aggressive energies" were secondary to the libidinal content of the ego: "Aggressive drives are elicited by pains and frustrations that arise out of libidinal excess and deficiency." Ostow, *Drugs in Psychoanalysis and Psychotherapy* (n. 6), p. 143.

8. Roy R. Grinker & John P. Spiegel, "Brief Psychotherapy in War Neuroses," *Psychosom. Med.,* 6:123–131, 1944, quoted at p. 130. Grinker and Spiegel note that the release of aggression provided by pentothal was only helpful for several inter-views, at which point convulsive shock treatment was employed. Even with these cathartic aids, the prognosis for soldiers with "repressed hostility" was poor. The most that could be hoped for, with follow-up psychotherapy, was reclassified (i.e., noncombatant) service. On the psychoanalytic rationale for narcotherapy "as an adjuvant in the exploration of repressed and dissociated psychological experiences" among soldiers with war neuroses, see also Lawrence S. Kubie & Sydney Margolin, "The Therapeutic Role of Drugs in the Process of Repression, Dissociation and Syn-thesis," *Psychosom Med.,* 7:147–151, 1945, quoted at p. 148 and Roy R. Grinker & John P. Spiegel, *Men Under Stress* (Philadelphia: Blakiston, 1945), pp. 390–394.

(EEG) in 1928, which transformed epileptology, did little to diminish psychodynamic theorizing about the epileptic personality, which gained expression in the 1935 (6th) edition of Jelliffe and White's *Textbook of Neurology and Psychiatry* and in the still later writings of Hendrick (1940), Diethelm (1946–47), Mittelmann (1947), and Glover (1949). Certain epileptic phenomena were thought to arise psychogenetically as late as 1956.[9]

As psychoanalytic theories of epilepsy waned in the 1950s, psychoanalytic explanations of compulsive ticcing continued to hold pride of place among North American psychoanalysts and psychiatrists. Rooted in Margaret Mahler's psychogenic theory of childhood tic syndrome, which Mahler and her residents at New York State Psychiatric Institute formulated in the early 1940s, psychoanalytic theorizing throughout the 1950s and 60s construed compulsive ticcing—the cluster of vocal and motor tics and impulsive cursing gathered together as Tourette syndrome—as the protopsychotic release of libidinal and aggressive energy in children whose motoric development had been derailed by intrusive, controlling, and/or overindulgent mothers. In the psychoanalytic jargon of the time, the syndrome was a neuromuscular manifestation of severe neurotic conflict that gave rise to an impaired ego unable to modulate the motoric and vocal release, via ticcing, of "erotic and aggressive instinctual impulses." Analysts held to this notion long after Mahler herself conceded that analytic treatment typically failed to remove or even ameliorate tics, and years after

---

9. Smith Ely Jelliffe & William Alanson White, "Classical Epilepsy," in *Diseases of the Nervous System: A Textbook of Neurology and Psychiatry*, 6th ed. (Philadelphia: Lea & Febiger, 1935); Ives Hendrick, "Psychoanalytic Observations on the Aurae of Two Cases with Convulsions," *Psychosom. Med.*, 2:43–52, 1940; Otto Diethelm, "Brief Psychotherapeutic Interviews in the Treatment of Epilepsy," *Am. J. Psychiatry*, 103:806–810, 1946–47; Bela Mittelmann, "Psychopathology of Epilepsy," in Paul H. Hoch & Robert P. Knight, eds., *Epilepsy: Psychiatric Aspects of Convulsive Disorders* (NY: Grune & Stratton, 1947), pp. 136–148; Edward Glover, *Psycho-Analysis, A Handbook for Medical Practitioners and Students of Comparative Psychology*, 2nd ed. (London: Staples, 1949), pp. 194–201; Louis A. Gottschalk, "The Relationship of Psychologic State and Epileptic Activity: Psychoanalytic Observation on an Epileptic Child," *Psychoanal. Study Child*, 11:352–380, 1956. For the history of psychoanalytic theorizing about epilepsy, see Peter F. Bladin, "'The Epileptic Constitution': The Psychoanalytic Concept of Epilepsy," *J. Hist. Neurosci.*, 9:94–109, 2000. Bladin discusses the disastrous consequences of psychoanalytic concepts of epilepsy, which "would continue to pose immense problems in all aspects of epilepsy well beyond the half-century mark" (p. 95).

the effectiveness of haloperidol (Haldol) and later dopamine-receptor blockers in managing Tourette syndrome had been conclusively established.[10]

As reserpine and chlorpromazine entered the American market, analytic insight was felt to be relevant not only to drug action but also to drug side effects, especially the motor agitation (in the form of dyskinesias and akathisia) associated with the neuroleptics. Led by the analysts, many American psychiatrists wondered whether the drugs destabilized patients' psychoenergic balance. Perhaps excessive motor restlessness, analysts mused, was not directly induced by reserpine or chlorpromazine, "but rather stemmed from their worries about the emergence of repressed material" secondary to drug use."[11] The emerging "psychiatric, electrochemical, and neuroanatomical" (Gottlieb) explanations of these side effects, which revolved around dopamine transmission in the brain, were deemed irrelevant to psychoanalytic understanding.

Now, a half-century later, American psychoanalysis is at a different place. Or is it? Psychoanalysts have by and large accommodated medication as adjunctive to, or coterminous with, talking therapy for patients with mood disorders, especially major depressions. From the early 1980s on, they have increasingly recognized that medication can facilitate, even enable, psychoanalytic treatment for certain of their

---

10. Mahler's psychogenic theory of ticcing was set forth in Margaret S. Mahler & Leo Rangell, "A Psychosomatic Study of Maladie des Tics (Gilles de la Tourette's Syndrome)," *Psychiat. Quart.*, 17:579–603, 1943 and Margaret S. Mahler, Jean A. Luke, & Wilburta Daltroff, "Clinical and Follow Up Study of the Tic Syndrome in Children," *Am. J. Orthopsy.*, 15:631–647, 1945. Mahler's admission that psychodynamic treatment usually failed to remediate tic syndrome came in her later papers, Margaret S. Mahler & Jean A. Luke, "Outcome of the Tic Syndrome," *J. Nerv. Ment. Dis.*, 103:433–445, 1946 and Margaret S. Mahler, "A Psychoanalytic Evaluation of Tic in the Psychopathology of Children: Symptomatic and Tic Syndrome," *Psychoanal. Study Child*, 3:279–310, 1949. Howard Kushner's excellent history of Tourette syndrome includes a thorough review of Mahler's work, and is especially compelling on Mahler's strained efforts to make her own dismal outcome data (as to the ineffectiveness of psychotherapy) subserve her entirely psychogenic explanation of the syndrome. See Howard Kushner, *A Cursing Brain? The Histories of Tourette Syndrome* (Cambridge: Harvard University Press, 1999), pp. 99–118, especially pp. 114ff.

11. David Healy, *The Creation of Psychopharmacology* (Cambridge: Harvard University Press, 2002), p. 114.

patients.[12] Few now feel called on, in the manner of Gottlieb, to hypothesize a unitary psychoanalytic *mechanism* of drug action. Fewer still deny the effectiveness of modern psychotropics in ameliorating symptomatic distress among patients whose profile is consistent with DSM-IV Axis 1 mood and anxiety disorders. All this being said, the tendency among many, probably most, analysts has been to pull medication into a psychoanalytic paradigm, wherein psychotropics acquire meaning as yet another type of analytic material, as "something that has meaning, involves both analysand and analyst, and becomes the focus of analysis. As something that affects the analysand, it must be acknowledged and dealt with by the analyst."[13]

Under what circumstances do analysts prescribe? A small-scale survey at the Columbia University Center for Psychoanalytic Training and Research found that, among respondees, 46% of then-current analytic candidates were prescribing medication to at least one of their analytic patients, whereas 62% of the teachers who supervised them (their training and supervising analysts) had prescribed to at least one of their own analytic patients over the past five years. More disturbing was the finding that the prescribing analytic candidates seldom based their medication decisions on established DSM-IV diagnostic criteria; indeed, they made little if any effort to differentiate the decision to prescribe from the "analytic process" they were intent on mobilizing.[14] As recently as 2001, one senior analytic contributor

12. Among statements of the facilitating role of medication in analytic work published in the 1980s, see, inter alia, N. L. Cohen, "Integrating Pharmacotherapy with Psychotherapy," *Bull. Menn. Clin.*, 44:296–300, 1980; Judd Marmor, "The Adjunctive Use of Drugs in Psychotherapy," *J. Clin. Psychopharm.*, 1:312–315, 1981; Arnold Cooper, "Will Neurobiology Influence Psychoanalysis?" *Am. J. Psychiatry*, 142:395–402, 1985; and William C. Normand & Harvey Bluestone, "The Use of Pharmacotherapy in Psychoanalytic Treatment," *Contemp. Psychoanal.*, 22:218–234, 1986.

13. George A. Awad, "The Effects of Medication on the Psychoanalytic Process: The Case of Selective Serotonin Reuptake Inhibitors," *Psychoanal. Study Child*, 56:263–285, 2001, quoted at p. 281.

14. Deborah L. Cabaniss & Steven P. Roose, "Psychoanalysis and Psychopharmacology: New Research, New Paradigms," *Clin. Neurosci. Res.*, 4:399–403, 2005. This article discusses the results of two separate surveys among candidates and training analysts, respectively, of the Columbia Center for Psychoanalytic Training and Research. Both surveys were conducted in the early 1990s, and the results were initially reported in Steven P. Roose & Robin Horwitz Stern, "Medication Use in Training

emphasized the manner in which the "affective, cognitive, and physical changes caused by medication" could undermine a psychoanalytic treatment agenda. For certain patients, that is, the ameliorative changes wrought by medication could induce patients to cling to "fantasies" about the organic factors that subtended their symptomatic distress. For these patients, facilitating symptomatic relief via medication served to militate against analytic exploration of these selfsame fantasies and thereby to "undermine psychoanalytic aims by strengthening defenses against patients' full integration of psychic experiences."[15]

Even among analysts who recognize that the stance involved in assessing symptomatology and prescribing medication is different from the stance involved in conducting psychoanalytic treatment, the emphasis is on minimizing these discrepant roles, and the pull is always toward an analytic paradigm. In the 1980s, the pull was expressed in the belief that medication might help patients traverse the rough spots in analytic work, including anxiety at the outset of treatment and anxiety attendant to imminent termination. And of course medication was always available for spot treatment of symptoms that arose during the course of the analytic work and could not be ameliorated through the work of interpretation. "If the symptom presents a serious threat to the patient," wrote Normand and Bluestone in 1986, "or if the treatment has bogged down and no purely analytic effort is effective, the use of drugs should be considered." More than a decade later, this kind of pull continues in the belief that prescribing medication during analytic treatment should be viewed as a "parameter" in the half-century-old sense of Kurt Eissler, i.e., as a departure from the normally "abstinent" and "neutral" position of the analyst toward the patient.[16] Viewed thusly, the introduction of medication into an

Cases: A Survey," *JAPA*, 43:163–170, 1995 (as to the candidates) and Stephen J. Donovan & Steven P. Roose, "Medical Use During Psychoanalysis: A Survey," *J. Clin. Psychiatry*, 56:177–179, 1995.

15. Mark H. Sworskin, "Psychoanalysis and Medication: Is Real Integration Possible?" *Bull. Menn. Clin.*, 65:143–159, 2001, quoted at p. 144.

16. Eissler set forth this concept of a "parameter" in a highly influential psychoanalytic paper of the 1950s: Kurt Eissler, "The Effect of the Structure of the Ego on Psychoanalytic Technique," *JAPA*, 1:104–143, 1953.

analytic treatment is warranted only if it is a small and manageable intrusion into the analytic frame, and only if the psychodynamic meanings of the medication will be analyzable later in the treatment.[17] Withal, from the very moment a medication is prescribed, the prescribing analyst is enjoined to encourage the patient to think psychologically about the medication intervention and the impact of the medication.[18]

Given this purview, it stands to reason that most analysts who write about psychotropics subordinate drug efficacy to a psychoanalytic modus operandi and psychoanalytic treatment goals. As analysts, they tend to view medication as yet another variable that complicates the treatment relationship, especially the transference, and requires a series of decisions about the impact of medication use over the projected course of a lengthy treatment. Medically trained analysts who write about medication tend to approach the matter tactically, i.e., they weigh the pros and cons of prescribing themselves against the pros and cons of split treatment arrangements in which their patients are seen by another psychiatrist who prescribes and monitors the medication. In contemplating the latter course, one salient *analytic* consideration is the special challenge of a three-way treatment alliance, with its triangular transference-countertransference possibilities.[19] Split treatment arrangements in which the analytic therapist lacks medical training heighten these possibilities, which include the patient's tendency to idealize one provider and denigrate the other and the two providers' tendency to lapse into a power struggle.[20] The most recent

17. Normand & Bluestone, "The Use of Pharmacotherapy in Psychoanalytic Treatment" (n. 12), p. 228; Kevin V. Kelly, "Principles, Pragmatics, and Parameters in Clinical Analysis: The Dilemma of Pharmacotherapy," *Psychoanal. Inq.*, 18:716–929, 1998, at pp. 726–727.

18. Mark H. Sworskin "Psychoanalysis and Medication," (n. 15), pp. 147, 144; Fredric N. Busch & Larry S. Sandberg, *Psychotherapy and Medication: The Challenge of Integration* (NY: Analytic Press, 2007), p. 38.

19. David. A. Kahn, "Medication Consultation and Split Treatment During Psychotherapy," *J. Am. Acad. Psychoanal.*, 19:84–98, 1991.

20. Fredric N. Busch & Edith Gould, "Treatment by a Psychotherapist and a Psychopharmacologist: Transference and Countertransference Issues," *Hosp. Com. Psychiatry*, 44:772–774, 1993; Marcia Kraft Goin, "Split Treatment: The Psychotherapy Role of the Prescribing Psychiatrist," *Psychiat. Svs.*, 52:605–609, 2001; and David L. Mintz, "Teaching the Prescribing Role: The Psychology of Psychopharmacology,"

and most balanced consideration of the host of issues attendant to integrating medication usage into psychodynamic talking treatment is Fredric Busch and Larry Sandberg's *Psychotherapy and Medication: The Challenge of Integration* (2007), which is especially strong in its consideration of both the tensions and the therapeutic benefits that inhere in "combination" (i.e., simultaneous pharmacological and psychodynamic) treatment and in its discussion of the range of psychodynamic meanings that may accrue to the prescribing and imbibing of psychotropic medication.[21]

Busch and Sandberg, both *psychiatrist*-psychoanalysts, concede instances in which "medication may diminish or avert the need for psychotherapy." For certain patients, that is, "medication alone will be satisfactory." Yet, as psychiatrist-*psychoanalysts*, they believe equally that "in many cases psychological as well as chemical vulnerabilities contribute to the onset of mood disorders and psychotherapy is indicated." And finally, as *psychoanalysts*, they are led to privilege the integrative, hence curative, potential of analytic treatment over pharmacotherapy insofar as certain patients "will decide that medication has been sufficiently helpful to curtail an introspective process that the therapist believes could have offered further benefit of integration."[22] Little corresponding attention is given to cases in which medication was shown to be the primary form of treatment, with psychodynamic therapy relegated to adjunctive status.[23]

Acad. Psychiatry, 29:187–194, 2005, esp. at p. 190: "Differences in therapeutic philosophy as well as personal and interdisciplinary tensions around such issues as competition and envy are ubiquitous."

21. Busch & Sandberg, *Psychotherapy and Medication* (n. 18). This book, incidentally, was one of the final projects I signed for The Analytic Press and the very last TAP book that I critiqued in manuscript (at the request of the authors) at the time of my resignation.

22. Busch & Sandberg, *Psychotherapy and Medication* (n. 18), pp. 30, 31, 157.

23. Writing a decade ago, Roose & Johannet deemed this scotoma with respect to indications for primary drug treatment a manifestation of the continuing "theoretical schism" between pharmacotherapy and psychoanalysis. See Stephen P. Roose & Christopher M. Johannet, "Medication and Psychoanalysis: Treatments in Conflict," *Psychoanal. Inq.*, 18:606–620, 1998, cited at pp. 616–617. Interestingly, in the same journal issue in which Roose & Johannet made this point, Larry Sandberg presented

Treatment success, analytically construed, typically acknowledges the "usefulness" of medication but subordinates it to one or another analytic paradigm. By helping to reduce the anxiety or depression attendant to a biologically grounded mood disorder, medications "allow the analysis to proceed." Analysts who acknowledge medication efficacy in positive treatment outcomes usually consider it one of several factors, all of which conjointly facilitate the kind of mutative dialogue specific to the talking cure.[24] In other instances, drug benefits, while acknowledged, are severed from drug action, pharmacologically construed. We read, for example, of Prozac's effecting a "softening" of a patient's superego that the prescribing analyst was at first inclined to relate "to the well-known pharmacological effects of fluoxetine on aggression,"

> but further reflection led me to realize that the transference meaning of reenacting crucial child experiences was a more likely explanation. . . . If it is true that the dramatic changes that began with the agreement to use medication were due mostly, or perhaps entirely, to the dynamic meaning of the reenactment and not to the effect of the drug at all, what can we learn from this case about the influence of the use of medication on the psychoanalytic process? Perhaps the most obvious conclusion to be drawn, but also the most important, is that the use of medication did not distort the analytic process to such an extent that the analysis became unmanageable.[25]

---

just such a case, i.e., a case in which initial assumptions about the need for psychoanalytic therapy yielded to medication, and "appropriate pharmacotherapy served to mitigate the need for intensive dynamic therapy." Larry S. Sandberg, "Analytic Listening and the Act of Prescribing Medication," *Psychoanal. Inq.*, 18:621–638, 1998, quoted at p. 628.

24. For example, Awad, "Effects of Medication on Psychoanalytic Process" (n. 13), p. 279: "I believe that there were three factors that account for the positive outcome of these two patients: analyzing the transference-countertransference interactions around the medications, the procedure used for prescribing the medications, and the effectiveness of the drugs."

25. Marshall A. Greene, "The Effects of the Introduction of Medication on the Psychoanalytic Process: A Case Study," *JAPA*, 49:607–627, 2001, quoted at pp. 624–625.

Unsurprisingly, psychoanalytic descriptions of the behavioral sequelae to drug administration evince little consistency and still less integrative force. Gottlieb imputes the effectiveness of SSRIs to their attenuation of behavioral aggression, to which Ostow replies that "any effective treatment of depression removes the aggression that accompanies it." Titelman, who surveyed patients receiving antipsychotics, put a different analytic gloss on the modulation of aggression effected by these particular drugs; *his* survey participants reported that, whereas their medication prevented them from acting on aggressive impulses, it left their aggressive, often angry, paranoid fantasies untouched and no less anxiety-inducing.

The global effort to make psychoanalytic sense of psychotropic action has left us with yet another subspecies of "theoretical pluralism" in its unedifying psychoanalytic sense. Awad, following Kantor, suggests that certain patients suffer from two discrete disorders, a biological one amenable to drug intervention and a psychological one rooted in conflict that requires psychodynamic treatment. Yet Cabaniss, like Kahn before her, insists that this Cartesian assumption, this need to construe symptoms as *either* organic *or* psychodynamic, is rendered obsolete by contemporary neuroscience. Analysts who prescribe medication, she avers, must utilize the same DSM-IV phenomenological criteria as their nonanalytic colleagues. Prescribing decisions are a matter of observable and/or reportable symptom clusters that have been shown to be responsive to medication, not of a priori analytic assumptions about the putatively "organic" or "psychodynamic" causes of these symptoms. To Sworskin's concern that pharmacological amelioration of symptoms may "reinforce" the patient's defenses against awareness of the "psychodynamic contributions" to these selfsame symptoms, Cabaniss replies that "The clinician who tries to determine the etiology of a given symptom before making a treatment decision reveals more about his or her countertransference than about scientifically based information."[26]

26. David Titelman, "A Psychoanalytic Understanding of Antipsychotic Drug Treatment: An Attempt at Applied Psychoanalysis," *Scand. Psychoanal. Rev.*, 22:67–84, 1999. Awad, "Effects of Medication on Analytic Process" (n. 13), p. 283; S. J. Kantor, "Transference and the Beta Adrenergic Receptor: A Case Presentation," *Psychiatry*, 52:107–115, 1989; S. J. Kantor, "Depression: When Is Psychotherapy Not Enough?" *Psychiat. Clin. N. Am.*, 13:241–254, 1990; Deborah L. Cabaniss, "Beyond Dualism: Psychoanalysis and Medication in the 21st Century," *Bull. Menn. Clin.*, 65:160–170, 2002, at pp. 161, 163; Kahn, "Medication Consultation and Split Treatment During Psychotherapy" (n. 19), p. 88; Sworskin, "Psychoanalysis and Medication: Is Real

Cabaniss may be unhappy with a dualistic approach to symptomatology, but she understands full well that adequate clinical care typically obliges the clinician to shift gears between psychopharmacologic and psychodynamic perspectives and, to that degree, to embrace two discordant models of mind. Sandberg equates the shift with "internal oscillations" in the service of "bimodal relatedness." "The essential task for the contemporary analyst," he holds, "is to have the capacity to oscillate, when indicated, between pharmacological and psychotherapeutic modes of relating." For Cabaniss, an analyst and psychiatric educator, teaching residents the "art" of shifting gears, of "allow[ing] oneself to put on a new pair of lenses through which to view any given case," is a primary goal of training.[27] It is not merely a matter of separating psychiatric diagnosis (as to medication needs) from psychoanalytic evaluation. More importantly, it is a matter of *epistemic* flexibility, of an ability to contain simultaneously the empirical knowledge involved in prescribing and monitoring medication usage and the heuristic knowledge that underwrites a notion of therapeutic progress within an "analytic process." The latter gear is engaged when, for example, "successful" drug management permits new layers of conflict or dysfunction to emerge and thereby provides the therapist with an enlarged arena for psychodynamic intervention.

Cabaniss's call for an analytic embrace of what amounts to epistemic dualism—a dualism that allows for fundamentally different kinds of clinical knowledge that guide, respectively, prescribing and analyzing—remains the exception to the rule.[28] The general trend

---

Integration Possible?" (n. 15), p. 147. The analyst Glen Gabbard, extrapolating from psychoanalysis to psychotherapy in general, rejects dualism in the same manner as Cabaniss: ". . . to think of psychotherapy as a treatment for 'psychological based disorders' and medications as a treatment for 'biological or brain-based disorders' is to make a specious distinction." Glen O. Gabbard, "Mind, Brain, and Personality Disorders," *Am. J. Psychiatry*, 162:638–655, 2005, quoted at p. 648 and "The Fate of Integrated Treatment: Whatever Happened to the Biopsychosocial Psychiatrist?" *Am. J. Psychiatry*, 158:1956–1963, 2001.

27. Larry S. Sandberg, "Analytic Listening and the Act of Prescribing Medication" (n. 23), p. 625; Deborah L. Cabaniss, "Shifting Gears: The Challenge to Teach Students to Think Psychodynamically and Psychopharmacologically at the Same Time," *Psychoanal. Inq.*, 18:639–656, 1998, quoted at p. 652.

28. Cabaniss, Sandberg, and Roose are in effect espousing what philosophers understand as "epistemic pluralism"—different "knowledges" or ways of knowing—as it pertains to the different knowledge bases that can and should be brought to bear

in the clinical reports of the past several decades, as noted, has been to pull drug action into a psychoanalytic orbit. Awad, while ceding the existence of discrete biological and psychological disorders, is quick to add that the former necessarily implicates the latter, since "A biological disorder will always create a mental state, and there is no mental state that does not have dynamic significance." Analytic commentators such as Wylie underscore the interwoven nature of dynamic and nondynamic aspects of disorder and recruit analytic expertise to distinguish between neurobiological "obstruction" and psychodynamic "resistance." Blatt calls attention to the psychological links between biologically grounded mood disorders and personality disorders.[29]

More tendentious are clinical reports in which interweaving and linking give way to psychodynamic reductionism; consider the report of Greene, whose patient's observable "softening" of the superego subsequent to administration of fluoxetine was deemed a transference phenomenon unrelated to drug action. Recent analytic contributors have argued that the act of prescribing and imbibing medication is *of necessity* an enactment between the analyst and analysand or, more discerningly, among the analyst, analysand, and the often personified medication.[30] In either event, transference gratifications and countertransference issues inhere in the process. As we approach the more extreme end of this spectrum, we encounter the claim that prescrib-

---

in understanding and treating analytic/psychiatric patients. On epistemic pluralism and its relation to ontological pluralism (the idea that there are many "real" things in the universe), see, e.g., Earl R. MacCormac, "Metaphor and Pluralism," *Monist,* 73:411–420, 1990; Walter Watson, "Types of Pluralism," *Monist,* 73:350–366, 1990; and Scott L. Pratt, "The Experience of Pluralism," *J. Spec. Phil.,* 21:106–114, 2007.

29. Awad, "Effects of Medication on Analytic Process" (n. 13), p. 283; H. W. Wylie & M. L. Wylie, "Resistances and Obstructions: Their Distinction in Psychoanalytic Treatment," *J. Clin. Psychoanal.,* 4:185–207, 1995; Sidney J. Blatt, *Experiences of Depression: Theoretical, Clinical and Research Perspectives* (Washington, DC: American Psychological Association, 2004); Greene, "The Effects of the Introduction of Medication on the Psychoanalytic Process" (n. 25).

30. Jay Abel-Horowitz, "Psychopharmacotherapy During an Analysis," *Psychoanal. Inq.,* 18:673–701, 1998; Barbara L. Milrod & Fredric N. Busch, "Combining Psychodynamic Psychotherapy with Medication in the Treatment of Panic Disorder: Exploring the Dynamic Meaning of Medication," *Psychoanal. Inq.,* 18:702–715, 1998; Adele Tutter, "Medication as Object," *JAPA,* 54:781–804, 2006.

ing medication is simply another analytic "intervention," and that patient communications regarding medication effects, whether positive or side, call for analytic interpretation no different from any other intervention "in which enactment may disturb the patient's psychological equilibrium."[31]

The issue here is not empirical. Certainly, it makes good sense to consider the transferential meaning of prescribing along with psychiatric factors in reaching a clinical judgment about the appropriateness of medication. And surely, it is an earmark of sound clinical judgment to consider the "intrapsychic, transferential, or interpersonal meanings" of medication-induced side effects. And finally, it may well be a common clinical reality that analytic interpretation of medication usage, including "the analysis of the object roles and representations contained and conveyed by medication[,] helps to expose covert transferences to the analyst, which can be split off and displaced onto medication, disguised in the service of defense."[32] What I am referring to is the analytic tendency to take such provisos, which typically grow out of individual case presentations, as a platform for categorical pronouncements that reduce psychotropic drug action to epiphenomena. We end up with an "analytic process" that effectively lyses medication into a garden-variety interpretable intervention (or parameter).

In this vein, we have Olesker's verdict that "medication *and all its effects* need hold no special status over the other interventions and enactments occurring daily in every analysis" and her insistence that "We can see the current state of the transference *whenever* the issue of medication or of medication consultation arises." And we have Glick and Roose's utter certainty that "with patients in analysis who are taking psychotropic medication, reports of 'side effects' are complex communications *requiring* analytic exploration, not simply a pharmacological response." "When a patient reports a side effect," they continue, "specific countertransference fantasies *are* evoked. The analyst's resistance to self-analysis of these countertransference

31. Wendy Olesker, "Thoughts on Medication and Psychoanalysis: A Lay Analyst's View," *JAPA*, 54:763–779, 2006, quoted at p. 775.

32. Milrod & Busch, "Combining Psychodynamic Psychotherapy with Medication" (n. 30), p. 702; Olesker, "Thoughts on Medication and Psychoanalysis" (n. 31), p. 774; Tutter, "Medication as Object" (n. 30), p. 803.

anxieties can derail the analytic process." And these axioms culminate in something tantamount to a psychoanalytic categorical imperative:

> Taking the side effect complaint at face value, and not as a meaningful transference experience, begins a process that may temporarily derail the analysis or even undermine it in its entirety, much as the introduction of a virus can degrade the hard drive of a computer.[33]

The cumulative effect of these and like-minded dicta is to trivialize drug action in an analytic setting by robbing it of pharmacologic integrity. If reports of side effects are ipso facto "complex communications requiring analytic exploration," then reports of drug effects and noneffects can be no less complex and no less in need of analytic decoding. So we end up in a situation where *any* communication about medication is *necessarily* analytic and not (or not primarily) pharmacologic in nature. This leaves prescribing analysts (or nonprescribing analysts in split-treatment arrangements) in a quandary. On the one hand, they are enjoined (by Cabaniss and Roose, among others) to embrace psychiatric phenomenology as embodied in DSM-IV Axis I disorders to make prescribing recommendations; such phenomenology is deemed independent of, and prior to, issues of psychodynamic meaning. Yet they are simultaneously told (by Roose, among others) that *any* patient communication about prescribed medication— whether or not it is helping, in what way(s) it is helping, what side effects it has engendered, how the patient feels about taking it, how the patient feels about the analyst for prescribing (or not prescribing) it, and so forth—has salience only as an interpretable *analytic* communication. This being so, how can analysts rely on what their patients report in making medication recommendations in the first place, since any such report can only be *heard* analytically? Why, for example, is a patient's communication of symptoms of major depression, up to and including suicidal ideation, any less "complex," analytically speaking, than a patient's communication of side effects subsequent to medication usage?

---

33. Olesker, "Thoughts on Medication and Psychoanalysis" (n. 31), pp. 764, 773; Robert Alan Glick & Steven P. Roose, "Talking About Medication," *JAPA*, 54:745–762, 2006, quoted at pp. 745, 747, 751. Emphases in quoted passages in this paragraph are added.

Analysts who invoke phenomenological DSM-IV criteria as a basis for prescribing and then insist that anything the patient reports about the medication is always and only an interpretable analytic communication want to have their epistemic cake and eat it too. And so we end up with case reports, such as that of Abel-Horowitz, in which a medical analyst's imputation of latent meaning to a 75-year-old male patient's request for medication led him to resist prescribing for analytic reasons, despite the fact that the patient had done well on medication (Prozac) during a preliminary period of therapy and despite the analyst's recognition, early in the analysis, that this patient's

> emerging depressive syndrome, as he described it over several sessions, would most likely have been considered an indication for pharmacotherapy by a general psychiatrist. But then, his obsessional symptoms, in and of themselves, would have been medicated for years, as well.[34]

When Abel-Horowitz finally decided to remedicate his patient, ending a long and fiery "resistance-counterresistance enactment," the latter, unsurprisingly, experienced relief. "The heat from the earlier 'battle' has been cooling," Abel-Horowitz remarked in his report, and "with it, his [patient's] capacity to reflect on his use of the medication is more available."[35] So why then did Abel-Horowitz resist prescribing until his patient was at the point of crisis? He was concerned that medicating his patient early in the analysis "would constitute a countertransference enactment," especially in the face of mounting evidence "that the patient's perceived need for medication masked and expressed a deeper need to engage me sadomasochistically." And since the treatment in question was a control case, he was also influenced by analytic supervisors who, in the mid-90s, urged him not to medicate whatever his patient's symptoms might be, since "being an analyst means being able to tolerate the patient's affects and impulses in all their intensity."[36]

34. Abel-Horowitz, "Psychopharmacotherapy During an Analysis" (n. 30), p. 684.

35. Abel-Horowitz, "Psychopharmacotherapy During an Analysis" (n. 30), p. 691.

36. Abel-Horowitz, "Psychopharmacotherapy During an Analysis" (n. 30), pp. 686, 687, 688, 696, quoted at p. 688.

When, in the face of his patient's suicidal panic on the eve of a summer break, Abel-Horowitz finally decided to remedicate him, it was not owing to a shifting of gears (Cabaniss) or an internal oscillation (Sandberg) that reoriented him to the phenomenological immediacy of the patient's deterioration. Rather it was because their mutual enactment had progressed to the point at which a "behavioral response" of one sort or another was called for. More specifically, Abel-Horowitz writes, the enactment had reached a juncture at which "the patient needed to enact dominance and experience me as 'giving in' to him at that point in treatment."[37]

Amid such disclosures, we search in vain for empirically established indications for psychotropic medication (as per Cabaniss, Busch, Sandberg, and Roose, among others). They have been lost amid ruminations that have less to do with the patient than with the analyst, whose concern about foreclosing interpretive (and hence analytically curative) possibilities down the analytic road trumps any phenomenological basis for medicating. Logically (and psychiatrically) speaking, the fact that an instance of prescribing is countertransferentially motivated has no bearing on the patient's need for medication. Nor does clinical evidence that a "deeper" relational need subtends a patient's "perceived need" for medication have any bearing on the existence (or nonexistence) of those signs, symptoms, and feeling states for which medication is frequently helpful. Nor, finally, in re Abel-Horowitz's supervisors, is a patient obliged to experience affects and impulses "in all their intensity" simply to validate the analyst's ability to tolerate them.

From such psychoanalytic absorption of psychotropic medication, it is only a small step to Gottlieb's psychoanalytic "hypothesis" about the therapeutic action of SSRI medications with which we began. Just as patient reports of drug efficacy (or nonefficacy or side effects) must be heard through analytic ears, so normal science explanations of drug efficacy must be re-visioned through psychoanalytic eyes. For Gottlieb, drug efficacy per se becomes an analytic matter that presents analysts with a normative burden: To provide "a psychoana-

---

37. Abel-Horowitz, "Psychopharmacotherapy During an Analysis" (n. 30), pp. 690, 698.

lytic hypothesis" of drug action that "is not psychiatric, electrochemical, or neuroanatomical."[38]

In the late nineteenth and early twentieth centuries, alternative medical providers of various persuasions found themselves with an analogous burden: They had to provide alternative accounts of bacteriology—which comprised microscopy, vaccination, and serum therapy[39]—that conveyed acceptance of the scientific findings that underlay the new discipline but pulled these findings into a conceptual orbit consistent with their idiosyncratic theories of etiology and therapeutic action. Physiomedicalists, naturopaths, homeopaths, osteopaths, and chiropractors—none could deny germ theory outright, but they could and did reframe it in ways consistent with their theories and clinical practices.

American homeopaths of the 1870s and 1880s did not reject the integration of Listerian antisepsis and bacteriology then ascendant within regular medical culture. Ingeniously, they embraced vaccination by developing "homeopathic vaccinations" out of the secretions of the patient's own diseased tissue, preparing the secretions by homeopathic dilution, and potentiating them according to homeopathic methods. In this manner, the new vaccine and serum therapies developed in German laboratories were taken to embody homeopathic law. Further still, the immunological and bacteriological paradigm in which these therapies were grounded provided fertile grounds for a new era of "scientific" homeopathic research. As to surgical antisepsis, it simply

38. Gottlieb, "A Psychoanalytic Hypothesis Concerning the Therapeutic Action of SSRI Medications" (n. 2), p. 970.

39. In serum therapy, antitoxins in the blood of immunized animals were extracted and purified to produce a serum that could selectively neutralize or destroy the bacteria that caused specific illnesses in human beings. The effectiveness of serum therapy was variable; it failed to affect the course of typhoid fever but saved the lives of many persons with tetanus and meningococcal meningitis and scored major triumphs in treating diphtheria and pneumococcal pneumonia. For an overview, see Harry F. Dowling, *Fighting Infection: Conquests of the Twentieth Century* (Cambridge: Harvard University Press, 1977), pp. 36–54 and for a more focal study, Paul Weidling, "From Medical Research to Clinical Practice: Serum Therapy for Diphtheria in the 1890s," in J. V. Pickstone, ed., *Medical Innovations in Historical Perspective* (London: Macmillan, 1992), pp. 72–83.

amplified their founder Samuel Hahnemann's injunction that physicians prevent disease.[40]

Andrew Taylor Still, who founded osteopathy in the mid-1870s on the basis of a crude, faith-grounded hypothesis of arterial blood flow as the curative medius, had no time for germ theory. Tuberculosis and other infections, so-called, resulted from the stagnation and fermentation of blood whose flow was obstructed by a bone displacement, an osteopathic "lesion." "Bacteria do not cause disease," he opined; they were merely "the 'Turkey Buzzards' of the body," scavengers that "live on dead cells" generated by osteopathic lesions. So much for Still. The faculty with which he surrounded himself at his American School of Osteopathy in Kirksville, Missouri, was more temperate in its claims, and it pulled bacteriology into an osteopathic orbit with greater scientific discretion. Bacteria might well be the active cause of disease, they argued in the early 1890s, but spinal lesions could still be predisposing factors that lowered resistance to infection. With this reasoning, they were at the point of a uniquely osteopathic hypothesis about the vulnerability to infection and the mobilization of bodily defenses to overcome it: Correcting osteopathic lesions via spinal manipulation would reduce the likelihood of infection, whereas correcting them after infection had already set in would allow the body's natural defenses to respond with maximal effectiveness against the bacterial invaders.[41] Germ theory might explain infectious disease, but it did not jeopardize an osteopathic mechanism of therapeutic action, which fell back on Still's injunction that "The Osteopathic physician removes the obstruction and lets Nature's remedy—Arterial blood—be the doctor."[42]

40. John S. Haller, Jr., *The History of American Homeopathy: The Academic Years, 1820–1935* (Binghamton, NY: Haworth, 2005), pp. 272–275; Naomi Rogers, *An Alternative Path: The Making and Remaking of Hahnemann Medical College and Hospital of Philadelphia* (New Brunswick, NJ: Rutgers University Press, 1998), p. 83; Nadov Davidovitch, "Negotiating Dissent: Homeopathy and Anti-Vaccinationism at the Turn of the Twentieth Century," in Robert D. Johnston, ed., *The Politics of Healing: Histories of Alternative Medicine in Twentieth-Century North America* (NY: Routledge, 2004), pp. 11–28, esp. pp. 14, 16–18, 20.

41. Norman Gevitz, *The DOs: Osteopathic Medicine in America*, 2nd ed. (Baltimore: Johns Hopkins University Press, 2004 [1982]), pp. 37–38; James C. Whorton, *Nature Cures: The History of Alternative Medicine in America* (NY: Oxford University Press, 2002), pp. 148, 159–160.

42. Andrew Taylor Still, quoted in Whorton, *Nature Cures* (n. 41), p. 150.

D. D. Palmer, the magnetic healer who founded chiropractic in 1895, was no less dismissive of bacteriology than Andrew Still. But, like osteopaths, chiropractors of the second generation were able to accommodate germ theory on strictly chiropractic terms. By the 1920s, bacteriology had entered the curriculum of all the chiropractic colleges, but with a uniquely chiropractic twist that mimicked the osteopathic solution of the faculty of the American School of Osteopathy. Steven Martin, who has written perceptively about the alternative vision of science that enabled chiropractic to co-opt elements of orthodox medicine while simultaneously presenting itself to the public as an unorthodox healing modality, puts the chiropractic solution thusly:

> Rather than wholeheartedly accepting the germ theory of disease, however, chiropractors accepted the association between pathogenic bacteria and disease but denied a causal relationship. Instead, they pointed to differences in susceptibility as the central issue in infectious diseases. They used their observational approach to note that not every person exposed to pathogenic bacteria became ill and argued that the difference between those who became sick and those who remained well was the presence or absence of vertebral subluxations. Thus, bacteriology could help confirm a diagnosis without explaining the disease.[43]

The nonmanipulative alternative healers devised their own hypotheses to address the challenge of germ theory. Nineteenth-century physio-medicalists, who espoused herbal cures of Indian, Shaker, or Thomsonian origin, preceded the osteopaths and chiropractors in questioning whether bacteria actually caused disease. At the second meeting of the American Physio-Medical Association in Cincinnati in 1884, where the germ theory of diphtheria was hotly debated, William H. Cook spoke for the majority of his colleagues in pronouncing that "Germs had nothing to do with the cause of disease and existed only because disease had damaged the tissues and the germs there 'find a place to exist, like maggots in bad meat.'" Early twentieth-century naturopaths, for whom all disease was a matter of internal poisoning and all therapy a matter of inner cleansing, responded in like manner

43. Steven C. Martin, "'The Only Truly Scientific Method of Healing': Chiropractic and American Science, 1895–1990," *Isis*, 85:207–227, 1994, quoted at p. 218.

but in language that reflected their own etiologic assumptions. Bacteria, they held, were "effect rather than cause, agents that established themselves in the body only after it had already begun to deteriorate owing to an unnatural mode of living." According to naturopathic etiology, disease followed from the clogging of tissue spaces (via, for example, impermeable clothing) that interfered with the natural elimination of waste through kidneys, bowels, lungs, and skin. Germs arrived only in the aftermath of such pathogenic clogging; they were "drawn to the feast of putrid fluids pooling in unpurified tissue."[44]

No more than Gottlieb's psychoanalytic hypothesis of SSRI action was directed to neuroscientists, pharmacologists, and psychiatrists were these hypotheses directed to bacteriologists, serologists, and regular clinicians of the day. They were specific to one or another alternative school and, as such, were intended to promote professional growth and solidarity among practitioners who, like psychoanalysts with their "theory and unique form of listening" (Gottlieb), felt they had something quite special to offer their patients. The proponents of these hypotheses gained a kind of backdoor entry to the world of scientific laboratory medicine, all the while circling back to alternative theories of etiology and therapeutic action. We see this development in late nineteenth-century homeopathy, where Almroth Wright's opsonic index[45] was recruited to sustain the claim that serums prepared from

44. John S. Haller, Jr., *Kindly Medicine: Physio-Medicalism in America, 1836–1911* (Kent, OH: Kent State University Press, 1997), p. 121; Whorton, *Nature Cures* (n. 41), pp. 194, 205–207.

45. The editors of the Jefferson Medical College Yearbook ("The Clinic") of 1935 quoted their physiology professor Lucius Tuttle's humorous definition of opsonin: "An opsonin is a substance, found in the blood, which seasons the bacteria and makes them more palatable to the leucocytes" (p. 277). In the language of bacteriology, opsonization is a process that facilitates phygocytosis (the engulfing and ingesting of bacteria by white blood cells) by coating the antigens with an antibody for which phagocytic cells express receptors. Opsonin is present in all serum, and the opsonic index measures the phagocytotic potency of serum as a ratio of the average number of bacteria ingested per white blood cell in bacterially infected serum versus the average number ingested in normal blood. For a period account of the opsonic index and its methods of calculation, see Edwin Henry Schorer, *Vaccine and Serum Therapy: Including Also a Study of Infections, Theories of Immunity, Opsonins, and the Opsonic Index* (St. Louis: Mosby, 1909), chaps. 3–5. The historian J. Rosser Matthews provides a lively account of the early twentieth-century debate between Almroth Wright (and other bacteriologists, physiologists, and clinicians) and the British bio-

a patient's own secretions raised the index and improved chances of recovery. We see it in chiropractic of the mid-1920s, where B. J. Palmer's "neurocalometer" measured temperature differentials on either side of vertebrae in an effort to demonstrate the existence of infection-promoting spinal subluxations. And we see it later still in osteopathy, where, beginning in the late 1930s, J. Stedman Denslow and his colleagues turned to the new field of electromyography to provide scientific evidence of the existence of osteopathic spinal lesions.[46] The trend continues in our own time, as chiropractic and osteopathy both move toward rapprochement with evidence-based medicine (EBM), even though—in the case of "straight" chiropractic—the move may only underscore "alternative" status by redefining the very notion of "evidence" within the alternative paradigm.[47]

These "alternative" applications of normal science bring us back to the continuing psychoanalytic efforts, from the mid-1950s on, to pull psychotropic drug action into an analytic etiological orbit. We have touched on the various instantiations of these efforts over the past half century. They begin with Kline and Ostow's attempt in the

---

metrician Major Greenwood (and other statisticians) on the status of the opsonic index as a reliable diagnostic tool in *Quantification and the Quest for Medical Certainty* (Princeton: Princeton University Press, 1995).

46. Davidovitch, "Negotiating Dissent" (n. 40), pp. 16–17; Steven C. Martin, "Chiropractic and the Social Context of Medical Technology, 1895–1925," *Tech. Cult.*, 34:808–834, 1993, at pp. 826ff.; Whorton, *Nature Cures* (n. 41), pp. 189–190; Gevitz, *The DOs* (n. 41), pp. 104–106.

47. Calls for alternative practitioners to embrace the challenge of evidence-based medicine include Brian Haynes, "Commentary: A Warning to Complementary Medicine Practitioners: Get Empirical or Else," *BMJ*, 319:1632, 1999; Kumanian Wilson & Edward J. Mills, "Introducing Evidence-Based Complementary and Alternative Medicine: Answering the Challenge, *J. Alt. Complem. Med.*, 8:104–105, 2002; and John C. Licciardone, "Educating Osteopaths to Be Researchers—What Role Should Research Methods and Statistics Have in an Undergraduate Curriculum?" *Int. J. Osteo. Med.*, 11:62–68, 2008. Yvonne Villanueva-Russell provides a discerning examination of the manner in which chiropractic's move toward EBM has been a mixed blessing, providing an avenue of legitimation that simultaneously jettisons the "vitalistic epistemological foundations of the profession," and thereby intensifies the split between the "straight" and "mixer" chiropractors. See Villanueva-Russell, "Evidence-Based Medicine and Its Implications for the Profession of Chiropractic," *Soc. Sci. Med.*, 60:545–561, 2005, quoted at p. 556.

mid-1950s to understand psychotropic action in terms of the binding of psychic energy, which might, depending on the drug, either release or diminish ego energy. Throughout the 1960s and 1970s, the psycho-energic line of cooptation blossomed into the analytic reconstrual of the symptomatic relief afforded by minor tranquilizers (the benzodiaz-epines) and antidepressants (monoamine oxydase inhibitors and tri-cyclics) as a damming up of repressed libidinal and aggressive energies that, absent analytic exposure and resolution of underlying conflicts, would inevitably erupt into new symptoms. More portentously still, the symptomatic relief offered by the second-generation psychotro-pics would sap the patient's ego of the motivation to enter into and maintain a rigorous "analytic process,"[48] the nature of which remains elusive.[49] Now, in the era of SSRIs, we have the more refined strate-gies of cooptation briefly considered above: (1) The effort to subordi-nate the phenomenological indications for medication to the dynamic requirements of analytic exploration, especially with respect to pre-liminary analytic judgment about the patient's defensive organization; (2) The effort to render the action of psychotropics secondary, or even epiphenomenal, to analytic work (especially transference analysis) coterminous with the use of medication; and (3) The effort to posit a mechanism of psychotropic action in the form of a "psychoanalytic hypothesis" that is unrelated to "psychiatric, electrochemical, and neuroanatomical" explanations that have evolved within a normal science framework.

To be sure, not all analysts embrace these tenets. The literature conveys a clear tension between analytic purists, such as Greene and

---

48. Most of the papers assembled in G. J. Sarwer-Foner, ed., *The Dynamics of Psy-chiatric Drug Therapy* (Springfield, IL: Thomas, 1960) exemplify this early analytic attitude toward medication. Judd Marmor writes about the opposition of most ana-lysts to pharmacotherapy in the 50s and 60s in "The Adjunctive Use of Drugs in Psy-chotherapy," *J. Clin. Psychopharm.*, 1:312–315, 1981.

49. "Despite the long-standing centrality of analytic process as a concept in clinical, educational, and research domains, there are a multitude of definitions of analytic process, many of which are contradictory. Before one could attempt to assess the impact of medication on analytic process, there would have to be an agreed-upon definition of the term and a way of rating analytic process using a scale with estab-lished interrater reliability and construct validity. Such an instrument is not currently available." Steven P. Roose & Robin Horwitz Stern, "Medication Use in Training Cases: A Survey," *JAPA*, 43:163–170, 1995, quoted at p. 168.

Sworskin, for whom the advisability of prescribing must be assessed within an analytic framework, and analytic eclectics, such as Cabaniss, Roose (for the most part), and Sandberg, who move toward the medical mainstream by accepting the effectiveness of psychotropics on its own epistemic and therapeutic terms. The purists are not opposed to medication, but they require that its use (including the symptomatic relief it affords) not distort or impede the analytic process to such an extent that analysis becomes "unmanageable" or that the possibility of analyzing defensive "structures" is foreclosed. Therapeutic methods and goals (e.g., symptomatic relief) are differentiated from analytic methods and goals (e.g., "psychic integration") in the time-honored manner.[50] For the eclectics, on the other hand, analytic patients, no less than other types of patients, are *entitled* to the symptomatic relief and mood regulation afforded by psychotropics *apart from* the psychodynamic meanings that may accrue to the drugs and those who prescribe them. It is *likely* that these meanings will be subject to analytic exploration, but the analyzability of medication issues is not a *precondition* of prescribing. Analytic eclectics allow for the possibility that patients may present with psychopathology for which the primary treatment modality is pharmacotherapy. Indeed, from their point of view, analysts who fail to discuss the potential benefits (and limitations) of medication with analytic patients with pharmacologically treatable Axis I mood and anxiety disorders are at the point of professional misconduct, since they have failed to obtain adequate "informed consent" as the concept is understood within a mainstream medical paradigm. To wit, they have not discussed alternative treatment options with patients prior to beginning psychoanalytic treatment—a consequential omission in the aftermath of *Osheroff v. Chestnut Lodge.*[51]

Of course, this same tension between purists and eclectics who reach out to normal science is a theme that runs through the history of all

50. Mark H. Sworskin, "Further Thoughts on Dualism, Science, and the Use of Medication in Psychoanalysis," *Bull. Menn. Clin.*, 65:171–178, 2001, cited at p. 172. The case presented by Abel-Horowitz in "Psychopharmacotherapy During an Analysis" (n. 30) is essentially a meditation on the difference between therapeutic and analytic goals.

51. Cabaniss & Roose, "Psychoanalysis and Psychopharmacology" (n. 14), p. 401. On *Osheroff v. Chestnut Lodge* (Civil Action No. 66024, Circuit Court for Montgomery County, Maryland, 1984), see chapter 1, p. 9.

the alternative healing modalities. We see it in the conflicts between homeopathic purists ("pure Hahnemannians") and homeopathic mixers in the 1880s; between "lesion osteopaths" and "broad osteopaths" in the 1890s and early 1900s; and between "straight" and "mixer" chiropractors throughout the twentieth century and right into our own time.[52]

As psychoanalysts ponder their future, not merely in relation to psychotropics but more broadly as licensed mental-health providers, they must ponder the desirability—professionally, socially, and politically—of a continued commitment to "straight" analysis versus an "eclectic" analysis that moves toward the medical and psychotherapeutic mainstream both scientifically and operationally. The decision will not be easily made, and a consensus may not be apparent for another decade or so. If medical history is any guide, the field will increasingly split between those who seek to align it with normal science and those who, in the manner of straight chiropractic, see psychoanalysis as a unique science (or nonscience), coherent and compelling on its own terms, but unlike the science of most scientists and laymen.

If psychoanalysts follow the historical path of other alternative providers, then a majority will gradually move to "eclectic" status. In doing so, they will be accommodating (or bowing to) social and economic pressures that militate against a methodologically rigorous insight therapy whose scientific foundations are (at best) shaky and whose results cannot be easily codified in the manner required by evidence-based, third-party reimbursers. Not all alternative therapies are eventually absorbed by normal science in the manner of osteopa-

52. Martin Kaufman, "Homeopathy in America: The Rise and Fall and Persistence of a Medical Heresy," in Norman Gevitz, ed., *Other Healers: Unorthodox Medicine in America* (Baltimore: Johns Hopkins University Press, 1988), pp. 99–123, cited at pp. 106–107; Haller, *History of American Homeopathy* (n. 40), pp. 268–271; Gevitz, *The DOs* (n. 41), pp. 69ff.; Whorton, *Nature Cures* (n. 41), pp. 161–163, 182–185; Martin, "Only Truly Scientific Method" (n. 43), pp. 222ff. Ernst attests to the persistence of straight (i.e., purist) chiropractic in the present in survey findings that "Today 88% of U.S. chiropractors believe the subluxation [spinal lesion] contributes to over 60% of all visceral ailments and 90% think it should therefore not be limited to musculoskeletal conditions." These purist beliefs fly in the face of the consistent scientific finding that "even severe nerve root compression does not cause organic disease." See Edzard Ernst, "Chiropractic: A Critical Evaluation," *J. Pain Sym. Man.*, 35:544–562, 2008, quoted at p. 548.

thy, but all of them eventually link up with normal science in meaningful ways or retreat to permanent cult status.

In medicine, the Flexner Report of 1910, which minced no words in condemning all 32 of the alternative medical schools examined by Flexner, proved the catalyst for the integration of homeopathy and osteopathy into the scientific mainstream. Traditional homeopathic practice was soon relegated to the status of a manual specialty that could be taught effectively in brief courses offered by homeopathic postgraduate schools. Only four homeopathic schools remained in existence 10 years after the report, and only two private institutions— New York Homeopathic Medical College and Hahnemann Medical College of Philadelphia—survived into the 1920s. NYHMC began phasing out the homeopathic part of its curriculum immediately after the Flexner report and dropped "homeopathic" from its name in 1936, becoming the New York Medical College. Hahnemann Medical College, the last medical school of homeopathic provenance, survived four years of "probationary" status (1945–1948) at the hands of the American Association of Medical Colleges and the AMA's Council on Medical Education and entered the 1950s fully accredited and fully mainstream. By the 1950s, when the last remnant of the split between purist and eclectic homeopaths was sealed with the merger of the "pure" International Hahnemannian Association and the "eclectic" American Institute of Homeopathy, only a handful of purists were left.[53]

The resurgence of homeopathy in the 1980s falls outside the orbit of medical education and reflects, albeit from another angle, the assimilationist dynamic at work, as the field successfully aligned itself with public demand for natural healing within a holistic framework that began in the 1970s and continues into the present. In the twenty-first century, homeopathy is alive and well because it follows a trend complementary to public pressure for individualized, holistic care— pressure that is particularly salient for patients with chronic and/or degenerative diseases that do not permit high-tech solutions. Now, during an era in which widespread patient dissatisfaction pulls mainstream "allopathy" toward the very "holistic" sensibility that typifies

53. Haller, *History of American Homeopathy* (n. 40), pp. 288–289; Rogers, *Alternative Path* (n. 40), pp. 87–90, 139ff.; Martin Kaufman, *Homeopathy in America: The Rise and Fall of a Medical Heresy* (Baltimore: Johns Hopkins University Press, 1971), pp. 169–171; Kaufman, "Homeopathy in America" (n. 51), pp. 114–115.

homeopathy, homeopathy has moved toward normal science by formulating homeopathic hypotheses in terms of "the more arcane reaches of modern physics, chemistry, and immunology," and by assessing the efficacy of homeopathic remedies through methodologically sound clinical trials and meta-analyses of those trials.[54]

The pull to normal science similarly typified twentieth-century osteopathy, excepting only a brief resurgence of strict "lesionists" in 1918–1919, when manipulative treatment evinced some success, relative to regular medicine, in treating victims of the swine flu. Earlier in the century, the incorporation of surgery into the osteopathic curriculum opened the door to drug therapy, which was utterly anathema to Andrew Still's vision of natural healing. In 1929, "broad osteopaths" definitively triumphed over their "straight" counterparts when the American Osteopathic Association approved a resolution requiring all osteopathic medical schools to include instruction in drug therapy in their curricula, and by the early 1930s the curriculum of osteopathic colleges closely resembled that of "regular" medical schools.[55]

Throughout the 1930s, osteopathy witnessed a steady decline of manipulative treatment and an increasing reliance on regular biomedicine. During World War II, osteopaths, who were denied medical status in the military, stepped into the breach left by departing M.D.s and provided comprehensive primary medical care on the home front. By war's end, manipulative care ceased to be employed in the postoperative care of patients in osteopathic hospitals. In private practice, osteopaths continued to fill the void in primary care occasioned by the postwar dearth of general practitioners; as medical providers, newly trained osteopaths were "deosteopathized." The assimilation of osteopathy into mainstream medicine received the imprimatur of the establishment in 1961, when the California Medical Association and California Osteopathic Association merged, and the AMA, accepting the new status quo, permitted the voluntary association of M.D.s and D.O.s and the staff appointment of osteopathic physi-

54. On the resurgence of homeopathy in America since the 1980s, see Whorton, *Nature Cures* (n. 41), pp. 272–276, quoted at p. 275. For references to current "normal science" trials and meta-analyses of homeopathic remedies, see Whorton's notes 12 and 13, pp. 352–353.

55. This was the finding of Louis Reed in *The Healing Cults* (Chicago: University of Chicago Press, 1932).

cians to accredited hospitals. Seven years later, in 1968, it opened up AMA-approved internships and residencies to graduates of osteopathic medical colleges and even provided for their membership in the AMA.[56]

Of greater relevance to psychoanalysis and its fate is chiropractic, which, like psychoanalysis for most of its history, came to embrace a science all its own. Not unlike analysts, chiropractors of the first six decades of the last century laid claim to the cultural authority of science while falling back on an alternative model of science that replaced laboratory investigation and controlled clinical trials with the naturalistic observation of patients before, during, and after treatment. And just as the clinical experience of countless analytic practitioners—and the testimonials of former analysands—have long attested to the therapeutic benefits of psychoanalytic treatment, so the clinical experience of several generations of "straight" chiropractors—and the testimonials of their spinally adjusted patients—have long attested to the therapeutic benefits of chiropractic.

"Straight" chiropractors, even more than analysts, have long responded to the imagery and rhetoric of normal science while disavowing its epistemology and conventional methodologies. For straight chiropractors, that is, chiropractic has always been a monocausal system grounded in metaphysics and immune to neurophysiological research and controlled outcome studies. The presence or absence of vertebral "subluxations"—which have never been proven to constitute a relevant pathogenic entity[57]—remains at the core of all musculoskeletal, and a significant amount of visceral, pathology, and spinal manipulation techniques are the surest *scientific* means to remediation. And just as "straight" psychoanalysts continue to express serious doubts about the ability of normal science to capture the nature of "psychic integration"—or the gains in adaptive ego functioning or the

56. Gevitz, *The DOs* (n. 41), pp. 101–103; Norman Gevitz, "The Sword and the Scalpel – The Osteopathic 'War' to Enter the Military Medical Corps: 1916–1966," *J. Am. Osteo. Assn.*, 98:279–286, 1998; Hans A. Baer, "Divergence and Convergence in Two Systems of Manual Medicine: Osteopathy and Chiropractic in the United States," *Med. Anthro. Quart.*, 1:176–193, 1987; Erwin A. Blackstone, "The A.M.A. and the Osteopaths: A Study of the Power of Organized Medicine," *J. Osteo. Phys. Surg. Cal.*, 5(3):34–39; 5(4):15–20, 41, 1979, cited at pp. 15–17.

57. Ernst, "Chiropractic: A Critical Evaluation" (n. 52), p. 548.

accretion of new self structure or the transference-mediated overcoming of maladaptive relational patterns—so chiropractors have long questioned the ability of normal science to comprehend the *kind* of healing that follows from the application of "their" science, a science that grows out of "a patient-centered system of values that embrace[s] the integration of mind, body, and soul."[58]

Willock, the proponent of comparative-integrative psychoanalysis considered in chapter 7, mentions with approval the "vibrant condition of conflict" experienced by graduates of his Toronto Institute of Contemporary Psychoanalysis, and he recruits the British analyst Adam Phillips in support of the belief that such conflict constitutes "the essence of the democratic mind." Democracy, writes Willock, is "The most difficult and cherished manner of containing multiplicity yet envisioned," and it "provides a suitable educational ethos for our time."[59] The appeal to "the democratic mind" as grounding for a particular philosophy of professional training takes us to a different time and place. We are back in the United States of Andrew Jackson, when democratic populism privileged the people's freedom of choice in the matter of healers and remedies against European canons of professional expertise. Medical care disintegrated into an epistemic and clinical free-for-all. The citizenry relied on personal predilection and common sense in the matter of its doctoring, most of which was self-doctoring, whereas state governments, for their part, rendered ineffectual or eliminated entirely licensing requirements in favor of a hands-off approach to claimants of every stripe and persuasion. In the Jacksonian era, the democratic mind led to "myriads of new therapeutic systems." We are in the realm of calomel-dosing, bloodletting-to-syncope "regulars," and such familiar and relatively benign "irregulars" as homeopaths, herbalists, Thomsonians, eclectics, hydropaths, phrenologists, Christian Scientists, folk healers, and faith healers. And we encounter heterodox exotica as well: Uroscopians who diagnosed through inspection of urine; chrono-thermalists

58. Martin, "Only Truly Scientific Method" (n. 43), quoted at p. 227.

59. Willock, *Comparative-Integrative Psychoanalysis: A Relational Perspective for the Discipline's Second Century* (NY: Analytic Press, 2007), p. 158; Adam Phillips, *Equals* (London: Faber & Faber, 2002).

who looked to electric energy as a cure-all; and natural bonesetters for whom massage and manipulation were universal remedies.[60] In the matter of philosophy, training, and practice, the democratic mind reigned supreme. Any effort to regulate medical training and licensing, so the Jacksonians held, "represented an 'aristocratic' restraint on the free practice of medicine."[61]

In antebellum America, no integrative force propelled the disparate communities of American practitioners toward integration. Despite islands of excellence and a smattering of gifted, European-trained clinicians, American medicine remained fragmented, weak, and tragically ineffectual. The Jacksonian period in particular emerges as a "Dark Age of the profession."[62] During this time, the nation laid claim to a medical elite only because a small monied intelligentsia—the surgeons John Collins Warren, Valentine Mott, Philip Syng Physick, and William Gibson; the gifted generalists David Hosack and Nathaniel Chapman; and a handful of others—found its way to European medical centers in London and Edinburgh. By the 1830s, the medical intelligentsia was drawn especially to Paris, where training informed by the democratic mind gave way to structured training grounded in pathoanatomical knowledge, the nascent application of such knowledge to the clinical setting via, for example, mediate auscultation,[63]

---

60. Robert E. Riegel, *Young America, 1830–1840* (Westport, CT: Greenwood Press, 1973 [1949]), pp. 314–315, quoted at p. 314.

61. Edward Pessen, *Jacksonian America: Society, Personality, and Politics* (NY: Dorsey, 1978), p. 64.

62. Joseph F. Kett, *The Formation of the American Medical Profession: The Role of Institutions, 1780–1860* (New Haven: Yale University Press, 1968), p. vii.

63. In the words of Jacalyn Duffin, "The stethoscope made it possible to reveal physical changes before the patient died. Disease no longer had to be defined by subjective symptoms felt and described by the patient; it could now be defined and classified as a physical change detected objectively by the doctor, sometimes even without the patient's knowledge. As a result, concepts of disease could be reformulated to incorporate anatomical observations. The stethoscope had finally ruptured the epistemological barrier that had prevented the seemingly useful pathological anatomy from finding applications in the clinical setting." Jacalyn Duffin, *To See with a Better Eye: A Life of R. T. H. Laënnec* (Princeton: Princeton University Press, 1998), quoted at p. 152; cf. pp. 298–299, 302–303. See also Stanley Joel Reiser, *Medicine and the Reign of Technology* (Cambridge: Cambridge University Press, 1978), pp. 25–31.

and an empirical approach to therapeutics informed by rudimentary statistical analysis.[64] American medicine writ large began to catch up with its advance guard of scientific practitioners only in the 1870s and 1880s, when European scientific and clinical advances, European standards of medical training, and a new wave of decidedly undemocratic licensing requirements began transforming the profession.

The canons of Jacksonian democracy, as appropriated by proponents of comparative psychoanalysis, provide a strange rationale for the training of twenty-first-century psychoanalysts, and we may reasonably ask whether all we can hope for are creative analysts whose ability to "contain" different theories and to fashion self-styled syntheses out of these theories exemplifies "the democratic mind" at work. Such an agenda leaves little room for the notion of valid knowledge.[65] As I hope to have made clear in chapter 7, I prefer a psychoanalysis that understands the desirability of moving toward the scientific mainstream and that devises a path to unity in order to propel such movement. But I see little evidence that psychoanalysis will embrace this

---

64. The outstanding study of the migration of antebellum American physicians to Paris and the impact of Paris medicine on these physicians is John Harley Warner, *Against the Spirit of System: The French Impulse in Nineteenth-Century American Medicine* (Princeton: Princeton University Press, 1998). The "rudimentary statistical analysis" in question refers to Pierre Louis's numerical method, which undertook to rationalize therapeutic decision-making by collating and analyzing data on the clinical outcome of different kinds of intervention (or nonintervention) in relation to specific types of illness. On the nationwide impact of Louis's call for the collection and mathematical analysis of clinical data, see T. D. Murthy, "Medical Knowledge and Statistical Methods in Early Nineteenth-Century France," *Med. Hist.*, 25:301–319, 1981. There is an English-language translation of Louis's early influential study of the impact of bloodletting on different illnesses, Pierre Louis, "Research on the Effect of Bloodletting in Several Inflammatory Maladies," trans. W. J. Gaines & H. G. Langford, *Arch. Int. Med.*, 106:571–579, 1960. On Louis's devoted American disciples and their role in American programs of reform, see Warner, *Against the Spirit of System*, pp. 127–131, 167–169, & 231ff. For a brilliantly succinct overview of Parisian empiricism, including Louis's numerical method and its location within the history of therapeutics, see Guenter B. Risse, "The Road to Twentieth-Century Therapeutics: Shifting Perspectives and Approaches," in Gregory J. Higby & Elaine C. Stroud, eds., *The Inside Story of Medicines: A Symposium* (Madison, WI: American Institute of the History of Pharmacy, 1997), pp. 51–76, at pp. 57–60.

65. "In science, of course, it is not only a matter of achieving democratic coexistence but of arriving at valid knowledge." Ricardo Bernardi, "On Pluralism in Psychoanalysis," *Psychoanal. Inq.*, 12:506–525, 1992, quoted at p. 518.

objective and travel this path. Perhaps the simple truth is that analytic subcommunities and the identities of their adherents are by now
so well entrenched that comparative examination of theories, paradigms, and even background assumptions cannot be a vehicle of professional unification, much less of progress. Nor do analysts seem to
care about devising new approaches to common ground. As clinicians,
they are by and large content with who they are and with what they
do. As to the field itself, absent a collective resolve to re-vision itself
in a manner that privileges professional unity over school-based part-
identities, it can only continue its retreat to the margins of medicine,
psychiatry, and psychotherapy. In the United States, the era of psychoanalysis as a unique method of treatment that relies on its own
theory of developmental psychopathology and its own theory of therapeutic action and cure, barring a metaphysical epiphany, is drawing
to a close.

This trajectory may represent a dire prospect for many analysts,
but it is also an opportunity for clinical and political renewal. Life at
the margins is not death. It is professional life of another sort, with its
own set of challenges and subtly transformative possibilities. If psychoanalysis embraces these challenges and acknowledges these possibilities, it may yet aspire to a condition of "optimal marginality" from
which to address the serious limitations that inhere in the mainstream,
viz., in mental health care under the aegis of managed care and governmental administrators and increasingly subject to evidence-based
outcome criteria.[66] It may yet become, to recur to the sociological

66. Marginality militates against the need to adopt evidence-based outcome criteria, and thus counters the advice given to psychosomatically oriented clinicians to
"get on board" the evidence-based express. See Michael Sharpe, David Gill, James
Strain, et al., "Psychosomatic Medicine and Evidence-Based Treatment," *J. Psychosom. Res.*, 41:101–107, 1996, quoted at p. 106. For an excellent discussion of
evidence-based medicine, which threatens not only psychoanalysis but the "art of
medicine" in general, see Howard Kushner, "The Other War on Drugs: The Pharmaceutical Industry, Evidence-Based Medicine, and Clinical Practice," *J. Pol. Hist.*,
19:49–70, 2007. More tendentious but still of psychoanalytic interest are feminist
and phenomenological critiques of evidence-based medicine (EBM) that question both
the "givenness" and the hierarchical ordering of the epidemiological evidence on which
EBM relies. See, for example, W. A. Rogers, "Evidence-based Medicine and Women:
Do the Principles and Practice of EBM Further Women's Health?" *Bioethics*, 18:50–
70, 2004, and Maya J. Goldberger, "On Evidence and Evidence-Based Medicine:
Lessons from the Philosophy of Science," *Soc. Sci. Med.*, 62:2621–2632, 2006. The

perspective invoked in chapter 1, an alternative source of clinical and cultural authority in dialectical interaction with the mainstream.[67]

Even today, the vast majority of fully trained psychoanalysts have little if any opportunity to practice psychoanalysis in any methodologically rigorous sense of the term. In the near future, they will likely have limited opportunities even to practice long-term analytically informed psychotherapy. But, operating at the margins, they may still have opportunities to bring one or another kind of psychoanalysis to bear on brief therapy and group therapy, on cognitive, behavioral, interpersonal, and supportive treatment modalities, and, certainly, on mainstream psychiatry with its near-total reliance on psychopharmacology.

To realize this new role, to maximize the possibilities of optimal marginality, American psychoanalysts must cease and desist in their quixotic quest for mainstream acceptance. The field must overcome its nagging tendency to recur to the glory era of the field as a marker of what once was and may yet again be. It must learn to accept its marginality if it is to exploit it to the full.

anthropologist Helen Lambert's "Accounting for EBM: Notions of Evidence in Medicine," *Soc. Sci. Med.*, 26:2633–2645, 2005 is much more suggestive of the manner in which psychoanalysts themselves might enter ongoing debates about the evidential base of EBM, especially as it pertains to the construal of patient and analyst narratives as qualitative evidence relevant to treatment decisions.

67. This is the sociological sense of marginalization as a "valuable strategic tool" that encourages self-definition, group cohesion, and innovative thought absent institutional constraints. See Neil McLaughlin, "Optimal Marginality: Innovation and Orthodoxy in Fromm's Revision of Psychoanalysis," *Sociol. Quart.*, 42:271–288, 2001 and Jaap Bos, David W. Park, & Petteri Pietikainen, "Strategic Self-Marginalization: The Case of Psychoanalysis," *J. Hist. Behav. Sci.*, 41:207–224, 2005.

Chapter 9
Life at the Margins

A closer relationship between psychoanalysis and society is a vista
which its adherents as well as its adversaries have traditionally
viewed with alarm.[1]

Throughout the nineteenth and into the twentieth centuries, alternative professions such as homeopathy and osteopathy, which,
unlike psychoanalysis, never enjoyed a period of mainstream dominance, grew skillful operating at the fringes of orthodoxy.[2] By the
1870s, homeopaths, formerly wed to Samuel Hahnemann's belief in
the curative action of similars and the effectiveness of minute doses,
were following their orthodox or "allopathic" colleagues to Germany
for training in one or another clinical specialty. By the turn of the century,
their own training programs in America incorporated bacteriology,

1. Victor H. Rosen, Presidential Address to the American Psychoanalytic Association, Atlantic City, NJ, May, 1966, quoted in Robert S. Wallerstein, "The Challenge
of the Community Mental Health Movement to Psychoanalysis," *Am. J. Psychiatry*,
124:1049–1056, 1968, at p. 1054.

2. Still earlier in the century, between 1840 and 1860, British hydropaths, many of
them medically qualified, perfected the art of thriving at the margins by limiting their
challenge to orthodoxy to received therapeutics at the same time as they embraced
conventional views of the body and disease. Furthermore, following the Gräfenberg
model of the founder of the water cure, Vincinz Priessnitz, British hydropaths transposed their treatment to special hydropathic institutions. The latter "provided a site
to carry out a potentially profitable form of medicine, aimed at a bourgeois clientele,
where the roles of other marginal practitioners like the spa physician, alienist, and
hospital specialist could be adapted to their own ends. In short, like these other positions, hydropathy provided opportunity on the edge of orthodoxy for the socially
marginal practitioners." See James Bradley & Marguerite Dupree, "Opportunity on
the Edge of Orthodoxy: Medically Qualified Hydropathists in the Era of Reform,
1840–1860," *Soc. Hist. Med.*, 14:417–437, 2001, quoted at p. 432 and James Bradley & Marguerite Dupree, "A Shadow of Orthodoxy? An Epistemology of British
Hydropathy, 1840–1848," *Med. Hist.*, 47:173–194, 2003.

microscopy, and serum therapy. But their educational institutions were inferior, and after Abraham Flexner documented the dismal state of American medical education in his Carnegie Foundation–funded report of 1910, they quickly folded. So the homeopaths, intent on remaining at the edge of orthodoxy, re-visioned homeopathy as one (among many) specialized techniques that could be taught within the framework of independent postgraduate schools. Beginning in 1924, these schools came under the sponsorship of the American Foundation for Homeopathy, an organization of former patients and lay supporters dedicated to preventing the disappearance of homeopathy.[3]

Osteopathy followed a similar course, except that it rose to the challenge of the Flexner Report, and its educational institutions were able to resist absorption into the mainstream. Osteopaths, heirs to Andrew Still's belief that manual adjustment of spinal lesions would restore arterial blood flow and revivify blood-starved organs, optimized their marginality by learning to work the legal system. Their lawyers were adroit in forcing a debate about the definition of medical practice. According to the osteopaths, mainstream medicine was legally constituted as the practice of administering drugs, a narrow reading that, prior to 1904, was accepted by the high courts of every state except Alabama and Nebraska. Eighteen ninety-seven witnessed the founding of the American Association for the Advancement of Osteopathy, renamed four years later the American Osteopathic Association (AOA); it became a platform for the legislative battle for independent boards of registration and examination. By 1913, 39 states had passed osteopathic practice laws. "Lesion osteopaths" continued to yield to "broad osteopaths," and in 1929 the profession, speaking through the AOA, directed osteopathic medical schools to provide all students with a course on supplementary therapeutics that included full instruction in pharmacology. From the 1930s on, osteopathy witnessed a steady decline of manipulative treatment and in 1943, now committed to integration with the mainstream, the AOA

3. Anne Taylor Kirschmann, "Making Friends for 'Pure' Homeopathy: Hahnemannians and the Twentieth-Century Preservation and Transformation of Homeopathy," in Robert D. Johnston, ed., *The Politics of Healing: Histories of Alternative Medicine in Twentieth-Century North America* (NY: Routledge, 2004), pp. 29–42; John S. Haller, *The History of American Homeopathy: The Academic Years, 1820–1935* (Binghamton, NY: Haworth, 2005), pp. 288–289.

launched the Osteopathic Progress Fund, which channeled money directly to osteopathic colleges.[4]

"Broad" or eclectic osteopathy, which by the outbreak of World War II differed little if at all from mainstream medicine, used the experience of the war virtually to co-opt one aspect of mainstream medical care: General practice. Denied medical commissions into the armed forces, osteopaths stepped into the breach left by departing M.D.s and became primary care physicians on the home front, a trend that continued after the war as biomedicine continued its wartime transformation into a capital-intensive endeavor revolving around specialist care. Meanwhile, chiropractors, whose naturalistic "science" of spinal manipulation to restore misaligned vertebrae (subluxations) remained robust at the margins of orthodox medicine, launched its own program of educational reform in the mid-1930s, when the "mixer" National Chiropractic Association appointed John Nugent—shortly referred to as chiropractic's own Flexner—director of education, with the charge of overhauling the profession's training system. Thus, chiropractic was well positioned to step into the breach left when osteopathy abandoned manipulative treatment and merged with the mainstream: It met the public demand for nonsurgical treatment of musculoskeletal disorders historically ignored by mainstream medicine.[5]

Chiropractic's gradual move toward the mainstream is a case study in optimal marginalization. Excluded by Congress from the Medicare reimbursement system established in 1965, chiropractic fought back by mobilizing its large patient base to demand "health freedom" from their elected representatives, who were barraged with an estimated 12,000,000 letters and telegrams. Inclusion in Medicare was granted a decade later in 1974. In the same year, the United States Office of Education authorized the Chiropractic Commission on Education to begin accreditation of chiropractic colleges, and Congress allocated two million dollars to the National Institutes of Health (NIH) for scientific study of the biomechanics of chiropractic manipulation. Two

4. Norman Gevitz, *The DOs: Osteopathic Medicine in America*, 2nd ed. (Baltimore: Johns Hopkins University Press, 2004 [1982]), pp. 46, 96–103.

5. James C. Whorton, *Nature Cures: The History of Alternative Medicine in America* (NY: Oxford University Press, 2002) p. 233; Hans A. Baer, "Divergence and Convergence in Two Systems of Manual Medicine: Osteopathy and Chiropractic in the United States," *Med. Anthro. Quart.*, 1:176–193, 1987 at pp. 180–181, 190.

years later, chiropractic went on the offensive, filing suit against the AMA and nine other medical organizations for violation of the Sherman Antitrust Act. A lengthy court battle ended in 1987, when the U.S. District Court for the North District of Illinois decided against organized medicine in *Wilk v. American Medical Association*. Continuing mainstream skepticism about the scientific credibility of chiropractic, the court held, did not justify a nationwide campaign to destroy the profession. An injunction was issued forbidding the AMA "from restricting, regulating or impeding" any members or hospitals from professional association with chiropractors.

As the AMA retreated from its policy of radical exclusion—as early as 1979 it had acknowledged that chiropractic treatment, despite its unscientific foundations, might benefit patients with certain kinds of musculoskeletal pain—so chiropractic itself edged toward normal science. Beginning in the early 70s, medical literature began citing workmen's compensation reports that attested to chiropractic's clinical effectiveness (and cost-effectiveness) in treating work-related neck and back injuries, and by the late 70s research on the biomechanics and neurophysiology of the spine was being pursued in order to provide a more scientific basis for chiropractic therapy.[6] Around the same time, clinical trial protocols were devised and implemented that provided support for chiropractic adjustments as a treatment of choice for lower back pain. These developments may herald the evolution of eclectic chiropractic—the portion of the profession that rejects the monocausal theory of spinal subluxations—into what Wardwell terms "a limited medical profession" like dentistry, podiatry, optometry, and psychology.[7]

6. "But therapeutic success alone cannot generate the necessary cultural authority for a modern movement to flourish. Without legitimacy achieved according to the rules of modern science, chiropractic, despite its record of success, would have remained only a marginal discipline consigned to the medical underworld inhabited by other heterodox healers." J. Stuart Moore, *Chiropractic in America: The History of a Medical Alternative* (Baltimore: Johns Hopkins University Press, 1993), p. 144.

7. These events in the recent history of American chiropractic are covered in Moore, *Chiropractic in America* (n. 6), chapter 6. Wikipedia provides an excellent summary of *Wilk v. American Medical Association* at http://en.wikipedia.org/wiki/Wilk_v._American_Medical_Association. For a succinct overview that brings American chiropractic into the twenty-first century and provides references attesting to chiropractic's turn to normal science, see Whorton, *Nature Cures* (n. 5), pp. 283–288.

For psychoanalysis, there are lessons to be learned from alternative professions that worked the system to their advantage, edging closer to the mainstream at the same time as they pulled the mainstream toward them.[8] How might psychoanalytic marginality be optimized? Even if psychoanalysts of different persuasions cannot lay down their theoretical arms and agree on a shared praxis, they might still appreciate the importance of a united sociopolitical front able to transform their public persona in therapeutically and socially responsible ways. To date, a small number of analysts have made individual forays into the community,[9] but their laudable initiatives have not coalesced into any kind of profession-wide mandate to bring the field into the trenches, where analytic insights could be brought to bear on various kinds of community violence and trauma. Among my final publications at TAP were applications of psychodynamic thinking to

---

Walter I. Wardwell discusses the evolution of chiropractors into "limited medical specialists" in "Chiropractors: Evolution to Acceptance," in Norman Gevitz, ed., *Other Healers: Unorthodox Medicine in America* (Baltimore: Johns Hopkins University Press, 1988), pp. 157–191 at pp. 186–191. Susan Smith-Cunnien illuminates the institutional history of chiropractic by examining the AMA's changing attitudes toward it and campaigns against it throughout the twentieth century. She concludes by examining chiropractic's role in the public discussions of health care reform during the early years of the first Clinton administration. See Smith-Cunnien, *A Profession of One's Own: Organized Medicine's Opposition to Chiropractic* (Lanham, MD: University Press of America, 1998), especially chaps. 5 & 6.

8. There is a substantial literature on mainstream medicine's movement toward complementary and alternative approaches to health care that began in earnest in the 1990s. The papers of Ted Kaptchuk and David M. Eisenberg are an excellent place to start, especially Ted J. Kaptchuk & David M. Eisenberg, "Varieties of Healing. 1: Medical Pluralism in the United States," *Ann. Intern. Med.*, 135:189–195, 2001. The highly politicized founding of the NIH's "Office of Alternative Medicine" in 1991, especially the role of Senator Thomas R. Harkin and his Iowa constituents Berkley Bedell and Frank Wiewel, is ably reviewed by James Harvey Young in "The Development of the Office of Alternative Medicine in the National Institutes of Health, 1991–1996," *Bull. Hist. Med.*, 72:279–298, 1998. For an excellent overview of the scientific evidence bearing on the effectiveness of mind-body (viz., alternative) interventions, see John A. Astin, et al., "Mind-Body Medicine: State of the Science, Implications for Practice," *J. Am. B. Fam. Prac.*, 16:131–147, 2003.

9. In the mid-90s, I was pleased to publish one noteworthy example of such a foray, Neil Altman's *The Analyst in the Inner City: Race, Class, and Culture Through a Psychoanalytic Lens* (Hillsdale, NJ: Analytic Press, 1995).

"streets, schools, [and] war zones"; to the psychodynamic issues attendant to assisted pregnancy; and to psychodynamic considerations in matters of divorce and custody. None of these books attracted significant interest among analytic readers; none has achieved even modest commercial success.[10]

The most laudable analytic initiative of the past decade is unquestionably SOFAR (Strategic Outreach to Families of All Reservists), initially an outgrowth of the Psychoanalytic Couple and Family Institute of New England. An organization of psychoanalysts and psychoanalytically oriented therapists (representing many schools of psychoanalytic thought), SOFAR, founded by Kenneth Reich and now codirected by Jaine Darwin, provides pro bono services to Reservists and National Guardsmen returning from Iraq and Afghanistan and to their families as well. SOFAR analysts not only provide individual therapy for returnees and their family members but also lead support groups at training sites for family members of Reservists and Guardsmen currently deployed.

SOFAR, which has attracted national publicity, has been honored by proclamation by the Governor's Office of the Commonwealth of Massachusetts and has expanded outside its native Boston. A "SOFAR Michigan," affiliated with the Michigan Psychoanalytic Institute, is now operational, as are branches in New York and Florida. SOFAR sites in Maryland, Texas, and Pennsylvania are in the early stages of development. The SOFAR Guide, a manual for helping children cope with the deployment of a parent in the military reserves, is available to all schools in Massachusetts, and is being reviewed for distribution throughout New England. Finally, and most promisingly, the American Psychological Association is considering a partnership with SOFAR.[11]

Sadly, however, the national psychoanalytic associations have done little in support of this rare and timely example of psychoanalysis in

---

10. Bruce Sklarew, Stuart Twemlow, & Sallye Wilkinson, eds., *Analysts in the Trenches: Streets, Schools, War Zones* (Hillsdale, NJ: Analytic Press, 2004); Allison Rosen & Jay Rosen, eds., *Frozen Dreams: Psychodynamic Dimensions of Infertility and Assisted Reproduction* (Hillsdale, NJ: Analytic Press, 2005); Linda Gunsberg & Paul Hymowitz, eds., *The Handbook of Divorce and Custody: Forensic, Developmental, and Clinical Perspectives* (Hillsdale, NJ: Analytic Press, 2005).

11. My thanks to Kenneth Reich for providing me with this information on the current status of SOFAR.

the service of the community. Expansion of SOFAR has been through individual contacts rather than organizational initiatives. Neither the American Psychoanalytic Association nor the Psychoanalysis Division of the American Psychological Association has mobilized its members to participate in what might become a widely publicized psychoanalytic initiative.[12] Nor has anything been done in a public context to underscore the value of the broadly analytic perspective that SOFAR volunteers bring to their therapeutic and psychoeducational work with reservists and their families.

Estimates of the number of Americans directly affected by the continuing war in Iraq now range from 63 to 92 million, with one-third of that number representing Americans aged 18 or younger. Why, in the face of a looming mental-health crisis, American psychoanalysts have not joined arms with Reich and his colleagues in demonstrating that psychoanalysis can be socially relevant and that psychoanalysts, as a community, are socially responsible, is disappointing but less than surprising. The roots of insularity and introversion that took hold in the aftermath of World War II remain deeply embedded. But it is just such roots that must be excised if analysts are to project a publicly united front that may yet earn them the attention of legislators, governmental agencies, and charitable foundations. A publicly united front does not remedy internal fractionation, but it may go some distance in offsetting the political and professional weakness attendant to it. Why have analysts not made SOFAR and like-minded community initiatives a profession-wide priority?

Marginalization can also be optimized by reframing one's relationship to neighboring professions, a strategy that leads us back to pharmacotherapy and the challenge it poses for psychoanalysis. The conflict between prescribing and talking, which is ultimately a conflict between different ontologies of mental "illness," different political and professional agendas, and different priorities in the allocation of limited financial resources, has never belonged to psychoanalysis alone. American psychiatry, and especially psychiatric training, has been rent by the conflict between medicating and doing therapy for more than three decades. The anthropologist Teresa Luhrmann, who conducted

12. The American Psychoanalytic Association, be it noted, did award SOFAR a grant of $3,500.00 toward the reprinting of the SOFAR Guide. Kenneth Reich to Paul Stepansky, September 24, 2008.

fieldwork at a mix of psychodynamic and biologically oriented psychiatric institutions in the mid-90s, resorted to something tantamount to Weberian "ideal types" in characterizing the "disorder" in American psychiatry as an irremediable divide between "psychoanalysis" and "psychiatric science." The divide commenced in the early 1980s, when hospital-based training programs witnessed "a sprawling confrontation between what were then thought of as the 'two camps.'" By the mid-1990s, the battle, no less than the search for an integrated psychiatry, was largely over. It had given way to a "muting" of psychotherapy under the impact of managed care; insurers ceased paying for in-hospital psychotherapy.[13]

Luhrmann, interestingly, did not hold biological psychiatry per se responsible for the threatened disappearance of psychodynamics in psychiatric training programs. The key problem, rather, was "a financial crisis in the context of lingering ideological tension." Under the financial constraints of managed care, that is, psychiatric residents and staff psychiatrists were forced to move from one-on-one relationships with patients to management positions on treatment teams or out of management positions altogether and into consultant roles. Psychiatric training was no longer conducive to "intense, unmediated relationships with patients," and residents, no less than patients, were the worse for it. "By the middle 1990s," Luhrmann observed, "I knew very few psychiatrists, regardless of their disciplinary commitments, who thought that reimbursement policies enabled most psychiatric patients to get adequate care."[14]

Luhrmann's research subjects echoed a criticism that has been made repeatedly by commentators over the past decade, viz., that the devaluation of psychotherapy in residency training compromises future psychiatrists' ability to diagnose and treat psychotherapeutically *or* pharmacologically. In the words of one of Luhrmann's interviewees, a self-described psychopharmacologist, "There's *no* question, you *cannot* be a good psychopharmacologist without being exposed deeply to psychotherapy." Psychiatric educators have joined in this complaint, even to the point of questioning the very viability of the psychopharmacologist

13. T. M. Luhrmann, *Of Two Minds: The Growing Disorder in American Psychiatry* (NY: Knopf, 2000), pp. 232ff.

14. Luhrmann, *Of Two Minds* (n. 13), quoted at pp. 249–250, 252.

role. According to the consultation-liaison psychiatrist Nicholas Kontos and his colleagues, the role is anathema to "good doctoring," which, for the psychiatrist, means embracing a medical model within which "decisions [are] based on thoughtful scrutiny of diagnoses, available science, and patient individuality." By imparting legitimacy and even prestige to the psychopharmacologist role, they observe, "psychiatry corrals part of itself off from all but a limited intervention-centered identity," as psychopharmacologists who believe that matching criteria with drugs is "clinically sufficient" can divorce themselves from the patient's personhood. In this manner, "the psychopharmacologist role ferments irrationally narrow practice strategies in physicians, unreasonably concrete expectations in patients, and, by extension, an inaccurately pat representation of the stuff of psychiatry to the rest of medicine."[15]

If "empathic and incisive scrutiny of a patient's experience is needed to match phenomenology to the DSM diagnostic scheme effectively," then it stands to reason that psychiatric residents need psychodynamic training. Equally, they need to be able to apply this training and the kind of thinking it cultivates to the prescriber's role, thereby working through the "illusion of simplicity that leaves residents unprepared to make sense of the complex and irrational processes that occur in the acts of prescribing and taking medication." To invoke the psychology of pharmacology is at once to summon psychoanalysis. Psychiatric residents, David Mintz, Director of Residency Training at the Austen Riggs Center, tells us, must learn how their patients' "own conflict[s] or dysfunctional attitudes are expressed in the pharmacotherapeutic relationships." They must learn that ambivalence, resistance, and transference to medications "may result in misuse of medication and noncompliance, lack of effectiveness, or the repeated emergence of untoward side effects." They must learn about the role of projective identification in the pharmacotherapeutic relationship. And they must learn, finally, that prescribers no less than their patients may act out unconscious issues through the latter's medication regimen.[16]

15. Luhrmann, *Of Two Minds* (n. 13), p. 246; Nicholas Kontos, John Querques, & Oliver Freudenreich, "The Problem of the Psychopharmacologist," *Acad. Psychiatry*, 30:218–226, 2006, quoted at pp. 224, 222.

16. Kontos et al., "Problem of the Psychopharmacologist" (n. 15), p. 222; David L. Mintz, "Teaching the Prescriber's Role: The Psychology of Psychopharmacology," *Acad. Psychiatry*, 29:187–194, 2005 at pp. 188, 189.

Who better than analysts to elaborate the psychology of psychopharmacology in its rational and irrational, conscious and unconscious, transferential and countertransferential, aspects? If analysts would stop pondering the compatibility of medication with an analytic frame and its conjectural impact on whatever they understand by an "analytic process" and bring their insights down to earth, they might optimize their marginality by contributing to medical education and psychiatric training. Analytic involvement in the forming of psychodynamically attuned prescribers could help ameliorate the "disorder" (Luhrmann) in American psychiatry.

Analysts might also play a role in family practice and internal medicine residencies.[17] Primary care providers have long been the frontline of psychiatric evaluation and psychotropic prescribing, and psychiatric educators have argued that primary care residencies should incorporate additional psychiatric training. By such training, they typically mean additional time in psychiatric services in which primary care residents would acquire experience "in timely diagnosis and treatment of psychiatric patients, as well as in the performance of an effective mental status examination." It is incumbent on primary physicians, they enjoin, to appreciate and understand the impact of comorbid

---

17. Contemporary analysts have distanced themselves from the psychodynamic challenges of primary medical care, although these challenges were substantively engaged in the 1940s by the American analyst Maurice Levine (*Psychotherapy in Medical Practice* [NY: Macmillan, 1944]) and again in the 1950s by the British analyst Michael Balint (*The Doctor, His Patient, and the Illness* [NY: International Universities Press, 1957]). Within the journal literature, efforts to reframe medical illness and illuminate doctor-patient relationships along analytic lines were highly speculative, in the manner of "wild" applied analysis. See, e.g., Ernst Simmel, "The 'Doctor-Game,' Illness and the Profession of Medicine," *Int. J. Psycho-Anal.*, 7:470–483, 1926; Herman Nunberg, "Psychological Interrelations Between Physician and Patient," *Psychoanal. Rev.*, 25:297–308, 1938; and Bertram D. Lewin, "Counter-Transference in the Technique of Medical Practice," *Psychosom. Med.*, 8:195–199, 1946. This tendentious literature, which posited, for example, that the physician's "compassion and healing intent" was ipso facto "based on guilt over aggressive and destructive impulses," was mapped into didactic articles of the 50s and 60s, e.g., Eric D. Wittkower, "The Psychiatric Role of the General Practitioner," in Norman Q. Brill, *Psychiatry in Medicine* (Berkeley: University of California Press, 1962), pp. 136–160, quoted at p. 148. For less analytic (and less tendentious) accounts of the psychodynamic dimension of primary care a decade later, see Paul E. Stepansky & William Stepansky, "Psychiatry in Family Medicine: An Old Role Restated," *Psychosomatics*, 13:380–387, 1972 and Paul E. Stepansky & William Stepansky, "Training Primary Physicians as Psychotherapists," *Comp. Psychiatry*, 15:141–151, 1974.

psychiatric illness on various medical disorders, diabetes and coronary heart disease among them.[18]

These recommendations are entirely reasonable, but they ignore one kind of knowledge associated with the kind of psychiatric evaluating and treating that primary physicians will do. Primary care residents who learn more psychiatry in hospital settings will only carry over to primary care settings the psychodynamic lacunae of psychiatric training, including enshrinement of the psychopharmacologist role, with its fomenting of "irrationally narrow practice strategies in physicians."[19] They, no less than psychiatric psychiatrists, will learn to rely on DSM diagnostic nomenclature, and their treatments will continue to consist, as they do now, entirely of prescribing. It stands to reason that primary care residents, no less than psychiatric residents, greatly need what psychoanalysts, medical or lay, can teach them about the psychodynamics of prescribing. Here is an arena for analytic engagement. By placing the psychodynamics of prescribing within a broader therapeutic context, analysts might optimize their marginality in a world in which the psychoanalytic method and long-term psychoanalytic treatment have become epiphenomenal, and the prescribing of psychotropic medication quite central, to the provision of mental health care, especially when that care is provided by nonpsychiatric physicians.

It would not be the first time analysts participated in the training of family practitioners and internists. During and after World War II, when American psychiatry, reshaped by its military mission, embraced psychoanalysis as its preferred explanatory paradigm, the psychodynamic dimension of primary care medicine came within the purview of analytically trained psychiatric educators. During the dark days of 1942, the psychiatric educator Maurice Levine, analytically trained at the Chicago Institute and destined to follow John Romano as chairman of the psychiatry department of the University of Cincinnati College of Medicine, published *Psychotherapy in Medical Practice*. A nontechnical, commonsensical exposition of the various psychotherapy

18. Eugene H. Rubin & Charles F. Zorumski, "Psychiatric Education in an Era of Rapidly Occurring Scientific Advances," *Acad. Med.*, 78:351–354, 2003, cited and quoted at p. 353.

19. Kontos et al., "Problem of the Psychopharmacologist" (n. 15), p. 222.

methods available to general practitioners, the book enjoyed enormous commercial success for its publisher, Macmillan, and was in its eigh-teenth printing at the time of Levine's death in 1971.[20]

Levine did what he could locally, conducting evening courses for senior Cincinnati internists who reached out to him for "psychiatric information that might be of value in the practice of internal medi-cine." But his sensibility only came to fruition when two of his University of Cincinnati colleagues, the psychiatrist John Romano and the internist George Engel, migrated to the University of Rochester in 1946. There, in a department of medicine already identified with psy-chosomatic medicine, the two initiated curricular innovations that worked psychodynamic psychiatry into all four years of medical school and extended it to postgraduate training through a program of Rocke-feller Foundation and Commonwealth Fund medical-psychiatric fellowships. The latter provided budding internists and later other nonpsychiatric specialists with two-year joint appointments in psy-chiatry and medicine in order to hone their skills as psychosomaticists able to serve as medical-psychiatric liaison consultants in general hospitals.[21]

Joined by pioneering psychiatric liaison services at the University of Colorado (under Franklin Ebaugh and Edward Billings), Massa-chusetts General Hospital (under Avery Weisman), Boston's Beth Is-rael Hospital (under Grete Bibring), New York's Mount Sinai Hospital (under Lawrence Kubie and M. Ralph Kaufman), and elsewhere, the Rochester Liaison Program brought psychoanalysis—in the guise of an analytically grounded psychosomaticism—to bear on hospital care in the decade following the end of World War II. But for many psy-chiatrists who served as military psychiatrists—the Army's William

20. Levine, *Psychotherapy in Medical Practice* (n. 17), especially chaps. 3 & 4, where Levine enumerates and discusses the various "methods" and "advanced methods" of psychotherapy available to the general practitioner. On the commercial success of the book, see George Engel, "Biographical Note," in Maurice Levine, *Psychiatry and Ethics* (NY: Braziller, 1972), pp. 255–262 at p. 257.

21. Maurice Levine, "Psychiatry for Internists," *Am. J. Orthopsy.*, 17:602–604, 1947, quoted at p. 602, reprinted in Levine, *Psychiatry and Ethics* (n. 20), pp. 286–291; Theodore M. Brown, "The Historical and Conceptual Foundations of the Rochester Biopsychosocial Model" (2000), www.human-nature.com/free-associations/engel2 .html, pp. 11–14.

Menninger and Lauren H. Smith, and the Army Air Force's (AAF) Roy Grinker, John Spiegel, and John Milne Murray among them—the wartime effectiveness of general medical officers, with at most three months of psychiatric training, provided a different psychoanalytically derived model for the kind of psychiatric aid that postwar generalists would be asked to provide.

Grinker in particular envisioned a postwar America overridden with psychiatric problems, especially among the waves of returning GIs, a great many "angry, regressed, anxiety-ridden, dependent men" among them. Addressing this postwar prospect had little to do with weaving psychoanalytic psychiatry into the inpatient medical service of general hospitals. The military psychiatrists were front-line men, in spirit if not in actuality, and they were less concerned with interspecialty fellowships for internists than with mobilizing office-based GPs into a psychiatric resource. "We shall never have enough psychiatrists to treat all the psychosomatic problems," intoned Grinker to the American Society for Research in Psychosomatic Problems in 1946. "Until sufficient psychiatrists are produced and more internists and practitioners make time available for the treatment of psychosomatic syndromes," he continued, "we must use heroic shortcuts in therapy which can be applied by all medical men with little special training." His assessment was echoed by Menninger, the Director of the Neuropsychiatry Consultants Division in the Office of the Surgeon General, and Murray, the AAF's Chief Consultant in Neuropsychiatry, both of whom addressed the annual convocation of the American Psychiatric Association that same year. "Even though we could train two or even five times as many psychiatrists," remarked Menninger, "the majority of minor psychiatry will be practiced by the general physician and the specialists in other fields." Murray, for his part, lauded the Army Air Force's "junior psychiatrists," whose wartime psychiatric training had been entirely "on the job" and whose ranks would be greatly expanded by the Veterans Administration in its program of postwar psychiatric care.[22]

22. Roy R. Grinker & John P. Spiegel, *Men Under Stress* (Philadelphia: Blakiston, 1945), pp. 428–434, and quoted at p. 450; Roy R. Grinker, "Brief Psychotherapy in Psychosomatic Problems," *Psychosom. Med.*, 9:98–103, 1947, quoted at pp. 100, 101; William C. Menninger, "Psychiatric Experience in the War, 1941–1946," *Am. J. Psychiatry*, 103:577–586, 1947, quoted at p. 584; John Milne Murray, "Accomplishments of Psychiatry in the Army Air Forces," *Am. J. Psychiatry*, 103:594–599, 1947. Milne's

Lauren Smith, who was appointed Psychiatrist-in-Chief to the Institute of the Pennsylvania Hospital prior to assuming his wartime duties, was more sanguine still, because he believed the community of stateside GPs was fully up to the psychiatric task before it. The great majority of returning veterans, after all, would present with psychoneuroses rather than serious psychiatric illness, and the majority of them "can be treated successfully by the physician in general practice if he is practical in being sympathetic and understanding, especially if his knowledge of psychiatric concepts is improved and formalized by even a minimum of reading in today's psychiatric literature." For Smith no less than Grinker, Menninger, and Murray, postwar general practitioners would be the foot soldiers of postwar psychoanalytic psychiatry; like their predecessors, the wartime general medical officers, they would summon the intuitive psychodynamic understanding that inhered in general practice to the task of learning and utilizing the "simpler techniques of psychiatry."[23]

The era of psychoanalytically grounded psychosomatic medicine ended in the 1970s, when psychoanalytic hegemony within American psychiatry gave way to biological psychiatry, and when the quest for a clinically grounded psychosomatics that sought to provide psychogenic explanations specific to one or another medical condition (in the tradition of Franz Alexander) gave way to a psychosomaticism grounded in animal models, stress studies, and neuroendocrine bench research. With the occasional heroic exception—such as the University of Rochester School of Medicine, where George Engel's pioneering "biopsychosocial model" continues to sustain a program of medical-psychiatric postgraduate fellowships—primary care medicine, in lockstep with psychiatry, has marched away from psychodynamically

---

vision of on-the-job psychiatric training for flight surgeons was set forth in his memorandum of April, 1943, to the Air Surgeon (medical director of the AAF) and shared with his colleagues in "Psychiatric Evaluation of Those Returning from Combat," *JAMA*, 126:148–150, 1944.

23. Lauren H. Smith & Horatio C. Wood, "The General Practitioner and the Returning Veteran," *JAMA*, 129:190–193, 1945, quoted at p. 192. Even before the war, Smith, who was analytically trained, developed a vision of community psychiatry that embraced the contribution of general practitioners. See Lauren H. Smith and Reynold A. Jensen, "The 'One-Contact' Case: A Problem in Community Psychiatric Practice," *Psychiat. Quart.*, 13:330–345, 1939.

informed history-taking and office psychotherapy. Primary care physicians, like their psychiatric colleagues, have reframed their psychiatric obligation: The postwar generation's mandate to practice "minor psychiatry," which included a broad range of supportive, educative, and dynamic interventions, has effectively shrunk to the simple act of prescribing a psychotropic agent.[24]

But is the act of prescribing really so simple, or so simply medical? It is here, in the margins of an entrenched pharmacological approach to "minor psychiatry" in the primary care specialties, that a marginalized psychoanalysis may find new interventional possibilities. If psychoanalysis, as diffused into psychoanalytic psychiatry, is no longer charged with guiding primary physicians in the practice of minor psychiatry, it is faced with a new charge: To introduce primary care physicians to the psychodynamic dimension of drug management in the face of a medicalized psychiatry straitjacketed by "the psychopharmacologist role." An excellent start in this direction was made more than a quarter century ago by the psychiatric educator Thomas Gutheil, whose notion of a "pharmacotherapeutic alliance" remains all too relevant to psychoanalytic, psychiatric, and nonpsychiatric prescribers of the present. The prescriber's vulnerability to a "delusion of precision"; the range of transference and countertransference meanings, positive and negative, that may attach to drug usage, including the administrative aspects of prescribing and monitoring (scheduling, dosage, and form of medication); the tendency of patients,

24. The rise and fall of psychoanalytically grounded psychosomaticism, the emergence of a new model of nonclinical psychosomatic research in the 1970s, and the demise of American psychosomatic medicine as a cohesive research field and clinical orientation in the decades thereafter are thoughtfully discussed by Theodore M. Brown in "Historical and Conceptual Foundations of the Rochester Biopsychosocial Model" (n. 21), an abbreviated version of which was published as "George Engel and Rochester's Biopsychosocial Tradition: Historical and Developmental Perspectives," in Richard Frankel, Timothy Quill, & Susan McDaniel, eds., *The Biopsychosocial Approach: Past, Present, Future* (Rochester: University of Rochester Press, 2003), pp. 199–219. Equally illuminating and more broadly gauged is Brown's "The Rise and Fall of American Psychosomatic Medicine," a presentation to the New York Academy of Medicine, November 29, 2000, www.human-nature.com/free-associations/riseandfall.html. For more focal consideration of the psychoanalytic aspects of Engel's biopsychosocial model, see Graeme J. Taylor, "Mind-Body-Environment: George Engel's Psychoanalytic Approach to Psychosomatic Medicine," *Aust. N. Zeal. J. Psychiatry*, 36:449–457, 2002.

and occasionally prescribers, to personify medication—these and other topics are all cogently set forth by Gutheil in a manner that has noth-ing to do with the analytic method or an "analytic process." Around the same time as Gutheil addressed the psychodynamic dimension of pharmacotherapy, another psychiatric educator, T. Byram Karasu, outlined an integrative model of combined psychotherapy and phar-macotherapy that remains edifying for the comprehensive list of di-agnostic, drug, psychotherapy, therapist, patient, and setting variables that it wove into an assessment of the differential effects and interac-tion of the two modalities. Stephen Adelman's illuminating study of the transitional properties of pills, including their function as "transi-tional objects" for borderline patients, dates from this same era.[25]

Analysts have added relatively little to this broadly psychothera-peutic literature in recent years, although contributions by Roose, Cabaniss, Sandberg, Tutter, and Rubin have a prescriptive (?) import that ranges beyond issues of analysis proper and are in the psychiat-ric tradition of Gutheil, Karasu, and Edelman.[26] Only Tutter, in an illuminating paper on "Medication as Object," makes explicit the relevance of psychoanalytic insights to prescribing outside the rari-fied world of long-term therapy:

25. Thomas G. Gutheil, "Improving Patient Compliance: Psychodynamics in Drug Prescribing," *Drug Ther.*, 7:82–83, 87, 89–91, 95, 1977; Thomas G. Gutheil, "Drug Therapy: Alliance and Compliance," *Psychosomatics*, 19:219–225, 1978; Thomas G. Gutheil, "The Psychology of Psychopharmacology," *Bull. Menn. Clin.*, 46:321–330, 1982; Toksoz B. Karasu, "Psychotherapy and Pharmacotherapy: Toward an Integrative Model," *Am. J. Psychiatry*, 139:1102–1113, 1982; Stephen A. Adelman, "Pills as Transitional Objects: A Dynamic Understanding of the Use of Medication in Psychotherapy," *Psychiatry*, 48:246–253, 1985.

26. Stephen P. Roose & Christopher M. Johannet, "Medication and Psychoanaly-sis: Treatments in Conflict," *Psychoanal. Inq.*, 18:606–620, 1998; Larry S. Sandberg, "Analytic Listening and the Act of Prescribing Medication," *Psychoanal. Inq.*, 18:621–638, 1998; Deborah L. Cabaniss, "Beyond Dualism: Psychoanalysis and Medication in the 21st Century," *Bull. Menn. Clin.*, 65:160–170, 2002; Deborah L. Cabaniss, "Shifting Gears: The Challenge to Teach Students to Think Psychodynamically and Psychopharmacologically at the Same Time," *Psychoanal. Inq.*, 18:639–656, 1998; Adele Tutter, "Medication as Object," *JAPA*, 54:781–804, 2006; Jeffrey Rubin, "Countertransference Factors in the Psychology of Psychopharmacology," *J. Am. Acad. Psychoanal.*, 29:565–573, 2001; Jeffrey Rubin, "Be Careful What You Wish For: Going Beyond Compliance," *J. Am. Acad. Psychoanal.*, 35:203–210, 2007.

The vast majority of patients who take medication do so outside of a psychotherapeutic context. Thus, the exploration of the unconscious meanings endowed with dynamic power that underlie questionable, often bewildering, behavior toward medication may be germane to such broad public health problems as medication noncompliance and chemical dependency.[27]

The role of "pharmacologic consultant" will surely not be superordinate in the professional lives of tomorrow's psychoanalysts, and I do not mean to exaggerate its significance. It is simply one example of how analysts may optimize marginality in a postanalytic era. Readers will hopefully adduce other optimizing clinical and consulting initiatives that take the field into wider therapeutic and public arenas. Such arenas, it may be hoped, will promote a kind of operational consensus that flattens theory-driven controversies and provides the field with much-needed breathing space outside the consulting room. They will be venues in which a pragmatic and intuitive psychoanalytic know-how—a know-how grounded not in one or another purchase on psychoanalytic theory and technique but in that insightful something that all well-trained analysts have in common—may come to the fore.

SOFAR is the largest such initiative to date, but it is preceded by noteworthy instances of individual initiative that have widened the orbit of psychoanalytic intervention in socially, educationally, and politically noteworthy ways. Kenneth Eisold has long argued for the relevance of psychoanalysis to organizational consulting and group work.[28] Vamık Volkan, who has focused on leader-follower relationships and the psychology of terrorism, utilizes a psychoanalytic perspective in devising strategies of inter-ethnic conflict resolution.[29]

27. Tutter, "Medication as Object" (n. 26), p. 802.

28. Kenneth Eisold, "Psychoanalysis Today: Implications for Organizational Consultations," *Free Assn.*, 6:174–191, 1996; Kenneth Eisold, "Psychoanalytic Perspectives on Organizational Consulting, Transference and Countertransference," *Human Rel.*, 56:475–490, 2003.

29. Vamık Volkan, *The Need to Have Enemies and Allies: From Clinical Practice to International Relationships* (Northvale, NJ: Aronson, 1988); Vamık Volkan, *Bloodlines: From Ethnic Pride to Ethnic Terrorism* (NY: Basic Books, 1998); Vamık Volkan, *Blind Trust: Large Groups and Their Leaders in Times of Crisis and Terror*

Back in the 1980s, Henri Parens and his colleagues began correlating mother-child relationships with the development of healthy "ego functions" in the child, and went on to develop and publish a workshop series aimed at the "prevention of experience-derived emotional disorders in children via parenting education."[30] Stuart Twemlow, a student of victim/victimizer/bystander interactive psychodynamics, has with his colleagues developed and implemented a multilevel, "pluralistic" psychoanalytic model for evaluating and treating violence in schools.[31] During my final decade at The Analytic Press, I was increasingly impressed with work that used the role of bodily experience in psychoanalytically oriented therapy as a basis for applying psychodynamic thinking to a variety of body-based treatment modalities as well as to pain management.[32]

(Charlottesville, VA: Pitchstone, 2004); Vamık Volkan, *Killing in the Name of Identity: A Study of Bloody Conflicts* (Charlottesville, VA: Pitchstone, 2006).

30. Henri Parens, "A Psychoanalytic Contribution Toward Rearing Emotionally Healthy Children: Education for Parenting," in J. M. Ross & W. A. Myers, eds., *New Concepts in Psychoanalytic Psychotherapy* (Washington, DC: American Psychiatric Press, 1988), pp. 120–138; Henri Parens, "Toward Preventing Experience-Derived Emotional Disorders: Education for Parenting," in Henri Parens & Selma Kramer, eds., *Prevention in Mental Health* (Northvale, NJ: Aronson, 1993), pp. 121–148; Henri Parens & Cecily Rose-Itkoff, *Parenting for Emotional Growth: The Workshop Series* (Philadelphia: Parenting for Emotional Growth, 1997); Henri Parens, Cecily Rose-Itkoff, Michael Pearlman, et al., "Into Our Fourth Decade of Prevention via Parenting Education: Where We Have Been, Where We're Going," *J. App. Psychoanal. Stud.*, 3:17–38, 2006.

31. Stuart W. Twemlow, Frank C. Sacco, & Preston Williams, "A Clinical and Interactionist Perspective on the Bully-Victim-Bystander Relationship," *Bull. Menn. Clin.*, 60:296–313, 1996; Stuart W. Twemlow, "The Roots of Violence: Converging Psychoanalytic Explanatory Models for Power Struggles and Violence in Schools," *Psychoanal. Quart.*, 69:741–785, 2000; Stewart W. Twemlow, Peter Fonagy, Frank C. Sacco, et al., "Creating a Peaceful School Learning Environment: A Controlled Study of an Elementary School Intervention to Reduce Violence," *Am. J. Psychiatry*, 158: 808–810, 2001; Stuart W. Twemlow & Jon Cohen, "Stopping School Violence," *J. App. Psychoanal. Stud.*, 5:117–124, 2003.

32. I have in mind Elaine Siegel, *Transformations: Countertransference During the Psychoanalytic Treatment of Incest, Real and Imagined* (Hillsdale, NJ: Analytic Press, 1996); Barbara Gerson, ed., *The Therapist as a Person: Life Crises, Life Choices, Life Experiences, and Their Effects on Treatment* (Hillsdale, NJ: Analytic Press, 1996);

These and similar initiatives exemplify the social conscience of individual psychoanalysts self-identified as "community psychoanalysts."[33] Their programs and the publications that describe them blur the line between psychoanalysis and psychodynamic thinking in heuristically valuable ways. They optimize the saliency of psychoanalytic insights to broader professional and lay constituencies and, in the process, provide venues for deploying marginality effectively. They garner psychoanalysis exactly the kind of public recognition it needs.

The problem is that these and other initiatives undertaken by American analysts have historically been marginalized within American psychoanalysis, where a tradition of community involvement and sociopolitical engagement never took root in the European manner. With the ascendancy of socialist-democratic governments following World War I, psychoanalytic free clinics were established in 10 European cities, Vienna, Berlin, Budapest, and London among them. The streamlining of analytic-type treatment (then termed "fractionary" psychoanalysis), teamed with the generosity of analysts who supported the clinics with donations in addition to providing no-cost and low-cost treatments, created a singular interlude in psychoanalytic history. "Between 1918 and 1938," observes Elizabeth Danto, who has chronicled the history of the free clinics, "psychoanalysis was neither impractical for working people, nor rigidly structured, nor luxurious in length."[34]

Alongside the free clinics, individual analysts spearheaded other programs under the sponsorship of reform-minded governments committed to the provision of social, educational, and medical services. In Vienna, where the Social Democrats controlled both municipal and

---

Lewis Aron & Frances Sommer Anderson, eds., *Relational Perspectives on the Body* (Hillsdale, NJ: Analytic Press, 1998); and Francis Sommer Anderson, ed., *Bodies in Treatment: The Unspoken Dimension* (NY: Analytic Press, 2008).

33. Stuart Twemlow is the principal exponent of the notion of the "community psychoanalyst." See Stuart W. Twemlow & Henri Parens, "Might Freud's Legacy Lie Beyond the Couch?" *Psychoanal. Psychol.*, 23:430–451, 2006, esp. at pp. 433–434 and 445–446.

34. Elizabeth Ann Danto, *Freud's Free Clinics: Psychoanalysis and Social Justice, 1918–1938* (NY: Columbia University Press, 2005), p. 2.

state governments from 1918 to1934,[35] the analyst August Aichhorn, with the financial backing of the Social Democratic Party, developed a network of child guidance clinics and later became chairman of the child guidance clinic of the Vienna Psychoanalytic Society.[36] A decade later, the Hungarian Franz Alexander journeyed to Boston's Judge Baker Guidance Center, where he spent nine months working with adolescent criminal offenders. In collaboration with William Healy, Director of the Judge Baker Foundation and pioneer of the American child guidance movement, Alexander published *Roots of Crime* in 1931; it remains one of the classic attempts to apply psychoanalysis to the practical management of delinquent behavior.

In Britain, the application of psychoanalysis to childhood emotional development in relation to mother-child bonding and wartime separation emerged during World War II, when Anna Freud, with her friend and colleague Dorothy Burlingham, founded the Hampstead War Nursery outside London in 1941, and then in 1947, with her colleague Kate Friedlaender, established the Hampstead Child Therapy Clinic and Course to treat children and their parents and to train a postwar generation of "child experts."[37] It was also in the postwar years that two British analysts, Siegfried Foulkes and Wilfred Bion, developed their respective frameworks for applying psychoanalysis to group therapy.[38]

35. After World War I, the shrunken Austrian state reorganized as a confederation of individual states, so that the city of Vienna became the state of Vienna in 1922 with administrative autonomy in education.

36. Aichhorn's work with delinquents in his clinics is detailed in *Wayward Youth* (NY: Viking, 1963 [1925]) and *Delinquency and Child Guidance: Selected Papers*, ed. O. Fleischmann et al., (NY: International Universities Press, 1964). For a discussion of Aichhorn's loosely psychoanalytic counseling techniques, which are compared with the techniques of Alfred Adler, who, beginning in 1920, established a parallel series of city-supported educational guidance clinics (*Erziehungsberatungsstellen*) in Vienna, see Paul E. Stepansky, *In Freud's Shadow: Adler in Context* (Hillsdale, NJ: Analytic Press, 1983), pp. 222–225.

37. For illuminating descriptions of the Hampstead War Nursery and Hampstead Child Therapy Clinic and Course, see Elisabeth Young-Bruehl, *Anna Freud: A Biography* (NY: Summit Books, 1988), pp. 246–257, 331–340.

38. S. H. Foulkes & E. J. Anthony, *Group Psychotherapy: The Psychoanalytic Approach* (London: Penguin, 1957); S. H. Foulkes, *Therapeutic Group Analysis* (Lon-

Even in France, where psychoanalysis carved its own torturously idiosyncratic path through the institutional and political thickets of worldwide psychoanalysis in the 1950s, a tradition of community involvement gained traction after the war. Immediately after the Liberation, prominent academics and psychoanalysts came together to establish an ambitious Center for the Study of the Sciences of Man. Funded by the analyst René Laforgue and with an active membership that included such analytic luminaries as Daniel Lagache and Jean Delay, the Center held weekly meetings and occasional retreats, where topics on the order of "The Destiny of Mankind" (October, 1947) were fearlessly tackled. The Center's journal, *Psyché: Revue Internationale de Psychanalyse et des Sciences de l'Homme*, edited by the novelist and psychoanalytic devotee Maryse Choisy, began monthly publication in November, 1946. Choisy's mission statement in the first issue foretold a new kind of psychoanalysis supremely well suited to war-torn France. Psychoanalysis, she held, was

> moving towards its constructive phase. According to the works of Jung and of Baudouin in Switzerland, of Laforgue in France and the researches of the British and American Schools, psychoanalysis offers interesting outlets into pedagogics, sociology, vocational training. Psychoanalysis allows one to glimpse, in some sort of a way, an unsuspected path towards collective happiness vainly beggared by moralists.[39]

In America, which escaped the ravages of both world wars, a *tradition* of community psychoanalysis failed to take hold. Nor was American psychoanalysis amenable to integration with alternative community-grounded visions that achieved prominence in the decades following World War II. The laudable and ill-fated community mental

---

don: Allen & Unwin, 1964); S. H. Foulkes, *Group-Analytic Psychotherapy: Methods and Principles* (London: Routledge, 1975); W. R. Bion, *Experiences in Groups and Other Papers* (NY: Basic Books, 1961); Malcolm Pines, ed., *Bion and Group Psychotherapy* (London: Routledge, 1985).

39. On France's postwar Center for the Study of the Sciences of Man, about which little has been written, see Alain de Mijolla, "France (1893–1965)" in Peter Kutter, ed., *Psychoanalysis International: A Guide to Psychoanalysis Throughout the World* (Stuttgart-Bad Cannstatt: Frommann-Holzboog, 1992), pp. 80–82, quoted at p. 81.

health movement of the 1960s is a case in point. A number of American analysts donated some time to community work, especially in the Los Angeles area.[40] But the APsaA distanced itself from the movement, and most APsaA members viewed it from the sidelines, content to pass judgment on the community psychiatrists, to applaud those few analytic colleagues who ventured into the community, and to underscore the analytic gifts the latter bestowed on their nonanalytic constituencies. Understanding of transference and countertransference between community psychiatrist and community groups was one such gift; it could only be understood, according to Irving Berlin, by those trained in individual psychotherapy and with the benefit of personal analysis.[41]

A few analysts of the time attempted to bridge the gap between psychoanalysis and community psychiatry, if only at the level of ideology. Consider the viewpoints of Bernard Bandler and Robert Wallerstein, both of whom addressed the American Psychiatric Association in May, 1967. Bandler juxtaposed the number of individual analysts who participated in community psychiatry with the official aloofness of their parent organization, which deemed the latter irrelevant to its central concern, i.e., the advancement of psychoanalysis, especially the maintenance of standards for training and practice. He contrasted this aloofness with the community-mindedness of analytic leaders of the 30s, 40s, and early 50s, especially analysts like William Menninger, Ralph Kaufman, and Roy Grinker, who were deeply identified with psychiatry and medicine and had adapted psychoanalysis to the needs of war. Bandler urged a return to this more embracing mindset. Just as postwar psychiatric educators understood the importance of analytic training for general psychiatric practice, so he now urged the value of analytic training, especially personal analysis, for psychiatrists destined for careers in the community. But he allowed that community psychiatry comprised areas of knowledge and competence far beyond what analysis had to offer. Indeed, the question of whether community psychiatry could scientifically advance psychoanalysis and contribute to analytic education was legitimate and open to exploration.[42]

40. Joseph G. Kepecs, "Psychoanalysis Today," *Arch. Gen. Psychiatry*, 18:161–168, 1968.

41. Irving N. Berlin, "Transference and Countertransference in Community Psychiatry," *Arch. Gen. Psychiatry*, 15:165–172, 1966.

42. Bernard Bandler, "The American Psychoanalytic Association and Community Psychiatry," *Am. J. Psychiatry*, 124:1037–1042, 1968.

Wallerstein, for his part, ceded that his analytic colleagues, defenders of "that bastion of individual treatment," were prone to react to the community mental health movement "defensively and negatively," and that this attitude accounted for the "real danger . . . that the new community mental health programs will grow up isolated from and conceptually antithetical to psychoanalytical thinking."[43]

Seeking, with Bandler, to dispel the widespread belief that community-related work was anathema to the analyst's identity, Wallerstein proffered his vision of a "psychoanalytically informed community mental health enterprise" that would be the hub of a consultative and referral network from which analysts would benefit. Such an enterprise, he held, would "generate more rather than less need for individual psychiatric care," so that analysis would retain "a very secure and unthreatened place in the shape of psychiatry during this new, hopefully successful, third revolution."[44] This accommodation was, to say the least, self-serving, since it urged psychoanalytic participation in community work by suggesting such work would generate referrals for psychoanalytic treatment.

Wallerstein sought an analytic outreach that would guide community mental health centers in professionally responsible ways, but the outreach never went beyond the role of analysts as mental health consultants and, more grandiosely, as "expert citizens" able to advise community centers on any and all areas of social policy that were health related. Beyond the gift of such guidance, analysts would remake community mental health centers in their image simply by remaining true to their analytic calling. Wallerstein conveys the sense of reaching for novel kinds of community participation that could not be articulated in a manner compatible with American psychoanalytic identity as it existed in the 1960s. What he leaves us with, therefore, is the appearance of novelty through verbal convolutions that evoke something grand but end where they begin: With the individual analyst bestowing psychodynamic largesse on others and taking referrals into analytic treatment:

If with this public health concept of a reaching out into the community, scrutinizing all of its institutional forms and the people who

43. Wallerstein, "Challenge of Community Mental Health" (n. 1), p. 1050.

44. Wallerstein, "Challenge of Community Mental Health" (n. 1), quoted at p. 1051.

fulfill them, with particular attention to the social breakdowns and the individuals at risk who comprise them, one combines a central available core of psychodynamically based individual treatment and a psychoanalytic guidance of the ramifying channels into the community along which the referrals for that individual treatment are made, then one has created what I am calling a psychoanalytic community mental health center.[45]

A year later, in May, 1968, the Executive Council of the American Psychoanalytic Association, perhaps heeding Bandler's and Wallerstein's advice, belatedly established a Standing Committee on Community Psychiatry, which proceeded to sponsor a Thursday discussion group on community psychiatry and psychoanalysis at subsequent annual meetings.[46] Wallerstein's sanguine vision of psychoanalysis in an era of community mental health centers otherwise had no discernible effect on the entrenched status quo. Certainly it did not prevent C. Knight Aldrich several years later from characterizing psychoanalysis and community psychiatry as antipodal forces whose collision was "as inevitable as that between free private enterprise and socialism."[47]

Unsurprisingly, the oxymoronic notion[48] of a psychoanalytic community mental health center never got off Wallerstein's drawing board. Indeed, his statement of intent only underscored the unnaturalness of analysts' assuming a therapeutic role *as analysts* outside the sacrosanc-

45. Wallerstein, "Challenge of Community Mental Health" (n. 1), p. 1053. Wallerstein borrowed the notion of analysts as "expert citizens" from H. Robert Blank, "Psychoanalysis and Community Mental Health," a position paper for the APsaA's committee on postgraduate development, presented in October, 1966.

46. On the APsaA's establishment of a Standing Committee on Community Psychiatry in 1968, See Ralph W. Wadeson, Jr., "Psychoanalysis in Community Psychiatry: Reflections on Some Theoretical Implications," *JAPA*, 23:177–189, 1975 at pp. 177–179. Incidentally, APsaA annual meetings run from Wednesday through Sunday morning, with many attendees arriving only for the weekend. A discussion group scheduled for Thursday would probably have attracted only a handful of attendees.

47. C. Knight Aldrich, "Some Issues in Community Mental Health – Psychoanalysis and Community Psychiatry: Confrontation or Collaboration?" *Contemp. Psychoanal.*, 7:138–146, 1971, quoted at p. 138.

48. It is not oxymoronic per se but oxymoronic in terms of how American psychoanalysts understood themselves and their profession in the 1960s.

tity of the 1960s consulting room. Despite occasional reports of psychoanalytically guided community interventions in the literature of the 1980s and 1990s, this self-limiting appraisal of the analyst's therapeutic potential (and obligation) persisted throughout the remaining three decades of the last century and into the new one. Then and now, analytic community initiatives tend to be filed away with other worthy marginalia as examples of "applied psychoanalysis," with some of the most promising recent instances of educational and community work sequestered away in small journals such as the *Journal of Applied Psychoanalytic Studies* or briefly noted in nonanalytic publications. *JAPA*, the *Psychoanalytic Quarterly*, and the *International Journal of Psycho-Analysis* have not exactly been at the frontlines in promulgating the work of those few analysts who are themselves at the sociopolitical frontlines.[49] Here, as in other respects, a fractionated journal literature has worked against the recognition of common interests, much less the creation of common ground.

The irony is that American psychoanalysis has marginalized the family of analytic initiatives that would help reposition the field's own global marginality in relation to the psychotherapeutic and psychoeducational mainstream.[50] The field, in the form of its institutions and

49. Among recent publications, the work of Mark B. Borg, Jr. deserves special mention. Borg, an interpersonal psychoanalyst, was a member of an intervention team that worked with residents of a South Central Los Angeles housing community for a four-year period following the Rodney King–related riots of 1992. In a series of illuminating studies—none of which appeared in *JAPA*, *Psychoanalytic Quarterly*, or *International Journal of Psycho-Analysis*—Borg utilized interpersonal concepts of community character, community-structured self system (per Harry Stack Sullivan), transference, countertransference, and enactment to understand the dynamics of change in community crisis intervention. See Mark B. Borg, Jr., "Community Group-Analysis: A Post-Crisis Synthesis," *Group-Anal.*, 36:233–246, 2003; "The Psychoanalyst as Community Practitioner," *Psychologist-Psychoanalyst*, 22:26–34, 2003; "Venturing Beyond the Consulting Room: Psychoanalysis in Community Crisis Intervention," *Contemp. Psychoanal.*, 40:147–174, 2004; and "Community Analysis: A Case Study Examining Transference and Countertransference in Community Intervention," *Int. Forum Psychoanal.*, 14:5–15, 2005.

50. "We have found that being helpful [within the community] may be the best way psychoanalysts can make their mission known to the lay public. When people feel they are being helped, they become appreciative, even respectful, of us, of our training and clinical background—by then being a psychoanalyst no longer makes us some 'ivory tower egghead.'" Stuart W. Twemlow & Henri Parens, "Might Freud's Legacy Lie Beyond the Couch?" *Psychoanal. Psychol.*, 23:430–451, 2006, quoted at p. 435.

leadership, has allowed allegiance to one or another psychoanalytic school to sustain a professional identity that is not only analytic but *intra-analytic*. Perhaps this is the most dire consequence of fractionation: That it has rendered analysts satisfied with part-identities and insensitive to the urgent need for self transformation in socially responsive ways that will command public respect and political attention.

What do analysts want? If they want to survive as a profession as opposed to a federation of schools whose individual members have something or other in common—the something depending on which faction provides the answer—then various strategies of medical and clinical outreach, pedagogical input, and conflict resolution must be woven into their professional identities. I am of a mind with Eisold, who adduces two strategies for reconsidering the "psychoanalytic project":

(1) The path of partner in the psychotherapies, offering the benefits of insight and inquiry in the treatment of psychiatric disorders; (2) A comparable partnership in the "applied fields" of organizational, family, and group work, allied with other disciplines and professions.[51]

However the psychoanalytic project is to be reconsidered, it must surely be reconsidered and then reconceived in one way or another. I am increasingly convinced that the survival of the profession in the foreseeable future lies beyond the couch and outside the consulting room.[52] Equally, it lies outside the realm of outcome studies and single-

---

51. Kenneth Eisold, "The Profession of Psychoanalysis: Past Failure and Future Possibilities," *Contemp. Psychoanal.*, 39:557–582, 2003, quoted at p. 579. Eisold adduces a third pathway that I consider too amorphous to serve as a survival strategy, viz., "The path of inquiry into false adaptations, social identities that block authentic and full human experience."

52. I share this decidedly minority viewpoint with Twemlow and Parens, who hold that "until psychoanalysis is recognized as a body of knowledge that can be applied to understanding and solving pressing community and social problems, rather than hold on to its limited application in the treatment of patients with specific psychiatric diseases, or in training those who treat them, it will lose its pioneering relevance in the 'social brain' initiative in the 21st century." Twemlow & Parens, "Might Freud's Legacy Lie Beyond the Couch?" (n. 50), p. 431. Several years earlier Renik suggested that analysts might attenuate their "pointless internecine squabbling" if they "re-

case research that strive to meet the ambiguous standards of evidence-based medicine, however useful such studies may prove over time.[53] Psychoanalysts, whose legal prerogatives and ethical obligations fall back on preanalytic professional identities as psychologists, social workers, or psychiatrists, may envision themselves as analysts of this or that type and characterize their therapeutic work as "psychoanalytic" to their hearts' content. They will survive. Indeed, training and supervising analysts and "senior" analysts of reputation may continue to have broadly "analytic" practices for another decade or two. But the survival of psychoanalysis as a self-sustaining profession hinges on a different set of factors. Ultimately, it will not be a matter of how psychoanalysts define their field(s) but of how sympathetically the public embraces them as alternative providers in an era of managed care, fiscal restraint, brief cognitive-behavioral treatment, and psychopharmacology. And the public (and the politicians it elects) will finally care less about how analysts think of themselves and of their field than with how analysts act as concerned citizens and psychotherapists who happen to enjoy the benefits of one or another kind of psychoanalytic training.

---

orient[ed] [them]selves toward filling a public need." At this point in time, I see no way of doing so without actually going public in the manner of Twemlow, Parens, and others. Owen Renik, "Commentary on 'Psychoanalytic Discourse at the Turn of Our Century: A Plea for a Measure of Humility,'" *JAPA*, 51S:119–121, 2003, quoted at p. 120.

53. Edelson pinned his hope for the eventual scientific validation of psychoanalytic hypotheses on the evidential value of single-case study, a methodological project of small interest throughout the 90s but now taken up by the Ulm Psychoanalytic Process Research Study Group. See Marshall Edelson, *Psychoanalysis: A Theory in Crisis* (Chicago: University of Chicago Press, 1988), chaps. 11 & 13; Horst Kächele, Joseph Schachter, & Helmut Thomä, *From Psychoanalytic Narrative to Empirical Single Case Research: Implications for Psychoanalytic Practice* (NY: Routledge, 2009).

Acknowledgments

A portion of this book was previewed in a series of presentations to the participants in an online symposium, "Uncommon Ground and the Possibilities for our Psychoanalytic Future: An Online Symposium with Paul Stepansky and Invited Guests," hosted by The Psychoanalytic Connection during the spring of 2007. It is a pleasure to thank Todd Essig, founder and owner of Psychoanalytic Connection, for his excellent job putting this event together and moderating the lively discussions that ensued. I am equally grateful to the "Uncommon Ground" participants for their discerning reactions, positive and negative, to my ideas. I learned much from them and my book, whatever its limitations, is stronger for their input. Among my several symposium interviewees were Stuart Pizer and Steven Cooper, who shared their experiences devising and implementing "comparative psychoanalysis" curricula at their respective training institutes. I thank them both for permission to quote from these interviews in chapter 7.

Chapter 3 on the rise and fall of psychoanalytic book publishing was a project unto itself. It relies on sales data generously provided by, among others, Joann Miller (Perseus Books); Justine Pierce and Melissa Nierman (Harvard University Press); Meredith Farmer Grubbs (Yale University Press); Eric Rohmann (Princeton University Press); Bill Foo (Other Press); Peter Dimock (Columbia University Press); Sara Sparger and Ellen Gibson (University of Chicago Press); and Zachary Woolfe (Farrar, Straus and Giroux). Kristopher Spring, formerly my assistant at The Analytic Press and now Assistant Editor at Routledge, was helpful in ways that far transcend the provision of sales data on TAP and Routledge titles. I thank him for keeping me in the loop, publishing wise, for his own astute reflections on psychoanalytic publishing, and for many acts of kindness in support of my research and writing.

I trust readers will understand that the sales data in chapter 3 are proprietary to the publishers and not to the authors of the many books in question. Once apprised of the scholarly grounds of my request, publishers were generally forthcoming with sales information when it was available. Often, particularly with books published more than 20 years ago, it was not. Withal, I have done the best I could with the data made available to me. The major university presses were most accommodating and typically assigned a member of the sales department to work with me ongoingly. Of all the publishers I contacted, only two—Johns Hopkins University Press and American Psychiatric Press—refused to cooperate. Johns Hopkins University Press deemed sales data a confidential matter and would not provide me with any information on their several psychoanalytic titles. American Psychiatric Press, Inc., after giving me a sales figure for Person, Cooper, and Gabbard's *American Psychiatric Publishing Textbook of Psychoanalysis* (2005), refused any further cooperation. APPI, through its Board of Directors, then took the unusual step of advising at least one of its authors not to supply me with sales information from royalties reports, thereby becoming the only publisher actively to obstruct my research.

Individual authors were otherwise most cooperative in consulting back royalties statements (as well as their memories) and occasionally contacting their publishers on my behalf. Among those individuals who helped me along in this manner were Jessica Benjamin, Morris Eagle, Rainer Funk (representing the estate of Erich Fromm), Arnold Goldberg, Adolf Grünbaum, Thomas Kohut (for his father, Heinz Kohut), Nancy McWilliams, Thomas Ogden, David Shapiro, Paul Wachtel, and Ernest Wolf.

Needless to say, the rounded sales numbers provided in chapter 2 are based on the information I received at a given point in time. In certain instances, I have sought and obtained updated figures over the course of this project, but books are bought and sold continuously, and the sales totals of recently published books will inevitably have increased since I obtained these data. I am satisfied this sales growth has been incremental, and that the data I provide are easily accurate enough to document the trends I discern and to sustain the argument I make.

An early version of chapter 3 on the rise and fall of psychoanalytic book publishing in America was presented to the Rapaport-Klein Study Group in Stockbridge, Massachusetts on June, 10, 2007, and I remain deeply appreciative both for the warm reception I received and for the stimulating commentary that my presentation elicited. I am especially grateful to Craig Piers, a member of the Study Group, for alerting me to the importance (and sales) of the books of David Shapiro and for putting me in touch with Dr. Shapiro, who kindly related to me the circumstances attendant to the writing and publishing of his classic *Neurotic Styles* of 1965 and also provided an estimate of total English-language sales.

For membership information on their respective organizations, which enters into other chapters of the book, I am grateful to Susan Kuper (American Psychiatric Association); Carolyn Gatto and Debbie Steinke (American Psychoanalytic Association); and Nancy McWilliams and Louis Rothschild (Psychoanalysis Division, American Psychological Association). I am also grateful to Nadine Levinson and David Tuckett, Directors of Psychoanalytic Electronic Publishing, Inc., for the information they provided and for their support of this project.

I am appreciative to the following scholars for sending me offprints of their articles, answering my queries, offering their thoughts, pointing me in promising directions, and otherwise providing collegial support: Susan Abrams, Edwin Beschler, Edward M. Brown, Theodore M. Brown, Sandra Buechler, John Burnham, Flurin Condrau, Margaret Crastnopol, Norman Daniels, Diana Diamond, Marguerite Dupree, Hendrik Edelman, James Edmonson, Howard Faulkner, John Gach, Ralph Harrington, Joel Howell, Leon Kamin, Douglas Lanska, Ruth Leys, Steven Martin, Jean Meike, Thomas Ogden, Arthur Pomponio, Kenneth Reich, Guenter Risse, Peter Rudnytsky, Oliver Sacks, Anthony Travis, Stuart Twemlow, and Margaret Winker. Special thanks to Professor Olga Damidova of Herzen State Pedagogical University (St. Petersburg, Russia), the editor of Abram Kagan's diaries, who patiently and thoroughly replied to my list of queries about Dr. Kagan who, as founder of International Universities Press in 1943, brought psychoanalytic book publishing to these shores.

My friends (and former authors) David Newman, Frank Summers, and Philip Bromberg generously found time to read my chapters and share their reactions. They have been unfailingly encouraging about the importance of my work, as has Nancy McWilliams, another gifted analyst and friend who read early versions of the chapters and urged me to continue with the project. I am grateful to Paolo Migone, whose close reading of "The Rise and Fall of Psychoanalytic Book Publishing in America," pursuant to translating it into Italian, alerted me to a number of small errors. Finally, I owe an immense debt of gratitude to John Kerr, my colleague of many years at The Analytic Press, who brought his luminous intelligence and discerning editorial eye to bear on the entire manuscript. He is a remarkable editor and a great friend.

Throughout this project, indeed throughout all my projects, I have been buoyed by a family holding environment of uncommon strength and resilience. It comprises, in addition to my wife and sons and daughter-in-law Jane Kohuth, my remarkable parents, Selma and William Stepansky, and my accomplished brothers and sisters-in-law: David Stepansky, Debra Schwartz, Robert Stepansky, Joyce Rubino, Alan Stepansky, and Elissa Sanders. My beloved father, William Stepansky, passed away in November, 2008, shortly before my manuscript entered production. He inspired me and guided me throughout my life, and he especially relished my scholarly achievements. Now, sadly, I must content myself with the memory of his delight and pride when I related to him, not long before his death, that I had found a publisher for this work.

The publisher in question is the estimable Other Press. I thank Judith Gurewich, the publisher, for her generous estimation of my work, Mimi Winick for her enthusiastic commitment to the project, and Yvonne Cárdenas and Don McConnell for skillfully seeing it through production. Finally, I thank my friend and designer of many years, Andrea Schettino, for lending her fine gifts to the cover design.

I am immensely proud of my sons, Michael Stepansky and Jonathan Stepansky, who have chosen to pursue careers of community service to disadvantaged groups in society—Michael as a Director of Housing and Employment in the Department of Mental Health of Massachusetts, and Jonathan as a professional counselor doing remedial work with convicts, perpetrators of domestic violence, delinquent adolescents, and individuals with cognitive impairments. Their lives inspire me on a daily basis and no doubt enter into the thoughts with which I conclude this book.

To my wife, Deane Rand Stepansky, who sustains me day in and day out, who is my *cara immortalis*, acknowledgment fails, since words journey but briefly down a well of feeling of inexpressible depth. Let me recur, though, to words offered her in tribute in New Haven in December, 1973. They come from Book I of Baldassare Castiglione's

Book of the Courtier (1528), where the author pays homage to the hostess of the conversations to ensue, my lady Duchess, Elisabetta Gonzaga:

> And impressing herself thus upon those about her, she seemed to attune us all to her own quality and tone; accordingly every man strove to follow this pattern, taking as it were a rule of beautiful behavior from the presence of so great and virtuous a lady; whose highest qualities I do not now purpose to recount, they not being my theme and being well known to all the world, and far more because I could not express them with either tongue or pen; and those that perhaps might have been somewhat hid, fortune, as if wondering at such rare virtue, chose to reveal through many adversities and stings of calamity, so as to give proof that in the tender breast of woman, in company with singular beauty, there may abide prudence and strength of soul, and all those virtues that even among stern men are very rare.

Journal Abbreviations in Notes

Acad. Med.	Academic Medicine
Acad. Psychiatry	Academic Psychiatry
Am. Anthro.	American Anthropologist
Am. Imago	American Imago
Am. J. Orthopsy.	American Journal of Orthopsychiatry
Am. J. Psychiatry	American Journal of Psychiatry
Am J. Sociol.	American Journal of Sociology
Am. Psychol.	American Psychologist
Ann. Intern. Med.	Annals of Internal Medicine
Ann. Neurol.	Annals of Neurology
Ann. Psychoanal.	The Annual of Psychoanalysis
Ann. Rev. Sociol.	Annual Review of Sociology
Antitrust Bull.	Antitrust Bulletin
Arch. Gen. Psychiatry	Archives of General Psychiatry
Arch. Int. Med.	Archives of Internal Medicine
Arch. Neurol.	Archives of Neurology
Arch. Neurol. Psychiatry	Archives of Neurology and Psychiatry
Austral. N. Zeal. J. Psychiatry	Australian and New Zealand Journal of Psychiatry
Austral. Psychiatry	Australasian Psychiatry
Bioethics	Bioethics
BMJ	BMJ (formerly British Medical Journal)
Brain Behav. Sci.	Brain and Behavioral Sciences
Brit. Heart J.	British Heart Journal
Brit. J. Anaes.	British Journal of Anaesthesia
Bull. Am. Psychoanal. Assn.	Bulletin of the American Psychoanalytic Association
Bull. Assn. Psychoanal. Med.	Bulletin of the Association for Psycho-analytic Medicine
Bull. Hist. Med.	Bulletin of the History of Medicine
Bull. Menn. Clin.	Bulletin of the Menninger Clinic
Can. Med. Assn. J.	Canadian Medical Association Journal

Chest	Chest
Chron. Rev.	The Chronicle Review
Circ.	Circulation
Clin. J.	Clinical Journal
Clin. Neurosci. Res.	Clinical Neuroscience Research
Comp. Psychiatry	Comprehensive Psychiatry
Contemp. Psychoanal.	Contemporary Psychoanalysis
Develop. Neuropsych.	Developmental Neuropsychology
Develop. Psychol.	Developmental Psychology
Drug. Ther.	Drug Therapy
Ethics Behav.	Ethics and Behavior
Found. Sci.	Foundations of Science
Free Assn.	Free Associations
Group	Group
Group-Anal.	Group Analysis
Hist. Theory	History and Theory
Hosp. Com. Psychiatry	Hospital and Community Psychiatry
Human Rel.	Human Relations
Infant. J. Men. Health	Infant Journal of Mental Health
Int. Forum Psychoanal.	International Forum of Psychoanalysis
Int. J. Osteo. Med.	International Journal of Osteopathic Medicine
Int. J. Psycho-Anal.	International Journal of Psycho-Analysis
Int. J. Psychoanal. Self Psychol.	International Journal of Psychoanalytic Self Psychology
Int. Pol. Sci. Rev.	International Political Science Review
Int. Rev. Psycho-Anal.	International Review of Psycho-Analysis
Isis	Isis
J. Alt. Complem. Med.	Journal of Alternative and Complementary Medicine
J. Am. Acad. Psychoanal.	Journal of the American Academy of Psychoanalysis and Dynamic Psychiatry
J. Am. B. Fam. Prac.	Journal of the American Board of Family Practice
J. Am. Hist.	Journal of American History
JAMA	Journal of the American Medical Association
J. Am. Osteo. Assn.	Journal of the American Osteopathic Association
JAPA	Journal of the American Psychoanalytic Association

J. App. Psychoanal. Stud.	Journal of Applied Psychoanalytic Studies
J. Can. Psychiat. Assn.	Journal of the Canadian Psychiatric Association
J. Clin. Psychiatry	Journal of Clinical Psychiatry
J. Clin. Psychoanal.	Journal of Clinical Psychoanalysis
J. Clin. Psychopharm.	Journal of Clinical Psychopharmacology
J. Contemp. Hist.	Journal of Contemporary History
J. Dem.	Journal of Democracy
J. Gen. Phil. Sci.	Journal for General Philosophy of Science
J. Hist. Behav. Sci.	Journal of the History of the Behavioral Sciences
J. Hist. Med. Allied Sci.	Journal of the History of Medicine and Allied Sciences
J. Hist. Neurosci.	Journal of the History of the Neurosciences
J. Kan. Med. Soc.	Journal of the Kansas Medical Society
J. Ment. Sci.	Journal of Mental Science
J. Nerv. Ment. Dis.	Journal of Nervous and Mental Disease
J. Neuropsy. Clin. Neurosci.	Journal of Neuropsychiatry and Clinical Neuroscience
J. Osteo. Phys. Surg. Cal.	Journal of Osteopathic Physicians and Surgeons of California
J. Pain Sym. Man.	Journal of Pain and Symptom Management
J. Physiol.	The Journal of Physiology
J. Pol. Hist.	Journal of Policy History
J. Psychiatry Law	Journal of Psychiatry and Law
J. Psychol. Anthro.	Journal of Psychological Anthropology
J. Spec. Phil.	Journal of Speculative Philosophy
Logos	Logos
Med. Anthro. Quart.	Medical Anthropology Quarterly
Med. Hist.	Medical History
Med. Rev.	Medical Review
Monist	The Monist
Move. Dis.	Movement Disorders
N. Eng. J. Med.	New England Journal of Medicine
NY State J. Med.	New York State Journal of Medicine
Neuro-Psychoanal.	Neuro-Psychoanalysis
Neurol.	Neurology

Neuron	Neuron
Noûs	Noûs
Osiris, 2nd ser.	Osiris, 2nd series
Phenom. Cog. Sci.	Phenomenology and the Cognitive Sciences
Phil. Sci.	Philosophy of Science
Phil. Soc. Sci.	Philosophy of the Social Sciences
Pract. Neurol.	Practical Neurology
Psyche	Psyche
Psychiat. Clin. N. Am.	Psychiatric Clinics of North America
Psychiat. Quart.	The Psychiatric Quarterly
Psychiat. Svs.	Psychiatric Services
Psychiatry	Psychiatry
Psychoanal. Contemp. Th.	Psychoanalysis and Contemporary Thought
Psychoanal. Dial.	Psychoanalytic Dialogues
Psychoanal. Inq.	Psychoanalytic Inquiry
Psychoanal. Psychol.	Psychoanalytic Psychology
Psychoanal. Quart.	Psychoanalytic Quarterly
Psychoanal. Rev.	The Psychoanalytic Review
Psychoanal. Study Child	The Psychoanalytic Study of the Child
Psychol. Clinic	The Psychological Clinic
Psychologist-Psychoanalyst	Psychologist-Psychoanalyst
Psychosomatics	Psychosomatics
Psychosom. Med.	Psychosomatic Medicine
Scand. Psychoanal. Rev.	Scandinavian Psychoanalytic Review
Soc. Forum	Sociological Forum
Soc. Hist. Med.	Social History of Medicine
Soc. Quart.	Sociological Quarterly
Soc. Rel.	Sociology of Religion
Soc. Sci. Med.	Social Science and Medicine
Stud. Hist. Phil. Sci.	Studies in the History and Philosophy of Science
Tech. Cult.	Technology and Culture
Theory Soc.	Theory and Society

Medical Glossary

A brief listing of technical terms, especially medical and biological terms, found in *Psychoanalysis at the Margins*.

Akathisia: Drug-induced motor restlessness, accompanied by quivering and an urge to keep moving about. It is a common side effect of antipsychotic medications.

Allopathy: Samuel Hahnemann, the founder of homeopathy, coined this term to designate orthodox or "regular" medicine and to differentiate it from his own system of homeopathy. According to Hahnemann, regular medicine was allopathic because it used medications that created effects different from the symptoms of the disease, unlike homeopathy, which prescribed minute quantities of drugs that created an effect similar to that of the disease.

Amines: Organic compounds in which nitrogen is the key atom.

Atrial fibrillation: In cardiology, disorganized electrical conduction in the upper heart chambers, or atria, which results in ineffective pumping of blood into the lower heart chambers, or ventricles. Atrial fibrillation manifests itself as a particular type of heartbeat (arrhythmia) characterized by an extremely fast, irregular rhythm; the heart quivers or fibrillates. This type of arrhythmia was discovered in 1898 by the Scottish physician James Mackenzie, who initially termed it "auricular paralysis."

Biopsychosocial model: Heir to the psychoanalytically grounded psychosomaticism of the 1940s and 1950s, the biopsychosocial model of the 1970s represented an attempt to conceptualize medical illness in terms of interacting psychological, social, and biological factors. This "systems"-based approach to patient care was a counterpoise to the biomedical reductionism that dominated medical training in the 1960s and 70s. The architect of the model was George Engel, and the model was implemented in medical education and in residency and fellowship programs at Engel's University of Rochester School of Medicine.

Catecholamine hypothesis: The theory that brain levels of catecholamines (biogenic amines such as norepinephrine, dopamine, and serotonin that function as neurotransmitters) account for mood disorders, especially depression. The theory was famously set forth in 1965 by Joseph Schildkraut, who cited research suggesting that diminished levels of norepinephrine were associated with depression.

Chiropractic: The alternative healing modality founded by David D. Palmer around 1897. According to Palmer, all disease is caused by vertebral misalignments (subluxations) that block the flow of "innate intelligence," the vital force which, according to the magnetic healers of the time, enabled the body to cure itself. Treatment of disease was through spinal manipulation (termed chiropractic "adjustment") to effect vertebral alignment and restore the flow of innate intelligence.

Chloroform: Volatile liquid haloform ($CHCl_3$), which is formed by treating alcohol with chlorine and an alkali. Chloroform was first used to induce general anesthesia in women in childbirth by James Young Simpson in 1847. In the decades that followed, its effectiveness was offset by its tendency to depress cardiac functioning, which often led to cardiac arrest and occasionally to chloroform death.

Clinical polygraph (aka Ink polygraph): Developed by James Mackenzie in 1906, the ink polygraph was a sphygmograph or blood-pressure reading device connected by rubber tubing to two separate Marey tambours (drums with elastic rubber heads), one placed on the jugular vein in the neck and the other on the radial artery on the forearm. The device allowed simultaneous recordings of venous and arterial pulse via tracings on a small smoked drum or strips of smoked paper. With this simple mechanical device, Mackenzie made significant observations on the origin of premature contraction of the heart (extrasystole), heart block, and the action of digitalis in atrial fibrillation.

Clinico-anatomical method (pathological anatomy): The effort to identify via postmortem dissection the tissular pathology that corresponded to the symptomatology and clinical course of hospitalized patients. It was developed in the first half of the nineteenth century by French pathologists of the Paris clinical school.

Connectionism: The neuropsychological theory that the connections among brain cells, which give rise to neural network systems, mediate thought and govern behavior.

Direct auscultation: The method of listening to the sounds of the heart and other internal organs directly with the human ear pressed against the body surface. It was superseded by mediate auscultation via the stethoscope, which René Laënnec introduced in 1816.

DSM: Shorthand for the American Psychiatric Association's *Diagnostic and Statistical Manual,* containing the official nomenclature for classifying mental disorders and behaviors in the United States. DSM has gone through four major revisions since its first publication in 1952, each of which retains its chronological position in referencing, i.e., DSM-I, DSM-II, DSM-III, DSM-IV. DSM-I and DSM-II adopted a system of classification that was broadly psychoanalytic, whereas DSM-III, published in 1980, was an effort to render psychiatric diagnosis more scientific by replacing psychodynamic categories with descriptive, behavioral categories associated with the approach of Emil Kraepelin. The "neo-Kraepelin" approach was carried over to DSM-IV, which was released in 1994.

Dudgeon sphygmograph: The sphygmograph invented by the British homeopath Robert Ellis Dudgeon in 1882 and widely used in the two decades to follow. It recorded and measured the pulse as a curve by transmitting movement from the radial artery onto a paper trace. The tiny movements from the radial artery were amplified through to the recording needle via a weighted pulley while a clockwork mechanism turned a roller of paper under the needle that recorded the amplified trace.

Dynamic systems theory (aka Chaos theory, Complexity theory): A scientific theory, derived from biology and mathematics, that explains the self-organization of systems in terms of interacting components that form evolving structures. These structures exhibit a hierarchy of properties that are emergent, i.e., that do not exist in any of the components that jointly form the system and only come into existence as higher-order properties of the system.

Dynamograph: In neurology, a dynamometer to which a device that automatically registers muscular force is attached.

Dynamometer: In neurology, a device that measures muscular force or power. Simple dynamometers typically utilize a spring to be compressed or a weight to be sustained by the force applied, with the force denoted by an index or measure.

Dyskinesia: In neurology, abnormal voluntary muscle movements, which often take the form of fragmentary or incomplete movements.

Electrocardiography (ECG or EKG): The recording of variations of electrical potential caused by the electrical activity of the heart muscle. These variations are detected at the body surface and registered graphically. Human electrocardiography was demonstrated by the British physician Augustus D. Waller around 1887, and the first clinically usable electrocardiograph, which utilized a string galvanometer, was invented by the Dutch physiologist Willem Einthoven, who described it in 1901.

Electroencephalography (EEG): The recording of electric currents in the brain via electrodes applied to the scalp, the surface of the brain, or within the brain. As a method of examining brain activity, EEG is characterized by its poor spatial resolution but very high time resolution. This activity was first recorded by Hans Berger, a Swiss inventor and aircraft manufacturer, in 1928.

Electromyography: Tests that measure muscle response to nerve stimulation, usually via surface or needle electrodes. Such tests are used to evaluate muscle weakness and to determine whether any such weakness is due to the muscles or to the nerves that supply them.

Evidence-based medicine (EBM): The approach to medical care according to which specific treatments must be justified on the basis of data derived from clinical trials and population studies. EBM represents the attempt to subordinate the allegedly unscientific art of medical decision-making to "hard" scientific criteria bearing on clinical efficacy.

Hemocytometer: An apparatus for counting the number of cells in a quantity of blood. A hemocytometer typically consists of a graduated pipette for drawing and diluting the blood and a ruled glass slide on which the cells are counted under a microscope.

Hemoglobinometer: An apparatus for measuring the hemoglobin content of blood by comparing the test sample with a solution of known strength and normal color.

Homeopathy: The alternative healing modality founded by Samuel Hahnemann at the end of the eighteenth century. According to Hahnemann, the treatment of disease followed two governing principles: (1) *similia similibus curantur*, or the curative action of "similars" that produced in attenuated form the same symptoms caused by the disease; and (2) the effectiveness of minute doses of such "similars," since in illness, according to Hahnemann, the body is vastly more sensitive to drugs than in health.

Hydropathy: The cold water cure. The alternative healing modality developed by the Austrian farmer Vincinz Priessnitz in Germany during the 1820s and introduced to the world via the hydropathic institution he opened in his native village of Gräfenberg in 1829. Priessnitz and his followers treated diseases by the copious use of water, administered both internally and externally, in the belief that skin bombarded by a battery of wet sheets, baths, and douches stimulated the nervous system and in the process mobilized the body's natural capacity to heal itself (the *vis medicatrix naturae*). Priessnitz's system reached Britain and America in the early 1840s and achieved considerable popularity. By the early 1850s, America had a national professional organization and a publication (*The Water-Cure Journal*) with a circulation of over 50,000; it would eventually grow to nearly 100,000.

Mediate auscultation: The method of listening to the sounds of the heart and other internal organs via an instrument (viz., the stethoscope) that amplifies sounds that would otherwise be less audible or totally inaudible. The French physician René Laënnec discovered the diagnostic use of mediate auscultation in 1816 and published his *Treatise on Mediate Auscultation* in 1819.

Mind-body therapy (MBT): Medical interventions that use various techniques to facilitate the mind's ability to affect bodily function and symptoms. Relaxation, meditation, imagery, hypnosis, and biofeedback are among the most widely used MBTs.

Monoamine: A molecule that contains one amine group, especially one that is a neurotransmitter. All monoamines derive from amino acids and the thyroid hormones.

Monoamine oxidase inhibitors (MAOIs): The group of antidepressant drugs that affect mood by preventing the enzyme monoamine oxidase (discovered in 1938) from oxidizing (breaking down) adrenaline, norepinephrine, epinephrine, and serotonin, thereby allowing these monoamines to build up in brain centers. The side effects of MAOIs, which include severe interactions with other drugs and food-derived amines, make their medical use difficult. The first MAOI, iproniazid (Marsilid, Wellbutrin), was synthesized by Herbert Fox and John Gibas at the Hoffman-La Roche laboratories in Nutley, New Jersey, in 1951 and released in the U.S. in 1957.

Naturopathy: The alternative healing modality founded by Benedict Lust in 1901. It held that all diseases were caused by internal poisoning, which meant that all therapy had to be directed toward inner cleansing.

Neural transmission, reticularist theory of: The theory of neural transmission, associated with Camillo Golgi and Joseph von Gerlach, that nervous impulses travel along neuronal chains in which individual nerve cells (neurons) make direct contact with one another.

Neural transmission, synaptic theory of: The theory of neural transmission, associated with Santiago Ramón y Cajal, according to which nervous impulses travel along neuronal chains in which individual nerve cells (neurons) are separated by a space (a synapse).

Neurocalometer: A handheld instrument introduced by chiropractor B. J. Palmer in 1924. The neurocalometer was claimed to measure temperature differentials on either side of the spinal column. According to Palmer, such differentials signified the presence of vertebral misalignment or "subluxation," since impinged nerves allegedly caused inflammation and hence higher temperatures.

Neuroleptics: Antipsychotic medications whose calming effect reduces confusion and agitation in psychotics but is also associated with apathy, lack of initiative, and limited range of emotion.

Neuronal group selection (aka **Neural Darwinism):** The theory of brain functioning put forth by the neuroscientist Gerald Edelman. According to the theory, the nervous system in each individual operates as a selective system resembling natural selection in evolution but operating through different mechanisms. The theory seeks to unify perception, action, and learning by positing a fundamental neural basis for the categorization of things in the world.

Osteopathy: The alternative healing modality developed by Andrew Taylor Still in the mid-1870s. According to osteopathy (from the Greek *osteon* [bone] and *pathos* [to suffer]), vertebral or other bony lesions caused disease by interrupting arterial blood flow. Therapy consisted of manipulation to relieve the obstruction and restore circulation.

Opsonic index: A measure of the phagocytotic potency of blood serum as a ratio of the average number of bacteria ingested per white blood cell in bacterially infected serum versus the average number ingested in normal blood. It was championed by Almroth Wright and other early twentieth-century bacteriologists as a reliable way of diagnosing infectious illnesses.

Opsonization: A process that facilitates phagocytosis (the engulfing and ingesting of bacteria by white blood cells) by coating the bacteria with an antibody for which phagocytes express receptors.

Percussion: In medicine, the act of tapping a body surface in order to obtain information about the organs beneath the surface via the sound emitted or the sensation conveyed to the fingers. The diagnostic value of thorax percussion (percussion of the chest) was discovered by the Viennese physician Leopold Auenbrugger in 1754.

Phagocytosis: The engulfing and digesting of bacteria or other foreign bodies in the bloodstream or tissues by phagocytes such as white blood cells.

Physico-Medicalism (Neo-Thomsonism): A mid-nineteenth-century variant of botanic medicine that espoused herbal cures of Indian, Shaker, or Thomsonian origin. Physico-Medicalism differed from Thomsonism in advocating formal education for its practitioners.

Presystolic murmur: A heart murmur heard at the end of ventricular diastole (i.e., the time between ventricular contractions when the ventricles fill with blood), which is usually due to obstruction at either the left or right atrioventricular opening.

Psychotropic: Literally a chemical substance that can influence human consciousness. Psychotropics, more commonly, "psychotropic drugs," denote the family of medications that influence mood, feeling states, and/or behavior. Psychotropic drugs are also referred to as psychoactive or psychiatric medications.

Radial pulse: The pulse at the radial artery, usually felt in the wrist.

Reflex hammer: In medicine, a small hammer that, on striking the patellar tendon, elicits the patellar (i.e., knee-jerk) reflex. The reflex was first described by the German neurologist Heinrich Erb in 1875, and the first reflex hammer was designed in 1888 by the Philadelphia neurologist John Madison Taylor.

Selective serotonin reuptake inhibitors (SSRIs): A class of psychotropic medications of which Prozac, released in the United States in December, 1987, is the best-known example. SSRIs regulate mood by preventing cellular reuptake of the neurotransmitter serotonin at receptor sites in the brain. All SSRIs are approved by the FDA for treating major depression, and specific SSRIs have also been approved for treating obsessive-compulsive disorder, bulimia nervosa, and panic disorder.

Semiotics: The subfield of philosophy that deals with the nature of signs and symbols in human communication.

Serology: The science that deals with the properties and reactions of serums, especially blood serum, in relation to disease.

Serum therapy: A precursor to antibiotic therapy in the early twentieth century, serum therapy involves the extraction and purification of antitoxins in the blood of immunized animals. These antitoxins were then administered to human beings via injection in the hope of neutralizing or destroying the bacteria that caused specific illnesses. The outcome of serum therapy was highly variable; it was effective in treating certain diseases but not others. The first two effective therapeutic serums (against diphtheria and tetanus, respectively) were developed in 1890 by Emil Behring and his collaborators Erich Wernicke (for diphtheria) and Shibasaburo Kitasato (for tetanus).

Sphygmograph: A blood-pressure recording apparatus modified to show pulse-beats as tracings on soot-blackened paper. The first usable sphygmograph was invented by Karl Vierordt in 1853.

Subluxation: The foundational chiropractic concept of disease, subluxation is a vertebral misalignment that allegedly impinges on spinal nerves. According to David D. Palmer, the founder of chiropractic, and first- and second-generation "straight" chiropractics, subluxations blocked the flow of "innate intelligence," which could be restored by spinal manipulation or "adjustment." According to more eclectic "mixer" chiropractors, subluxations exist, but they cause disease in a nonmetaphysical, biomechanical way.

Syncope: A spontaneous loss of consciousness owing to insufficient blood to the brain; fainting.

Tendon reflex: A stretch or "myotatic" reflex in which a muscle involuntarily contracts when its tendon is struck. The mechanism of contraction is a two-neuron reflex arc that involves the spinal or brainstem segment that innervates the muscle in question. The biceps reflex, patellar tendon (or knee-jerk) reflex, ankle jerk reflex, and plantar (Babinski) reflex are examples of tendon reflexes.

Thomsonianism (botanical medicine): The alternative healing modality developed by an uneducated New Englander, Samuel Thomson, in the final years of the eighteenth century. Thomson believed that the human body is composed of the elements earth, air, fire, and water; that disease represents a lessening of heat; and that herbs and other vegetable medicines restore that heat. In 1813, Thomson obtained a patent on his herbal remedies and proceeded to form a network of "friendly botanic societies" where laymen, who paid $20 for access to Thomson's patented cures, gathered to exchange information. The movement peaked in the 1830s and 1840s, and had its widest following in New England, Ohio, and certain regions of the South.

Tricyclic antidepressants: A family of antidepressants named after their three-ring molecular structure. Tricyclics treat depression by preventing cellular reuptake of the neurotransmitter norepinephrine at receptor sites in the brain. Certain tricyclics, such as amitriptyline (Elavil), amoxapine (Asendin), and imipramine (Tofranil) are further believed to prevent reuptake of the neurotransmitter serotonin and to function as histamine antagonists. The antidepressant properties of imipramine (Tofranil), the first tricyclic, were discovered by Geigy field investigators, especially Roland Kuhn, in the period 1953–1955, and the drug was released in Europe in 1958 and in the U.S. in 1959.

Ventricular fibrillation: In cardiology, very rapid uncoordinated fluttering contractions of the lower heart chambers, or ventricles. Ventricular fibrillation disrupts the synchrony between the heartbeat and the pulse beat and may lead to sudden cardiac death within minutes. It is commonly associated with heart attack or scarring of the heart muscle from previous heart attack. August Hoffman published the first electrocardiogram of ventricular fibrillation in 1912.

Index

Bowie, M., 64
Bowlby, J., 190
Bowman, K, 97
Boyd, D., 101–102
brain, 179n17, 222n11. *See also*
    mind-brain models
    attachment theory and, 186, 208–209
    centers of, 175–176, 201
    chemistry of, 4–5
    dynamic systems theory and, 209
    mirror neurons in, 198–199, 201–
        202
Brain and the Inner World, The
    (Solms & Turnbull), 68
Brandchaft, B., 70, 162n54
Brenner, C., 42, 62
Brigham, A., 117
Brill, A. A., 48, 77, 79, 87
Britain, 283n2, 306
British Independent Group, 60
British Journal of Psychiatry, medical
    focus of, 124n37
British Psycho-Analytic Society, 238–
    239
Broca, P., 176n10
Brockway, G., 43n9
Brody, E., 120
Bromberg, P., 64
Bromberg, W., 95n38
Brosin, H., 95
Brown, B., 17
Bruce Publishing Company, 52
Brunner-Mazel, 38
Brunton, T. L., 134
Bucci, W., 178, 204n63
Bühler, K., 18
Burden-Sanderson, J., 150
Burlingham, D., 306
Burnham, J., 122n34
Busch, F., 262

Cabaniss, D. L., 264–265, 277
Cajal, S. Ramón y, 112n15
Can Love Last? (Mitchell), 70
Carfago, V., 46

Cariello, N., 7n11
"Catecholamine Hypothesis of
    Affective Disorders, The"
    (Schildkraut), 4–5
Center for the Study of the Sciences
    of Man, 307
Character Analysis (Reich), 46
Charcot, J., 117n22, 152–153
Charles, M., 57
Chessick, R., 11
Chestnut Lodge, malpractice suit
    against, 9, 277
Chicago Institute of Psychoanalysis,
    47–48
*Chicago Journal of Nervous and
    Mental Disease*, 119–120
child guidance clinics, 306
Childhood and Society (Erikson), 37,
    43–44, 43n8
children, 306. *See also* attachment
    theory
    mentalization of, 180–181
    psychologists working with, 98–
        99, 125
chiropractic, 273, 275
    lawsuit against AMA, 290
    moving toward mainstream
        medicine, 275n47, 289
    psychoanalysis compared to, 281–
        282
    relation to mainstream science of,
        278, 281–282, 290
chloroform death, in relation to
    theoretical pluralism, 133–138,
    140
Choisy, M., 307
Clark, L. P., 256
*Clinical Introduction to Lacanian
    Psychoanalysis, A* (Fink), 65
clinical psychology
    roles of, 97, 125–127
    training and certification in, 126–127
*Clinical Studies in Neuro-
    Psychoanalysis* (Kaplan-Solms &
    Solms), 175
clinico-anatomical method, 175–176

formal logic, Freudian
metapsychology and, 221
Fosshage, J., 170
Foulkes, S., 306
Foundations of Psychoanalysis, The
(Grünbaum), 8, 56
fractionation
analysts' response to, 83n14, 312
causes of, 76, 130n46
changing journal policies with
regard to, 105, 108
comparative-integrative approach
not cure for, 240, 250
effects of, 62–63, 67–68, 72–73
efforts to accommodate, 76, 83,
108
integrative strategies as efforts to
counter, 203–204, 206, 212–
213
in psychoanalytic publishing,
57n38, 62–63, 67–68, 72–73
role of journals in, 76, 105, 108,
129–130
symptoms of, 72–73, 129–130
France, psychoanalysis in, 307
Frank, K., 54n34
Frankfurt School, New School of
Social Research and, 18
Frazier, S., 17
Free Press, 38
Frenkel-Brunswik, E., 18
Freud, A., 12, 43, 83n14
general-interest psychoanalytic
books by, 54–55
work with children, 177, 306
Freud, S., 7, 82n13, 139n8, 189,
201, 219
"analyzing instrument" of, 137,
141–142, 146–147
changing theories of, 139, 141
definition of psychoanalysis, 127–
128, 130, 212n74
influence of, 16n27, 19, 127–128
Jung as disciple of, 78, 128–129
Library of Congress exhibit on, 11
loyalty to, 130–131

Menninger and American
popularization of, 34–36
no longer center of psychoanalysis,
1, 4, 19
and politics over psychoanalytic
journals, 77–78, 128–129
role in fractionation of
psychoanalysis, 130n46, 131–
132
seduction theory of, 7n10, 136–
138, 158–159
support for lay analysis, 89, 103
vision of psychoanalysis, 19, 78,
103, 127–128
Freud and Beyond (Mitchell &
Black), 59, 61, 69–70
Freud Encyclopedia, The (Erwin),
66
Freudians, vs. Kleinians, 238–239
Friedlaender, K., 306
Friedman, L. J., 35, 44n10
Fromm, E., 18n33
commercial success of books by,
33–34, 35n52, 45, 47
on crisis in psychoanalysis, 3–4
Frozen Dreams (Rosen & Rosen), 74
Function of the Orgasm, The (Reich),
46
Funk, R., 45

Gabbard, G. O., 66, 178, 264n26
Galatzer-Levy, R. M., 192–193, 196–
197
Gallese, V., 198–199
Garza-Guerrero, C., 12
Gaskell, W. H., 135
Gedo, J., 12, 37, 55, 233n28, 234–
235
Gergely, G., 68
germ theory, alternative medicine
reframing of, 271–274
Gerson, M.-J., 54n34
Ghaemi, S. N., 246n50
Ghent, E., 194–195, 197
Gill, M., 24n41

Schiffrin, A., 30–31
Schilder, P., 79n7
Schildkraut, J., 4–5
Schiller, F., 146
Schlesinger, H., 65
Schneiderman, S., 64
Schocken Books, 42–43
School of Clinical Psychology, 93
Schore, A., 182–183, 186
science, 122n34, 156
  alternative medicine and, 271–275,
    277–281
  chiropractic and, 273, 281–282, 290
  nineteenth-century medicine's
    rhetoric of, 207–208
  pluralism in, 110–115, 133–138, 140
  psychoanalysis and, 172–174,
    206–209
  psychoanalysis as, 3, 8, 56, 111n12,
    127–128, 155n41, 206–207
  psychoanalysis moving toward
    mainstream, 217, 219–221,
    284–285
  psychoanalytic integrative
    strategies tied to, 208–209
  psychology as, 125–126
Science in Action (Latour), 156
Search Within, The (Reik), 45
Seashore, C., 99n44
*Seduction, Surrender, and
  Transformation* (Maroda), 64
seduction theory, Freud's, 7n10,
  136–138, 140, 158–159
Seguin, E., 151–152
self psychology, 4, 55–58, 66, 103, 186
Seligman, S., 195–196
semiotics, 179, 209
September 11 (Coates, Rosenthal, &
  Schechter), 74
Severe Personality Disorders
  (Kernberg), 63
Sexual Revolution, The (Reich), 46
Shadow of the Object, The (Bollas),
  60–61, 70
Shakow, D., 93
Shane, E., 169

Shapiro, D., 53, 72, 192
Shapiro, T., 106
Shengold, L., 60, 71n47
Shepherd, R., 62n41
Shore, L. E., 135
Shortt, S. E. D., 207n66
Sigerist, H., 82n13
Sigmund Freud Archives, Masson's
  dismissal from, 7
Silbersweig, D. A., 200
Silverman, M., 169
Simon & Schuster, 46
Simpson, J. Y., 134
Sklarew, B., 74
Slade, A., 182–185, 198
Smith, H., 13, 107–108
Smith, L. H., 298–300
Smith-Cunnien, S., 290n7
social activism
  by analysts, 37n56, 98, 291–293, 308
  opportunities for optimal
    marginality through, 303–306
  by psychiatrists, 37n56, 94–96
sociology, marginalization as
  understood within, 13
SOFAR (Strategic Outreach to
  Families of All Reservists), 292–
  293, 303
SOFAR Guide, 292, 293n12
Solms, M., 68, 175–176, 199–201
Soul Murder (Shengold), 60, 71n47
Spence, D., 56, 166
Spiegel, J. P., 256n8, 299
Spitz, R., 18, 177
Spitzer, R., 6
SSRIs, 11, 251–254, 264, 270–271.
  See also medications
Standing in the Spaces (Bromberg), 64
Stekel, W., 78, 128–129
Stern, Daniel, 55, 70
Stern, Donnel, 56, 64
Stern, E., 200
Stern, R. H., 276n49
Stevens, R., 88
Stevenson, G., 94
Still, A. T., 272, 280, 287–288